The Pessimism
of
THOMAS HARDY

Thomas Hardy
c 1880

The Pessimism
of
THOMAS HARDY

G. W. Sherman

RUTHERFORD · MADISON · TEANECK
Fairleigh Dickinson University Press
LONDON: Associated University Presses

Associated University Presses, Inc.
Cranbury, New Jersey 08512

Associated University Presses
108 New Bond Street
London W1Y OQX, England

Library of Congress Cataloging in Publication Data

Sherman, G. W.
The Pessimism of Thomas Hardy.

Bibliography: p.
Includes index.
1. Hardy, Thomas, 1840–1928—Criticism and interpretation. I. Title.
PR4754.S5   823'.8   74–4982
ISBN 0–8386–1582–1

The author thanks the University of Nebraska Press for permission to reprint extracts from Walter F. Wright, *The Shaping of The Dynasts*, 1967. Reprinted by permission of University of Nebraska Press.

to

Mrs. S., and

Maurice, Jenny, and Molly,

affectionately

Contents

Preface

In this study the reader may find an interpretation of Thomas Hardy different from that in any of the studies hitherto.

It has been too easily forgotten that the Victorians had other problems than the conflict between the New Science and the Old Religion—"bread and butter" problems arising from the conflict between Capital and Labor—the development of monopoly capitalism and of rival imperialisms leading up to World Wars I and II, which, to a person with "an observing eye" and a sensitive temperament like Hardy, clouded one's hopes and tried one's faith. In his poem "In Tenebris II" (1895–96), Hardy repudiates the Samuel Smiles philosophy of the apologists for Progress and Expansion, who cry "Our times are blessed times . . . there are many smiles to a tear," and the like. In Hardy's case, it is not quite so simple as dividing Victorian writers into the orthodox and unorthodox; into those who went to Oxford or Cambridge, and those who did not, or could not; into expatiating on Darwinism and disregarding Social Darwinism. One may make a compact little syllogism of Hardy's pessimism from his novel *The Return of the Native* and his poems "Hap" and "The Convergence of the Twain"—about the meeting of the Iceberg and the s.s. *Titanic*—but it can hardly be passed off as understanding Hardy. To do that one must cease immersing himself "voluptuously in the pessimism of Hardy," as Randolph Bourne observed in his *History of a Literary Radical* (1924), and "must see him in his age," as Dr. Arnold Kettle has observed of Shakespeare.

Hardy's critics have failed to see him in his age; this goes for the belleletrists, the regionalists, the philosophical critics, the Marxists to a lesser degree, and finally the New Critics. The first have been concerned with his art, the last with his lack of art; neither have approved of his philosophy. The second and third were interested in whether his pessimism was indigenous to Wessex or a German importation. The Marxists have either regretted with Granville Hicks "that so little was known about his youthful years in London," or regarded him as one who prolonged England's "long bourgeois summer" (Caudwell) by idealizing a country pocket and who stayed "art's movement to surréalisme."

The official biography (*The Early Life of Thomas Hardy* [1928] and *The Later Years of Thomas Hardy* [1930]), which should have been of value to the later critics had they utilized it, has been discounted by the New Critics, who declare (Albert J. Guerard) "that the facts of Hardy's life are irrelevant to an understanding of his novels." The philosophical critics have not benefited from Helen Garwood's study either, *Thomas Hardy: An Illustration of the Philosophy of Schopenhauer* (1911), which showed that the two men are not at all alike in the conclusions to which they came; nor from W. R. Rutland's study, *Thomas Hardy: The Backgrounds of His Thought* (1938), which reestablished. in historical sequence, the influence of his earlier reading of Spencer, Darwin, and Mill over that of the German philosophers, whose works were not available in English translation till after Hardy's thought was shaped and most of his novels were written.

The teleological bias has been persistent, from the Romanist of Hardy's time who complained of Hardy's "refusal of consolation and the dark gravity of his thoughts," to T. S. Eliot, of our own time, who found Hardy "a symptom of decadence . . . whose matter of communication is not particularly wholesome or edifying." I. A. Richards, on the other hand, praises Hardy as the poet "who has most courageously accepted the contemporary background . . . and reflects the neutralization of nature," while Delmore Schwartz considers that Richards has "inverted the truth" about Hardy in the interest of his thesis. Samuel C. Chew comments that "the modern critic is inclined to accept and even admire Hardy's stories provided a symbolic interest or at any rate a susceptibility to symbolic interpretation may be detected." One might go on and on, but perhaps it is enough to cite Hardy's remark, "How strange one may write a book without knowing what one puts into it—or rather what the reader puts into it."

The studies since World War II, except for Harvey Curtis Webster's *On a Darkling Plain* (1947), have added little or nothing to what was already known in Carl Weber's centenary study, *Hardy of Wessex* (1940), reissued in 1960, and constitute a retreat into the private world of academe, which Caudwell defined as surréalisme and is as completely separated from life as the *fin de siècle,* or what Henry Adams called at the beginning of the century "this dead water."

I have used documentation where it seemed important and omitted it in certain references to the official biography, referred to as *The Early Life* and *The Later Years,* giving the date in the context because the chronological arrangement is easy to follow in both volumes.

The chart of Hardy's serialized novels has been arranged from Purdy's *Thomas Hardy: A Bibliographical Study* (1954), an indispensable book. Hardy's adeptness in contriving installment endings matches Marty South's ingenuity (*The Woodlanders*) at improvising a tool for a blade in a horse bone for barking trees. I leave this task to some one interested in tracing Hardy's mastery of the serial-writer's trade beyond the tabu and reticences treated in Mary Ellen Chase's study. Because it was available in a one-volume Modern Library edition, I have used Constance Garnett's translation of Tolstoy's *War and Peace* in comparisons between it and Hardy's *The Dynasts,* rather than the Dole translation that, according to Walter Wright, Hardy read.

I take this opportunity to express my appreciation to those who have, in one way or another, given me help on a work with which I have been occupied, off and on, for more than twenty years. It has involved the exploration of the related fields of history and economics, to which I first had an introduction in Professor Parrington's course in Eighteenth Century literature and Professor Joseph Harrison's course in American literature at the University of Washington, and again took up at Syracuse University under Dr. A. McK. Terhune during World War II, when graduate study was at a low ebb. I am indebted to Dr. H. G. Merriam of the University of Montana for entrusting the teaching of a course in Hardy during my stay there (1946–1950) as English instructor. Also to my colleagues there, the late Dr. Robert W. Albright, Dr. Rufus Coleman, Professors Byron Bryant, Edmund Freeman, John Moore, Dr. John Wolfard, and the late Dr. Joseph Kramer for their interest in my interest in Hardy, and to students of mine while there. Also to a few who read earlier versions of the manuscript, in full— Dwight Mitchell of Palo Alto and Dr. Arnold Kettle of the University of Leeds, or in part, in the article stage (chapter 3)—Dr. Edwin Berry Burgum, Dr. Bradford Booth, Dr. John E. Jordan, the late Dr. Carl Weber, Paul Linderman, and Dr. E. K. Brown, who suggested that I needed to read more widely, which I have since done. Also to old friends of the middle twenties and early thirties, when our excitement over literature was deflated by reading Shaw and Mencken, among whom, besides Paul Linderman, are Sverre Arestad, Harold Woolford, Theodore and Martha Cederberg, George Summers, Walter Moberg, Mary Hutchison (Banks), the late Lester E. Larson, who gave me a Modern Library edition of Hardy's *The Mayor of Casterbridge,* the late Mike Clary, who liked "Hardy's yokels," and George Caraker for sending me a postcard from Dorchester. And to my sister Miriam, the late Mrs. David Anderson, who gave me a deluxe copy of *Tess,* and to my artist friend Mrs. Inez McCurdy, who pleased me by reading Hardy's *Dynasts.*

Also to a few literary-minded friends, who, after I gave up college teaching for social work, have kept my interest alive in things literary when it was flagging; they know who they are without my naming them.

I am very grateful to the editors of *Science & Society* magazine for publishing some of my reviews of books on Hardy during the past twenty years and, still more recently, to Herbert Aptheker and the late Sidney Finkelstein for their interest in the manuscript about six years ago; also to Professor Arthur Adrian and Professor Jacob Korg, who took the trouble to answer an inquiry of mine, and finally to Dr. Charles Angoff and the members of the Editorial Committee of Fairleigh Dickinson University Press for accepting the manuscript for publication, and to Mathilde E. Finch for her competent editing of it. Also to Percy McNutt and Eve Smith for double-checking my proofreading of the galley-proof, and the Mitchells for a whole afternoon on the same.

I wish to thank the librarians at the University of California (Berkeley), Stanford University, San Jose State University, and the San Jose Public Library for making books available to me, and Wanda Brockman of the Seattle Public Library, who provided a Xerox copy of Ella Higginson's review of Hardy's *The Dynasts* in the *Seattle Times.*

And last, but not least to my wife, Martha, and our children, for their inspiration of a kind that endureth.

I shall be grateful to anyone who discovers errors of fact or in judgment in my study for calling them to my attention. I feel a special debt to Christopher Caudwell and Randolph Bourne for their milestones in literary criticism—*Illusion and Reality* (1947) and *The History of a Literary Radical* (1924), respectively, without which I should never have ventured on the task.

For the critical opinions expressed in this book, *The Pessimism of Thomas Hardy*, I must assume full responsibility, which I cheerfully do.

San Jose, California   G. W. Sherman

Acknowledgments

I would like to thank the following publishers and individuals for permission to quote from copyrighted material:

George Allen & Unwin Ltd. (London) for permission to quote from Sidney and Beatrice Webb, *History of Trade Unionism*, 1924; Simon Maccoby, *English Radicalism 1853–1886*, 1935; and Franz Mehring, *Karl Marx: The Story of His Life*, 1951.

Adam and Charles Black for permission to quote from Simon Maccoby, *The English Radical Tradition*, 1952.

Basil Blackwell Publisher (London) for permission to quote from W. R. Rutland, *Thomas Hardy: A Study of His Writings and Their Backgrounds*, 1938.

Clarendon Press (Oxford) for permission to quote from Isaiah Berlin, *Karl Marx: His Life and Environment*, 1963, from Richard L. Purdy, *Thomas Hardy, a Bibliographical Study*, 1954, and from E. L. Woodward, *The Age of Reform 1815–1870*. By permission of The Clarendon Press (Oxford).

Columbia University Press for permission to quote from Susanne Howe, *Novels of Empire*, 1949; J. M. Park, *The English Reform Bill of 1867*, 1920; Lionel Trilling, *Matthew Arnold*, 1958; and Carl Weber, *Hardy of Wessex*, 1960.

J. M. Dent & Sons Ltd. (London) and the Trustees of

the Joseph Conrad Estate, for permission to quote from Joseph Conrad. *Heart of Darkness,* 1924, and *The Mirror of the Sea,* 1924.

Duckworth & Company Ltd. for permission to quote from Vere H. Collins, *Talks with Thomas Hardy at Max Gate,* 1928, and from K. B. Smellie, *A Hundred Years of English Government,* 1937.

Eyre & Spottiswoode Publishers Ltd. (London) for permission to quote from Norman St. John-Stevas, *Walter Bagehot,* 1939.

Grosset & Dunlap, Inc. for permission to quote from Georg Lukács, *Studies in European Realism,* copyright © 1964, by Grosset & Dunlap, Inc., Publishers.

Harcourt Brace Jovanovich, Inc. for permission to quote from Vernon Louis Parrington, *Main Currents in American Thought,* 1939.

Harper & Row, Publishers for American rights to quote from Arnold Kettle, *Introduction to the English Novel,* vols, 1 and 2, 1951 and 1953 respectively.

Haskell House Inc., Publishers and Haskell House Publishers, Ltd. for extracts for J. W. Mackail, *Life of William Morris,* 1901.

A. M. Heath & Company Ltd. for extracts from Giles Dugdale, *William Barnes of Dorset,* 1953.

David Higham Associates, Ltd. (London) for permission to reproduce the photograph of Serge Youriévitch's bust of Thomas Hardy from Evelyn Hardy's *Note Books of Thomas Hardy* (London: Hogarth Press, 1955), with appreciation of Miss Hardy's courtesy for the same.

Hutchinson Publishing Group (London) for permission to quote from Arnold Kettle, *Introduction to the English Novel,* vols. 1 and 2, 1951 and 1953 respectively.

Indiana University Press (Bloomington, Ind.) for permission to quote from Norman St.-John Stevas, *Walter Bagehot,* 1959.

International Publishers Company, Inc. for permission to

quote from Christopher Caudwell, *Illusion and Reality,* 1947; T. A. Jackson, *Charles Dickens: The Progress of a Radical,* 1931; *Marx-Engels Correspondence 1846–1895,* edited by Dona Torr, 1936, and from George Plekhanov, *Essays in Historical Materialism,* 1940.

Nicholas Kaye (London) for permission to quote from Simon Maccoby, *The English Radical Tradition 1763–1914,* 1952.

Alfred A. Knopf. Inc. for permission to quote from Samuel C. Chew, *Thomas Hardy, Poet Novelist,* 1919, and from *Journal of Leo Tolstoy: 1895–1899,* translated by Rose Strunsky, 1927.

Macmillan & Company Ltd. for extracts from *The Life of Thomas Hardy 1840–1928,* by Florence Emily Hardy, © 1962, Macmillan & Co. Ltd. Reprinted by permission of Macmillan, London & Basingstoke, and the Macmillan Company of Canada Limited. This Life includes *The Early Life of Thomas Hardy: 1840–1891,* and *The Later Years of Thomas Hardy, 1892–1928.* Also for the reproduction of the photograph of Thomas Hardy, *c.* 1880 (facing p. 192), as frontispiece.

Macmillan, London and Basingstoke, for extracts from Charles Morgan, *The House of Macmillan 1843–1943,* 1944. Also for extracts from Florence Emily Hardy, *The Early Life of Thomas Hardy 1840–1891* and *The Later Years of Thomas Hardy, 1892–1928,* 1928 and 1930 respectively. Reprinted by permission of the Trustees of Hardy Estate and Macmillan, London and Basingstoke.

Macmillan Publishing Company, Inc. for permission to quote from Thomas Hardy, *Collected Poems,* 1940; *The Dynasts,* 1944; and *Winter Words,* 1928; Florence E. Hardy, *The Early Life of Thomas Hardy,* 1928, and *The Later Years of Thomas Hardy,* 1930. Also from Granville Hicks, *Figures of Transition,* 1938, and Barbara Tuchman, *The Proud Tower,* 1966.

Modern Library, Inc. for permission to quote from Karl

Marx, *Capital*, 1936, translated by S. Moore and E. Aveling, and from Leo Tolstoy, *War and Peace*, 1931, translated by Constance Garnett.

Monthly Review Press for permission to quote from Robert Blatchford, *Merrie England*, 1966, and from Paul Sweezy, *Theory of Capitalist Development*, 1942.

John Murray (Publishers) Ltd. for permission to quote from Monypenny and Buckle, *The Life of Benjamin Disraeli*, vol. 2, 1929.

Octagon Books for permission to quote from Amiya Chakravarty, *The Dynasts and the Post-War Age in Poetry*, 1970.

Oxford University Press (London) for permission to quote from Richard Purdy, *Thomas Hardy, Bibliographical Study*, 1954, and from Eugene Tarlé, *Napoleon*, translated by John Cournos, 1970.

Pergamon Press, Ltd. for permission to quote from Johann Von Thunen, *Von Thunen's Isolated State*, translated by Carla Wartenberg, 1966. Reprinted with permission.

Princeton University Press (Princeton, N.J.) for permission to quote from David V. Erdman, *Blake: Prophet against Empire*, rev. ed., 1969. Reprinted by permission of Princeton University Press.

Progress Publishers (Moscow, USSR) for permission to quote from Maxim Gorki, *On Literature*, translated by Ivy Litvinov, n.d.; Friedrich Engels, *Paul and Laura LaFargue Correspondence*, vols. 1 and 2, 1959 and 1960 respectively, translated by Yvonne Kapp; and *Marx and Engels Selected Correspondence*, translated by the late I. Lasker, 1965.

Random House, Inc. for permission to quote from A. L. Morton, *A People's History of England*, 1938; from Leo Tolstoy, *War and Peace*, translated by Constance Garnett; and from Karl Marx, *Capital: A Critique of Political Economy*, edited by Frederick Engels and translated by S. Moore and E. Aveling, 1936.

Russell & Russell Publishers (New York) for permission

to quote from Thomas Hardy, *An Indiscretion in the Life of an Heiress,* Carl J. Weber, ed. (oringinally published by the Johns Hopkins University Press, 1935), New York: Russell & Russell, 1965; from Randolph Bourne, *The History of a Literary Radical,* 1956; and from Joseph Warren Beach, *The Technique of Thomas Hardy* (originally published by the University of Chicago Press, 1922, New York: Russell & Russell, 1962.

St. Martin's Press, Inc. for permission to quote from Evelyn Hardy, *Thomas Hardy, a Critical Biography,* 1954.

Science & Society for permission to quote from Royden Harrison, "Beesly's St. James Speech" (Fall 1963) and from Henry Collins, "Karl Marx, The International and the British Trade Union Movement" (Fall 1962).

Charles Scribner's Sons for permission to quote from Lloyd Eshelman, *A Victorian Rebel,* 1940.

Irving Shepherd for permission to quote from Jack London, *People of the Abyss* (New York: Macmillan, 1904).

The Shoe String Press (Hamden, Conn.) for permission to quote from Harvey Curtis Webster, *On a Darkling Plain,* 1973 (originally published by the University of Chicago Press, 1947).

Simon & Schuster, Inc. for permission to quote from Edgar Johnson, *Charles Dickens: His Tragedy and Triumph,* 1952.

Alfred McK. Terhune for permission to quote from *The Life of Edward FitzGerald* (New Haven, Conn.: Yale University Press, 1947).

University of Michigan Press (Ann Arbor) for permission to quote from K. B. Smellie, *Great Britain since 1688,* 1947.

University of North Carolina Press (Chapel Hill) for permission to quote from J. O. Bailey, *The Poetry of Thomas Hardy,* 1970.

University of Washington Press (Seattle) for permission to quote from Jacob Korg, *George Gissing, a Critical Biography,* 1963.

The Viking Press for permission to quote from Siegfried Sassoon, *Siegfried's Journey 1916–1920,* 1946.

A. P. Watt & Son for extracts from G. M. Trevelyan, *The Life of John Bright,* 1925. Quoted by permission of The Estate of G. M. Trevelyan.

The Pessimism
of
THOMAS HARDY

The pale pathetic peoples still plod on
Through hoodwinkings to light!
                                    —*The Dynasts:* III, 4, iv.

1

A Critic of a Critic

On August 8, 1927, Thomas Hardy wrote in a letter to J. B. Priestly, who had sent him his book on George Meredith, that he was "not at all a critic, especially *of* a critic when the author he reviews is a man who was, off and on, a friend . . . for forty years." Their acquaintance began in 1869, when Meredith, a reader for the publisher Chapman & Hall, explained why the firm was reneging on its promise to publish his radical novel, *The Poor Man and the Lady*. The friendship lasted till Meredith's death in 1909. With all due respect to Hardy's judgment, I shall attempt to be both a critic and a critic of his critics and shall try to "hold the scales very fairly," as Hardy thought Priestly had in his criticism of Meredith, Hardy's first critic.

There is no question in any one's mind but what Hardy was a pessimist, but there has been a great deal of disagreement as to the cause of his pessimism, which most critics have finally agreed was the influence of Darwin's *Origin of Species* (1859). In 1921 Hardy remarked to Vere Collins, "Why are people always talking about 'pessimism?'" adding, "I suppose 'pessimism' is an easy word to say and remember. It's only a passing fashion;" [1] and in the official biography he is said to have observed humorously that taking a gloomy view of things was the surest way of protecting oneself against the many disappointments in life—or words to that effect. Much of his gloom arose from the miasma of a mercantilist society and the exploitation of the poor by the rich, particularly at the expense of farmworkers, or "workfolk," as he called them. Hardy protested in his Wessex novels long before Conrad did in his essay "Autocracy and War" (1905), against "Commercialism and Industrialism," in which the Western nations had "put their faith." Hardy criticized the proponents of "Progress, Expansion and Prosperity"—those optimists who were saying "All's well when all was not well," who "blind the eyes to the real malady and use empirical panaceas to suppress the symptoms," declaring that "if a way to the Better there be, it exacts a full look at the Worst," [2] as he wrote in 1898 and again on January 16, 1918. He did not have to go out of his way to have a full look at the Worst, as Granville Hicks [3] suggests he was wont to do. Hardy's long life (1840–1928) embraced a record of depressive cycles and imperialistic wars leading up to World War I, which all but destroyed his hope for mankind. The cause of his pessimism was not his loss of faith in God from having read Darwin's *Origin of Species* as a young man, but his loss of faith in the leaders of society, both Whig and Tory alike, after 1867.

Not that Darwin's book, which he was reading in 1865 in London lodgings, along with Newman's *Apologia pro Vita Sua* (1864), did not have a profound effect on his already scientifically inclined mind, which was stimulated by his use of his grandfather's telescope on the heath, and by Professor Last's microscope in school, invented in 1836. Indeed, his friend Horace Moule had in 1857 given him a book titled *Experimental and Natural Philosophy* (1853), by Jabez Hogg,[4] a British ophthamologist who also wrote *The Microscope* 1854), which went through three editions. These experiences early liberated him from the "old articles of faith held by our grandfathers," [5] and, what is more important, provided an insight into his own youthful struggle in London (1862–1867).

Bourgeois society was teeming with industrial conflicts at home and erupting into imperialistic wars abroad. The struggle for manhood suffrage in England culminating in the passage of the Second Reform Bill (1867) fired Hardy's youthful idealism, and he envisioned in his little poem "1967" (1867):

> A century which, if not sublime,
> Will show, I doubt not, at its prime,
> A scope above this blinkered time.[6]

It had seemed to him that "the Darwinian theory and 'the truth [that] shall make you free!'" were potent forces in 1867, but not so in 1922, "when men's minds appear to be moving backwards rather than on."[7] There had been no political enlightenment in Germany in 1867. Marx, writing to Engels on 3 February, 1865, in defense of their efforts for manhood suffrage, observed of Bismarck's and Lasalle's "treachery" that they would have "at least [to] express themselves as favourable to the restoration of universal suffrage which was set aside in Prussia by *coup d'état*° and repeal of the Combination Laws (1845)," which had "prohibited every form of combination between bodies of workers . . . and provided punishment by fines and imprisonment . . . where workers were disobedient or rebellious."[8] The working classes in England had realized, in part at least, two of the major demands of the Chartists' platform (1848): the secret ballot and manhood suffrage, which had increased the base of the electorate threefold. These were straws in the wind toward a melioristic society.

The Reform League[9] was organized by Marx and trade-

° Similarly, in our own time Diem, by a presidential decree in June 1956 "abolished elected Village Councils and Mayors. This imposed directly on the Viet-nam peasantry, the dictatorial regime which he had already welded at its center."See Bernard Fall, *Viet-nam Witness* (New York: Praeger, 1966), p. 237.

union leaders for this express purpose. Blomfield's offices where Hardy was employed were located in rooms above the League's headquarters, thus Hardy was in an advantageous position to observe the reform movement. The League staged mass meetings and demonstrations in Hyde Park and Trafalgar Square to make the working classes politically as well as wage conscious, and largely deserves the credit for the passage of the Reform Bill of 1867. It is significant, I think, that Hardy not only has his protagonist Will Strong speak to a crowd of workingmen in Trafalgar Square, in his never-published novel *The Poor Man and the Lady* (1868), there having been much opposition by both the Home Secretary Spencer Walpole and the septugenarian Metropolitan Chief of Police, Richard Mayne to the League's holding the meeting in the Park, but also sets the time of the action back to the 1840s—a criticism that John Morley, Macmillan's reader,[10] censured him for as an anachronism.

In 1848 revolution was rearing its head in Europe, and Disraeli was exhorting the country "that the palace is not safe when the cottage is not happy." [11] The Whigs called for 5,000 additional troops to put down Chartism under the command of the aged Duke of Wellington, the hero of Waterloo and mock-hero of Peterloo (1819), who had lived to see his country supporting Louis Napoleon. At the later time Robert Lowe, M.P. from Calne, who hated the working classes of England as much as Bismarck° did those of Germany, thought "that they were within twenty-four hours of a revolution." [12] A Tory parliament was scared into passing a more liberal reform bill than the Whigs had rejected a year before.

Hardy's sympathies for the working classes are evident in his choice of his heroes and heroines for his novels and scarcely need recapitulating: Gabriel Oak (*Far from the*

° Engels wrote Schmidt (July 9, 1891): "The conspiracy of the bourgeois press in 1859 was one thousand times more effective than Bismarck's contemptible Socialist Law (Marx-Engels Correspondence, ed. Dona-Torr (New York: International Publishers, 1936), p. 398).

Madding Crowd), Clym Yeobright (*The Return of the Native*), Giles Winterborne and Marty South (*The Woodlanders*), Michael Henchard (*The Mayor of Casterbridge*), Ethelberta Petherwin, the daughter of a butler to high society (*The Hand of Ethelberta*), the poor architect George Somerset (*A Laodicean*), the dairymaid Tess and finally Jude, the poor student and stonemason who, deprived of an education, recognizes that something is basically wrong with society and beyond the individual's power to change it. Moreover, Hardy shows them as having fared better in their homespun clothes under the Household system than in the cottons and worsteds of their new industrial masters for whom "the mildly liberal Forster, M.P.," Marx noted "shed tears over the blessings of free-trade and the profits of the eminent men of Bradford who deal in worsteds" (p. 728).

It is true that Hardy did not choose to write of the industrial working classes as did George Gissing in England and Maxim Gorki in Russia, because he did not know them as they did. His working people are country artisans, farmers, agricultural laborers, or the "work folk," but he saw the effects of the Industrial Revolution on their lives nonetheless, by the introduction of the corn-drill (*The Mayor*) and the steam-thresher (*Tess*), "the *primum mobile* of this little world, whose substitution for man," as Marx observed, "worked wonders in the line of drainage . . . and gives in this, as in all similar revolutions, the finishing blow." [13] "Nothing in Zola or Dreiser," Irving Howe says of Hardy's description of Tess's feeding the thresher at Flintcomb-Ash farm, "surpasses these pages . . . for a portrayal of human degradation, a portrayal compassionate through its severe objectivity" (p. 25). Hardy notes in his Dorsetshire Labourer essay (1883) a further effect of the steam-engine on the emigration of the workfolk to the larger towns, comparing it to water being forced uphill by the pressure of machinery. Evicted from the land, they could not find employment in the larger towns and they had no share in either adversity or prosperity and no voice in government under either Whig or Tory management. The borough franchise, which was extended to all rate-payers as well as to lodgers occuping rooms at the annual rent of £10, did not affect the males in the rotten agricultural boroughs, which were still controlled by the landed aristocracy, nor did it include the women who, after the defeat of Mill's amendment (196 to 73) in 1866, had to wait until after World War I for the franchise, and it was a far cry from the Chartists' demands of 1840 for the abolition of any property qualification.

The rural laboring classes turned to the National Agricultural Workers Union of Joseph Arch (1872) for redress of their grievances, as they had turned to the Friendly Society of Agricultural Labourers of the Loveless brothers in 1830. Arch's Union asked for

> an increase of wages from 12s to 14s. for a 54-hour week. The farmers' answer was a lockout, which "victimized" no fewer than 10,000 members. . . . With the decline of prosperity of British farming (1876–77), men were everywhere dismissed . . . and soon even Joseph Arch advised the local branches to acquiesce in lower wages. By 1881 the National Union could claim only 15,000 members, and in 1889 only 4,524.[14]

At the end of 1872 it had boasted of a membership of 100,000! The decline began in 1874, when they paid £21,365 in strike pay, which was a ruinous drain on their funds but they had succeeded in raising the wages and standard of living of the farmworkers, as Hardy observes in his essay "The Dorsetshire Labourer," noting,

> That the maximum of wage has been reached for the present is, however pretty clear; and indeed it should be added that on several farms the labourers have submitted to a slight reduction during the past year, under stress of representations which have appeared reasonable.

In the thirties the attempts of the Loveless brothers to improve the farmworkers' lot had been put down with greater severity than those of the Chartists in the towns during the hungry forties. From his parents Hardy had learned about the time of the Peasants Rebellion of the eighteen-thirties, when workfolk had burned the corn ricks and broken machinery under Captain Swing in the southern counties and threatened to go after the parsons and the statesmen for redress of their grievances.[15] He had heard the story of the Loveless and Stanfield brothers, who in 1830 had organized their Friendly Society of Dorchester Labourers ("the Tolpuddle Martyrs," [16] as Marx calls them) and who had engaged the village painter to paint a figure of Death six feet high as a symbol of their desperation, and asked for a wage increase from 7 to 10 shillings a week, the amount paid by farmers in the neighboring counties.[17] They were arrested, incarcerated in the Dorchester jail, tried on March 18, 1834, before Judge John Williams, a recent appointment to the bench, who in his charge "dwelt at length on the enormity of trifling with oaths" and exacting membership fees from farmworkers. They were found guilty and sentenced to seven years' imprisonment at Botany Bay,[18] the English penal colony. Lord Melbourne expressed the opinion that "the law has in this case been most properly applied," and by 15 April "lord Howick was able to say in the House of Commons that their ship had already sailed for Botany Bay," with which Dickens's Boundersby agreed (*Hard Times*, chap. 5).

The London *Times*, editorializing on the severity of the sentence, pronounced it "a useful deterrent for the more acute and powerful disturbers of the town population throughout England." The Webbs have called the case "the best known episode in trades-union history." [19] The sentence caused the oath to be dropped out of trade-union ceremonies, and set back the collective bargaining movement for forty years. Most of those joining the Society were dispossessed yeomen whose forebears had been "the backbone of Cromwell's army," as Marx called them, and "the bold

peasantry of England, the country pride," as Oliver Goldsmith eulogized them in "The Deserted Village" (1770).
They had been kept in subjugation at a subsistence level
by the farmers and landlords, and looked to the leadership
of the Loveless brothers to remedy the injustice. William
Cobbett and Feargus O'Connor worked indefatigably on the
case of the Dorchester Labourers, to rouse public opinion.
Cobbett presented the petition of the London Trades Union
against the injustice of the sentence, and O'Connor defended them in the House of Commons. Robert Owen, who,
Hardy's mother explained to him, was a manufacturer of
printed calicos, had led a monster parade in London in their
cause. Through their continuous efforts the labourers were
pardoned in 1836, but their pardon in no way ameliorated
the deplorable agricultural condition in Dorset.

Their plight "down to 1850 or 1855 was one of great
hardship," [20] Hardy recalled in March 1902 in a letter to
Rider Haggard; Edward Beesly, history professor at the
University of London and Hardy's friend of a later date,
compared it at a meeting in St. James Hall* on March 26,
1863, to that of Negro slaves in America. Hardy declared

*Marx wrote: "I gave in the 'New York Tribune', the facts about the
Sutherland slaves [epitomized in part by Carey in The Slave Trade, London,
1853, pp. 202–3]. My article was reprinted in a Scotch newspaper,
and led to a pretty polemic between the latter and the sycophant of the
Sutherlands. When the present Duchess of Sutherland entertained Mrs.
Beecher Stowe, authoress of 'Uncle Tom's Cabin', with great magnificence
in London, to show her sympathy for the negro slaves of the American
republic—a sympathy that she prudently forgot with her fellow-aristocrats,
during the civil war, in which every 'noble' English heart beat for the
slaver owner." She "had appropriated 794,000 acres of land that had from
time immemorial belonged to the clan," and had "divided it into 29 great
sheep farms, each inhabited by a single family, for the most part, imported
English farm servants," Marx notes, and "British soldiers enforced their
eviction and came to blows with the inhabitants" (Capital, pp. 801–2).
Incidentally, Conrad "embarked as an ordinary seaman in the wool-
clipper Duke of Sutherland, on 12 Oct. 1878, among the officers of the
great wool fleet" [London to Sydney] and on Aug 21, 1880, "he got
a berth of the wool-clipper Loch Etive." See Norman Sherry, Conrad's
Eastern World, p. 255n). The Duke of Sutherland and his party docked
in their yacht La Peur Feb. 16, 1886, just as Conrad was embarking on
the Melita to command the fever-striken ship Otago.

in 1879 that "if a farmer can afford to pay thirty per cent. more wages in a time of agricultural depression, and yet live, and keep a carriage while the landlord still thrives on the reduced rent which has resulted, the Labourer must have been greatly wronged in prosperous times,[21] a point emphasized by Marx on the dissolution of the family under the capitalistic exploitation (*Capital,* p. 536).

Hardy's observations of the condition of the peasantry offer a sequel to Blake's description of "the hard toil of Albion's daughters and their needles" and of "his sons at their Smitheys" in his "Visions of the Daughters of Albion":

How different far the fat fed hireling with hollow drum,
Who buys whole cornfields into waste, and sings upon the heath.°
How different their eye and ear! how different the world to them!
With what sense does the parson claim the labour of the farmer?
What are his nets and gins and traps, and how does he surround him,
With cold floods of abstractions and with forests of solitude,
To build him castles and high spires, where kings and priests may dwell
Till she who burns with youth, and knows no fixed lot, is bound
In spells of law to one she loaths? And must she drag the chain
Of life in every lust? [22]

His observation also invites comparison with a later period still, after the Repeal of the Corn Laws (1846), which had split the Tory party into Peelites and Protectionists, and what is more important, "gave a marvellous impulse to

---

° It will be recalled that Clym, cutting furze, sings on the heath, and that his seeming not to care much about social failure" angers Eustacia "as an educated lady-wife," although he explains, "It is only a little song which struck my fancy when I was in Paris, and now just applies to my life with you: *Le point du jour à nos bosquets rend toute leur* parure". (*The Return of the Native* (p. 299).

English manufacture," as Marx notes, at the expense of Ireland, which no longer enjoyed "the monopoly of the free importation of corn into Great Britain." In Ireland it resulted in "the conversion of arable land into grazing land and the eviction of small cultivators;" in England, Marx notes:

> As far as the actual agricultural labourers of both sexes and of all ages are concerned, their number fell° from 1,241,396 in 1851 to 1,163,217 in 1861 (the number of shepherds increased from 12,517 to 25,559). If the English Registrar-General therefore, rightly remarks: 'The increase of farmers and farm-labourers, since 1801, bears no kind of proportion to the increase of agricultural produce', this disproportion obtains much more for the last period, when a positive decrease of the agricultural population went hand in hand with increase of the area under cultivation, with more intensive cultivation, unheard-of accumulation of the capital incorporated with the soil and devoted to its working, an augmentation in the products of the soil without parallel in the history of English agriculture, plethoric rent-rolls of landlords, and growing wealth of capitalist farmers. If we take this, together with the swift unbroken extension of the markets, viz., the towns,

° Marx notes further: "The decrease of the middle-class farmers can be seen especially in the census category: 'Farmer's son, grandson, brother, nephew, daughter, grand-daughter, sister, niece'; in a word, the members of his own family, employed by the farmer. This category numbered, in 1851, 216, 851 persons; in 1861, only 176, 151. From 1851 to 1871, the farms under 20 acres fell by more than 900 in number; those between 50 and 75 acres fell from 8,253 to 6,370; the same thing occurred with all other farms under 100 acres. On the other hand, during the same twenty years, the number of large farms increased; those of 300–500 acres rose from 7,771 to 8,410, those of more than 500 acres from 2,755 to 3,914, those of more than 1,000 acres from 492 to 582." (p. 744n).

The New York *Tribune* was a radical newspaper founded by a group of American followers of Fourier (1772–1837), with a circulation at its peak of 200,000. It was broadly progressive—anti-slavery and anti-autocracy, pro-freetrade, and found itself in opposition to virtually every government in Europe. Marx, who was hired by Charles Dana as foreign correspondent, wrote articles on a wide range of subjects. for which he was paid 1 pound sterling per article until the paper was taken over by Horace Greeley, who in trimming the paper's policy to his westward expansion program ("Go West") fired Marx against Dana's advice. Unemployed, Marx tried to get work as a booking-clerk in a railway station, but his shabby appearance and the illegibility of his handwriting ruled him out. (See Berlin, pp. 198–201.)

and the reign of Free Trade, then the agricultural laborer was at last, *post tot discrimina rerum,* placed in circumstances that ought, *secundum artem,* to have made him drunk with happiness. (*Capital,* pp. 744–45)

Many of the rural poor had migrated to London, swelling the ranks of the urban proletariat. In 1815, after the peace ending the Napoleonic wars, there was a heavy slump and widespread unemployment in both imports and exports. In Shropshire alone, twenty-four out of thirty-four blast-furnaces went out of production; the price of iron fell from £20 to £8 a ton,[23] and thousands of iron-workers and colliers were thrown out of work. Blake accuses the Empire of promoting war, intensifying exploitation, and stultifying the lives of its slaves," Erdman remarks, to which he "now adds the charge of divisive malice," that is, "Imperialism."[24] In his poem "A Song of Liberty," Blake envisioned a time when "Empire is no more!" And now the Lion and Wolf shall cease."

Hardy of course knew Blake's poem

> Tiger, tiger burning bright
> In the forests of the night—

but having read Darwin's *Origin of Species,* he could not accept Blake's answer to the mysterious contradiction of creation:

> Did he smile his work to see?
> Did he who made the Lamb
> Make thee?

although Blake had described with impressionistic power the process of primitive accumulation, whose "sovereign eyes" Marx's documentation in *Capital** had made so very

---

* "No period of modern society is so favourable for the study of capitalist accumulation," says Marx, "as the period of the last 20 years (1846–1866). It is as if this period had found Fortunatus' purse. But of all the countries England again furnishes the classical example, because

real. The basis of Hardy's pessimism is not only "the pessimism of the Wessex peasant who sees his world and values
being destroyed," as Kettle [25] declares, despite Morrell's
criticism of his politico-economic stand; but it is also Hardy's
realization that the ruling classes had learned nothing and
forgotten nothing from the lessons of the Napoleonic Wars
in their conquest for control of the world market. John
Bright, the free-trade advocate, condemned the ruling
classes in a speech at Glasgow on October 16, 1866, in support of manhood suffrage:

> Probably what I call the Botany Bay view of their country-
> man would be got rid of, and we should have a sense of
> greater justice and generosity in the feeling with which they
> regard the bulk of the nation. And if there was more knowl-
> edge of the people, there would assuredly be more sympathy
> with them; and I believe the legislation of the House, being
> more in accordance with the public sentiment, would be wiser
> and better in every respect. The nation would be changed.
> There would be amongst us a greater growth of everything
> that is good. . . . The class which has hitherto ruled in this
> country has failed miserably. It revels in power and wealth,
> whilst at its feet, a terrible peril of its future, lies the multitude
> which it has neglected. *If a class has failed, let us try the
> nation.*[26]

Hardy was affected by the political struggle for manhood
suffrage during the militant sixties as Engels was affected
by the struggle of the Chartists (1838–48), who had demanded a living wage, universal suffrage, the secret ballot,
annual parliaments, and salaries for members. Chartism
waned after 1842. There was nothing much left for the
working classes after that except agitation for the repeal of
the Corn Laws (1846), by which the importation of foreign
grain had been forbidden since 1815 till wheat reached

it holds the foremost place in the world-market . . . because the introduction of the Free Trade millennium since 1846 has cut off the last
retreat of vulgar economy" (*Capital*, trans. Ernest Untermann (New York:
Modern Library, n.d.) pp. 711–12).

famine prices in the interest of the big landowners. The Repeal proved only a panacea, as the Chartists had maintained in their debates with the Leaguers. The Hardys appear to have been free-traders, at least, and possibly disappointed Chartists, judging from a family incident at this time. In 1844, young Hardy dipped a wooden sword that his father had made for him in the blood of a freshly butchered pig and brandished it about the garden, exclaiming, "Free Trade or blood!" [27] A common expression heard from farmhands at Anti-Corn Law League meeting was "I be protected, and I be starving," [28] which might have come straight from any of Hardy's rustics.

It is meaningful that Hardy associated the achievement of manhood suffrage with the "Darwinian theory and the truth [that] shall make you free" in 1867. Hardy as well as Marx was one of the earliest acclaimers of the *Origin of Species*. Marx, who was reading Darwin's book "within four weeks of its publication," and during his wife's serious illness, wrote to Engels (Dec. 19, 1860): "This is the book which contains the basis in natural history for our view," and in a letter to Lasalle (Jan. 16, 1861) he declared: "Darwin's book is very important and serves me as a basis in natural science for the class struggle in history." [29] Marx was so impressed by Darwin's book that he offered to dedicate *Das Kapital* (1867) to him, but Darwin declined the honor. He commented in his letter to Engels (June 18, 1862) that "it is wonderful how Darwin has rediscovered English society in the plant and animal world." [30]

Hardy witnessed the same betrayal of youthful idealism following the passage of the Second Reform Bill (1867) as Tennyson had following the First Reform Bill (1832). I quote two stanzas from Hardy's poem "A Young Man's Exhortation" [31] (1867):

> Exalt and crown the hour
> That girdles us, and fill it full with glee,

> Blind glee, excelling aught could ever be
>   Were heedfulness in power.
>
> If I have seen one thing
> It is the passing preciousness of dreams;
> That aspects are within us; and who seems
>   Most kingly is the King.

His health had become so impaired physically and mentally by the end of the summer of 1867 that he quit his job at Blomfield's architectural office on the eve of the passage of the Reform Bill and returned home to Wessex, seeking the curative power of nature in Little Hintock forest of *The Woodlanders;* there he found mirrored the condition of society—sad to say—from which he had just escaped, and all the more ironically so, since man, unlike nature, was capable of exercising some control of his society. This experience is described in his little poem "In a Wood" [32] (1887–1896), which is a recollection of his youthful struggle in London and the malaise resulting from it:

> Heart-halt and spirit-lame,
>   City-opprest,
> Unto this wood I came
>   As to a nest;
>
> Dreaming that sylvan peace
>   Offered the harrowed ease—
> Nature a soft release
>   From men's unrest.
>
> But, having entered in,
>   Great growths and small
> Show them to men akin—
>   Combatants all!

In these lines Hardy depicts the competitive struggle empirically, as he had experienced it in London, in terms of the Darwinian struggle in nature without benefit of Marx or Engels, though Marx's *Capital* was first published in

English in 1886 and he may have read it then but have had his interest whetted by the review of the German edition of it in *The Saturday Review*, January 18, 1868 (p. 97).

Hardy's despondency over his work and prospects is set down in a diary note of July 1 (1868), when he prescribed as "Cures for Despair" the reading of Wordsworth's "Resolution and Independence," Mill's "Individuality," and Carlyle's "Jean Paul Richter." This reading, however, served no better as a stimulant for his depressed spirits than attending church had as an opiate after his reading Darwin's *Origin of Species* (1859). Political reform was only a politicians' game of Hare and Hounds, and the Great Exhibitions of 1851 and 1862 concealed behind their dazzling façade of peace and amity Bessemer's revolutionary converter, which had performed patriotic and profitable service in the Crimean War (1853–1856) and Krupp's steel cannon, which blasted France in the Franco-Prussian War, and which was shortly to be supplied to the Boers in South Africa in the contest of rival imperialisms for the subjugation of rich undeveloped countries. The Portuguese were bent on reestablishing their pristine hold in Africa; even Hooper Tolbort, Hardy's friend during their architect-apprenticeship days with Mr. Hicks of Dorchester, had gone to India and written a treatise on the Portuguese in India, which "just before his death" he commissioned Hardy to publish.[33] Parliament, after abolishing imprisonment for debt (1869) and nationalizing the telegraph under the post office system (1868) "settled down into the mould of its vulgarity," as Robinson Jeffers describes the United States at a later period of capitalist development in his poem "Shine Perishing Republic," "heavily thickening to empire and protest only a bubble in the molten mass, pops and sighs out and the mass hardens." Marx observed a similar solidification in the assembly of Louis Philippe (1848) whose "legislative activity . . is summarized during this period in two laws: the law reestablishing the *wine tax* and the *education law* abolishing unbelief." [34] The peasants of France had been subjugated by the restoration of the monarchy of Louis Philippe and "were disappointed more than ever by the low level of grain prices on the one hand and by the growing burden of taxes and mortgage debts on the other." [35] The situation was not unlike that in England, which had produced a last and futile flare-up of Chartism in 1848, which the Duke of Wellington was called upon to subdue, and the way was cleared for the conquest of the world market. [36]

"During the age of colonial expansion, that is roughly up to 1900," Morton observes, "Britain had been most frequently in conflict with France, the most active colonizing Power," but after "that date the main rival became Germany, which left well behind in the race for colonies, began to penetrate what the British bourgeoisie had long [been] accustomed to regard as their own markets," or became commerce, "that greatest of all political interests," [37] in the words of Joseph Chamberlain, M.P. from Birmingham. Germany's victory over France in 1870 and the unification of the Reich in 1871 made her a world power, and the payment of a huge indemnity by France enabled her to enter on a career for colonies in Africa. The French, humiliated by defeat and impoverished financially, sought to rehabilitate themselves by colonizing Algeria and Cochin China. England, fearful of encroachments on her colonial domain, dispatched troops to protect her holdings and enlarge her possessions. Each nation coveted a solid block of territory in Africa, as Leonard Woolf later observed. The Germans wanted a Mittel-Afrika, stretching in "a solid block" from the Atlantic to the Indian Ocean; M. Etienne and his supporters wanted "a solid block" of French territory, stretching from the Mediterranean to the Gulf of Guinea; Rhodes and his followers "a solid block" from the Cape to Cairo, running from south to north "and therefore necessarily shaking all the other solid blocks which ran from west to east."

As early as 1857 Livingstone had exhorted Cambridge

students, "I beg to direct your attention to Africa," and he had rationalized his missionary zeal for conquest thus: "If such men must perish by the advance of civilization as some races of animals do before others, it is a pity; God grant that ere this time they may receive the Gospel—a solace for the soul in death." The explorers and the missionaries were succeeded by the soldiers and the merchants, and idealism hardened into realism in 1880, when the alien intruders wanted not only "the native's soul," as Mrs. Howe points out, but also "his services and his wealth" (*Novels of Empire*, p. 116). To be sure, they always advanced under the guise of benefiting the natives; the Germans and their Kulturmission; the French and "their effort civilisateur;" and the English and their WhiteMan's Burden, which were later to recall the Japanese and their Co-prosperity sphere; and, more recently, the Americans and their Operation Beefsteak. No wonder that the native was confused and wondered, as did some poets of the thirties like Auden in "the fattening forties" ("Under Which Lyre"), whose side they were supposed to be on, and as Mrs. Howe* observes of Grimm in his story *"Der Leutnant und der Hottentot,"* who made a similar mistake.

"The favorite nineteenth century mystique of blood and race" provided the psychological milieu, according to Mrs. Howe (p. 94) and the mouthpieces of the governments—Bismarck, M. Etienne, and Rhodes—found the Master's voice in Nietzsche and Bergson and above all in Kipling, whose poem "The Recessional" was a chaplain's clarion call to the colors:

> God of our fathers, known of old,
> And of our far-flung battle-line,
> Beneath whose awful Hand we hold

---

* Mrs. Howe says: "If anyone can doubt that imperialism played a large part in leading the world down the great slide to 1914, and thence to 1939, let him read some of these French and German contributions to the 'genre' of the colonial novel. They shriek aloud with national rivalries, grudges, jealousies, antipathies, and misunderstandings" (*Novels of Empire* (New York: Columbia University Press, 1949), p. 31).

> Dominion over palm and pine—
> Lord of Hosts, be with us yet,
> Lest we forget—lest we forget.

Kipling's bombast was most ably answered by William Watson, an opponent of the Boer War and one of the pallbearers at Tennyson's funeral, in his lines:

> Best by remembering God, say some,
> We keep our high imperial lot;
> Fortune, I think, has mainly come
> When we forgot, when we forgot.

But the will of the expansionists prevailed over the protests of the anti-imperialists like William Morris, John Morley, W. L. Courtney, and other members of the *Fortnightly* group, including Hardy, who was a frequent contributor, and William Watson.

By 1900 the United States had well outstripped both Britain and Germany in coal, iron, and steel production. The rate of British industrial growth after 1880 fell to less than 2 percent per annum, while that of Germany had risen to 3.9 percent, and that of the United States to 4.8 percent. "Henry Strakers were in the wings," says historian Smellie, "to do their turn after Hardy's yokels." [38] The expansionists were clamoring for the annexation of Canada and Cuba, against which Whitman, whom Hardy admired; Thomas Reed, Republican Congressman from Maine (1877–1899); Mark Twain; and later Edgar Lee Masters protested in vain. Even Goldwin Smith, professor of modern history at Oxford and later at Cornell University (1872–1874), whose articles favoring the American North Hardy had read in the *Saturday Review* (1863–1865), argued for the annexation of Canada to the United States in his book *Canada and the Canadian Problem* (1891). There was a hue and cry raised in Congress to build "a navy equal to Great Britain's or shut up about the Monroe Doctrine"—a situation reflected on the other side, Mrs. Howe states, in "Meredith's *Beauchamp's*

Career [which] is concerned about England's backward navy and about the harsher air blowing from the continent toward England." [39] The military occupation of the Philippines filled American novelist William James with loathing, and he called President McKinley's euphemism "benevolent assimilation" "the cold-pot grease of McKinley's eloquence."[40] Joseph Conrad deals with the former period in *Heart of Darkness,* in which Marlow observed a man-of-war anchored off the coast: "The French had one of their wars going on thereabout, and there she was firing into a continent," [41] and with the later period in *Nostromo* (1904) about the American capitalist Halroyd, who is dictating with his money, with the operation of the Gould concession, the San Tomé mine in Costaguana, and the political regime there, of which Irving Howe [42] declares: "Conrad has struck exactly upon the note of fanatical solemnity which is to vibrate through the bloody comedies of Latin American politics"—which only superficially treats the situation.

Hardy had seen with his own eyes both in Wessex and in London the exploitation of the working-classes by the ruling classes, regardless of whether Whigs or Tories were in office, and the reckless gambling with their lives in imperialistic wars abroad. During the Franco-Prussian War (1870–71), Hardy, like Clym Yeobright of *The Return of the Native* (1878), "had reached the stage in a young man's life when the grimness of the general human situation first becomes clear; and the realization of this causes ambition to halt awhile" (p. 222). In *The Poor Man and the Lady,* he had championed the cause of the working classes for the ballot but, following the reaction soon afterwards, he became as disillusioned with the pretense of politicians in England as Victor Hugo did with the supporters of the monarchist pretender Napoleon III and the bourgeois republic after him, and as Dostoevsky did in 1862 on his visit to Paris and London. In London as in Paris, he observed in his *Winter Notes on Summer Impressions,* the same frantic struggle to preserve the status quo, to wring from oneself all one's desires and hopes, to curse one's future, in which even the leaders of progress do not have enough faith perhaps, and to worship Baal.[43]

Hardy faced the realities of his times with "blank misgivings and obstinate questionings," as he states in the preface to *Late Lyrics and Earlier*, viewing the future with diminishing hope. This has been mistakenly called his pessimism. It was not the result of an intellectual crisis over religion and science, as Granville Hicks [44] suggests in his observation that "Harrison and Morley made the transition to agnosticism at Oxford and Leslie Stephen at Cambridge," lamenting that "if we knew more about Hardy's life between 1862 and 1866, we should be better able to answer the questions that have been posed." It was the result of a social and economic crisis, as Professor Bowra has suggested. To attribute the origin of Hardy's pessimism to religious crisis is as specious a kind of argument as attributing his somber view of life, as some regional critics have done, to a black humor of temperament or to staring at the heath as a child. Because these contemporaries are agreed that the times—"say from 1860 to 1890 . . . in spite of its perpetual polemics," were a "happy time," and that Hardy was not happy, is insufficient evidence to support Granville Hicks's conclusion. It "was not a Golden Age or Belle Epoque except to a thin crust of the privileged class," as Mrs. Tuchman [45] remarks. Neither Conrad nor his friend Cunninghame Graham, to whom he dedicated his novel *Typhoon* (1903), found it a happy time. In a letter (August 27, 1898), Conrad wrote Graham:

> Sometimes I feel deeply distressed, at times, a little angry. But I think and think *et la terre tourne.* How long? O Lord! How long? If this miserable planet had perception, a soul, a heart, it would burst with indignation or fly to pieces from sheer pity.[46]

Hardy, in his poem "In Tenebris III" (1896)—the same date

as Conrad's letter—expresses a similar feeling about the
state of affairs:

> There have been times when I well might have passed and
>   the ending have come—
> Ere I had learnt that the world was a welter of futile
>   doing. . . .
> Say, on the noon when the half-sunny hours told that April
>   was nigh . . .
> Or on that winter-wild night when, reclined in the chimney-
>   nook quoin,
> Slowly a drowse overgat me, the smallest and feeblest of
>   folk there,
> Weak from my baptism of pain; when at times and anon I
>   awoke there—
> Heard of a world wheeling on, with no listing or longing to
>   join.[47]

Neither was it a happy time to William Morris, who wrote
during the Haymarket riots in Chicago: "Just think of the
mixture of tyranny and hypocrisy with which the world is
governed. These are the sort of things that make thinking
people so sick at heart that they are driven from all interest
in politics save revolutionary politics; which I must say
seems like to be my case." [48] Nor to George Gissing.[49] Hardy
was concerned with the injustices and evils of society in his
London novels—*The Hand of Ethelberta* and *A Laodicean*
and *Jude,* as were Dickens and Gissing, but they did not
touch on the agricultural malaise, which was the source of
Hardy's pessimism and his concern in the Wessex novels.
Nor in France did Victor Hugo find it a happy time before
his self-exile on the Isle of Guernsey at Hauteville during
the Third Empire of Louis Napoleon (1852–70), nor after
his return to France during the bourgeois third republic;
nor did Anatole France, whose profound pessimism, like
Hardy's, was reinforced by World War I. Hardy himself
noted in his journal on May 9, 1880 :

> If Law itself had consciousness, how the aspect of its creatures
> would terrify it, fill it with remorse!

Hardy was no Panglossian, and the height of his hope in 1867 was as deep as his despair in 1898. This is recorded in a personal letter to his friend Mrs. Arthur Henniker (June 5, 1919): "I should care more for my birthdays if at each succeeding one I could see any sign of real improvement in the world—as at one time I fondly hoped there was." Nor was he alone in this feeling.

George Lukacs notes that "the defeat of the 1848 uprisings in the most important western Europeon countries and in England the collapse of Chartism brought about a profound general ideological depression. The turning-point in historical development," he observes, "is mirrored in literature. This is the epoch of Napoleon III, the emergence of Bismarck's 'Bonapartist Monarchy,' the Prussification of Germany, the great pause in the democratic evolution of England. A universal despairing pessimism descends on the greatest writers," which in Flaubert and Baudelaire "degenerates into nihilism." [50] "Others again—and these are the majority—choose to enter into an ideological compromise with triumphant reaction." [51]

The events since Hardy's death in 1928 would dye his pessimism a darker hue if he were alive today on account of the same triumphant reaction. He was apprehensive about the future of mankind after World War I, as was C. Wright Mills[52] after World War II. The world, historically,*

---

* Marx's chronology of the period from 1815 to 1863 is enlightening: "From 1815 to 1821 depression; 1822 and 1823 prosperity; 1824 abolition of the laws against Trades' Union, great extension of factories everywhere; 1825 crisis; 1826 great misery and riots among the factory operatives; 1827 slight improvement; 1828 great increase in power-looms and in exports; 1829 exports, especially to India, surpass all former years; 1830 glutted markets, great distress; 1831 to 1833 continued depression: the monopoly of the trade with India and China withdrawn from the East India Company; 1834 great increase of factories and machinery, shortness of hands. The new poor law furthers the migration of agricultural labourers into the factory districts. The country districts swept of children. White slave trade; 1835 great prosperity, contemporaneous starvation of the hand-loom weavers; 1836 great prosperity; 1837 & 1838 depression and crisis; 1839 revival; 1840 great depression, riots calling out the military; 1841 and 1842 frightful suffering among the factory operatives; 1842 the manu-

is not a very stable planet, as Conrad observed, and the treaties following wars from the Napoleonic wars till now have hardly added to its stability. Such artists as Hardy and Conrad, who are sensitive to the human condition in their time, have much to communicate to their fellow men about the injustices of society and the tragic consequences if they are not remedied. Blake tried just that when he observed in his time that "the eye sees more than the heart knows" ("Daughters of Albion"). It is not that they were seers—in fact both Conrad and Hardy, unlike Blake, had no religious creed—but, like Blake, they knew that "we are led to believe a lie," as Blake says in his poem "Proverbs," "when we see *with* not *through* the eye," and they show, consequently, some understanding of the lives of their characters in the

facturers lock the hands out of the factories in order to enforce the repeal of the Corn Laws. The operatives stream in thousands into the towns of Lancashire and Yorkshire, are driven back by the military, and their leaders brought to trial at Lancashire; 1843 great misery; 1844 revival; 1845 great prosperity; 1846 continued improvement at first, then reaction. Repeal of the Corn Laws; 1847 crisis, general reduction of wages by 10 and more per cent, in honour of the "big loaf"; 1848 continued depression; Manchester under military protection; 1849 revival; 1850 prosperity; 1851 falling prices, low wages, frequent strikes; 1852 improvement begins, strikes continue, the manufacturers threaten to import foreign hands; 1853 increasing exports. Strike for 8 months, and great misery at Preston; 1854 prosperity, glutted markets; 1855 news of failures stream in from the United States, Canada, and the Eastern markets; 1856 great prosperity; 1857 crisis; 1858 improvement; 1859 great prosperity; increase in factories; 1860 Zenith of the English cotton trade, the Indian, Australian, and other markets so glutted with goods that even in 1863 they had not absorbed the whole lot; the French Treaty of Commerce, enormous growth of factories and machinery; 1861 prosperity continues for a time, reaction, the American civil war, cotton famine; 1862 to 1863 complete collapse" (Marx, *Capital*, pp. 497–98).

Marx comments on how the industrialists "had entered upon the contest for the repeal of the Corn Laws, and needed the workers to help them to victory. They promised, therefore, not only a double-sized loaf of bread but the enactment of a Ten Hours Bill in the Free Trade Millennium" (*ibid.*, pp. 308–9).

Hardy in the preface to *The Mayor of Casterbridge* asks his readers "who have not yet arrived at middle-age . . . to bear in mind that, in the days recalled by the late tale, the home Corn-Trade, on which so much of the action turns, had an importance that can hardly be realized by those accustomed to the sixpenny loaf of the present date and to the present indifference of the public to harvest weather" (p. vii).

crucial time of history about which they write. They do not write in a historical vacuum, and they record the human situation with the empirical observations of fidelity to truth.

This book, however, is concerned with Hardy, not with Conrad.

2

Wessex

One is struck by Hardy's interest in the family, beginning
with his own family, as is shown by the family tree prepared
in his own hand of "The Hardy Pedigree," [1] and in the
family as a social and economic group in his novels, and
finally in the family of man in his epic of the Napoleonic
Wars, *The Dynasts*. I shall restrict myself to the essential
experiences in his life that found expression in his writings
and that shaped his philosophy, and shall try to avoid carrying coal to Newcastle as so many critics have done who have
reiterated the well-known facts of his life without seeing
him in his age.

Thomas Hardy was born about eight o'clock in the
morning of June 2, 1840, in a seven-room gabled house with
thatched roof and three chimneys, in a lonely spot between
woodland and heathland, at Upper Bockhampton,* Dorset.

---

* In a "speech" made by Hardy at the opening of the Bockhampton
Reading Room and Club (Dec. 2, 1919), erected almost on the very spot
where had stood Robert Reason's shoemaking shop when Hardy was a
boy (described in *Under the Greenwood Tree*) as 'Mr. Robert Penny's,' "
Hardy recalled: "The village of Bockhampton has had various owners.
In the time of the Conqueror, it belonged to a Norman countess; later to
a French Priory; and in the time of Queen Elizabeth to the Dean and
Chapter of Exeter, who at the beginning of the last century sold it to
Mr. Morton Pitt, a cousin of Pitt the Premier. What a series of scenes

The place was sometimes called Veterans Valley on account of the number of Napoleonic war pensioners living there, and sometimes Cherry Alley on account of the lane of cherry trees on the hill.

On his father's side Hardy was of French stock, and on his mother's Anglo-Saxon. His father's people were descended from Clement le Hardy, Baily of Jersey, whose son John navigated to England in the fifteenth century and settled at Wareham, then a port. His mother's people—the Chiles, Childs, or Childses—had married into families by the name of Hann or Hands, and Swetman, and resided in the Pidele Valley and the Vale of Blackmore, Dorset, since the time of Charles the First.

His great-grandfather Thomas I had built the house for his son John, who had "married improvidently" at the age of twenty-one, and who had served in the Home Guard during the threat of Napoleon's invasion—an incident related in Hardy's poem "The Alarm," inscribed to him. Hardy's father was a master-mason and contractor, like his grandfather Thomas and his grand-uncle James.° Thomas I died three years before Hardy's birth, and although James was the elder son, the business came into the possession of Hardy's father, Thomas II, who carried it on. Hardy's forebears had built bridges, dwellings, and crypts in the parish as well as supplying stringed music in church and for weddings and christenings and at Christmas time, never accepting any money for their musical performances. These activities "did not, to say the least, assist their building business," Mrs. Hardy says, and it was "somewhat of a relief" to Hardy's mother "when ecclesiastical changes . . . led to her

does this bare list of owners bring back!" (*Later Years*, p. 199). The rustic Coggan, in *Far from the Madding Crowd*, remarks, "New lords, new laws, as the saying is, I suppose" (p. 75).

° Rebecca West's remark that "Hardy came half from the yeoman class and half from the labouring class" (*Literary Digest*, Feb. 21, 1931) is true, but her statement that "he was anxious to be above criticism and arrange himself with the yeoman class" is false.

husband's abandoning in 1841 or 1842 all connection with the choir." [2]

The Hardys had been large landowners and burgesses of towns during Elizabethan times, but their possessions had shrunk after the Enclosure Acts and the beginning of the Industrial Revolution. Of one of the more influential members of the family, whom his mother had pointed out to him when he was a child, Hardy observed (Sept. 30, 1888): "So we go down, down, down." [3] Hardy's father at the time of his death in 1892 was the only landowner by that name left in the county. His holdings consisted of a homestead of an acre-and-a-half with garden and orchard, a horse paddock, and sand and gravel pits at Bockhampton, and also a freehold farm at Talbothays, with some houses and a brick yard and a kiln elsewhere.

His maternal ancestors had suffered reverses. Christopher Childs, Hardy notes, "the brother of my great grandmother who left Dorset was a Jacobite, which accounted for the fall of his fortunes"; the Swetmans had sided with the Duke of Monmouth against James the Second in the rebellion of 1685, and though better off economically than the majority of small farmers and miners among Monmouth's supporters, their adherence to the lost cause "seems to have helped becloud the family's prospects . . . if they had ever been bright." [4] Swetman had been brought before Judge Jeffreys "for being absent from home att the tyme of the Rebellion," [*] which had been crushed by William of Orange sending back the troops stationed in Holland. Hardy's maternal grandmother Elizabeth Swetman (1778–1847) had undergone trying experiences in raising her family of seven after her husband's death and her father's cutting her out of his in-

[*] In the fall of 1907 Hardy and Sir Frederick Treves, the Serjeant-surgeon, both being Dorset men, frequently discussed the question of the "poor whites" in Barbados," descendants of the Dorset and Somerset "rebels" banished there by Judge Jeffreys, who had become "a degenerate and decadent race" (*Later Years*, p. 126). Hardy asks in his first serialized novel, *A Pair of Blue Eyes:* "How shall Monmouth's men fight when Monmouth runs away?"

heritance, "which she could never speak of without pain," [5] and she never wished to revisit her birthplace, the village of Fawley, which Hardy took for Jude's surname. Jemima, the eldest daughter, became skilled at mantua-making and tambouring gloves, and was on the point of going to work as a cook in a London clubhouse when, attending Stinsford Parish Church one Sunday, she glimpsed, in the musician's gallery, Thomas Hardy Sr. She was a woman slightly below average height, with a Roman nose, chestnut hair, and gray eyes, and she thought him rather amusingly old fashioned in his "red and black flowered waistcoat, Wellington boots, and French trousers, but decidedly good-looking" with his Vandyke beard. The incident is described in Hardy's poem "A Church Romance (Mellstock: *circa* 1835)":

> She turned again; and in her pride's despite
> One strenuous viol's inspirer seemed to throw
> A message from his string to her below,
> Which said: "I claim thee as my own forthright!" [6]

They were married in 1836, and the question of moving to town arose—"was indeed always arising," Mrs. Hardy says, after the birth of each child—Thomas, Mary, Henry, Katherine. Mrs. Hardy favored moving for the children's sake, but his father opposed it, so they stayed on "wealth-wantless," in their old home, as Hardy says in his poem to his father, "On One Who Lived and Died Where He Was Born." [7] His grandmother, sixty-two at the time of Hardy's birth, who lived with them, had helped his grandfather plant the east belt of trees around their house—the woodland part—and they had lived through the good times and anxieties of the Napoleonic Wars and the anxieties and bad times of The Peasants' Rebellion afterwards. His grandmother had doctored half the village, "her anchor sheet being Culpepper's *Herbal Dispensary*," and she was called on as an unerring authority" if there was any question as to where a parishioner was buried. Hardy recalls in his poem about his birthplace "Domicilium" (1857–1860), how "[my] father's mother would take me out to walk," and her answer, "which I remember well," to his question on "how looked the spot when first she settled there":

> Fifty years
> Have passed since then, my child, and change has marked
> The face of all things. Yonder garden-plots
> And orchards were uncultivated slopes
> O'ergrown with bramble bushes, furze and thorn;
> That road a narrow path shut in by ferns,
> Which, almost trees, obscured the passer-by.
> Our house stood quiet alone, and those tall firs
> And beeches were not planted. Snakes and efts
> Swarmed in the summer days, and nightly bats
> Would fly about our bedrooms. Heathcroppers
> Lived on the hills, and were our only friends,
> So wild it was when first we settled here.[8]

In *Far from the Madding Crowd* and *The Woodlanders*, he pictures the later time, after the sheep-enclosures, when the sheep, as if in protest, "as they ruminated, looked quietly in the bedroom windows" of Mrs. Charmond's house at the village of Little Hintock, about fourteen miles northwest of Dorchester.

Hardy had a very happy and normal childhood, enriched by an early interest in the family's books,* fostered by his mother, and in music, fostered by his father. The Hardys had a piano and a violin and several song books. His father played old songs on his violin (which afterwards hung in Hardy's study at Max Gate), such as "Enrico," "Miss Mac-Leod of Ayer," "My Fancy Lad," and "Johnny's Gone to Sea," while his mother sang, for like Tess's mother she had an ear for a tune, and he danced in the middle of the room, or improvised on the little accordion his father had given

---

* Addison and Steele, Richardson, Fielding, *Paradise Lost, Pilgrim's Progress*, Dumas Père (in translation), Shakespeare, Johnson's *Rasselas*, and *Paul and Virginia*, and Dryden's *Virgil*, which his mother gave him in 1848 (*Early Life*, pp. 8, 21, 31).

him on his fourth birthday. As a child he played at being "a parson," with his grandmother acting as the congregation and his cousin as the clerk, to the amusement of the family except his mother, who did not want her son to be a parson, but to become one "had been his dream." [9] At other times he watched while the setting sun blazoned the crimson staircase with a certain chromatic effect, when he would fervently recite a line from Dr. Watt's hymn, "And now another day has gone." [10]

He early developed a great interest in nature, both his parents being great outdoor livers. His mother took him on walks along the Via Vicenza, which ran across the heath "straight and bare, as a pale parting line in hair"—an image described in his poem "The Roman Road"—when she had knelt down beside him. His father showed him defense ramparts on Rainbarrow Tumulus dating back to Napoleonic times, and the Coliseum, or "Ring," in Dorchester, a relic of the Roman occupation. Nature and history were inseparable companions on these walks in the woods and on the heath. Seeing a bustard was a rare occurrence, but his father remembered a time, not many years before, when he had seen five-and-twenty at one time. An imaginative boy, Hardy had listened to the wind on the heath and in the woods and investigated afterwards the damage done to trees by the storm. He had observed the mistletoe on the oak trees and noticed how "the chimney of the house was enlarged by the boughs of the parasite to the aspect of a ruined tower." [11] He had seen the snakes sloughing off their winter skins, had worried about birds going "to bed, supperless," and had never forgotten a half-frozen fieldfare he had seen in the garden with his father at the end of a winter day.[12]

The outdoors improved his health, and in 1848, at the age of eight, he was enrolled in the model Church-of-England school, at Lower Bockhampton, just opened by the Grand Dame of the Manor, Mrs. Julia Augusta Martin, who employed his father part-time as caretaker of her estate,

Kingston-Maurward. It was a three-story, "mid-Tudor and early Georgian" mansion, which had once belonged to the Dorset Greys and the Pitts, whose arms, quartered with the Stawells, commemorated "the marriage of Angel Grey," [13] Miss Hardy notes (pp. 20ff), and were carved over the porch. Mrs. Martin indulged him in a godmotherly way and, being childless, took a benefactress's interest in him and in her school. In a hollow near the roadside and the school was Mr. Penny's shoeshop, outside the window of which was "the upper-leather of a Wellington boot, pegged to a board as if to dry," [14] and not far away a blacksmith shop, a tranter's place, and "several old Elizabethan houses with mullioned windows and doors of Ham Hill stone." Farther on were some little Stephen Foster homes, dwellings of "the parish paupers before workhouses were built," and "the Poor-houses just at the corner turning down to the dairy." [15]

The following year his mother took him on a trip to visit her sister in Hertfordshire, where he attended for a short time a school on the "Squeers" model of Dickens's *Nicholas Nickleby*. On their return home his parents considered him strong enough to walk to the Grammar School in Dorchester, some two-and-a-half miles distant, founded by his namesake, Thomas Hardy of Melcombe Regis, who died in 1599 before Milton was born. Mrs. Martin became angry at the Hardys for sending "Tommy" to a nonconformist school—which they had not known it was at that time—in preference to her Church-of-England school, and discharged Hardy's father from her employ. This quarrel created some financial anxiety and hard feelings. The Hardys would have left the parish altogether, but because they enjoyed lifehold to the property, they remained, Mrs. Hardy says. The boy was torn between loyalty to his parents and affection for "her ladyship," who ceased to welcome him in her home. Something of his feeling is expressed in his poem "In Her Precincts," when seeing her house dark "from the foggy lea," he imagined that she missed him as much as he did her, but seeing it lighted and "glee within" one night, felt "the gloom of severance mine alone." [16]

He soon came to like the Nonconformist school better, for they had only to learn the Ten Commandments, on which they were drilled once a week, instead of the boring catechism, which had been a daily drill at Mrs. Martin's school. He remained there for three years (1849–1852), studying out of the textbooks of the time—Walkingame's *Arithmetic,* Tate's *Mechanics,* and Nesbitt's *Mensuration;* and in 1852 he followed his teacher Isaac Glandfield Last, who "opened a more advanced school, called an Academy, where boarders were taken." Mr. Last° allowed him to take Latin as an extra subject and awarded him as a prize "Beza's Latin Testament, for his progress in the tongue." [17]

Hardy had the usual adolescent attachments—Elizabeth, a gamekeeper's daughter with beautiful bay-red hair (commemorated in his poem "To Lizbie Browne," who despised him because he was a year or two younger than she; and Louisa (Louisa Harding), a farmer's daughter, who had smiled at him on the way home from school (commemorated in his poems "To Louisa in the Lane" and "The Passer-By") and who, he learned later, had gone to a boarding school for young ladies in Weymouth. There was also a young girl from Windsor, in whom he was disappointed because she showed no interest in Herne or Anne Boleyn of Ainsworth's *Windsor Castle.* He was popular with his classmates—"almost too popular," Mrs. Hardy says, and he disliked having anyone walking home with him, or laying a hand on his shoulder. One lad asked him, "Hardy, how is it that you do not like us to touch you?" His reply is not given, but "this peculiarity never left him," [18] Mrs. Hardy says. He played the violin at weddings and christenings, being showered on one occasion

---

° Mr. Last's son, W. J. Last, Director of the Science Museum, South Kensington, London, whose obituary notice in *The Times* (June 1911) "gave details of a life more successful than his father's," Mrs. Hardy says, "though not of higher intellectual ability than that by which it had been Hardy's good fortune to profit" (*Later Years,* p. 149).

with "a hatful of pennies." With the money he bought a book about games, *The Boys Own Book,* which he had seen in a Dorchester shop, despite the Hardys' practice of never accepting pay for their musical performances; and some time later he bought a writing-desk in Treves's store. Treves's son Frederick attended the same school as Hardy's sister Mary.

His formal education ceased in 1856 on his graduation from Mr. Last's school, and Hardy was articled to Mr. John Hicks, a Dorchester architect, whom his father had known when he and another contractor carried out Hicks's restoration plan of Woodsford Castle. Hicks offered to take Hardy "for somewhat less than the usual premium," payable in the middle of a term of three years," but Hardy's father being "a ready-money man," he paid the full amount (£40, according to the extant receipt) [19] at the start of the term, and on July 11, 1856, Hardy began his apprenticeship with Hicks, whose family lived in rooms above his office at 30 Church Street, Dorchester. The last year of his apprenticeship Hardy took lodgings in town, but up till then he walked back and forth daily from home to Hicks's office.

In Hicks Hardy found a man who, in many ways, was like his own father—kindly, good-natured, easy-going ("A milder-mannered man never scuttled a sacred edifice," [20] he remarked on Hicks's death), and who preferred Dorchester to Bristol, where he had formerly practiced, finding a country town less competitive. Hicks had other pupils besides Hardy under his tutelage—Fippard, a dandyish "comet-like young man," who was just finishing his apprenticeship; Hooper Tolbort, the orphan nephew of one of the partners in a firm of mechanical engineers, who had attended a good school in London and regretted having to give up his classical studies; and Henry Bastow, an ardent Baptist youth, also interested in the classics. A dispute over a knotty problem in syntax was always taken to William Barnes, the Dorset poet and philologist, who was keeping school next door, and who was also tutoring Tolbort for his examination for the Indian Civil Service, which he passed with an outstanding grade according to the list of names in the *Times*.[21] Barnes may well have loaned Hardy some of his *Poems of Rural Life in the Dorset Dialect* (1844) and *Hwomley Rhymes* (1858). In the former collection were six poems under Latin titles dealing sympathetically with the farm-workers' plight, originally published in *The Dorset Chronicle* (1833–1834), which was read in homes of landowners and laborers alike—poems disproving E. M. Forster's accusation that Barnes "could live through the Labourers Revolt in 1830 without its shadows falling across his verse." [22] Hardy would have been attracted by the Latin titles, and he admired Barnes's speaking out in the farmworkers' cause when doing so involved the risk of losing his teaching job at Mere. The following lines would not have fallen on deaf ears:

> For to breed the young fox or the heare,
>   We can gi'e up whole eacres o'ground,
> But the greens be a-grug'd, vor to rear
>   Our young children up healthy an' sound.
> Why, there woont be a-left the next age
>   A green spot where the veet can goo free;
> And the goocoo wull soon be committed to cage
>   Vor a trespass in zomebody's tree.
> Vor 'tis lock'en up, Thomas, an' blocken up,
>   Stranger or brother,
> Men mussen come nigh woone another.

Barnes also protested against the free-enterprise system, in *Views of Labour and Gold* (1859), as had Thomas Hodgskin, a retired naval lieutenant on half pay, in *Labour Defended against the Claims of Capital* (1825). Barnes summarizes the situation:

> The Kindness which is done by Capital when it affords employment to people, from whom, by a monopoly, it has taken their little businesses is such as one might do to a cock by adorning his head with a plume of feathers pulled out of his own tail.[23]

One may be sure that Barnes and Hardy discussed other
things than Latin grammar and the classics.

In this congenial atmosphere Hardy acquired a draughtman's skills and also kept up his interests in the classics,
doing most of his studying between five o'clock and breakfast; in this way he got through "several books of the
Aeneid, some Horace and Ovid," after which he took up
Greek, "which he had not learnt at school," beginning with
the *Iliad.* His friend Bastow, to whom he had written, replied from Hobart Town (May 1861): "I have scarcely
touched a book—Greek, I mean since. I see you are trying
all you can to cut me out." Hardy's thirst for knowledge
and his perseverance at his studies remind one of Jude's.
He had abandoned "the heathen authors" temporarily to
look into the subject of paedobaptism, reading up on it in
Hooker's *Ecclesiastical Polity* (1594) and in a *Handbook,*
borrowed from a priest in order to argue "one against three"
with Bastow and the two Perkins brothers, sons of the Baptist minister and students at Aberdeen University. Sometimes
they "waxed so polemical" that Mrs. Hicks would call down-
stairs for them to quiet down. "His convictions on the
necessity of adult baptism gradually wore out of him," Mrs.
Hardy says, "and while perceiving that there was not a shred
of evidence for infant baptism in the New Testament, he
saw that Christianity did not hang on temporary details
that expediency might not modify, and that the practice of
an isolated few in the early ages could not be binding on
its multitudes in differing circumstances, when it had grown
to be the religion of continents." [24] His feelings about the
subject come out in the scene between Tess and the clergy-
man, who at first objects, on liturgical grounds, to recognizing Tess's baptism of her dead baby, and even more so
to granting it a Christian burial, reluctantly assuring her,
"My dear girl it will be just the same" [25] at last.

One "unusual incident" occurred that left a lasting impression on Hardy. One summer morning before breakfast,

he suddenly remembered that a man was to be hanged at eight o'clock at Dorchester. Taking his grandfather's big brass telescope, he hastened to a hill on the heath a quarter of a mile away and looked toward Dorchester. "The sun behind his back shone straight on the white stone façade of the gaol," and he could see the gallows, the form of the murderer in white fustian, the executioner and officials in dark clothing and the crowd below "at this distance of nearly three miles." As he placed the glass to his eye, the white figure dropped downwards, and the town clock struck eight. He felt as if he had been "alone on the heath with the hanged man," and the "whole thing had been so sudden that the glass nearly fell from [his] hands." "It was the second and last execution he witnessed," Mrs. Hardy says, "the first having been that of a woman two or three years earlier, when he stood close to the gallows."

There were more mundane questions to disturb a young man of military age in the international situation in 1859 when the French invaded Sardinia. On May 1, while the pacification of India was being observed publicly in the churches, England was on the brink of war* with France and feverishly building ironclads to meet the threat of France's steam-driven navy. Parliament passed a Volunteer Act mobilizing the country's manpower, to which Tennyson, in the official capacity of Poet Laureate, contributed his poem "Riflemen Form!" (*The Times*, May 9, 1859), and tens of thousands of Englishmen, William Morris among them, joined up. Hardy, nineteen, was wondering whether the

---

* Sidney Herbert, then at the war office, wrote privately to Gladstone (Nov. 23, 1859) "that he was convinced that a great calamity was impending in the shape of a war provoked by France. Officers who had visited that country told him that all thinking men in France were against war with England, all noisy men for it, the army for it, and above all the government for it. . . . The general expectation was for next summer. French tradesmen at St. Malo were sending in their bills to the English, thinking war coming. 'We have to do with a godless people who look on war as a game open to all without responsibility or sin; and there is a man [Napoleon III] at the head of them who combines the qualities of a gambler and a fatalist" (Morley's *Gladstone*, 2:43).

history of his grandfather's time was going to repeat itself. The crisis was narrowly averted by the signing of a commercial treaty (1860) favorable to free trade.°

This situation most certainly brought back to Hardy the excitement over the Crimean War, when he was sixteen and England had lost her Wellington only two years before. Wellington, without chagrin, had put down the Chartists and supported the restoration of Louis Napoleon in 1848, when Metternich fled Vienna and was living in a London hotel and the Prussian Crown Prince had taken refuge in Strothfield Saye.°° During his residence in England, Louis Napoleon courted a Miss Damer, who lived with her parents at Winterborne-Came House, near Dorchester and near William Barnes, who told Hardy (Oct. 17, 1885) an amusing incident involving himself and Hardy's "peppery" grandfather Hann. They were promenading on the South Walk in full dress, as was the custom of Dorchester people on a Sunday afternoon. "For a freak," Louis Napoleon slipped his cane between Hann's legs as they passed each other in opposite directions, and Hann, "almost before Barnes knew what was happening had pulled off his coat, thrown it on Barnes, and was challenging Louis Napoleon to a fight." [26] The latter apologized profusely and the walk was resumed without further incident.

He heard other stories from old timers; how,

> when Jack Ketch had done whipping by the Town Pump [Dorchester], the prisoners' coats were thrown over their bleeding backs, and, guarded by the town constables with their long staves, they were conducted back to prison. Close at their heels came J. K., the cats held erect—there was one cat to each man—the lashes were of knotted whipcord.[27]

and how, James Bushrod [28] of Broadmayne had seen

° In 1860 the number of articles bearing custom duties was reduced from 371 to 48, of which only 14 were important: sugar, tea, tobacco, wine, coffee, corn currants, timber, cheese, figs, hops, peppers, raisins and rice (*ibid*).

°° See Richard Aldington's *The Duke,* p. 360.

two German soldiers of the York Hussars shot for desertion on Bincombe Down in 1801, "and there was a mark" on the spot, according to James Selby, one of his father's old workmen, who had engaged in the illicit business of rum-running.

These "occurred between 1825 and 1830," Hardy says in the preface to *Wessex Tales* (p. 4), "and the lawbreakers were brought to trial before Baron Bolland," who had practiced in the Old Bailey and was the Baron of the Exchequer (1829-1839). He had also heard a smuggling story from the landlord, Captain Masters, at Swanage in November 1875, which he "always remembered":

The narrator was in a fishing-boat going to meet a French lugger half-Channel-over, to receive spirit-tubs and land them. He and his mates were some nine miles off Portland, which was the limit allowed, when they were sighted by the revenue-cutter. Seeing the cutter coming up, they said "We must act as if we were fishing for mackerel." But they had no bait, and the ruse would be discovered. They snapped up the stems of their tobacco-pipes, and unfastening the hook from a line they had with them slipped on the bits of tobacco-pipe above the shank. The officers came—saw them fishing, and merely observing that they were a long way from shore, and dubiously asking why, and being innocently told because the fish were there, left them. Then, as if the bait had been genuine, to their surprise, on pulling up the sham line they began to haul in mackerel. The fish had made their deception truth.

These tales stirred Hardy's imagination and he drew on them for his short stories "The Melancholy Hussar of the German Legion" and "The Distracted Preacher" (1879), the latter an audacious tale of rum-smuggling—Cherbourg to Weymouth—involving a mild-mannered landlady, a Wesleyan minister, and a smuggler, Jim, of which he says in a footnote that "the ending of the story, with the marriage of Lizzy and the minister was almost *de rigeur* in an English magazine at the time of writing." But he restored the original version in which Lizzy, much to her credit, "stuck with Jim," and after their marriage they emigrated to Wisconsin. One suspects that Hardy used Selby's nickname for his smuggler and that it suggested his having the furmity-woman of *The Mayor* refer to herself as "a land-smuggler in a large way of business" in her trial on a drunkenness charge before the judge for the day, Henchard, who had sold his wife in her furmity-tent eighteen years before. The former is embittered by the decline in her fortunes and the rise of his.

The agitation for the repeal of the Corn Laws was something else, and by far the most important experience of Hardy's early boyhood. His father took him to anti-corn law demonstrations in Dorchester's Roman Coliseum, at which he heard recited or sung some of Ebenezer Elliot's *Corn Law Rhymes* (1834), "dedicated to Jeremy Bentham, our second Locke," of which "The Ranter" [29] was typical during the time when "work grew scarce while bread grew dear":

> Yes, when our country is one vast disease,
> And failing fortunes sadden every door—
> These, O ye quacks! These are your remedies:
> Alms for the rich! A bread tax for the poor.

He may have recalled the lines in London in 1866 when Parliament indemnified millionaire landlords during the cattle-disease epidemic and did nothing for the London poor. "Song," sung to the tune of "Land of the Leal," would have appealed to young Hardy because of his father's stories about poachers like K. Troyton, caught in the great fray at Westwood Barn near Lulworth Castle, about 1825. He was led past his own door in chains, riveted on by Dick Facey,[30] the journeyman for Clare the Smith, to say goodbye to his family, who never heard of him again:

> No tax in despair,
>   No tyrant, no slave;
> No bread tax is there
>   With a maw like the grave.

> But the poacher thy pride,
> Whelm'd in ocean afar,
> And his brother who died
> Land-butchered in war.

This was a very different picture of Heaven from the one hymned to him in Stinsford Parish Church, or described by the catechism teacher in Lady-of-the-manor Mrs. Martin's Church-of-England school:

> The rich man in his castle,
> The poor man at his gate,
> God made them high and lowly
> And ordered their estate.[31]

In 1850 Hardy had attended with his father a No-Popery riot in Dorchester, in protest against the establishment of a Catholic hierarchy in England by Papal Bull, ordaining Fr. Wiseman as Cardinal and Archbishop of Westminster. He had been shocked to recognize, in the hooded procession of marchers burning the Cardinal in effigy, one marcher whose cowl blew aside, as one of his father's workmen. England had been a Protestant nation since Henry VIII had disenfranchised the Catholic church and confiscated the Papal lands in 1534, and priests ever since were as obsessed with getting them back as Fr. Corbelan in Conrad's *Nostromo*.[32] The Vatican's edict provoked ire among the populace, and the English magazine *Punch,* edited by Mark Lemon, "a champion of the under-dog," [33] which Hardy read, had campaigned against Papal aggression.

In 1861 Bastow completed his apprenticeship with Mr. Hicks and departed for Tasmania. Hardy, as senior pupil, was given more responsibilities and duties by Hicks in the church restoration business, "which was at this time in full cry in Dorsetshire and the neighbouring counties." Hardy had become acquainted with Horace Moule, son of the Vicar of Fordington and a graduate of Queen's College, Cambridge, who was just beginning to write for the *Saturday Review*, a Benthamite periodical, which advocated "the greatest happiness to the greatest number." Hardy's interest shifted from Homer to contemporary writers, and he read and discussed with Moule Bagehot's *Literary Estimates* (1860) and *Essays and Reviews* (1860) by "the Seven Against Christ," "these two works impressing him much." [34] The latter, Dean Church wrote to the American scientist Asa Gray, created "a greater row" [35] between the supporters of the old religion and the new science than *The Origin of Species* (1859). Moule, who recognized Hardy's promise, continued to bias him in the direction of books and gave him a copy of Jabez Hogg's* *Experimental and Natural Philosophy* (1853), Evelyn Hardy says (p. 52), and in 1862 a copy of Palgrave's *Golden Treasury* (1861), a poetry anthology. Hardy consulted Moule on whether he should continue his Greek studies, and Moule reluctantly advised, Mrs. Hardy says, that "if Hardy really had (as his father had insisted and as indeed was reasonable, since he never as yet had earned a farthing in his life) to make an income in some way by architecture in 1862, it would hardly be worthwhile

* Editor of the *Journal of British Opthalmology* and author of a treatise on cataracts, which went through three editions, and of a book *The Microscope: Its History* (1854), and of a letter "Who's to blame: The Poor-Law Board or the St. Pancras Guardians," which appeared in *The Examiner & London Review* (1869).

"At Lyme, Sept," (1882), Hardy· notes: "met on the Cobb an old man who had undergone a cataract operation," who said. "It was like a red-hot needle in yer eye whilst he was doing it. . . . He wasn't a minute mor than three-quarters of an hour at the outside. When he had done one eye, 'a said. 'Now my man you must make shift with that one and be thankful you bain't left wi' narn.' So he didn't do the other, and I'm glad 'a didn't I've saved half-crowns and half-crowns out of number in only wanting one glass to my spectacles. T'other eye would never have paid the expenses of keeping en going" (*Early Life*, p. 200). Hardy has Dr. Fitzpiers show Grace" a fragment of old John South's brain which I am investigating under the microscope" (*The Woodlanders*, p. 156).

** Contained several of Shakespeare's poems, a few anonymous poems, and the following poets: K. Barnfield, T. Campion, C. Cibbey, C. Dancet, J. Donne, W. Drummond, R. Herrick, J. Herbert, J. Milton, T. Shirley, P. Sidney, E. Spenser, and W. Wordsworth, but nothing by Byron or Tennyson, who were added to later editions, however.

for him to read Aeschylus and Sophocles in 1859–61." "He had secretly wished," Mrs. Hardy says, "that Moule would advise him to go on with Greek plays in spite of the serious damage it might do to his architecture," but he followed Moule's advice. "The copy of his *Iliad* bears the notation," Evelyn Hardy [36] says, "Left off, Bockhampton, 1860."

Hardy, having completed his apprenticeship with Hicks in April 1862, bought a round-trip ticket to London, boarded the train in Dorchester on Thursday, April 17, to look for a job in the profession his father had chosen for him and to take in the Great Exhibition, which was opening on May 1.

3

London

Hardy paused on Waterloo Bridge to gaze at the city of London—the largest metropolis in the world, with a population of four million—overcome with the vastness of it, "with a vivid sense of his own insignificance in it." [1] "The greyness creeping over green fields" had increased considerably since 1848, when he and his mother had gazed at London from Swiss Cottage, a suburb then, on their trip to his maternal aunt in Hertfordshire. They had stayed overnight at a coaching-inn, The Cross-Keys, St. John Street, Clerkenwell—the same one at which Shelley and Mary Godwin used to meet on weekends "not two score years before," [2] and little changed since then. They had speculated on whether the room at the top of the oval stairway might not have been the same one that Shelley, like themselves, took for economy's sake, and it may have been the reason why he took a copy of Shelley's poems with him on the train.

Searching for lodgings, Hardy met a bachelor in his thirties whose cousin he had known, who questioned the advisability of anyone's coming to London. "Wait till you have walked the streets a few weeks," he warned, "and your elbows begin to shine, and the hems of your trousers get frayed, as if nibbled by rats! Only practical men are wanted here." [3] "Hardy began to wish," Mrs. Hardy says, "he had thought less of the Greek Testament and more of iron girders." [4]

With the letters of recommendation from "a gushing lady" and from Mr. Hicks, he went to see the persons to whom they were addressed. Mr. Ferrey, of Trinity Place, Charing Cross, who had designed a Dorset mansion on which Hardy's father had worked, and also the Gothic-styled All Saints Church in Blackheath suburbs, erected in 1859, received Hardy civilly and inquired about his father and offered to assist. Mr. Norton, whom Hicks had known during their Bristol days, and a former pupil of Ferrey's, welcomed him "with great kindness," telling him "he must on no account be doing nothing in London." He offered him the use of his office in Old Bond Street, a bottleneck of traffic, and referred him to a possible opening with Arthur W. Blomfield, of 8 St. Martin's Place. Blomfield was favorably impressed with Hardy and asked him to report for work on May 5. Delighted at obtaining a job within a fortnight after his arrival, Hardy returned to his lodgings at 1861 Clarence House, Kilburn, and wrote his parents of his good fortune, but held onto his return ticket for six months.

Hardy commuted daily by train from Kilburn station, with the conductor's voice ringing in his ears, "Any more passengers for London!" to Blomfield's architectural office in the City. He puts something of the hurly-burly at the station in his description of Stephen and Elfride, who, re-gretting their elopement, are as anxious to get a train home as they had been to get there. Stephen, inquiring, is brushed aside by a guard, but Elfride is harkened to by another guard.

"Is there a train for Plymouth tonight?" said Elfride.
"Yes, miss; the 8 : 10—leaves in ten minutes. You have come to the wrong platform; it is the other side. Change at Bristol into the night mail. Down that staircase and under the line."
They run down the staircase—Elfride first to the booking-

office, and into a carriage with an official standing beside the door. "Show your tickets, please." They are locked in—men about the platform accelerate their velocities till they fly up and down like shuttles in a loom—a whistle—the waving of a flag—a human cry, a steam groan and away they go to Plymouth again, just catching these words as they glide off.

"Those two youngsters had a near run for it, and no mistake." [5]

But Hardy had as yet found no sweetheart in London and left none at home. His days were spent bending over the drawing-board at Blomfield's and his evenings reading Shelley and other English poets at his lodgings, or playing, on a secondhand fiddle he had bought, arias from Italian romantic operas with a fellow-lodger who played the piano.

Mr. Blomfield was the son of the recently deceased Dr. C. J. Blomfield, Bishop of London, whose salary was £10,000 per annum,[6] and at a later date became the architect for the Bank of England. He employed several young assistants and enjoyed a lucrative practice. One may judge of the extent and success of his business by the fact that at one time he had five cathedrals as established customers and he designed many public buildings, libraries, and schools. A lithe, athletic man of thirty-three, a graduate of Rugby and Trinity College, Cambridge, where he had been "a great boating man," Blomfield had served his apprenticeship under Philip G. Hardwicke, who had built the elegant hall of the Goldsmiths Company in Foster Lane. He was also "a genuine humorist like his father the Bishop," Mrs. Hardy says, and possibly this ameliorated some of Hardy's sensitivity about his own working-class origin and the feelings an intellectually inclined young man who had only finished grammar school is apt to have toward an employer who is a university graduate and an influential businessman.

Hardy had come to London at a prosperous time of great bulding activity, stimulated partly from the discovery of gold in California and Australia, which had depleted the labor supply, and partly from the removal of tariff barriers, which had upped imports and exports. The building trades, which agreed with Marx[7] that "a working day should be shorter than a natural day," had won a nine-hour day by their prolonged strike (1859–1862), in spite of the government's having intervened in July 1861 by sending troops to work at Chelsea Barracks on the £100,000 project to house one thousand Napoleonic War veterans. Cotton manufacturing, which had yielded in 1860 five-thirteenths of the total English export at 6d a pound, was at its zenith in 1861, and Iron had become "the daily bread of all industries," as Cobden remarked, and had already made its own "Divine Image" of cruelty and terror on "the human heart" as well as on the human dress in Blake's poem of that name, in which even the punctuation contributes its sledgehammer blows:

> The Human Dress. is forged Iron
>   The Human Form. a fiery Forge,
> The Human Face. a furnace seal'd
>   The Human Heart. its hungry Gorge.

The blast furnaces, shipyards, and railroad construction were at an all-time high from the government's spending on war industries, with the specter of a cotton famine on account of the American Civil War, yet with such an overproduction of cotton goods that the government was intriguing with the Confederacy.[8] The national expenditure increased from 52 million pounds in 1859, when Gladstone had framed his famous budget, to seventy million pounds in 1862. Hardy must have recalled Marcellus's words to Horatio on why Hamlet's father's ghost "at this dead hour with martial stalk hath gone by our watch."

> And why such daily cast of brazen cannon
> And foreign mart for implements of war;
> Why such impress of shipwrights whose sore task

Does not divide the Sunday from the week?;
What might be toward, that this sweaty haste
Doth make the night joint-labourer with the day?

The textile workers starved or worked at roadmaking rather than aid the Confederacy.° "The English *ateliers nationaux* of 1862 and of the following years, established for the benefit of the destitute cotton operatives," Marx notes, "differ from the French of 1848 in this, that in the latter the workman had to do unproductive work at the expense of the state; in the former . . . productive municipal work to the advantage of the bourgeois, and that, too[,] cheaper than the regular workmen, with whom they were in competition." English workshops in the open—that is what these national workshops were Marx declared (*The Class Struggle in France*, p. 299).

The London of Dickens and Thackeray was in the process of reconstruction. The new houses of Parliament, of Tudor Gothic design, which combined Barry's knowledge of functionalism and Pugin's of Gothic decoration, were only ten years old; Ruskin called them "eternal foolscap in freestone." [9] Westminster Bridge, on which Wordsworth composed his famous sonnet "Earth has not anything to show more fair," had been torn down in 1861, and a new

° In Oct. 1862, 60.3% of the spindles and 58% of the looms were standing; few mills worked full time (60 hours a week), the remainder worked at intervals. Wages shrank, owing to good cotton being replaced by bad, Sea Island by Egyptian (in fine spinning mills), American and Egyptian by Surat, and pure cotton by mixing of waste and Surat." Manufacturers "reduced rate of piece-wage by 5, 7½, and 10 per cent and made wage deductions for rent in their miserable shacks and for defects in the finished article that were really due to the bad cotton and unsuitable machinery (see Marx, *Capital*, pp. 498–99). Marx condemned the ruling classes for supporting the slaveowners during the American Civil War and for the conniving at the suppression of Caucasians and Poles by Russia (see Harrison's "Beesly's St. James Speech" (*Science & Society*, Fall, 1963). The *Daily News* and the *Spectator* were pro-North, the London press predominantly Southern. Hardy's friend Moule advised him to read Goldwyn Smith on American slavery and Kinglake's Invasion of the Crimea (see Evelyn Hardy's "Thomas Hardy & Horace Moule," London *Times Literary Supplement*, 23, 1, 1969, p. 59.

bridge nearly completed, which was opened on May 24, 1862. Hungerford Market, a large rambling two-story building with vegetable, fruit, meat, and fish stalls on the banks of the Thames, rebuilt in 1833, was demolished in August 1862 for the erection of the Embankment and Charing Cross Bridge. Hardy had occasionally "lunched at a 'Coffee house' there"—probably Gatti and Morica's [10] small foreign café with an orchestra, for he was fond of music. Blackfriars Bridge was torn down in 1863. The blocks of buldings known as the Law Courts were still in the blueprint stage of their designer C. E. Street. Some four hundred dwellings, in the space of eight acres and housing four thousand persons, were slated for demolition between 1866 and 1868. One of the reasons for the overcrowding in this area was the dispensing of coals, tea and bread, sugar, and other commodities to the poor at Christmas time.[11] Business was expanding and rapidly replacing residences. The restaurant in St. Martin's Street, Leicester Square, called Newton House, had been the residence and observatory of Sir Isaac Newton and later of the Burneys, who had entertained Johnson, Reynolds, and other celebrities at the time, and was now the dining spot of the Cannibal Club, to which Swinburne belonged. Holborn Hill was a steep and noisy thoroughfare, on which omnibus horses slipped on the greasy street and struggled to get up the hill. Skinner Street ran close by, with presumably Godwin's house yet standing on it, Mrs. Hardy says, "at which Shelley first set eyes on Mary." London, or the "Great Wen," as Johnson had called it, had grown considerably since his day; urban development had wrought changes in "At a House in Hampstead: Sometime the Dwelling of John Keats," [12] described in Hardy's poem "At a House in Hampstead":

> O Poet, come you haunting here,
> Where streets have stolen up all around
> And never a nightingale pours one
>   Full-throated song?

and :

> What will you do in your surprise
> At seeing that changes wrought in Rome
> Are wrought yet more on the misty slope
> One time your home?

Another house on the heath, called the Upper Flask Inn, was once the resort of the Kit-Cat Club,[13] where Steele, Addison, Richardson, and other literary men had met. Marx and his wife occasionally picknicked on Hampstead Heath of a Sunday with their small children,° Guido, Franziska, and Edgar.[14] He gave them a ride on his back and recited poetry of which he was fond—Heine, Shakespeare, Goethe —substituting the name of Liebig for Hamlet in "Liebig can a tale unfold (*Capital,* p. 422 n), who, he explained, was a German agronomist who had studied the value of fertilizers to the soil that produced the food they ate; or on a windy day changing John Oxenham's lines "To whom shall the world henceforth belong?" to "Who owns the wind?" while they scampered around his knees.

The bridge across Ludgate Hill, which Hardy later thought "disfigured St. Paul's and the neighbourhood," had not yet been built. Paxton's Crystal Palace of 1851 had been removed to Sydenham, where Hardy visited it. The Cider Cellars, next to the stage door of the Adelphi Theater, in Maiden Lane, and Evans's Rooms, at the western corner of

° The children "died largely as a result of the conditions in which they lived," in a Soho slum in London. A French refugee gave Marx the money to buy a coffin for his daughter Franziska. Edgar's death in 1856 broke Marx's "iron reserve." "I have suffered every kind of misfortune," he wrote his friend Engels, "but I have only just learned what real unhappiness is . . . in the midst of all the suffering which I have gone through in these days the thought of you, and your friendship, and the hope that we may still have something reasonable to do in the world, has kept me upright." (See Isaiah Berlin, *Karl Marx: His Life & Environment,* pp. 196–97.) Marx studied daily at the British Museum Reading Room from 9 A.M. to 7 P.M.; wrote articles on a wide range of subjects for the New York *Tribune* for ten years, for which he was paid 1 pound sterling per article; was dismissed by Horace Greeley in 1860 against the plea of Charles Dana; became socially unemployable (*ibid*).

the Covent Garden Piazza, both underground, were popular supper clubs offering musical entertainment of the vaudeville type. Hardy visited Evans's Rooms at least once, Mrs. Hardy says. The Coal Hole, in a court off the Strand, was another combination music hall and restaurant. Both establishments featured "Judge and Jury" mock trials, with Baron Nicholson, or his successor, in "full wig and gown," parodying recent criminal court actions in a farcical manner for the pitlike crowd. Dr. Donovan, the phrenologist, "gauged heads" in the Strand, and told Hardy "that his would lead him to no good." [15]

In a letter to his sister Mary dated August 17, 1862, 9 P.M., Hardy wrote, "I have not been to a theater since you were here. I generally run down to the Exhibition for an hour in the evening two or three times a week."

The Great Exhibition, which was one reason for Hardy's going to London when he did, was larger than the First Exhibition (1851), but its huge pair of domes scarcely matched the grandeur of the Crystal Palace, built of iron and glass, which FitzGerald, revisiting it at Sydenham in the early sixties called "the sight of the Century," and Dostoevsky, seeing it there the week of July 9, 1862, called "Baal— an Apocalyptic monster." [16] A gloom was cast on the spectacle by the phenomenally wet weather on which Hardy remarked in a letter to his sister Mary—"Such a disappointment to Londoners, whose holiday is Sunday"*—and by the death from typhoid fever the previous winter of Prince Albert, who had suggested an International Exhibition to ease the tension between France and England and promote international amity. An arrangement had even been made for a delegation of French workers, "half tourists, half representatives of the French proletariat," [17] to attend, and doubt-

---

* The London day-labourers in fish and poultry shops asked for the abolition of Sunday labour (August 1863); they had averaged 15 hours a day for the first six days a week and on Sunday 8 to 10 hours (*Capital*, p. 291n) "The hand-nail makers . . . on account of the low price of labour worked 15 hours a day, 6 a.m. to 8 p.m." (*ibid*)., p. 600n).

less they were under surveillance there. Poet Laureate Tennyson eulogized the "mourned monarch" and the century's achievement in his "Exhibition Ode," which was sung at the opening:

> All of beauty, all of use
> That one fair planet can produce.

For the first time the foreign exhibitors were in the majority. There were two innovations—an art gallery, which Hardy visited with his friend Horace Moule on May 18, being much impressed by Gérôme's paintings "The Death of Ney," and "Jerusalem"; and a section devoted to educational equipment; but in other respects it was divided, like the Exhibition of 1851, into four great classes: 1) Raw Materials, 2) Machinery, 3) Manufactures, and 4) Sculpture and Fine Arts. There were all the things exhibited before:

Applegarth's vertical printing press, Stephenson's locomotive, Shephard's electric clock, Rosse's telescope, Nazsmyth's steam-hammer,° Jacquard's looms, Bessemer's penny postage stamp cancellater, steel pens, McCormick's reaper, Krupp's steel cannon, Bolton & Watts steam navigation engines of colossal size, produced at the Krupp Works, according to the Essen Chamber of Commerce [Marx, *Capital,* p. 427n], Goodyear's vulcanized rubber, and revolutionary new inventions—Bell's telephone, Bessemer's converter, Faraday's dynamo, Edison's electric light, which amazed Londoners and rural folks, accustomed to gas.

° Hardy describes the tranter Reuben Dewey's objection to his son Dick's putting "the romantic teaspoonful of elder wine in Fancy's glass, which she couldn't drink by trying ever so hard in obedience to the nightly arguments of the tranter, his hand coming down upon her shoulder the while like a Nasmyth's hammer" (*Under the Greenwood Tree,* p. 60). The bull from which Henchard rescues Lucetta has "nostrils like the Thames Tunnel as seen in the perspective toys of yore" (*The Mayor of Casterbridge,* pp. 236–37).

Marx describes one of Nasmyth's hammers that weights over 6 tons and strikes on an anvil weighing 36 tons, which enabled him to reduce the number of grown-up men from 1500 to 750, "with a considerable increase in my profits" (*Capital,* pp. 421, 476).

Before he went to London, Dickens's Pip had heard about the steam-hammer "that can crush a man or pat an egg-shell" (*Great Expectations,* chap. 18).

A triumph of science and materialism! To these were added objects of art and household furnishings from abroad as well as two stalls of furniture, embroideries, and green glass and tile from the firm of William Morris,° which the rich could buy and the poor could look at. Morris's first job was the re-decoration of the green dining-room at South Kensington Museum, then nicknamed "the Brompton Boilers," where Hardy often dropped in on the reading room after leaving the Exhibition to obtain material for an essay on terra cotta that he submitted to a contest of the Royal Institute of British Architects (RIBA) that fall. There were revolutionary exhibits in the art of Mars and in the art of Paracelsus (Simpson's chloroform, Lister's antiseptics, Pasteur's microbiology), which could preserve human life or blow the world to hell, besides appetizing condiments like Brand's A-1 Steak Sauce from Hartford, Connecticut, and the American machine for making paper coronets "which cut the paper, pasted, folded and finished 300 in a minute" (*Capital,* p. 413). In short, as Tennyson declared in his Exhibition Ode, everything was

> Brought from under every star,
> Blown from every main,
> And mixed as life is mixed with pain
> The works of peace with works of war.

You might say of the Great Exhibition of 1862 what Flaubert said to Ernest Chevalier of the Exhibition of 1851, that "despite the universal admiration, it was really fine," [18] or what Hardy has the old gentleman narrator of his story, "The Fiddler of the Reels," say: "It was the parent of them all . . . when a noun substantive went so far as to become an adjective, and it was 'exhibition' hat, 'exhibition' razor-

---

° Walter Bagehot, the economist, had his library and other rooms at Herd's Hill decorated with Morris wallpapers and leather upholstery. "They bring sample threads every two or three months, but the curtains don't come," he wrote (see Norman St. John-Stevas, *Walter Bagehot* (Bloomington, Ind.: University of Indiana Press, 1959), p. 20.

strap, 'exhibition'-watch, nay even 'exhibition' weather."
Ned's sweetheart Car'line gets drenched in an open excursion-train going to see Ned, who had worked on "the monstrous greenhouse," as the *Times* had called it.

Hardy called on Mrs. Julia Martin, the "grand dame" of the parish, then living in an apartment on Bruton Street, on the east side of Berkeley Square, who invited him to call again, although he did not respond to her invitation. In the fall Hardy went home to assist his father in the cider-making as usual—"a proceeding he always enjoyed from childhood till 1873, the last time he ever took part in a work," Mrs. Hardy says, "whose sweet smells and oozings in the crisp autumn air can never be forgotten by those who have had a hand in it." These, he described in the seasonal occupation of Giles Winterborne of *The Woodlanders*, "who looked like autumn's very brother," as well as in his poem "Great Things," beginning "Cyder is a great thing," and in the conversation between the dying Nelson and Captain Hardy, who replies to Nelson's question, "What are you thinking of:

> Thoughts all confused, my lord:—their needs on deck,
> Your own sad state, and your unrivalled past;
> Mixed up with flashes of old things afar—
> Old childish things at home, down Wessex way,
> In the snug village under Blackdon Hill
> Where I was born. The tumbling stream, the garden,
> The placid look of the grey dial there,
> Marking unconsciously this bloody hour,
> And the red apples on my father's trees,
> Just now full ripe.[19]

In the winter of 1862 Blomfield moved his office from 8 St. Martin's Place, which he had shared with the Alpine Club, to larger rooms at 8 Adelphi Terrace, described in Hardy's letter of February 19, 1863, to his sister Mary:

> You see that we have moved, so for the future my address will be as on the other side. We have not recovered from

the confusion yet, and our drawings and papers are nohow.

The new office is a capital place. It is on the first floor and on a terrace that overlooks the river. We can see from our window right across the Thames, and on a clear day every bridge is visible. Everybody says that we have a beautiful place.

To-day has been wretched. It was almost pitch dark in the middle of the day, and everything visible appeared of the colour of brown paper or pea-soup.

He wrote at some length about the forthcoming royal marriage (that of Princess Alexandra to the prince regent Edward) on March 10, on the eve of which "there will be an illumination," and mentioned, "I tried the Underground Railway [it had opened on Jan. 10, 1863] one day—Everything is excellently arranged," besides giving some office news and asking for some from home.

Adelphi Terrace facing the Thames was a handsome row of buildings, built by the Adam brothers in 1779, and the rooms were richly furnished with "fine Adam mantelpieces in white marble, on which we used to sketch," Hardy recalled, "caricatures in pencil." Hardy sat at his drawing-board at the easternmost window, with Whatman paper* within reach, and sometimes idled on the balcony from which he saw "the Embankment and Charing Cross Bridges built and, of course, used to think of Garrick and Johnson." [20] On a clear day he could see "the snow-white scrolls of steam from the tall chimneys of Lambeth, rising from the livid sky behind, as if drawn in chalk on toned cardboard," and "the rows of hideous zinc chimney pipes in dim relief against the sky"; or at night "the lights along the riverside toward Charing Cross sent an inverted palisade of gleaming swords down into the shaking water, and the pavement ticked to the touch of pedestrians' feet . . . most of whom held handkerchiefs to their mouths to strain off the river mist from

* James Whatman, and eighteenth-century English manufacturer of high-quality architectural paper and drawing boards (*Webster's Unabridged Dictionary,* 1968).

their lungs." [21] Londoners appeared to be automatons like "Amabel" of his early poem, who with

> Her step's mechanic ways,
> Had lost the life of May's;

or somnambulists like the crowd in the Strand that he describes in *Desperate Remedies,* his first published novel:

tall men looking insignificant; little men looking great and profound; lost women of miserable repute looking as happy as the days are long; wives, happy by assumption, looking careworn and miserable. Each and all were alike in this one respect, that they followed a solitary trail like the inwoven threads which form a banner, and all were equally unconscious of the significant whole they collectively showed forth.[22]

Hardy got along very well with his employer and his co-workers. Blomfield encouraged "singing-glees" among his pupils for relaxation, and organized an office choir, in which they all waited till he had "got his low E." [23] There were serious moments and humorous ones. One morning Blomfield greeted Hardy on his arrival with: "Hardy, that tower has fallen," indicating a drawing of a new church just then finished on the opposite wall. Another well-known architect some years earlier had been sentenced to a year's imprisonment for manslaughter, but fortunately no one had been killed or injured by Blomfield's fallen tower. On another occasion, Blomfield sent the office boy to the Strand to buy a bottle of port and to the housekeeper to borrow a glass for a builder-caller, whom he had jokingly greeted with, "Well, Mr. T— What will you take this morning—sherry or port?" During the noon hour "every day for many months," Hardy hurried to the National Art Gallery, which was enlarged in 1866 to the rear of Trafalgar Square, and possibly was sometimes a little late in getting back to his drawing-board. He attended the theater, seeing Buckstone in *The American Cousins,* at the Haymarket, and Charles Kean and his wife in Shakespeare, and Phelps* whom he thought "had never received his due . . . as Falstaff," at the Drury Lane, where the play would pause a moment to the audience's murmur of "half-price coming in." He recalled to Charles Morgan in 1922 how "with his text in his hands, seated in the front row, he would follow the dialogue by the stage light." He also took in Dickens's later readings at Exeter Hall and the foreign operas (Rossini, Donizetti, Verdi, Meyerbeer, and Bellini) at the Covent Garden and Her Majesty's. He heard Miss Louisa Pyne* and William Harrison* (in *Maritana* and the *Bohemian Girl*), who were trying desperately to compete with foreign opera, and was much affected by the breakdown of Harrison's voice, admiring the courage with which he went on singing "Let me like a soldier fall" in *Maritana*.

Hardy sometimes dined and danced at the Willis Rooms, formerly known as Almack's—an anagram of Macall, its previous owner, and frequented by chaperoned girls from Bayswater looking for an eligible husband. Hardy found them "lighter on the arm than their Weymouth sisters," an

---

* Samuel Phelps (1804–1878): English actor and manager; in 1826 married Sarah Cooper, who died in 1867; accepted a theatrical engagement in the York circuit at 18s a week; later rivaled Edmund Kean in tragic roles in south-of-England towns; made first London appearance Aug. 28, 1837, at Haymarket as Shylock; was with William McCready for about six years at Covent Garden and Drury Lane. In 1844 co-leased Sadler's Wells theater with Thomas L. Greenwood and Mary Amelia Warner (1804–54); retired in 1862, unable to cope with the business management after Greenwood's death; went back to acting, achieving success in Andrew Halliday's dramatic versions of Sir Walter Scott's novels, *The Fortunes of Nigel* and *Ivanhoe,* and as Sir Pertinax Macsyphant in Charles Macklin's *The Man of the World;* last appearance was in 1878 as Cardinal Wolsey in *Henry VIII.* Published an annotated edition of Shakespeare's plays (2 vols., 1852–1854), which Hardy may have read.

Louisa Fanny Pyne (1832-1900), soprano singer, student of Sir Gèorge Smart; in August 1849 made her first appearance on stage at Boulogne as Amina in Bellini's "*Somnambula*"; the following October at Princess's Theater, London, as Fanny in Macferren's *Charles the Second;* in 1854 in company with her sister Susan, William Harrison, and Borrani toured principal cities in America for three seasons; then in English opera with Harrison,

William Harrison (1813–1868), English tenor; made his first appearance ni Rooke's opera *Henrique,* May 2, 1839, at Covent Garden, and principal role in Balfe's *Bohemian Girl.*

experience recalled in his poem "Reminiscences of a Dancing Man" (1866). Almack's held not only terpsichorean associations of the days of Johnson and Addison—"powdered Dears from Georgian years" of the poem—but also political associations with the age of Gladstone, the Liberal Party having been organized there in 1859. It boasted of a supper room and ballroom that would accommodate 1,700 guests.

Sometime in 1863 Hardy moved from Clarence House to Westbourne Park Villas, Kilburn, where he lived the remainder of his time in London.[24] He enjoyed browsing in the bookstalls of Holywell Street—Stephen's Book Shop and others—buying Nutalls Dictionary, Walker's *Rhyming Dictionary* to which he added additional rhymes, and Swinburne's *Atalanta in Calydon* (1865), and a year later *Poems and Ballads* (1866)—"new words in classic guise" [25]—which he read in the hazards of London traffic. Swinburne's hexameters might have "their dull subterrene reverberations," but the thought had a far from soporific effect on his already Darwin-awakened mind:

Wilt thou yet take all, Galilean? But these thou shalt not take—
The laurel, the palms, and the paen; the breasts of the nymphs in the brake.[26]

And:

Ye shall sleep as a slain man sleeps, and the world shall forget you for kings—
Though these that were Gods are dead, and thou being dead art a God. . . .
Yet thy kingdom shall pass, Galilean, thy dead shall go down to the dead.

On Swinburne's death (April 10, 1909), Hardy recalled how the press had reviled him in 1866 "when we did care," and "how it made the blood of some of us young men boil." In 1879 he read Swinburne's poem to Walt Whitman;

> Reincarnate with fresh generations—
> the great god Man, which is God.

Later (1905), the critics in a Scottish paper condemned both free-thinkers juridically, which must have made Pope Pius X smile with a wan beatitude: "Swinburne planteth, Hardy watereth, and Satan giveth the increase." [27]

During these years Hardy came to know London "like a born Londoner and as only a young man can get it," [28] Mrs. Hardy says. He continued going to church on Sunday as he had been brought up to do, but found the services at Westminster Abbey (July 5, 1865) "a very odd experience amid a crowd of strangers compared to those at Stinsford Parish church at home; and he sometimes thought of François Hippolite Barthélémon, first fiddler at Vauxhall Gardens, "returning from his nightly occupation of making music for a riotous throng, lingering on Westminster Bridge to see the rising sun and being inspired to the composition of music ("Awake My Soul"), voiced every Sunday in most churches to Bishop Ken's words, but is seldom now heard." The contrast between the wealth of the West End and the poverty of the East End stirred Hardy to the marrow of his bones. He saw what a gaping gulf existed between the rich and poor—between the theatergoers and supper diners at the clubs—"men in evening clothes, ringed and studded, and women much uncovered in the neck and heavily jeweled, their glazed and lamp-blacked eyes wandering" [29]—and the gaping throngs at Piccadilly and the families living in the slums of St. Giles and Soho. These last must have been like the two bootblack urchins who pointed to Blomfield's and his muddy boots on their way back from measuring a building site in Soho, or like the two shoeblacks in the Strand "who began to importune" Edward and Owen on their way to the unemployed carpenter Higgins' lodgings in St. Giles, which presented "a depressing picture of married life among the very poor of the city" (*Desperate Remedies*).[30] Neither the flower-vendors nor the costermongers' carts in the spring, nor the boys shoveling snow for tuppence a house in the winter could hide the poverty of St. Giles and Soho. On his daily shortcuts to Blomfield's office, past the Seven Dials, he saw "wretched mothers," as Robert Blatchford observed in his *Merrie England,*

> feed young Faradays and Miltons on gin, or send them out ignorant and helpless to face the winter wind and the vice and disease of the stews.[31]

He glimpsed the ex-prizefighters (Alec Keene and Tom King in West Street and Nat Langahm at the top of St. Martin's Lane) in the saloons behind their respective bars, not loth to sell a quartern of gin to a man like Higgins, or the man who said to him (May 9, 1890):

> When one is half-drunk London seems a wonderfully enjoyable place, with its lamps, and the cabs moving like fire-flies.

"Between the Thames and the Kensington Squares," Hardy passed "the premises of builders and contractors," whose yard with "its workshops formed part of one of those frontier-lines between mangey business and garnished domesticity that occur in what are called improving neighbourhoods." [32] Often wealth and poverty were juxtaposed, as in Knight's lodgings at Bede's Inn (*A Pair of Blue Eyes*), which "faces, receives from, and discharges into a bustling thoroughfare speaking only of wealth and respectability, whilst its postern abuts on as crowded and poverty-stricken a network of alleys as are to be found anywhere in the metropolis." [33] "Those who occupy chambers in the Inn," Hardy adds, "may see a great deal of shirtless humanity." Theodore Parker (1810–1862), an American minister and reformer, called London "the paradise of the rich, the purgatory of the wise, and the hell of the poor," and Herman Melville (1819–1891), standing on one of its bridges, amid "the clouds of smoke," thought "of the damned and the City of Dis" in

Dante's *Inferno,* reflecting, "Its marks are left upon you, &C. &C. &C": [34] Morris described it as "a beastly congregation of smoke and dried swindlers and their slaves whom one hopes someday to make their rebels," and Hardy as "that *hot-plate* of humanity [italics his] on which we first sing, then simmer, then boil, then dry away to dust and ashes!" "Poverty in the country is a sadness," he says in *The Hand of Ethelberta,* "but poverty in town is a horror"; and in *Desperate Remedies,* another London novel, he changes a quotation from Keats's "Ode to a Nightingale" to read " 'Hungry generations' soon tread down the muser in a city," [35]—a reflection that may be found in Thomas Chatterton, and Thomas Hood, in Wordsworth's *Excursion,* and in statistically documented facts in Engels and Marx. Hardy may have reflected on Keats's lines in his poem "Teignmouth" to his friend B. R. Hayden in Devonshire : "Why go to dark Soho," and thought of his parents at home, and pondered sometimes on Blake's lines, "Pity would be no more/ If we did not make somebody poor," and sat down as Blake, in his poem "The Human Abstract,"

> Sits down with holy fears,
> And waters the ground with tears;
> Then Humility takes its root
> Underneath his foot.

Hardy has Tom Fool say, in a Shakespearean vein, to the Milkman in the opening of *The Hand of Ethelberta:* "I've tended horses fifty year that other folk might straddle 'em. When I see so many good things about, I feel inclined to help myself in common justice to my pocket." He concludes with :

> "Work hard and be poor,
> Do nothing and get more."

The class disparity was particularly impressed on Hardy 1863; the gorgeous splendor of the royal wedding that

spring and the "sensational" heading in all the London
daily papers in the last week of June 1863: "Death from
simple overwork" of the milliner Mary Ann Walkley, 20
years of age, who "worked 16½ hours a day in a highly
respected dressmaking establishment of Madame Elise,"
which Marx says "conjured up in the twinkling of an eye
the gorgeous dresses for the noble ladies bidden to the ball
in honour of the newly imported Princess of Wales" (*Capital*,
p. 280). The effect of this tragedy, which Hardy certainly
read and heard discussed, may be heard in his poem "The
Dream of the City Shopwoman" (1866), which ends:

> O God, that creatures framed to feel
> A yearning nature's strong appeal
> Should writhe on this eternal wheel.
> > In rayless grime;
> And vainly note, with wan regret,
> Each star of early promise set;
> Till Death relieves, and they forget
> > Their one Life's time!

Yes, God was dead; long live Man! was in the thoughts if not
on the tongues of many Londoners, including J. S. Mill,
who said, "The world would be astonished if it knew how
great a proportion of its brightest ornaments are complete
skeptics in religion." Macaulay "once said that not two
hundred men in London believed in the Bible." [36]

Progress was no respecter of the living or the dead. The
Industrial Revolution was creating a nomadic population
that could not support itself on the land or find employment
in the towns. The process that statisticians described as "the
tendency of the rural population toward the large towns,"
Hardy pointed out in his Dorsetshire Labourer essay was
"really the tendency of water to flow uphill when forced by
machinery." "The English working class," Marx observed,
"was precipitated without any transition from its golden age
into its iron age," and had become "the light-infantry of
capitalism" (*Capital*, pp. 799, 728). The machines were not

only the "creators of commodities," as Ricardo had declared, "but also of redundant population;" Marx corrected him by showing that "the pressure of population is not upon the means of subsistence but upon the means of *employment* and that "mankind is capable of increasing more rapidly than bourgeois society can stand" (*Correspondence,* p. 198). Hordes of dispossessed, ragged Irishmen and farmworkers from decaying villages, living like beasts in wagons on wheels in Ague Town, which Dickens described as "an English Connemara," were digging the road beds and laying the shining rails made in Bessemer's revolutionary blast-furnaces, into "the milk-teeth of a suburb." [37] The five thousand miles of shining rail opened to traffic in 1859 had more than doubled by 1862. The Midland Railway had obtained a right-of-way from the City to extend its lines through Old St. Pancras cemetery, which by the summer of 1868 wiped out the whole of Agar Town, and the rumor of "this lamentable upheaval," Mrs. Hardy says, had led Percy Shelley to have the bodies of his mother's parents moved therefrom to St. Peter's, Bournemouth, where Mary Shelley had been buried in 1851.

Because Hardy's employer, Mr. Blomfield, was the son of the recently deceased Bishop Blomfield, he was engaged as "the right and proper person" for superintending the job, which was carried out at night in old St. Pancras cemetery. On an earlier job of similar nature, Blomfield had concluded from a careful inspection of the site that the bodies had not been reinterred as the Company had agreed to, telling Hardy grimly, "I believe these people are all ground up!" Resolved that the Company should not put something over on him again, he engaged a clerk-of-works in the churchyard and delegated Hardy to drop in at unexpected times. The work, which involved the removal of hundreds of coffins and pro-
ding new ones for the bones of the old ones that had fallen
was carried out in the winters of 1865 and 1866. Clad
tcoat, Hardy dropped in "after nightfall at differ-

ent times," and "supervised these mournful proceedings" by
the flare of lamps that cast lurid shadows on the high hoardings. On one occasion a coffin fell apart and disclosed "a
skeleton and two skulls." [38] The mixed feelings with which
Hardy viewed these macabre exhumations are expressed in
his poem "The Levelled Churchyard," in which the spirits
protest to no avail to a "Passenger" against being "half stifled
in this jumbled patch/ of Wrenched memorial stones," and
that their corpses "pave some path or porch or place/ We
have never lain." Marx quotes the *Morning Star* on a reporter's visit in 1866 to a stone pile in an East London shed
where he saw 3,000 unemployed,

> each man seated on a big paving stone, while he chipped away
> at the rime-covered granite with a big hammer until he had
> broken up five bushels of it . . . [for which he] got his day's
> pay—threepence and an allowance of food. (*Capital,* p. 734)

In another poem, "The Cemetery," Hardy has the sexton
reflect on the mothers' looking for their children's graves,
"buried like sprats in a tin," and say that they may as well
cry "over a new laid drain" as anything else to ease their
pain. All three poems lead to his observation in *A Pair of
Blue Eyes,* his first serialized novel, that "we are only the
leaseholders of our graves."

Hardy must have felt disgust when he read Prime Minister Gladstone's panegyric in his budgetary speech (April 16,
1863) in the *Times* that "this incredible . . . intoxicating
augmentation of wealth and power . . . must be of indirect
benefit to the labouring population, because it cheapens the
commodities . . . when the cost of living was rising and
wages were at a standstill." The situation of the proletariat
during a similar period of progress and prosperity at the
turn of the century was compared to that of Tantalus, by
Jack London in *The People of the Abyss,* and to "advising
a man who is starving to eat less" by Oscar Wilde (quoted
by London [pp. 50, 300] from Wilde's *The Soul of Man*

under Socialism). Hardy must have been even more shocked by Gladstone's speech a year later (April 7, 1864), which Marx called "a Pindaric dithyrambus on the advance of surplus-value-making° and the happiness of people tempered by poverty;"[39] Gladstone reconciled pauperism and wealth as compatible companions in progress since "human life is but, in nine cases out of ten, a struggle for existence." In consequence of the cotton famine (pauperism) grew in the years 1863 and 1864.

> to 1,079,382 and 1,014,978 [creating] in this centre of the world market [London] . . . an increase in pauperism for the

° The increase of profits liable to income tax (farmers and some other categories not included) in Great Britain from 1853 to 1864 amounted to 50.47% or 4.58% as the annual average (*Tenth Report of the Commissioners of H.M. Inland Revenue*, London, 1866, p. 38), that of the population during the same period to about 1.2%. The Augmentation of the rent of land subject to taxation (including houses, railways, mines, fisheries, etc.) amounted for 1853 to 1864 to 38% or 3 5/11% annually. Under this head the following categories show the greatest increase:

Houses, 38.60%	3.50%
Quarries, 84.76%	7.70%
Mines, 68.85%	6.26%
Iron-works, 39.92%	3.63%
Fisheries, 57.37%	5.21%
Gas-works, 126.02%	11.45%
Railways, 83.29%	7.57%

"If we compare the years from 1853 to 1864 in three sets of four consecutive years," Marx says, "the annual rate of augmentation of the income is: 1853–1857, 1.73%; 1857–61, 2.74%; 1861–64, 9.30%. The sum of the incomes of the United Kingdom that come under the income tax was in in 1856, £307,068,898; in 1859, £328,127,416; in 1862, £351,745,241; in 1863, £359,142,897; 1864, £362,462,279; in 1865, £385,530,020 (*Capital,* pp. 712–13).

These figures are sufficient for comparison, but, taken absolutely, are false, since, perhaps, £100,000,000 of income are annually not declared. The complaints of the Inland Revenue Commissioners of systematic fraud, especially on the part of the commercial and industrial classes, are repeated in each of their reports" (*ibid.,* n2). Marx declared that "The public debt becomes one of the most powerful levers of primitive accumulation" (p. 827), and notes "William Cobbett's remarks that in England all public institutions are designated 'royal' as compensation for this; however, there is the 'national' debt" (p. 827n).

According to the census of 1861 for England and Wales, "there were employed in the gas-works "15,211 persons; in telegraph, 2,399; in photography, 2,366; steam navigation, 3,570, and in railways, 70,599 . . . a total number of 84,145 in these five new industries" (*Capital,* p. 487).

year 1866 of 19.5% compared with 1865, and of 24.4% as compared with 1864, and a still greater increase for the first few months of 1867, as compared with 1866. (p. 717)

Marx, investigating the period of capitalistic accumulation between 1846 and 1866, notes that "improvements of towns accompanying the increase of wealth, by the demolition of badly built quarters, the erection of palaces for banks, warehouses, &C., the widening of streets for business traffic for the carriages of luxury, and the introduction of tramways, &C., drive the poor into even worse and more crowded hiding places." [40] Ruskin, whom Hardy read, regarded all great art as Gothic, but questioned how "the lofty lines express the spirit of a devout and sturdy nation of shopkeepers who above everything else were devoted to trade." Everywhere Hardy looked he saw what Ruskin condemned in *The Stones of Venice* (1851–1853): "There is scarcely a public-house near the Crystal Palace but sells its gin and bitters under pseudo-Victorian capitals copied from the Church of the Madonna of Health and of Miracles," or saw mushrooming villas of every cheap builder between this and Bromley surrounded "by the accursed Frankenstein monsters of, indirectly, my own making." [41] Hardy, incensed, describes a gingerbread domicile "in which Pugin would have torn his hair," and the propinquity of "antiquity and beehive industry" at Milton's tomb, where Ethelberta takes out her *Milton* and reads the lines beginning "Mammon led them on": "not many yards from the central money mill of the world." [42] In his poem "The Temporary and All," he writes, presumably about his London lodgings: "Tenements uncouth I was fain to house in/ Soon a more seemly"; and he observes of suburbia—Farnfield—in *The Hand of Ethelberta:*

Waggons laden with deals came up on this side, and landaus came down on the other—the former to lumber heavily through the old established contractors' gates, the latter to sweep fashionably into the square.

and again with a Blakean touch (of *The New Jerusalem*) combined with Hogarth:

> We are accustomed to regard increase as the chief feature in a great city's progress, the well-known signs greeting our eyes on every outskirt. Slushponds may be seen turning into basement-kitchens; a broad causeway of shattered earthware smothers plots of budding gooseberry-bushes and vegetable trenches, foundations following so closely upon gardens that the householder may be expected to find cadaverous sprouts from overlooked potatoes rising through the chinks of his cellar floor. But the other great process, that of internal transmutation, is not less curious than this encroachment of grey upon green. Its first erections are often only the milk-teeth of a suburb, and as the district rises in dignity, they are dislodged by those which are to endure. Slightness becomes supplanted by comparative solidity, commonness by novelty, lowness and irregularity by symmetry and height.[43]

Marx notes that the persons displaced by this redevelopment "do not go beyond the same or the next parish," and that the packing of laborers together in smaller, worse, and more expensive quarters led to endemic diseases, with laborers' families being "prosecuted in the name of Sanitation!" (*Capital*, pp. 724–25). In one of the parishes of the Strand, "a main thoroughfare which gives strangers an imposing idea of the wealth of London," Marx notes:

> the Officer of Health reckoned 581 persons per acre, although half of the width of the Thames was reckoned in.

These conditions had created epidemics that do not even spare "respectability" and that had brought into existence from 1847 to 1864 no less than ten Acts of Parliament on sanitation. Dr. Julian Hunter, in his 7th and 8th reports on Public Health° (1864–1865), which Hardy undoubtedly read

---

° *The Economist* refused to go into details of the public health bill of 1847, and the London *Times* rebuked a Parliamentary committee for asking a woman if she had ever mis-carried (see Hicks, *Figures of Transition*, pp. 20–21).

in *The Times,* observed of the evil situation (as Marx notes [p. 723]) that

> there was such exposure of animal and sexual nakedness as is rather bestial than human, and that to be children who are born under its curse it must often be a very baptism into infamy.

One recalls Hardy's poem "To an Unborn Pauper Child":

> Thou wilt thy ignorant entry make
> Though skies spout fire, and blood and nations quake.

and his "Lines Spoken by Ada Rehan . . . at a performance on behalf of Lady Jeune's* Holiday Fund for City Children," which are a sobering answer to the capitalistic accumulation that had so intoxicated Gladstone:

> Why should Man add to Nature's quandary,
> And worsen ill by thus immuring thee?

In London's East Side the Salvation Army in 1865 opened its doors to the poor, and soon afterward

> Booth led boldly with his big bass drum,
> *Are you washed in the blood of the Lamb?* [44]

---

* "Mary Jeune says that when she tries to convey some sort of moral or religious teaching to the East-end poor, so as to change their views from wrong to right, it ends by their convincing her that their view is the right one, not of her convincing them" (*Early Life,* p. 272). Hardy's friend Horace Moule was the Poor Law Inspector at Ipswich (*Ibid.,* p. 123). Dickens wrote Wilkie Collins (July 12, 1861) about W. H. Wills, an associate at the periodical *Household Words,* telling him "a story that I thought very ridiculous about a charity boy who persisted in saying to the Inspector of Schools that Our Saviour was the only forgotten son of his father and that he was forgotten by his father before all worlds, etc., in an Athanasian and Theological dogmatism" that Hardy would have understood (*Letters of Dickens,* 2:72). Engels tells about children's ignorance of geography, religion, and simple arithmetic, that they did not know where London was, who the Apostles were, and could not add two and two (pp. 127–28). The Boy in Hardy's *Dynasts,* hearing two citizens discussing Pitt's "spirits" after Trafalgar, asks: "Is it because Trafalgar is near Portingal that he loves port wine?" (I, 5, v).

Hardy, coming home from Regent Circus the "wet evening" of October 18, "saw the announcement of the death of Lord Palmerston whom," he noted, "I heard speak in the House of Commons a year or two ago." He wrote his sister Mary (Oct. 28, 1865) in great detail about Palmerston's funeral in Westminster Abbey, which "I would not have missed for anything," having obtained tickets through Mr. Blomfield, and he sent his father copies of the *Times,* for "these things interest him."

Lord Palmerston (1784–1865), who was Prime Minister at the time of his death, "has been connected with the gov.," Hardy wrote his sister, "off and on for the last 60 years"; his foreign policy, historians have written, was one of neutrality and his domestic policy one of inaction toward the pressing needs for reform. And with his death one obstacle to it was removed. Lord Russell, a Whig, who succeeded him, was more receptive to reform, and Disraeli, foresaw (Oct. 23) "tempestuous times and great vicissitudes in public life. Hardy had witnessed the ferment during these years created by the Reform League, which had put the heat on Parliament. They were a body of extreme reformers, of some note and power for a time," Mrs. Hardy says, quoting Swinburne, "which had solicited me to sit in Parliament as representative of more advanced democratic or republican opinions than represented there. Mazzini,° whom Swinburne

° The League was regarded by Howell and Cremner "first and foremost as a means of check-mating those employers who might attempt to break strikes by using the new transport facilties to import French, Belgian, German or Italian labour rapidly and cheaply" (See S. Maccoby's *English Radicalism,* 3 : 87 on The League), as the Iron-Masters had done in 1864, employing the lockout to successfully import Belgian workers, and the following year claiming falling prices and foreign competition, they further imposed a wage reduction upon their men (*ibid.,* p. 109). Marx writes, "As it is the fashion amongst English capitalists to quote Belgium as the Paradise of the labourer because 'freedom of labour', or what is the same thing, 'freedom of capital,' is there limited neither by the despotism of Trade's Unions, nor by Factory Acts, a word or two on the 'happiness' of the Belgian labourer," which he refutes (*Capital,* p. 737). Benjamin Lucraft, former Chartist, referred to the Government's using troops as strikebreakers at Chelsea Barracks' project as a "new and powerfull argument for the workers' franchise," writing in *Reynold's* newspaper consulted, "dissuaded him from consenting." "The heads of the League were familiar personages to Blomfield's pupils who, as became Tory and Churchy young men, indulged in satire at the League's expense, letting down ironical bits of paper on the heads of members, and once nearly coming to loggerheads with the worthy resident secretary, Mr. George Howell—to whom they had to apologize for their exasperating conduct." [45] It is hard to believe Mrs. Hardy's statement about their conduct's "being unknown to Mr. Blomfield himself."

The Reform League was avant-garde, a threat to Conservatives and Liberals alike. A reference to its purpose and scope is given in a letter of Marx's (Jan. 13, 1866) to Dr. Kugelmann:

> We have succeeded in drawing into the movement the one really big workers' organization, the English Trades Union, which formerly concerned themselves *exclusively* with wage questions. With their help the English Society (The Reform League), which we founded for achieving universal suffrage (half of the central committee consists of members—workers—of our Central Committee) held a monster meeting a few weeks ago, at which only workers spoke. You can judge of the effect by the fact that the *Times* dealt with the meeting in the leading articles in two consecutive issues.[46]

The meeting referred to by Marx was the Trades Reform demonstration of December 3, 1866, in which some 23,000 persons of the League's fifty-three societies marched with banners inscribed with slogans of general import such as "Taxation without Representation is Tyranny" or relating to specific trades, such as the tallow makers' "Bright and

(July 28, 1861): "I should hope that the operatives builders are by this convinced that political power has something to do with the social conditions of the people." (see Henry Collins's article (*Science & Society* [Fall 1962]). The London Trades Council emerged from the struggle. Disraeli refused to meet Garibaldi; he sympathized with the 1863 Polish insurrection, "but saw no reason why England should engage in a war for a cause that was so little hers" (Monypenny & Buckle, *Life of Disraeli*, 2:61, 70).

Light," the shoemakers' boot elegantly inscribed with "It's the wearer that feels where the shoe pinches," and the Workingman's Association's "To procure the political enfranchisement of the industrial classes." [47]

It takes one back to the American Revolution and the Colonies' demands of King George III, and farther to the Great Charter (1215–1217) and the Barons' wresting promises in writing from King John, which have been honored more in the breach than the observance. Blake's poem "Thames and Ohio" offers a comment on the little-changed situation for the common people between the rule of the barons and the new industrial capitalists:

> Why should I care for the men of Thames,
> And the cheating waters of chartered streams
> Or shrink at the little blasts of fear
> That the hireling blows into mine ear?
>
> Though born on the cheating banks of Thames—
> Though his waters bathed my infant limbs—
> The Ohio shall wash his stains from me;
> I was born a slave, but I go to be free.

Toward the emancipation of the industrial serfs, the League* held many meetings and staged many demonstrations. The most famous of these was the one scheduled in Hyde Park for July 23, 1866, forbidden by the Home-Secretary Walpole and the septuagenarian Metropolitan Chief of

---

* The League's president was Edmund Beales, a barrister. It had a strong trade-union membership: Robert Applegarth and George Potter of the Carpenters Union, Edward Coulson and George Howell of the Bricklayers Union, George Odger of the Shoemakers Union and secretary of the London Trades Council 1860–67, "who had the rare gift of making his minutes interesting." (see Webbs's *History of Trade Unionism*, p. 247) Charles Bradlaugh resigned his office in the League "in order to deprive the enemies of reform of the pretext for attacks on the League afforded by my irreligion and to save some of the friends of the League from the pain of having their names associated with my own" (Maccoby, p. 99.). The League disbanded in 1867. Hardy heard Bradlaugh speak in H. of C. Apr. 13, 1886, and in the Bradlaugh-Hyndman debate in St. James Hall in 1890 (see *Early Life*, pp. 233, 299).

Police Mayne.* John Stuart Mill who, Disraeli wrote Queen
Victoria on July 24, 1866, "rose and delivered a speech
hardly worthy of a philosopher, but rather more adapted to
Hyde Park," tried to dissuade the League officers from holding it there, but the members insisted on their right of
assemblage in Hyde Park.** They marched in orderly procession to the entrance gates, and finding them closed and
guarded by police, they withdrew to Trafalgar Square,
where they held a protest meeting and adopted a resolution
viewing "with alarm the advent of the Tories to power as
being destructive to freedom at home and favourable to
despotism abroad." 48 Meanwhile, the restless crowd outside
the Park broke through the palings and swarmed inside.
Some of them, later, surged into Chester Square and stoned
the windows of police commissioner Mayne's home. Matthew Arnold, who had witnessed the incident with his
family from the balcony of their home across the street,
thought "the men should have been horsewhipped"—a view,
one may be sure, that would have appalled Hardy, and
the *Saturday Review* and *The Times* joined hands in abus-
ing Bright and spreading English fear of their fellow man.49
A militant demonstration had occurred three weeks be-

* Disraeli wrote to Lord Derby: "I have spoken with Hardy (Gawthorne Hardy) who says he 'wishes to God he (Mayne) would resign' but
surely when even the safety of the state is at stake there ought to be
no false delicacy on the point" (*Life of Disraeli*, 2:307).
** Mill resorted to *"les grand moyens,"* he says, with the officers of the
League against their holding this meeting. He told them "that a proceeding
which would certainly produce a collision with the military could only
be justifiable on two conditions: if the position of affairs had become
such a revolution was desirable, and if they thought themselves able
to accomplish one" (see Lionel Trilling, *Matthew Arnold*, p. 246). Trilling
thinks "the fear was unwarranted, for not only was the power of the
working class soon minimized, but the old spiritual ascendancy of the
upper classes remained strong" (*ibid*, p. 249). "Here in London," Marx
wrote Engels (July 27, 1866) "the government has nearly produced a
rising. The Englishman first needs a revolutionary education, of course,
and two weeks would be enough for this if Sir Richard Mayne had
absolute control . . . if the railings had been used offensively and defensively against the police, the military would have had to 'intervene' instead
of only parading, and then there would have been some fun" (*Correspondence*, pp. 212–13).

fore, on June 29, 1866, on the defeat of Lord Russell's more moderate reform bill, and Robert Lowe, M.P. from Calne, who had manipulated its defeat by his Cave of Addulam conspiracy, thought "that they were within twenty-four hours of a revolution." [50] Ten thousand people assembled in Trafalgar Square and marched to Gladstone's house to cheer and to the Carlton Club to jeer. Phillimore, minister of Indian affairs, observed that "the whigs hate Gladstone. The moderate Conservatives and the radicals incline to him. The old tories hate him." He regretted Gladstone's taking his name off the Carlton as "a marked and significant act of entire separation from the *whole* party," and predicted that it would strengthen Disraeli's hand.[51] And so it did.

We do not know whether Hardy attended any of these meetings or not, considering his frightening experience in the Mansion House Crush (March 10, 1863), on the occasion of the marriage of the Prince of Wales to Princess Alexandra of Denmark, in which six people were killed and Hardy narrowly escaped with his life, along with Mosely and Harris, pupils of Ferrey's and friends of his. Many children of the poor, according to the report of the Children's Employment commission, did not know the Queen's name, or thought that Princess Alexandria was Queen (*Capital,* p. 285n.), and concerned persons testified that the poor were denied relief if their children were in school (*ibid.,* p. 529). In 1865 Hardy accompanied Blomfield to New Windsor for the ceremony of laying a memorial stone of a church there, at which the Crown Princess of Germany (the English Princess Royal) and her husband, afterwards Frederick, participated, of which he recollected:

> Blomfield handed her the trowel, and getting her sleeves daubed with the mortar . . . in distress, she handed it back to him, saying, "Take it take it!"

About this incident Weber observes: "two years later Hardy transferred the words to Miss Allamont" of *An Indiscretion in the Life of an Heiress,* in the scene of her father's "laying a foundation stone of a tower . . . on his estate to the memory of his brother, the General." Hardy also used the incident of his protagonist, Will Strong, addressing a crowd of working men in Trafalgar Square, to the distress of Miss Allamont, to whom, till then, he was engaged.

During the year 1866 political tension reached its height, aggravated by the unrest and misery caused by the migration of the shipbuilding industry from East London to Tyne and Clyde, "the next place after London in the housing inferno," according to Marx (p. 726), and by the panic precipitated by the failure of the investment firm of Overend & Gurney on May 10, with liabilities of £10,000,000, which Bagehot, the banker-economist, in a letter to Gladstone, attributed to "a drain on deposits rather than on notes," and Marx to "the collapse of swindling companies." [52] The discount rate was pushed up to ten percent. The misery of the poor was increased by the poor harvest and the rinderpest* plague; the price of meat and milk rose a quarter. Matthew Arnold, wandering through Spitafiels and Bethnal Green that summer, conversed with Mr. Tyler, the Nonconformist, who told him that

> the parish workhouse was full . . . pawnshops loaned "but trifling sums" for the borrower's few possessions. Provident workmen** fought for three hours' work on the workhouse

* Disraeli spoke in favour of compensation to owners, whose cattle were slaughtered for the public good," but not for the labourers (Monypenny and Buckle, 2:162).

** During the depression in trade occasioned by this, the Ironfounders levied "to extent of 15s. a week, or 1/6 of their whole weekly earnings to maintain their union," and some "actually took the savings of years to the amount of £2,500 and deposited it to save the union from insolvency and to enable it to meet all dues and demands" (see George Howell's *Conflicts of Capital and Labour,* 1:161).

Marx quotes a *Morning Star* correspondent "who at the end of 1866 and beginning of 1867 visited the chief-centers of distress," and found in the East-end districts 5,000 workmen's families in destitution, and 3,000 skilled mechanics breaking stones in the workhouse yard (after distress of over half a year's duration) (*Capital,* p. 734).

stonepile that would give them threepence and a loaf of bread.[53]

Arnold's poem "East London" (1866), inscribed to Tyler, is pertinent:

> 'Twas August, and the fierce sun overhead
> Smote on the squalid streets of Bethnal Green,
> And the pale weaver, through his windows seen
> In Spitafields, looked thrice dispirited.

Hardy may have thought with Shakespeare's Timon of Athens:

> You take my life when you do take the means whereby I live.
> . . .

A Parliamentary Committee previously reported that of 14,000 children in Bethnal Green, only 2,000 attended school; the others went to the public market on Mondays and Tuesday and hired themselves out to silk manufacturers —children from nine and older.[54]

Hardy's poem "The Two Men" (1866), written the year of the financial disaster, is revelatory. In it he relates the lives of two men with similar backgrounds—one who "joined the fortune-finding rout" and the other who "despised the Market's sordid war," both of whom perished in the pauper-stye." * Booth of the Salvation Army reported later that "32 percent of the population were living in a state of chronic poverty . . . incompatible with physical health, and industrial efficiency";[55] and Jack London, still later, noted that "one in every four 'descendants of the Sea Kings'

---

* See Blake's poem "The Defiled Sanctuary," beginning, "I saw a chapel all of gold/That none did dare to enter in," except a serpent stretched "his shining length" along the pavement and forcing his entrance, "vomited his poison out/on the bread and on the wine," ending: "So I turned into a stye,/And laid me down among the swine." Hardy thought Blake "a poet who benefits by selections—like Wordsworth," and Mrs. Hardy admired Blake more than her husband, who "is always a little repelled by the evident streak of insanity in him" (Vere Collins, *Talks with Thomas Hardy at Max Gate*, pp. 66–67).

(Hengist and Horsa) in London dies on public charity and 939 out of every 1,000 in the United Kingdom die in poverty, while 8,000,000 simply struggle on the ragged edge of starvation." [56] He describes Dorset Street in Spitafiels as "the worst street in London." The population had nearly doubled since Hardy's youthful years in the metropolis: "Four million forlorn hopes!" [57] he called London.

Hardy had read nothing but the daily papers and English poetry during these years and written nothing since 1862, except the essay "On the Application of Terra Cotta to Modern Architecture," and an article "How I Built Myself a House," for the amusement of his co-workers at Blomfield's. For the one he was awarded the silver medal by the R.I.B.A. (Royal Institute of British Architects) in March 1863, and for the other he was paid £3 15s. by *Chamber's Journal,* in which it appeared March 18, 1865. In this way he had gotten through a large body of English poetry from Milton's *Paradise Lost* to Shelley's *Mask of Anarchy,* in which Shelley had attacked the Castlereagh government for the massacre of workers at Peterloo in 1819. He was quite unhappy about the Muses' desertion of him (see poems "A Young Man's Epigram on Existence" and "A Young Man's Exhortation" on the lighter and darker side of his literary life between 1863 and 1865). He had started turning the Book of Ecclesiastes into Spencerian stanzas, but finding the original "unmatchable", he abandoned the task. Although he was living within walking distance of Swinburne and Browning, to whom he might have obtained "introductions," and from whom he might have received "encouragement," Mrs. Hardy says, "through literary friends of Blomfield's," he did not seek to meet them, "and if he had cared, possibly have floated off some of his own poems in a small volume." [58] One afternoon during Blomfield's absence he talked to his co-workers on poetry, but did not mention his desire to be a poet, nor that he had sent out his poems to editors who had rejected them, and who, he concluded,"did not know good poetry from bad."[59] They would have preferred to talk about the sensational Tichborne case,* or about women—Cora Pearl,** "Skittles," Agnes Willough-by, Ada Isaacs Menken, and others of whom they professed to know many romantic and *risqué* details," Mrs. Hardy says, "but really knew nothing at all." [60] Or about the trial of Governor Eyre for the murder of George William Gordon, a Negro victim of his martial law suppression of the Jamaica rebellion, for which Huxley and Mill condemned him, and Carlyle and Tennyson contributed to the subscription fund for his defense. The risk of failure in literature seemed more desirable to Hardy than the price of success in architecture. His poem "The Dead Man Walking" [61] reads like an obit of his struggle to be a poet:

> —A Troubadour-youth I rambled
> With Life for lyre,

* The attempt of Arthur Orton (1834–1898) the son of a Wapping butcher, who had deserted a sailing-vessel at Valparaiso in 1850, to obtain the heritage of Roger Tichborne (1829–1862), whose death at sea his mother refused to believe. A judicious advertisement on Nov. 1, 1865, had resulted in the claimant calling on Christmas day 1866 at Tichborne House. The insurance had been paid and the will proven, and the baronetcy and estate had passed in 1862 to a younger brother, Sir Alfred Joseph Doughty-Tichborne, who died in 1866. The family descended from Sir John de Tichborne, sheriff of South Hampton, knighted by James I in 1621. The imposter would gladly have dropped his claim on the death of Lady Tichborne but for the pressure of his creditors. An ejectment action against the trustees of the estate to which the heir was the twelfth baronet finally came before Chief Justice Bovill on May 11, 1871. The claimant's case collapsed when his solicitor Ballantine refused to allow Orton's sisters to testify, and on the 188th day of the trial the jury found the claimant to be Arthur Orton. He was sentenced on Feb. 28, 1874 to fourteen years' penal servitude and died in obscure lodgings in Marylebone, April 2, 1898. The trial cost £200,000, and the Tichborne estate was mulcted of £90,000.

Hardy's lawyer friend Hawkins told him at "an interesting legal dinner at Sir Francis Jeune's [Dec. 17, 1892] his experiences in the Tichborne case, and that it was by a mere chance that he was not on the other side. Lord Coleridge [the cross-examiner in the same case, Hardy says, with his famous, "Would you be surprised to hear?"] was also anecdotic" (*Later Years*, p. 14).

** Cora Pearl had been notorious in her day for her affair with Prince Napoleon (1822–1891), the son of Jerome, nicknamed "Plon-Plon." She and the Archbishop of Paris, Monseigneur Guibert, died on the same day, July 8, 1886.

The beats of being raging
  In me like fire.

But when I practiced eyeing
  The goal of men,
It iced me, and I perished
  A little then.

He thought he might try his hand at reviewing or writing blank-verse plays and gain a knowledge of stagecraft by serving as a supernumerary, if necessary. Toward this end, he consulted with Mark Lemon, then editor of *Punch* magazine and an ardent amateur actor himself, and also with Mr. Coe, the stage-manager of the Haymarket Theater. Hardy was adversely influenced less by Mr. Coe's disrespectful remarks about the theater, Mrs. Hardy says, than by the disillusionment when confronted by the sight of stage paraphernalia. He played the part of "a nondescript" in the pantomime of "The Forty Thieves," at the Covent Garden theater, and also in a reproduction of the Oxford and Cambridge boat race, obtaining the latter part through his acquaintance with the smith who, besides doing the iron work for the pantomime, executed the designs for the church metal work for Mr. Blomfield, and who made crucifixes and harlequin traps," Mrs. Hardy says, "with equal imperturbability." [62] He also thought about entering the church, like Jude, and also, like Jude, could not reconcile the beliefs he had come to hold with the ecclesiastical doctrine, and wrote in his journal of "A certain person"—obviously himself— "who feels himself shrinking into nothing when contemplating other people's *means* of working. When he looks upon their ends, he expands with triumph." It is possible that he became disillusioned with a career in architecture by the reading of Ruskin during these years as he had with religion by the reading of Darwin's *Origin of Species*. He may have winced on reading the following passage in Ruskin and have reflected deeply over it:

Your present system of education is to get a rascal of an architect to order a rascal of a clerk-of-the-works to order a parcel of rascally bricklayers to build you a bestially stupid building in the middle of the town, poisoned with gas, and with an iron floor which will drop you all through it some frosty evening; wherein you will bring a puppet of a cockney lecturer in a dress coat and a white tie, to tell you smugly there's no God, and how many messes he can make of a lump of sugar.

Mrs. Hardy describes Hardy's situation at this time as that "of an isolated student cast upon the billows of London with no protection but his own brains, the young man of whom it may be said more truly than perhaps of any"—quoting Swinburne—"that 'save his own soul he hath no star.' " [63]

Hardy's health grew steadily worse during the first six months of 1867, and his voluntary confinement in his rooms from six to midnight evenings, and breathing the contaminated air from the Thames daytimes at low tide—it being so bad before the days of the Metropolitan Sewage System that Parliament sometimes had to adjourn—further lowered his resistance. The *Daily News* had called them "Stink-Traps." He scarcely had the strength to hold his drawing pencil at his drawing-board at the office. Mr. Blomfield advised him to take a few months' vacation in the country; Hardy was beginning to think he should go into the country altogether.

At the end of July 1867, Hardy left his belongings in his lodgings at 16 Westbourne Park Villas and went home, possibly muttering over his most recent poem "1967" [64] (1867), in which he looked forward gloomily to

A century which, if not sublime,
Will show, I doubt not, at its prime
A scope above this blinkered time

and thinking of his real, or imaginary beloved—perhaps the "sweet liberal lady" of the poem "Discouragement," whom he had met at the Willis Rooms:

With nothing left of me and you
In that live century's vivid view
Beyond a pinch of dust or two;

—Yet what to me how far above?
For I would only ask thereof
That thy worm should be my worm, Love!

The Second Reform Bill, drafted by Henry Thring,* was
passed at the instigation of Disraeli, whose watchword *Sanitas sanitatum, omnia sanitas* the Liberals called "A policy of
sewage," by a Tory parliament in August, with mixed feelings—jubilation by some, direful forebodings by others.
Peel, Cranborne, and Lord Carnarvon,** Hardy's acquaintance at a later date, resigned in protest on March 3, 1867.
The *Times,* which had supported the measure, declared that
"the sturdiest Conservative would have to admit that the
more intelligent mechanics were at least the equals of the
small shopkeepers who did possess the franchise," and the
Earl of Derby pronounced the legislation "a great experiment and a leap in the dark," which he confidently hoped
"would increase the loyalty and contentment of a great
portion of Her Majesty's subjects." [65] It seemed to Lord
Goschen,*** later chancellor of the exchequer, however,
that "the whole center of gravity of the constitution had
been displaced," and Gawthorne Hardy, Disraeli's chief
counsellor and president of the Poor Law Board in Derby's
Third Cabinet (June 1866), wrote: "What an unknown world

*Henry Thring, Baron Thring, (1818–1907), drafted other bills, and
composed the War Office Manual.
** Lord Carnarvon (Henry Howard Molyneux: 1831–1890) was Viceroy
to Ireland in Gladstone's Cabinet; Disraeli referred to him as "little Carnarvon who feeds the radical press" (Monypenny & Buckle, *Life of Disraeli,*
2:815). In 1890 he proposed Hardy for membership in the Athenaeum
(*Early Life,* p. 298).
*** Hardy met Lord Goschen at a Savile Club dinner on June 8, 1887;
also Lord Lytton, A. J. Balfour and others (*Early Life,* p. 262); and in
December 1890 "he was a fellow guest of Goschen, then Chancellor of
the Exchequer, and the "I forgot Goschen' story was still going about"
(*ibid.,* p. 301).

we are to enter." [66] Walter Bagehot, editor of *The Economist* and advisor to the Bank of England, who, said Morris, "is composing the drawing-room in blue damask as he would an ode," [67] predicted gloomily that "the adaptation of democratic theory would make the parliamentary system unworkable," [68] and Carlyle, who had earlier complained about the "Bitch Goddess of Commercialism" and the "gambling society," lashed out later in his essay "Shooting Niagara and After?" (1867) at the "traitorous politicians grasping at votes, even at votes that the rabble have brought on." Dickens, on the other hand, in a speech at the Leeds Mechanics Institute on December 1, 1868, defended education against those who feared putting the power of knowledge into their hands.[69]

The Reform Bill* increased the base of the electorate from about two hundred twenty thousand to about six hundred seventy thousand in a population of fourteen million. On leaving office Gladstone declared to Fould, Minister of Finance (July 11, 1866): "The statesmen of to-day have a new mission opened to them: the mission of substituting the concert of nations for their conflicts, and of teaching them to grow great in common and to give to others by giving to themselves." [70]

At home in Wessex, Hardy "easily fell into the routine he had followed before," Mrs. Hardy says, "though with between five and six years superadded of experience as a young man at large in London, it was with very different ideas of things" (p. 74). He decided "to abandon poetry as a waste of labour," and try his hand at a novel while employed part-time for Mr. Hicks in Dorchester. That winter he read in

---

* After 1867 one man in 14 was an elector in counties in contrast to one man in 7 in boroughs; the ratio before had been 1:21 and 1:16, respectively (see Joseph H. Park's *English Reform Bill of 1867*, p. 252). Disraeli is said to have said: "The pot was on the point of boiling over, and that those who kept it seething would get scalded" (*ibid.*, p. 234). Hardy observed in Mar.–Apr. 1890: "Tories will often do by way of exception to their principles more extreme acts of democratism than Radicals do by rule—such as help on promising plebeians, tolerate wild beliefs . . . (*Early Life*, p. 294).

the *London Times* about the Fenians blowing up Clerken-well Prison (Dec. 13, 1867) and on February 25, 1868, of the House of Representatives impeaching President Johnson. Many Fenians had been imprisoned for the murder of Police Sergeant Brett in Manchester on September 18; many had en-listed and fought on the side of the North in the American Civil War against the Confederacy, which Palmerston had favored. A few days later he read of the Gunpowder Plot to dynamite the Houses of Parliament, about which Disraeli wrote to Queen Victoria "Most secret, December 16, 1867":

> You remember Mrs. Montgomery and her strange, but not improbable information a year ago. She now informs me that on Saturday morning last, a dying Irishman in one of the London hospitals confessed that, early in the sessions there was a plot, quite matured, to blow up the Houses of Par-liament by gunpowder introduced through gas-pipes; but it failed through the House being too well watched. They are going, however, to blow up another prison,* but which, though pressed he refrained from declaring. . . . Gunpowder through gas-pipes is a new idea, and worth attention.[71]

Following the Sheffield outrages, the *Daily News* declared "the Unions must be stamped out as a public nuisance." Edward Beesly, Hardy's friend at a later date, nearly lost his professorship at the University of London over his state-ment "that a trades-union murder was neither better nor worse than any other murder." [72]

These things Hardy read in the papers while he was working half-time for Mr. Hicks and making "a fair copy" of his novel *The Poor Man and the Lady* at home "to submit to a London publisher." A statue of Richard Cobden, who had died on April 2, 1865, was erected in Harrington Square, London, in 1868, by public subscription, and the long-

---

* Marx had been, most active in promoting agitation among the English workers on behalf of the Fenian prisoners but "disapprovel of its terroristic manifestations (blowing up of Clerkenwell prison, etc." (*Correspondence,* p. 231n).

promised lions by Edward Landseer were placed at the base of Nelson's pedestal in Trafalgar Square to complement the statue of Wellington* at the Marble Arch entrance to Hyde Park, opposite Apsley House, wearing upon his breast the Waterloo medal and the horses crowned with laurel. Possibly the scene of the wealthy squire in Hardy's aforementioned novel erecting a statue to "the memory of his brother the General" was suggested by this event.[73] Hardy doubtless read the review of Marx's *Das Kapital* (1867) in the *Saturday Review* (Jan. 18, 1868) "always hostile to my views," Marx wrote—admitting that "the presentation of the subject invests the driest economic questions with certain peculiar charm." [74] That summer, while waiting for a report from the Macmillan publishers on his manuscript, Hardy reflected on J. S. Mill's speech of July 22, 1868, on which Mill had progressed as far as Hamlet:

> But the statemanship of the country has much more to do nowadays than merely to abolish bad institutions. It has to make good laws for a state of society which never existed in the world before. . . . A vast manufacturing and commercial industry has thrown itself up . . . and from the necessities of the case, a hundred evils have sprung up along with it. There are now many things to be done which demand long and patient thought. . . . For instance, let us take the question which is in every one's mind at the present—the proper relations between capital and labour**. . . . how far has the public

* On June 18 the Duke of Wellington held his annual Waterloo dinner at Apsley House, with covers laid for 85 guests: "a silver plateau, 27 feet long and 4 feet wide, occupied the center of the table"—the gift of the King of Portugal, and Dresden porcelain dessert service, the gift from the the Emperor of Russia. The military band played "The Old Roast Beef of England," and many toasts were offered while a vast number of people clustered around the entrance gates. Prince Albert left at a quarter past ten, and the party broke up (see John W. Dodds, *The Age of Paradox*, p. 140).
** During the cotton famine (1863) cotton-workers protested against the masters' allowing some to work overtime, "while others, for want of work, are compelled to exist upon charity (*Capital*, p. 698n). "The relation of masters and man in the blown-flint bottle trades amounts to a chronic strike" (*ibid.*, p. 475); in 1865 the Sheffield file-cutters engaged in a savage revolt against machinery" (*ibid.*, p. 464); in 1867 there was a strike

mind advanced on the subject? It has got thus far: that the old relation between workmen and employers is out of joint.

and on Gladstone's oath when he took office (1868), "My mission is to pacify Ireland" (Morton, p. 383).[75] He thought perhaps with Hamlet: "O cursed spite that ever I was born to set it right." On July 1 Hardy had written down "in all likelihood after a time of mental depression over his work and prospects," Mrs. Hardy says; "Cures for despair: "To read Wordsworth's 'Resolution and Independence'; Stuart Mill's 'Individuality' (in *Liberty*); Carlyle's 'Jean Paul Richter.'" They may well have been prescribed by his friend Horace Moule, who had written him in Dorchester on July 2, 1868, on his writing:

> The grand object of *all* in *learning to write well* is to gain or generate *something to say* . . . [with] Don't read anybody for his style, but for his thoughts, for you must in the end write your own style.[76]

To glance at the record on some of the questions raised by Mill:

> In 1869 Parliament passed the Debtors Act abolishing imprisonment for debt, which Dickens had attacked in his novel *Little Dorrit* (1855–1857) and more symbolically in *A Christmas Carol* (1843), of which he said that "the emancipation of the working class must be conquered by the working class *itself!*" [77] A century lacking eleven years had passed since a London crowd counting Blake in its numbers had battered down the gates of Newgate Prison (June 6, 1780), a debtors' prison. On October 17, 1869, the Suez Canal was opened, giving Great Britain access to India, where Clive of the East India Company had already established a foothold, and also a monopoly of the cotton plantations in Egypt, in which the Sudan Plantation Syndicate virtually made vassals of the original peasants, and its director Baring ruled Egypt during the twenty-five years of his consulship as if "the interests of

of 20.000 men at Preston against a 5 percent reduction in wages (*ibid.*, p. 497).

the bondholders and those of the Egyptian people were identical." [78] Lord Derby pointed out that as the "Suez Canal would form a link with the chain of fortresses which we possess on the road to India"—nearly four-fifths of the shipping through it was British—"by the purchase we gained a great additional security, which we should prize for the free intercourse of navigation." [79] Congratulations came from almost every European nation except Russia, and the King of the Belges, Leopold II, who had put down the strike of the Belgian miners at Marchiens by powder and lead in February 1867, hailed the canal as "the greatest event of modern politics," adding relievedly, "Europe breathes again." The introduction of the Arkwright power-loom, Marx notes, decimated the ranks of Indian weavers, and in 1866 millions of Hindoos died of famine. In 1856, after the signing of a commercial treaty with France, Parliament, at the behest of the mercantilists, adopted a liberal immigration policy, but would not appropriate a farthing for emigration at the request of the suffering English textile workers. (*Capital*, p. 632)

Hardy was witnessing a phase in the development of British imperialism comparable to that of American imperialism in South America depicted in Conrad's novel *Nostromo* (1905) and Belgian imperialism in the Congo in his *Heart of Darkness*. Leopold's cruelties are treated with poetic justice in Vachel Lindsay's *The Congo: A Study of the Negro Race* (1914):

> Listen to the yell of Leopold's ghost
> Burning in hell, for his hand-maimed host.
> Hear how the demons chuckle and yell
> Cutting his hands off down in hell.

And Mark Twain, in his essay "King Leopold's Soliloquy," scathingly indicts the United States for its recognition of the Congo Free State (April 22, 1888) in the face of British and American missionary reports of Leopold's having his soldier-police cut off the right hand of blacks

> as punishment for not bringing in enough rubber, and who, in the shadow that he cast across the Congo Free State, boasts as his protection, "I know the human race."

Everywhere there was recoil in horror at the development of bourgeois man from feudalism into colonialism. Hardy was all the more sensitive to man's inhumanity to man because he had been impressed hopefully by the achievements of science and manhood suffrage, which were signs of men's awakening to a new sense of truth and responsibility toward their brothers.

Hardy still had not found a marriage partner. Mary Waight had turned down his proposal in 1862 before he went to London, and his cousin Tryphena Sparks, then seventeen, gave him back his ring on his return to Wessex, having been persuaded by a new suitor, Charles Gale, a hotelier of Topsham, that cousins should not marry. Hardy appears to have fathered a son by Tryphena—Randal, who went into architecture and died in 1924; but there is no "official record" and only old wives tales, as F. E. Halliday [80] says. Tryphena died on March 17, 1890, and Hardy and his brother Henry bicycled down to Topsham to lay a wreath on her grave, and Hardy finished a poem "Thoughts of Phena" in memory of her. The secret hushed up for so long gives a piquancy to the incident in Hardy's first published novel *Desperate Remedies* (1871) of Edward Springrove's telling Cytherea that his cousin had jilted him for Bollens, and he was free to marry her. This may have influenced his giving up poetry for prose and going back to London in 1872, a job having been offered him by T. Roger Smith, a wellknown architect and professor of Architecture at the Royal Institute of British Architects.

4

The Novels

The most outstanding thing about Hardy's novels is the constancy with which he returned to his satire of London society begun in *The Poor Man and the Lady* (1868). It was not easy to shape one's own literary career against the circumstances over which authors, "as representatives of Grub Street have no control," [1] as both Hardy and Gissing complained. They both wrote in an age when "the novel breeds a characteristic escape from proletarian misery," [2] Caudwell states discerningly. Hardy and Gissing resisted this degrading tendency.

Hardy did not have any intention of restricting his literary horizon to the sheepfolds of Wessex, when he had already widened it to the thoroughfares of London, although "the acquisition of something like a regular income had become important since his marriage" in 1874, and the popularity of *Far from the Madding Crowd,*° published in that year, "had made him aware of the pecuniary value of a reputation for a speciality," [3] but he was opposed to capitalizing on his first literary success. For this reason he laid aside

---

° Title from Thomas Gray's "Elegy written in a Country Churchyard" (1751), stanza XX, beginning "Far from the madding Crowd's ignoble strife."

his story *The Woodlanders* (1887) for thirteen years, and attempted a further criticism of London society in *The Hand of Ethelberta* (1876), despite the discouragement from editors, publishers, and the reading public, who were most disappointed in the novel. *The Hand of Ethelberta,* Mrs. Hardy says, "was too soon for a Comedy of Society of that kind—just as *The Poor Man and the Lady* had been too soon for a socialist story." [4]

Indeed, every Wessex novel, from *Far from the Madding Crowd* on, was followed by a London novel; the novels, properly speaking, should be considered in the order Hardy conceived them rather than in the order of their publication, "the printing of a book" being in Hardy's mind "but an accident in the life of a literary creation and the least individual occurrence in the history of its contents," [5] which is true. However, I shall first take up Hardy's apprenticeship novels, "when he was feeling for a method,"[*] and then the Wessex and London novels separately, considering *Far from the Madding Crowd* and *The Mayor of Casterbridge* together because the setting for both is laid in Casterbridge, though the time is a generation apart. Hardy, ingeniously and with much misgivings, endeavored to scourge London society in lighter thrusts and parries than the mortal blows he had tried to deal in *The Poor Man and the Lady,* which had fanned to life the sparks of the Chartist cause, which Grub Street, for obvious reasons, preferred to let die.

[*] Carl Weber, *Hardy of Wessex* (1940). Weber's chronology (p. 182) of Hardy's novels is very helpful: but it omits the time of. *Desperate Remedies:* 1865–1867:

Trumpet-Major	*Jude*
1800–1808	1855–1874
Under the Greenwood Tree	*Two on a Tower*
1835–1836	1858–1863
Mayor of Casterbridge	*Far from the Madding Crowd*
1846–1849	1869–1873
The Well-Beloved	*The Woodlanders*
1852–1892	1876–1879
The Return of the Native	*Tess*
1842–1843	1884–1889

Some attention to *The Poor Man and the Lady* is necessary for understanding what Hardy was up against in trying to buck the trade demands and maintaining, at the same time, his self-respect as a man and his freedom as a writer. *The Poor Man and the Lady* was "a sweeping dramatic satire of the squierarchy and nobility, the vulgarity of the middle class, modern Christianity, church restoration, and political and domestic morals* in general," [6] in Hardy's own words. Needless to say, it was rejected. Hardy was surprised that "in the opinion of such experienced critics he had written so aggressive and even dangerous a work." [7] He must have been puzzled by Macmillan's ambiguous letter [8] (August 10, 1868) saying that he "liked his tone better than Thackeray's, yet he meant fun, you mean mischief," and his recommending, at the same time, that he emulate Thackeray. He must have been similarly puzzled by the report of Macmillan's reader John Morley,** who had cited to Macmillan portions of the manuscript: "For queer cleverness and hard sarcasm—*e.g.* p. 280—a little before and after: p. 333–p. 352"; and "for cynical description half-worthy of Balzac pp. 358–9," yet recommending that "he must study

---

* "One instance he could remember was a chapter in which, with every circumstantial detail, he described in the first person his introduction to the kept mistress of an architect who 'took in washing' (as it was called in the profession)—that is worked at his own office for other architects—the said mistress adding to her lover's income by designing for him the pulpits, altars, reredoses, texts, holy vessels, crucifixes and other ecclesiastical furniture which were handed on to him by the nominal architects who employed her protector—the lady herself being a dancer at a music-hall when not engaged in designing Christian emblems—all told so plausibly as to seem actual proof of the degeneracy of the age" (*Early Life,* pp.81–82).

** Hardy did not see Morley again till "July 8 or 9" (1879), when he went "with E. (Mrs. Hardy) to Mrs. (Alexander) Macmillan's garden party at Knapdale, near our house," where he "talked to Mr. White of Harvard University, and Mr. Henry Holt, the New York publisher . . . and also to John Morley, whom I had not seen since he read my first manuscript," who "remembered it, and said in his level un-interested voice: 'Well, since we met you have . . .' etc., etc." (*Early Life,* pp.167–68). Morley had criticized the scene in the manuscript of Will Strong's addressing a crowd of workingmen in Trafalgar Square as "absurd and impossible."

form and composition in such writers as Balzac and Thackeray, who would I think come as natural masters to him," and later warned him of "letting *realism* grow out of proportion to his *fancy*."

Macmillan had praised his "description of country life among working-men as admirable" and "palpably truthful," and found "the scene in Rotten Row . . . full of real power and insight." He admitted that "the utter heartlessness of *all* the conversation you give in drawing-rooms and ballrooms about the working-classes has *some* ground of truth . . . but your chastisement would fall harmless from its very excess." Morley was moved by "the real feeling in the writing, although now and then," it seemed to him, "it is commonplace in form as all feeling turning on the insolence and folly of the rich in face of the poor is apt to sound," for which he cited to Macmillan "*eg.,* p. 338." Macmillan had found "Will's speech" to the working-men in Trafalgar Square, "full of wisdom," but declared that "nothing could justify such a wholesale blackening of a class but large and intimate knowledge of it," which he admitted that he did not have since his "own experience of fashionables is very small," and "probably the nature of my business brings me into contact with the best of the class."

It is possible that the publisher and his reader might have taken a different attitude toward Hardy's novel if the manuscript had borne a London postmark instead of a Dorset one. Neither of them seems to have realized that he prefaced a chapter in his manuscript of *The Poor Man and the Lady* with this from Thackeray's *Book of Snobs* (1846–47): "Come forward some great Marshall, and organize equality in society"; or that he had visited the originals of the "Cave of Harmony" [9] in Thackeray's *The Newcomes* (1853) and the "Black Kitchen" in *Pendennis* (1850), and recognized them as the originals of the Coal Hole and the Cider Cellars. Macmillan's question, however, "Would you be willing to consider any suggestions?" was hopeful, and Hardy, after waiting a months, wrote the following letter to Macmillan:

> Bockhampton, Dorchester *Sept.* 10, 1868
>
> Dear Sir,
> I have become anxious to hear from you again. As the days go on, and you do not write, and my production begins to assume that small and unimportant shape everything one does assumes as the time and mood in which one did it recedes from the present, I almost feel that I don't care what happens to the book, so long as something happens. The earlier fancy, that *Hamlet* without Hamlet would never do, turns to a belief that it would be better than closing the house.
> I wonder if your friend meant the building up of a story, and not English composition, when he said I must study composition. Since my letter, I have been hunting up matter for another tale, which would consist entirely of rural scenes and humble life, but I have not courage enough to go on with it till something comes of the first.[10]

On December 7, Hardy made "a flying visit" to London to see Mr. Macmillan, who advised him that *The Poor Man and the Lady* was "a class of book which Macmillan himself could not publish—it would be looked on too much as a Reynolds' ° Miscellany affair"—and he referred him, with a letter of introduction, to Chapman & Hall as "a likely publisher," located in Piccadilly, on whom Hardy called. Chapman, "ignoring Hardy's business," pointed out to him" an

° Is Macmillan's referring to *Reynolds Weekly*, edited by C. W. M. Reynolds, an old Chartist, "receptive to all and every variety of literature . . . if illustrating some wholesome principle"; or *Reynolds* newspaper, controlled by Sir Henry Dalziel, which set fourth in much detail . . . as might prejudice aristocratic institutions with many readers and amuse them all, and was anti-imperialist in tone." (See Walter Graham, *English Literary Periodicals* and Viscount Camroe, *British Newspapers and their Controllers.*) The issue of Jan. 20, 1867, featured broadsides on the walls of London; "Fat Oxen! Starving Men," and observed "while English workmen with their wives and children are dying of cold and hunger, there are millions of English gold—the produce of English labour—being invested in Russian, Spanish, Italian and other foreign enterprises" (Marx *Capital*, p. 734n). "The best of it is that Reynolds has now come out in his paper as a furious opponent of the middle class" (John W. Dodds, *The Age of Paradox*, p. 124.)

aged figure in an inverness cape and slouched hat . . . "You see that old man talking with my clerk? He's Thomas Carlyle. Have a good look at him. You'll be glad I pointed him out to you some day." Chapman told Hardy that "they could not purchase the MS outright," but agreed to publish it if Hardy "would guarantee a small sum against loss—say £20," [11] to which Hardy agreed. When the proof-sheets did not come, Hardy wrote the publisher again and was invited to call (March 1869) and meet "the gentleman who read your manuscript." This was George Meredith, who, in a back room "piled with books and papers," with the manuscript in his hand, "began lecturing Hardy upon it in a sonorous voice." He strongly advised Hardy "not to 'nail his colours to the mast' so definitely in a first book if he wished to do anything practical in literature; for if he printed so pronounced a thing, he would be attacked on all sides by the conventional reviewers, and his future injured." Its final rejection by Tinsley Brothers was the end of Hardy's trial of hope. In this matter, all three publishers had acted less from a wish to protect Hardy's literary reputation—he had none as yet—than from seeking to avoid any pecuniary risk or endangering the reputation of their own firms.

This experience had a profound effect on Hardy's construction of his next two novels: *Desperate Remedies* (1871) and *Under the Greenwood Tree* (1872). *Desperate Remedies* was about a bigamist, Aeneas Manston, the natural son of Miss Aldclyffe, whom she hires as bailiff on her estate, and he, Hardy says, "like Curius at his Sabine Farm, he had counted his glory not to possess gold himself, but to have power over her who did." [12] Miss Aldclyffe persuades her lady's maid, Cytherea, to marry Aeneas rather than her poor tenant's son, Edward Springrove. Cytherea's brother Owen and Edward rescue Cytherea from Manston in a London hotel and, tracking down his past, discover that he was previously married to a woman named Eunice, whose corpse they unearth "stuffed in a common corn-sack in the mouth of an old oven, mortared up by Manston in one of the out-buildings on the estate, formerly used as a workshop and brew-house." *Desperate Remedies* was the result of Hardy's having followed Meredith's advice to construct a novel with a complicated plot, and is patterned somewhat after Wilkie Collins's *The Woman in White* (1860). Macmillan found *Desperate Remedies* of "far too sensational an order for us to think of publishing," [13] and Chapman and Hall reneged on their promise to publish it. For an advance of £75 Tinsley Brothers published *Desperate Remedies*, which Mr. Tinsley told Hardy was "a bloodcurdling story" and "'Pon my soul, you wouldn't have got another man in London to print it. Oh, be hanged, if you would!" [14]

The novel showed glints of promise not usually found in a novel of this kind: a description of nature, or an insight into character such as:

> Miss Aldclyffe's visit to Cytherea's bedroom, Parson Raun-ham's yeoman services in putting out the brush-fire, which burned the elder Springrove's cottage Inn to the ground, Ed-ward's reflecting on "the vanishing figure of Cytherea with the disconsolation of Adam, when he first saw the sun set," or look-ing at Cytherea on their walk to the railroad station "as a waiter looks at the change," and the flash of poetry in their looking "at the river, then into it: a shoal of minnows was floating over the sandy bottom, like the black dashes on miniver."

There is already the characteristically Hardyan passage in Farmer Springrove's remark to Farmer Baker on seeing two carpenters bearing "an empty coffin, covered by a thin black cloth":

> "Why should we not stand still, says I to myself, and fling a quiet eye upon the Whys and Wherefores, before the end of it all, and we go down into the mouldering-place, and are forgotten? [15]

Macmillan likewise rejected *Under the Greenwood Tree*

(the novel of "humble life") on the grounds that he was afraid "the public will find the tale very slight and rather unexciting." [16] Tinsley, however, was delighted with the story and pronounced it as "sweet as new mown hay," [17] accepting it on a royalty basis. This novel creates a sort of pastoral island in Wessex of the time of Hardy's forebears and has a lyrical quality of Shakespeare's *Tempest*. It is a romance of Christmas minstreling, beehiving, cider-making, and love-making, following the seasons, at the time just before the barrel organ displaced the stringed band in church; the stringed instrumentalists call on Parson Maybold and ask

> not to be choked off quiet at no time in particular [which] would seem rather mean in the eyes of other parishes, sir. But if we fell glorious with a bit of a flourish at Christmas, we should have a reasonable end, and not dwindle away at some nameless paltry second Sunday . . . that's got no name of his own.[18]

This was more socially accepted behavior than Strong's political activities among the workingmen in London in *The Poor Man and the Lady*. One of the musicians, Reuben, holds up his fist playfully and says to Maybold:

> "If you or I, or any man of the present generation at the time music is a-playing, was to shake your fist in father's face this way and say, 'William your life or your music!' he'd say, 'My life!' "

The parson is reported as saying, "I don't wish to change the church music in a forcible way." It is a novel in which Death takes a holiday.

The critic's review of *Desperate Remedies* in the *Spectator* (April 22, 1871), epithetized the novel as "a desperate remedy for an emaciated purse" (he had advanced £75 of £123, which was all he had in the world), and castigated Hardy for "daring to suppose it possible that an unmarried lady owning an estate could have an illegitimate child," and also for his anonymity, declaring that "the law is hardly just which prevents Tinsley Brothers from concealing their participation also." [19] Hardy had read the review "as he sat on a stile leading to the eweleaze he had to cross on his way home to Bockhampton," and "wished that he were dead." [20] Seeing his book listed in Smith and Son's surplus catalog at 2s.6d. at Exeter Station the day after his thirty-first birthday (June 3, 1871), he thought "that the *Spectator* had snuffed out the book," and Tinsley's statement (Feb. 22, 1872) remitting £60 represented a loss of £15 on his literary venture.[21] *Under the Greenwood Tree* was reviewed in the *Athenaeum* (June 15, 1872), in the *Pall Mall Gazette* (July 15, 1872), and in the *Saturday Review* (Sept. 20, 1872), the last being written by his friend Horace Moule, who resolved never to review a friend again. Neither Hardy nor Tinsley* had made any money on the book, despite Tinsley's advertisements of it in "railways and street hoardings so that your works will be well before the public." [22]

Hardy decided to "banish novel writing forever," and concentrate all his time on architecture. The reason for his decision was his desire to marry Emma Lavinia Gifford, whom he had met in the spring of 1870, on an assignment of church restoration for Mr. Crickmay, who had taken over Mr. Hicks's practice after his death, which Hardy had learned of in London. How Hardy felt about Miss Gifford and she about him the evening of March 7, 1870, when he arrived at the rectory of the Reverend Caddell Holder (M.A. Oxon), Miss Gifford's brother-in-law, with a blue paper sticking out of the pocket of his great coat, which was not the plan for a church after all, but a "Ms. of a poem," to her

---

* "He was a shrewd chap when dealing with young authors," Hardy remarked to Vere Collins (Oct. 29, 1921). "However, I always think that on a first novel (*Desperate Remedies*), a writer must not expect to make money. Old Tinsley must have sunk into poverty in his later years, for he asked me to help him to obtain a Civil List grant" (*Talks with Thomas Hardy at Max Gate,* p. 55).

surprise (*Early Life*, pp. 92–93) are the subject of Hardy's poem "When I Set Out for Lyonnesse" (his name for Cornwall) and "A Man was Drawing Near to Me." Miss Gifford, whom he was soon calling "Em," wished him, however, to adhere to a career of authorship, and his friend Moule, whom he accidentally encountered the following summer in London, "hoped he still kept a hand on the pen, since, supposing anything were to happen to his eyes from the fine drawing, he could dictate a book, article, or poem, but not a geometrical design"; in a letter, later, he recommended an eye specialist to Hardy and the reading of Kinglake's *Invasion of the Crimea* and Goldwin Smith's *American Slavery*.[23] Moule's words came back to him one morning soon afterward, "by his seeing for the first time in his life, what seemed like floating specks on the white drawing-paper before him."

During the winter of 1871-72, Hardy buckled down to architecture as the quickest means to marriage, working for T. Roger Smith, a London architect, who was busy designing schools in competition with other London architects for the London School Board. Running one day into Tinsley, whose office in the Strand was not far from Smith's on Bedford Street, Hardy rashly agreed to supply a story for *Tinsley's Magazine*. He "reflected on the novel he had abandoned" (*A Pair of Blue Eyes*), Mrs. Hardy says, "considered that he could do it in six months, but to guard against temptation, multiplied by two the utmost he could expect to make at architecture in the time," which Mr. Tinsley thought "very reasonable, Mr. Hardy," [24] and led him to his office to sign the contract. After the completion of the school-board drawings, Hardy left Smith's and began writing *A Pair of Blue Eyes* (originally entitled "A Winning Tongue Had He"—undoubtedly a reference to Tinsley's persuasiveness) and, finding he could not get on with it in London lodgings, went home to Dorset and on September 30 (1872), according to his diary entry, "Posted MS. of *A Pair of Blue Eyes* to Tinsley up to Page 163." Just before that he had received a letter from Mr. Smith "informing that another of the six Board-school competitions . . . had been successful," and inviting him back on "any more liberal terms if he felt dissatisfied." "This architectural success for which he would have given much had it come sooner," Mrs. Hardy says, "was now merely provoking." [25] He had published his first three novels anonymously because he did not want to be known as an author who had failed at architecture, or as an architect who had failed at literature, the literary architect "always being suspect" [26] in the profession in those days.

From that time on Hardy "sat writing away as if his life depended upon it—which it did," [27] like the journalist Knight in *A Pair of Blue Eyes*. While Hardy was completing that novel, he started working on *Far from the Madding Crowd* for the *Cornhill* magazine. Its editor, Leslie Stephen, thought the descriptions in *Under the Greenwood Tree* "admirable," but advised him it was "not a magazine story, and though he did not want a murder in every number"— probably thinking of *Desperate Remedies*—reminded him that it was "necessary to catch the attention of readers by some distinct and well arranged plot." [28] Hardy soon found himself committed to novel writing as a trade, as he had formerly been to architecture, and he felt harassed into "the unfortunate course of hurrying forward a further produc-tion, before he was aware of what had been of value in his previous one; before learning, that is, not only what had attracted the public, but what was of true and genuine substance on which to build a career as a writer with a real literary message." [29] The appearance of *Far from the Mad-ding Crowd* in the *Cornhill's* January issue (out in Decem-ber) made Miss Gifford feel "that her desire of a literary course for Hardy was in a fair way of being justified," and Hardy having finished the last chapter "at a gallop," they were married on September 17, 1874—a day she described as "not brilliant sunshine, but wearing a soft sunny luminousness, just as it should be," and an event beside which, it seemed to him, "a high repute as an artistic novelist loomed even less important." [30] Living at Surbiton, a London suburb, on their return from their honeymoon in Rouen, they had not fully realized the popularity of the novel, until seeing, on their frequent journeys to London, ladies carrying about copies of it with Mudie's lending library label on the cover.

Hardy had all at once become a producer of fiction for the popular libraries and the lending library public, whose object was not "upward advance but lateral advance." He must either fictionize his characters "to produce the spurious effect of their being in harmony with social forms and ordinances, or, by leaving them alone to act as they will, he must bring down the thunders of respectability upon his head." [31] He deplored "arranging a *denouement* . . . indescribably unreal and meritricious, but dear to the Grundyist and subscriber," * and he believed "that, in representations of the world, the passions ought to be proportioned as in the world itself, life being a physiological fact." George Gissing, who found "refreshment and onward help" in Hardy's novels, wrote him (June 30, 1886): "That aid is much needed now-a-days by anyone who wishes to pursue literature as distinct from the profession of letters," declaring, "the misery of it is that, writing for English people, one may not be thorough:

---

* Stephen reminded Hardy that the seduction of Fanny Robin (*Far from the Madding Crowd*) must be treated "in a gingerly fashion, owing to an excessive prudery of which I am ashamed" (*Early Life*, p. 130). Mr. Locker, editor of *Macmillan's* magazine, recommended toning down Dr. Fitzpiers' affair with Suke Damson (*The Woodlanders*), and his reader James Payn criticized *The Mayor* "that the lack of gentry among the characters made it uninteresting"—"a typical estimate," Mrs. Hardy says, "of what was, or was supposed to be mid-Victorian taste" (Purdy, pp.53–55 and *Early Life*, pp. 235–36). Editors' decisions were not always of their own making, Hardy learned from his call on Arthur Locker at the *Graphic* office, who told him that he did "not object to the stories (*A Group of Noble Dames*) but the Directors do" (*Ibid.*, p. 297). Even Tinsley and his reader objected to Hardy's putting forward Mrs. Manston's *substitute* so prominently as his *mistress* in *Desperate Remedies* (Purdy, p.5). Charles Edward Mudie, who began a bookselling business in 1840, by 1852 had 25,000 subscribers (see Jacob Korg, *George Gissing*, p. 154).

reticences and superficialities have so often to fill places where one is willing to put in honest work."

The time of Hardy's Wessex novels is after the unsuccessful efforts of the Loveless brothers in 1834 to organize the workfolk, and before the successful one of Joseph Arch's National Agricultural Workers Union (1872). Pauperized on the one hand by the Speenhamland system of outdoor relief (1795–1834) and cowed into submission, on the other hand, by commissions of assize and the constabulary, their distress was further intensified by the Poor Law of 1834, which was written, historian Smellie says, "in the purest milk of the Benthamite word;" [32] by abolishing outdoor relief it had created a million complete paupers out of three or four million semi-paupers, until an English peasant, as E. K. Wakefield observed, "and a pauper were synonymous." Whitbread, in 1796, had proposed a minimum wage for agricultural workers; Pitt had opposed it. The workfolk are still dependent on Providence in *Far from the Madding Crowd,* or on Pa'son Thirdly,

> who shared his " 'taties with them," or are forced to use up their own seedling potatoes for food like Tess's evicted family —"that last lapse of the improvident," or they are forced to "traipse up to the vestry . . . when the use-money is gied away to the second-best poor folk," as Billy Smallbury had seen Gabriel Oak's Uncle Andrew's family do "only last Purification Day (February 2) in this very world." [33]

Hardy draws on the amendment of 1847 to the Poor Law of 1834, which had allowed farmers to recruit workers from the workhouse for eleven months, as the Old Malter remarks:

> "Old Twills wouldn't hire me for more than eleven months at a time, to keep me from being chargeable to the parish, if so be I was disabled,"

and on the Guardians of the Poor House rescinding "that harsh order"—the segregation of the sexes—as Hardy depicts in his dramatic monologue "The Curate's Kindness (A Workhouse Irony)." [34] An indigent old fellow, who had worked hard and "gone to Communion O'Zundays these fifty years past," is looking forward to an escape from his wife by consoling himself that "Life there will be better than t'other . . . with *the men in one wing and their wives in another*," en route to Casterbridge Union. "Just then, one pa'son arriving, steps up out of breath to the side o' the waggon," and informs them that he has persuaded the Board that "they shall abide in one wing together." The old fellow "sank" and "knew 'twas quite a foredone thing that misery should be to the end," and had a suicidal impulse:

> I thought they'd be strangers aroun' me,
>   But she's to be there!
> Let me jump out o'waggon and go back and drown me
>   At Pummery or Ten-Hatches Weir.[35]

Much domestic incompatability must have resulted from low wages and exploitation by farmers and landlords "that caused the 'Complaint of Piers the Plowman' to be echoed in his heart," as Hardy remarks in his essay "The Dorsetshire Labourer" (*Longman's Magazine*, July 1883). In the essay he contrasts the laborers improved condition after their affiliating with Arch's National Agricultural Workers Union, noting that they were no longer treated like "thralls of Cedric" by a farmer astride a horse, and that "though they are losing their individuality they are widening the range of their ideas, and gaining freedom." [36] He had heard Arch speak on one of his numerous campaigns through Dorset, and describes an old man who raised his hand and said, "Here's a zixpence toward that, please God." Hardy's essay throws considerable light on the farm-laborers'* plight

---

* "Now the crowd is as dark as a London crowd," Hardy observes in the essay. "The genuine white smock-frock of Russia duck and the whity-brown one of drabbet, are rarely seen now afield. . . . Where smocks are worn by the young and middled-aged, they are of blue material. The mechanic's 'slop' has also been adopted." And "That peculiar-

in the Wessex novels, particularly in *The Mayor of Caster-bridge,* "immediately before foreign competition had revolutionized the trade in grain":

> the wheat quotations from month to month depended entirely upon the home harvest. A bad harvest, or the prospect of one, would double the price of corn in a few weeks; and the promise of a good yield would lower it as rapidly. Prices* were like the roads of the period, steep in gradient, reflecting in their phases the local conditions, without engineering, levelling, or averages.
>
> The people, too, who were not farmers, the rural multitude, saw in the god of weather a more important personage than they do now. Indeed, the feeling of the peasantry was well-nigh to prostrate themselves in lamentation before untimely rains and tempests, which came as the Alastor of those households whose crime it was to be poor.[37]

Some of the references to laborers' migrations during the long agricultural depression are touched on more sociologically in *Tess* than in any of the other novels. *Far from the Madding Crowd* is about the later time, when workfolk no longer had to labor in the fields on Sundays, and "farmers' wives are beginning," Gabriel Oak remarks to Bathsheba Everdene, "to have pianos now." Indeed some of the farmers like Boldwood of *Far from the Madding Crowd* appear as young men in *The Mayor of Casterbridge:*

> Each with an official stall in the corn-market room with their names painted thereon—"Henchard", "Everdene", "Shiner",

ity of the English urban poor (which M. Taine ridicules, and unfavourably contrasts with the taste of the Continental working-people)—their preference for the cast-off clothes of a richer class to a special attire of their own—has, in fact, reached the Dorset farm folk" (p. 176). At the Alma-Tademas (May 20, 1889), Hardy met M. Taine—"a kindly, nicely trimmed old man with a slightly bent head" (*Early Life*, p. 287).

* Marx notes in his letter to Engels (Jan. 7, 1851): "Since 1815 the price of corn has dropped irregularly but steadily—from 90 shillings to 50 shillings and lower—this before the repeal of the Corn Laws. Rent has steadily risen. . . . In every country we find, as Petty has already noticed, that when the price of corn dropped the total rental of the country rose (*Correspondence* p. 28).

"Darton", to which Farfrae's in staring new letters, was added, from which Henchard, stung into bitterness, like Bellerophon, wandered away from the crowd.[38]

There are no acts of incendiarism or destruction of machinery in either novel as there had been at the height of the Labourers Revolt (1830), and again during the bitter winter of 1843–1844. The hayrick fire, which Gabriel puts out for Bathsheba when he happened by looking for work, and the lightning storm on the eve of the harvest, are acts of God, or Nature, and Farfrae's display of the new corn-drill in *The Mayor*, Hardy says, "created as much sensation in the corn market as a flying machine would create at Charing Cross." But in *The Mayor* there are the smoldering ashes from the suppressed Labourers Revolt that had furnished the sparks of Anti-Corn Law agitation and Chartism, albeit hidden, and gave rise perversely to the attacks on the morals of their overseers in the skimmington ride (p. 324), timed after Royalty's visit to Casterbridge, which saddens Farfrae, ruins Henchard, and kills Lucetta. "Effigies, donkey, lanterns, band, all had disappeared like the crew of *Comus*," and no one feigns to know anything about the perpetrators of the crime. Henchard, going home alone, dumbly realizes:

So much for man's rivalry. . . . Death was to have the oyster, and Farfrae and himself the shells.[39]

The two novels should be considered together; because *The Mayor* deals with Casterbridge of the earlier time, I shall take it up first, although *Far from the Madding Crowd* was the first of Hardy's Wessex novels.

The Mayor depicts the rivalry between two grain merchants: the older Henchard, who conducts his business by "the old crude *viva voce* system"—"I'll do't" and "you shall hae't it," and the younger Farfrae, a Scotchman from Edinborough, who can cipher, keep ledgers, and court the ladies. Farfrae, with his "inventions useful to the corren trade," is on his way "to Bristol—from there to the other side of the worrld, to try my fortune in the great wheat-growing districts of the West." [40] Henchard, realizing his value to him, persuades him "to give up his American notion" and stay with him as manager of his corn department. They have a falling-out, and Farfrae sets up his own business, prospers, buying cheap and selling dear, while Henchard, buying dear in "the war of prices," goes bankrupt. His creditors decline to accept his gold watch, which he offers them, and "moved by a recollection,"

> he took the watch to the makers just opposite, sold it there and then for what the tradesman offered, and went with the proceeds to one among the smaller of his creditors, a cottager of Durnover in straitened circumstances, to whom he handed the money.[41]

After hearing from Jopp that "Farfrae had bought his furniture," Henchard goes to a suicidal spot on Gray's bridge, and stares "down into the racing river till the bridge seemed moving backward with him." Hardy writes:

> The miserables included bankrupts, hypochondriacs, persons who were "out of a situation," from fault or lucklessness, the inefficient of the professional class—shabby genteel men . . . [whose] eyes were mostly directed over the parapet upon the water below . . . or those whom the world did not treat kindly for some reason or other.[42]

Henchard's exclusion by Farfrae, now mayor, from the celebration honoring the King's visit, fills him with rancor, and he resolves to settle their differences in a life-and-death wrestle in the barn. Yet, when he has Farfrae at his mercy, and can easily push him through the door to his death with one hand, his affection for the young Scotsman, who resembles his dead younger brother, stays his hand, though Farfrae charges him with wanting to kill him. He says:

> "O Farfrae! that's not true! . . . God is my witness that no man ever loved another as I did thee at one time. . . . And

now—though I came here to kill 'ee, I cannot hurt thee! Go and give me in charge—do what you will." [43]

Henchard is "a vehement gloomy being," Hardy says, "who had quitted the ways of vulgar men without light to guide him on a better way." He is superstitious to the point of believing in demons and conjurors, and is driven by a fierce conscience that does not spare himself and that brings about his downfall. The day he is serving his turn as judge and the furmity woman is brought before him on a drunkenness charge,[44] he cannot deny her accusation that he sold his wife years before in her tent. He is torn apart between his compassion for Abe Whittle, a fatherless boy whose mother he has "kept in coals and snuff," [45] and his role as employer. On losing Lucetta to Farfrae, he bursts out in a drinking spree after twenty years' sworn abstinence. A "headstrong man whose diplomacy was as wrong-headed as a buffalo's," he brings to mind Dylan Thomas's poem to his father, "Do Not Go Gentle into that Goodnight," with a great deal of the laborer's repressed wrath of Mixen Lane in him, "the slum and Addulam of all the surrounding villages."

[Mixen Lane] was the hiding-place of those who were in distress, and in debt, and trouble of every kind. Farm-labourers and other peasants, who combined a little poaching* with their farming, and a little brawling and bibing with their poaching, found themselves sooner or later in Mixen Lane. Rural mechanics too idle to mechanize, rural servants too rebellious to serve. . . .
A brook divided the moor from the tenements, and to outward view there was no way across it. . . . But under every householder's stairs there was kept a mysterious plank nine inches wide; which plank was a secret bridge.*

* Hardy recalled how when at Bockhampton a home was pulled down, "a pair of swingels was found under a thatch—'an instrument of defense' used by poachers and capable of killing a man" (see *Later Years*, p. 262).
Charlotte tells her brother Captain De Stancy, that "the poachers had it all (the game) in Mr. Wilkins' time." Wilkins was a blind man,

> Families from decayed villages—families of that once bulky, but now nearly extinct, section of village society called "liviers", or life-holders—copy-holders and others, whose roof-trees had fallen for some reason or other, compelling them to quit the rural spot that had been their home for generations—came here, unless they chose to lie under a hedge by the wayside . . . who would not stick at a trifle.[46]

They are men like Christopher Coney, who had lived in the county forty-five years, and had "no more love for my country than I have for Botany Bay," [47] or like Joseph Poorgrass of *Far from the Madding Crowd,* who thinks he is "too good" for his country;[48] both represent the alienated worker who has come to recognize, in Marx's words, that "the worker has no fatherland" (*Communist Manifesto*). Henchard's selling his wife and infant daughter to the sailor Newson for £5 in the furmity-woman's tent—a matter of record (given in the preface) supports Marx's statement that the worker who formerly sold only his labor now sold his wife and family into slavery.[49] They are victims of the revolutionary changes in agriculture and the ascendancy of mercantilism, resulting in the increasing army of the unemployed—and no one realizes this more fully than Henchard at the exhibition of the brightly colored corn-drill out of which a metallic voice is pouring the strains of "The Maid of Gowie," and Lucetta remarks, "Why, it is a sort of agricultural piano?" and Farfrae predicts it will "revolutionize agriculture hereabouts," [50] and Henchard is silent.

Far from the Madding Crowd is the best known and least understood of Hardy's Wessex novels; it is the story almost never alluded to when anyone speaks about his pessimism. It is only superficially a pastoral romance "about a shepherd, a woman-farmer and a sergeant of the cavalry," [51] which Hardy sketched to Stephen, but it has an elegaic

from whom Paula's father purchased the castle (*A Laodicean*, p. 171). Lord Mountclere instructs his men, "You go and keep watch by the further lodge: there are poachers about" (*Hand of Ethelberta*, p. 445).

quality of the Twenty-Third psalm and of the Christmas scenes in Tennyson's *In Memoriam* (1859), as if Hardy were saddened by the suicide of his friend Horace Moule° as Tennyson had been by the sudden death of his friend Arthur Hallam, and both were searching for their lost faith. There is a pervasive harmony between Nature and society in the novel; Gabriel Oak exhibits all the New Testament virtues of patience, loyalty, forbearance, and forgiveness toward humanity, as if they were his sheep, for which he is finally rewarded with the hand of the coquettish Bathsheba, after the shooting of her husband, Sergeant Troy, by Farmer Boldwood at Boldwood's Christmas party. Goodness leads to marriage and happiness, justice is tempered with mercy, evil is forgotten in the children's singing Newman's "Lead Kindly Light" at Troy and Fanny's graves; even the peasant Coggan, who is "staunch Church of England," exclaims on the commutation of Boldwood's death sentence to life imprisonment: "Hurrah! God's above the Devil yet!"

In *The Mayor of Casterbridge* one is reminded not only that "The farmers' income is ruled by the wheat crop within his own horizon and the wheat crop by the weather"—this is only suggested in *Far from the Madding Crowd* in Farmer Boldwood's failure to cover his wheat-ricks—but also that the competitive rivalry between Henchard and Farfrae is being taken up by their drivers in the clash between Henchard's hay-loaded waggon and Farfrae's empty waggon in the rivalry of their masters. Henchard's driver, in backing up, brought "the rear hind wheel against the churchyard wall, and the whole mountainous load went over;" "instead of considering how to gather up the load the two men closed in a fight with their fists;" Henchard sent them staggering, and after extricating the horse that was down and

---

° September 24, 1874: "It was a matter of keen regret to him now," Mrs. Hardy says, "and for a long time after, that Moule and the woman to whom Hardy was warmly attached had never set eyes on each other, and that she could never make Moule's acquaintance or be his friend" (*Early Life,* p. 126).

"seeing the state of his waggon and its load, began hotly berating Farfrae's man." Lucetta and Elizabeth-Jane both side with Farfrae's man; Henchard reminds them "The other's is the empty waggon, and he must have been most to blame for coming on." Henchard's man says, "You can't trust their senses!" referring to the women—and to Henchard's "Why not?" he replies:

> "Why, you see, sir, all the women side with Farfrae—being a damn young dand—of the sort that he is—one that creeps into a maid's heart like the giddying worm into a sheep's brain—making crooked seem straight to their eyes!"

There is a counterpoint to the antiphonal tone of the Twenty-Third Psalm prevailing in *Far from the Madding Crowd* in some of the peasant dialogue with its dissonance of religious skepticism and humor toward institutionalized religion, which supports the London Morning *Chronicle*—then the most important Liberal organ—in its reporter's interview by "One who Has whistled at the Plough" [52] (July 1843): that the farm workers' religion was a bread-and-butter question. The reporter, quoted by Engels, asked the farmworkers "why they went to Church?" and received the answer, "Why go at all? We be like to go, and we wouldn't lose everything, work and all." The reporter explains, "I learned later they could get a few privileges in regard to fuel and ground for potatoes (to be paid for)"—Hardy calls them 'perquisites' in his essay—"if they went to church." Hardy's rustics talk more like the farm laborers interviewed by the *Chronicle,* on which Dickens was a reporter in 1834, than they do like Shakespeare's rustics. Cain Ball remarks on the two religions going on in the nation now: "And thinks I, I'll play fair, so I went to High Church in the morning and High Chapel in the afternoon. Well, at High Church they pray singing and worship all the colours of the rainbow; and at High Chapel they pray preaching, and worship drab and whitewash only." Joseph Poorgrass observes that

"Chapel-folk be more hand in glove with them above than we"; while Jan Coggan, who has "stuck like a plaster to the old faith [he] was born in," would "as soon turn King's evidence for the few pounds you get." [53] Jan observes, "A man can belong to the Church and bide in his cheerful old inn, and never trouble his mind about doctrines at all," to which Mark Clark replies, "But we Church-men you see must have it all printed aforehand, or dang it all, we should no more know what to say to a great gaffer like the Lord than babes unborn." Poorgrass, in one of his more perspicacious moments, declares, sitting down, "Your next world is your next world and not to be squandered off hand." And Coggan, reprimanded by Gabriel for drinking while they are waiting for Fanny's corpse, replies, "If she now wanted victuals and drink, I'd pay for it, money down. But she's dead and no speed of ours will bring her to life." Mark Clark says to Poorgrass, "I'm sure your face don't praise your mistresses' table." One can gather something of their hand-to-mouth existence from Coggan's reply, "Why neighbours, when everyone of my 'taties were frosted, our Pa'son Thirdly were the man who gave me a sack for seed, though he hardly had one for his own, and no money to buy 'em." [54] When they finally reached the old manor house, they are met by a man at the gate, whose voice Gabriel recognized" through the fog, which hung between them like blown flour," "as that of the parson," to whom Gabriel says, "The corpse is here, sir."

One can hardly agree with the *Chronicle* reporter's conclusion that "they were hypocrites, ay, dangerous ones . . ." or his assertion that "the condition of these people, their poverty, their hatred of ecclesiastical despotism is the rule among the parishes of England and its opposite the exception." They had been dangerous when "the Swing riots, in 1830 revealed by the light of blazing corn-stacks, that misery and black mutinous discontent smoulders quite as fiercely under the surface of agricultural as of manufacturing England" (*Capital,* p. 742), but the time of *Far from the Madding Crowd* is in the seventies, when the condition of the work-folk was much improved. But even then, there are hundreds of unemployed farmworkers every Lady Day (April 6) in that novel, "waiting upon Chance," or upon those "beating up for recruits through the four streets" of Casterbridge. Gabriel Oak has only 15 shillings and the clothes on his back after selling "the stock, plant and implements which really were his own" to pay the dealer who had stocked his farm ten years previous to his young dog's driving his un-insured sheep over the cliff. He had risen into the *métayer* class to become a small, encumbered sheep farmer and, after the pastoral tragedy, falls into the unemployed class to start all over again as a shepherd and then a bailiff for Bath-sheba. Winterborne loses his house and land but preserves his cider-making equipment and becomes an itinerant cider-maker. Gabriel, however, does not lose his faith in God or man, while Winterborne, after the loss of his house and in-tended bride, "had never gone near a church latterly and had been sometimes seen on Sundays with unblacked boots, lying on his elbow under a tree, with a cynical gaze at surrounding objects." [55]

The death of Fanny Robin and her unborn child in Cas-terbridge Poor House sounds a tragic note in the harmony between Nature and Society. Nature and the Newfoundland dog are kinder to her than the custodians of the Poor House, who admitted her through a small door, stoning the dog away—a passage objected to by some members of the American Humanitarian Society—and discharged her body through a similar one, "used solely for the passage of articles and persons to and from the level of a vehicle standing on the outside which seemed to advertize itself as a species of Traitor's gate translated to another sphere." "The door then opened, and a plain elm coffin was slowly thrust forth," Hardy says, on which one of the men "took from his pocket a lump of chalk and wrote upon the cover the name and a few other words in a large scrawling hand," and adds in a parenthesis "(We believe that they do these things more tenderly now, and provide a plate.)" One detects an irony in Hardy's comment, since there are less than four years between the date of Fanny's death and the novel's publication, but Hardy has a tendency to soften things of this kind. "I've got poor little Fanny Robin in my waggon outside," says Joseph. "And so she's nailed up in parish boards after all," says another rustic, "and nobody to pay the bell shilling and the grave half-crown." Joseph replies:

> The parish pays the grave half-crown, but not the bell-shilling, because the bell's a luxury, but 'a can hardly do without the grave, poor body.

Hardy attacks both the sacrosanct aura of the small bourgeosie in his explanation of Boldwood's friends' difficulty in obtaining signatures on their petition of clemency, and also the Victorian-Elizabethan system of welfare of the day:

> It was not "numerously signed" by the inhabitants of Casterbridge, as is usual in such cases, for Boldwood had never made many friends over the counter. The shops thought it very natural that a man who, by importing direct from the producer, had daringly set aside the first great principle of provincial existence, namely, that God made country villages to supply customers to country towns, should have confused ideas about the Decalogue.

It is every bit as cynical as Charles Lamb's remonstrating with Robert Southey in one of his essays written during his tenure as a clerk for the East India Company:

> A moral should be wrought into the body and soul, the matter and tendency, of a poem, not tagged to the end, like a "God send the good ship into harbour," at the conclusion of our bills of lading. (*Works*, 6: 144)

or of Paul Lafargue's comment on Beaulieu's extolling the

manufacturers for there being fewer poor on relief in Wales in 1883 than there were in 1849 in his letter (25/7/1884) to Engels:

Do you know who profits? The consumer. The capitalist is but a poor devil who exerts himself to the utmost to provide the well-being of that idler, the consumer.

Christopher Coney remembers that Mrs. Cuxom's mother was "rewarded by the Agricultural Society° for having begot the greatest number of healthy children without parish assistance, and other virtuous marvels." [56] " 'Twas that kept us so low upon ground," she replies, and he retorts, "Ay, where pigs be many the wash runs thin." Farfrae, Hardy says, "like John Gilpin had been detained by important customers, whom even in the exceptional circumstances [moving and having a "bride of two days"] he was not a man to neglect." [57] William Cowper treats the shopkeeper's avarice more humorously in his poem "John Gilpin's Ride," in which Gilpin is thus delayed in making the change from apron to wig.

The class cleavages are presented more sharply in *The Mayor of Casterbridge* in Hardy's description of the hiring fair: "What these ghibbous human shapes represented was ready money, not ready next year like a nobleman's . . . nor merely ready at the bank like a professional man's but ready in their large plump hands," and also in the "minor tradesmen" at the luncheon at the Royal Arms, "a little below the social level of the others," carrying on discussions "not quite in harmony with those at the head; just as the west end of a church is sometimes persistently found to sing out of time

° The Anti-Corn Law Leaguers frequently quoted such a "labourer's certificate": "West Suffolk Agricultural Association: President, the Duke of Grafton. This is to certify that that a prize of £2 was awarded to William Burch, aged 82, labourer of the Parish of Stowapland, County of Suffolk, 25th of Sept., 1840, for having brought up nine children without relief except 'when flour was very dear' " (G. M. Trevelyan *Life of John Bright* [New York: Houghton Mifflin, 1914] p. 93n2).

and tune with the leading spirits of the chancel." [58] It will be recalled all of them, who a few moments before were blaming the Mayor for the bad bread resulting from the green flour he had sold to the bakers, had "gone in for comforting beverages to such an extent, that they had quite forgotten, not only the Mayor, but all those vast politcal, religious, and social differences which they felt necessary to maintain in the daytime, and which separated them like iron grills." [59]

The psychology of the characters of *The Mayor*, likewise, is more deeply related to the socioeconomic status, or lack of it, than in *Far from the Madding Crowd.* Henchard's rise and fall in business and in love are more grippingly told than Shepherd Oak's fall and rise in these matters. Farfrae pays his workers "a shilling less a week," and they "work harder," but "there is no meddling with your eternal soul and all that," as Whittle says; Hardy remarks that "Farfrae had lost in the eyes of the poorer inhabitants something of that wondrous charm which he had had for them as a light-hearted penniless young man, who sang ditties as readily as the birds in the trees" (pp. 255, 309). Lucetta is a more sophisticated and designing woman than Bathsheba in engaging Elizabeth-Jane as a maid and companion, while entertaining Henchard and Farfrae without suspicion. One suspects that her appeal to Farfrae not to separate the young married couple at the Hiring Fair is more a ploy to advance her own place in his affections over Elizabeth-Jane, who had bitterly tasted the affliction of a separation from her father as a child and could not speak of it. The love triangle is developed with deeper insight and conflict than in *Far from the Madding Crowd.* Elizabeth-Jane is a more completely realized character than Fanny Robin, who flits in and out of the novel, in her clandestine meetings with Sergeant Troy. Although the meetings are similar to Henchard's and Lucetta's at the Casterbridge Amphitheatre, they are not fraught with the social and economic implications of those of Farfrae in his courting of either Elizabeth-Jane or Lucetta. In many respects, Henchard is more protective of his employee Abe Whittle than Bathsheba is of her maid-servant Fanny Robin, on the occasion of whose disappearance she makes quite a stir, and tries, too late, to save. The business rivalry between Farfrae and Henchard is "a commercial combat—a war of prices"—whereas there is no conflict of this kind in *Far from the Madding Crowd*, even in Bathsheba's visits to the Corn Exchange. Her romance with Boldwood is a mixture of coquetry and compassion for an older man, who is "the nearest approach to aristocracy that this remoter quarter of the parish could boast of" (p. 136). *The Mayor of Casterbridge* is the strongest of Hardy's "novels of character and environment," as he subtitled them, and the richest in the paleontology of society.

The Return of the Native (1878), written after the discovery of diamonds in Kimberley, Africa (1867), is the only novel in which "the unities are strictly observed, whatever virtue there may be in that," * he wrote on November 15, 1923, and its action compressed into a year is literarily what Engels's *The Condition of the Working Class in 1847* is historically. It is the most depressing of Hardy's novels. There is an atmosphere of doom impending over humanity in the final conquest of Nature, which is as indifferent to Man's existence as to the flora and insects of the heath that have disappeared during the millions of years that preceded Man's appearance on the earth and that will return after his final disappearance. The love story of Clym and Eustacia, Wildeve and Thomasin and Diggory Venn, the reddleman,

---

* "I, myself, am old-fashioned enough to think there *is* a virtue in it, if it can be done without artificiality." He also observed the unities in his *The Famous Tragedy of the Queen of Cornwall*, a play (1923) of which he wrote, "I have tried to avoid turning the rude personages of say, the fifth century, into respectable Victorians, as was done by Tennyson, Swinburne, Arnold, etc. On the other hand, it would have been impossible to present them as they really were, with their barbaric manners and surroundings" (*Later Years*, pp. 235–36).

is the farthest expression from Hardy's love lyric "Amabel" (1865):

> Knowing that, though Love cease,
> Love's race shows no decrease;
> All find in dorp or dell
> An Amabel.

The tragic prelude in the novel is sounded in the opening chapter describing the heath, "a near relative of night . . . and when night showed itself" an apparent tendency "to gravitate together could be perceived in its shades and the scene." It continues with:

> Every night its Titanic form seemed to await something; but it had waited thus, unmoved, during so many centuries through the crises of so many things, that it could only be said to await one last crisis—the final overthrow.

Clym's looking down at the heath while cutting furze and up at the sky expresses a deceptive feeling about the time given for man's fulfilment of himself and his kind. *The Return of the Native* has a significance in the post-World War II world that it did not have when Hardy wrote it, and more especially so since the competitive struggle that Hardy observed developing along imperialistic lines prior to World War I was augmented to such frightful proportions as to disturb his later years and menace our times with the Iron Heel, to use Jack London's term, until the evolution of the species seems a slow process compared with the capacity of rival imperialism to annihilate humankind. Thus it is related to writings as far apart yet as close together as the lines from William Blake: "The fire, the fire is falling" ("A Song of Liberty") and James Baldwin's novel *The Fire Next Time*. *The Return of the Native* and *The Woodlanders* are the most Darwinian expressions of Hardy's writings, and both contain his Marxist interpretation of the struggle for supremacy projected into Nature expressed in his early poem "In a

Wood," which says the same thing that Marx observed to Engels on Darwin's book, only in the manner of poetry.

It is significant, I think, that Hardy describes the flora of the heath, which is "awakening with feline stealth," in images of tool-making man and of machinofacture. Clym, while waiting for Eustacia, is reminded of a state of Nature before man's appearance on the scene:

> He was in a nest of vivid green. The ferny vegetation round him though so abundant, was quite uniform; it was a grove of machine-made foliage, a world of green triangles with saw-edges, and not a single flower. The air was warm with vapor-ous warmth, and the stillness was unbroken. Lizards, grass-hoppers, and ants were the only living things to be beheld. The scene seemed to belong to the ancient world of the car-boniferous period, when the forms of plants were few, and of the fern kind, when there was neither bud, nor blossom, nothing but a monotonous extent of leafage, amid which no bird sang.[60]

Clym's Keatsian, pteridophytic fantasy vanishes on the ap-pearance of Eustacia, and he promises here that he will give up the idea of educating the workfolk on the heath, and instead open a school for farmers' sons at Budmouth, where there are a watering place, a band, dances, and urban life. As he watches her out of sight, he is reminded by the "oppressive horizontality" of the heath of "the arena of life, with a sense of his bare equality with, and no superiority to, a single living thing," and his old depression returns.

Clym's life prior to his coming home was the product of accidents in society like those in Nature on the heath—'accidents of situation" in bourgeois society, which was the complement to blind Nature. "That waggery of fate," Hardy says, "which started Clive as a writing clerk, Gay as a linen-draper, Keats as a surgeon and thousands of others in a thousand odd ways, banished the wild and ascetic heath lad to a trade whose sole concern was with the especial symbols of self-indulgence and vainglory." [61] "Much of his development," Hardy tells us of Clym, "he may have owed to his studious life in Paris where he had become acquainted with the ethical systems popular at the time" (St. Simon, Comte, Mill, Thoreau).This has disturbed his rational conscience and caused him to rebel against bourgeois society. "Mother, I hate the flashy business. Talk about men who deserve the name, can any man deserving the name waste his time in that effeminate way, when he sees half the world going to ruin for want of somebody to buckle to and teach them the misery they are born to? I get up every morning and see the whole creation groaning and travailing in pain, as St. Paul says, and yet there am I, trafficking in glittering splendours with wealthy women and titled libertines, and pandering to the meanest vanities—I, who have health and strength enough for anything. I have been troubled in my mind about it all the year, and the end is that I cannot do it anymore." [62]

The tragedy hinges on the conflict not only between Clym and Eustacia's likes and values but also between Clym and his mother's. To his mother's question, "Why don't you do as well as others?" he explains that "there are many things other people care for which I don't."

> "And you might have become a wealthy man [she says disappointedly] if you had only persevered. Manager to that large diamond establishment—What better can a man wish for? What a post of trust and respect! I suppose you will be like your father; like him, you are getting weary of doing well."

On Clym's telling her that he wants to educate the workfolk on Egdon Heath, she exclaims, "Dreams, dreams! If there had been any system left to be invented they would have found it out at the universities long before this date." To this Clym replies,

> "Never, mother. They cannot find it out, because their teachers don't come in contact with the class which demands

such a system—that is, those who have had no preliminary training. My plan is one for instilling high knowledge into empty minds without first cramming them with what has to be uncrammed again before true study begins."

In this Hardy limns the conflict between School Inspector Arnold's *Twice Revised Code* (1862) and his superiors Robert Lowe and Ralph Lingen, of which E. K. Brown says

> The issue was nothing less than a choice between the older order, of Lansdowne and Kay-Shuttleworth [Arnold's predecessor] by which the common people might at least take first steps in a rudimentary civilization and the new order which cynically condemned the common people to unenlightened drawer-of-water and hewer-of-wood ignorance.[63]

Eustacia Vye despises the heath and the workfolk as much as Clym loves them and is willing to be the first unit sacrificed. She longs for the City and the bright lights and wants to be the last unit sacrificed. Eustacia embodies the decadence of the bourgeoisie, who, for want of anything better, glorify the individual; her position is well summed up in Hardy's observation:

> Had it been possible for the earth and mankind to be entirely in her grasp for a while, had she handled the distaff, the spindle, and the shears at her own free will, few in the world would have noticed the change of government. There would have been the same inequality of lot, the same heaping up of favours here, of contumely there, the same generosity before justice, the same perpetual dilemmas, the same captious alternation of caresses and blows that we endure now.[64]

Hardy describes her as "the raw material of a divinity." She is a more voluptuous and indolent woman than Fancy Day or Bathsheba Everdene, and resembles Lucetta and Fanny Robin more than she does the women aforementioned, as is evinced by her assignations on the heath with Damon Wildeve, the husband of Thomasin, Mrs. Yeobright's niece and

Clym's cousin. She does not care to be flattered or praised, but only "to be loved to madness." Clym is forced, on account of the threat of blindness, to postpone his teaching plans and takes to cutting furze on the heath, to the dismay of his mother and of his wife, who does not understand how he can lower himself to peasant work and even sing* at his task.

The novel opens in the darkness of dotted bonfires on Egdon Heath—"a resistant act of man when, at the winter ingress, the curfew is sounded throughout Nature"—and it closes a year later, in darkness on the heath, in the recovery of the drowned bodies of Eustacia and Wildeve from the swollen weir, seen by lantern light. Hardy's observation of a sunset at Sturminster-Newton when he was writing the novel is diffused meaningfully in the darkness and intensity

---

* The song, which he knows by heart, is (p. 299):

"Le point du jour
A nos bosquets rend toute leur parure;
Flore est plus belle à son retour;
L'oiseau reprend doux chant d'amour,
Tout célèbre dans la nature
Le point du jour.

"Le point du jour
Cause perfois, cause douleur extrême;
Que l'espace des nuits est court
Pour le berger brûlant d'amour
Forcé de quitter ce qu'il aime
Au point du jour!

I have not been able to trace the authorship of the poem in Hardy criticism or elsewhere. James Ginden, in his edited edition of *The Return of the Native* (New York: W. W. Norton, 1969) says in a note (p. 198): "This song, about the coming of dawn, describes both the beauty and the sadness of the change from night to day." It possibly dates from Hardy's class in French under Professor Stievenard at the University of London (1863–64) and may have been suggested by Molière's faggot cutter Sganarel singing at his work (*The Mock-Doctor*, I. vi). I did find in Marx's *Capital* (1:652 in USSR ed.) a quotation from Boileau's by an English writer in connection with the "continual crying contradictions in Gladstone's budget speeches of 1863 and 1884," as follows:

"Voilà l'homme en effet. Il va du blanc au noir,
Il condamne au matin ses sentiments du soir.
Importun à tout autre, à soi-même incommode,
Il change à tout moment d'esprit comme de mode."

of the summer heat on the heath, from which Mrs. Yeobright dies of heat prostration, feeling cast off by her son:
"End of November (1877): This evening the west is like
some vast furnace where new worlds are being cast," as it
is later, in his description of "an evening of exceptional
irradiations and the west heaven gleamed like a foundry of
all metals common and rare." [65] At this time the competition
in the manufacturing of steel* was forcing British capitalists to scrap outmoded equipment to vie with the rising
industrialists in the United States and Germany, and rival
imperialisms were extending their power to Africa and Asia.
British exports had declined from 256 million pounds in
1872 to 192 million pounds in 1879, and unemployment had
increased from one to twelve precent. Hardy's observations
on the insecurity of Clym, who had arrived at that stage in
his life when "the general grimness of the situation causes
ambition to halt and wait awhile" may be applied to himself
as substantiated by his journal entry of "November 28
(1878): Woke before it was light. Felt that I had not enough
staying power to hold my own in the world."

The Return of the Native offers an interesting comparison with The Woodlanders in that it presents a transitional
study of character and environment from a peasant society
to a bourgeois society emerging from the handicraft stage,
which is exploited by the rising timber merchant Melbury
in the wooded area of the Hintock villages. With its woodland setting it is a more explicit presentation of Darwinism
than The Return of the Native with its heath setting, being
in this respect like his poem "In a Wood."

On older trees still than these huge lobes of fungi grew like
lungs. Here, as everywhere, the Unfulfilled Intention, which

---

* In 1879 Percy Gilchrist and Sidney Thomas showed how to line a
blast furnace to take up the phosphorus in iron, a detrimental component
(Smellie, Great Britain since 1688 (Ann Arbor, Mich.: University of
Michigan Press, 1962), p. 215.

makes life what it is, was as obvious as it could be among the depraved crowds of a city slum. The leaf was deformed, the curve was crippled, the taper was interrupted; the lichen ate the vigour of the stalk, and the ivy slowly strangled to death the promising sapling.[66]

One is arrested by the similarity of the sentence, "Here, as everywhere . . . ," and Marx's observation on the disfiguring effects of the capitalist system on the handicraft workers in the following quotation from *Capital* (p. 461), which gives social import to Hardy's "Unfulfilled Intention":

> Here as everywhere else, we must distinguish between the increased productiveness due to the development of the social process of production and that due to the capitalistic exploitation of that process.[67]

Hardy has projected the market in the woodland scene in which Giles Winterborne, "to justify his presence there began bidding" against his prospective father-in-law

> for timber and faggots he did not want, pursuing the occupation in an abstracted mood in which the auctioneer's voice seemed to be one of the natural sounds of the woodland . . . and when the auctioneer said every now and then, with a nod towards him, "Yours, Mr. Winterborne," he had no idea whether he had bought faggots, poles, or log-wood.[68]

The class cleavage between the poor and the rich is stronger in *The Woodlanders* than in any of Hardy's other Wessex novels, and the affluence of Mrs. Charmond and the Melburys and the increasing misery of the Souths and of Winterborne depict poignantly the emergence of capitalism from feudalism at the laissez-faire stage, which exploited the dispossessed cottagers at piece-work and accumulated surplus capital wrung from their hands. Mr. Melbury, "the timber, bark and copse-ware merchant," for instance, pays Marty South "eighteenpence a thousand" for making spars; by working all day and half the night in a dingy smoky cottage, she can make three bundles, for which she is paid "two and threepence." This is not enough to support herself and her sickly father, who is "all skin and grief." She doesn't want to sell her hair to Barber Percombe, "Perruquier to the Aristocracy," to make a wig for Mrs. Charmond, the divorced wife on an iron manufacturer in the North, whose hair matches her own, but he offers two sovereigns, with,

> "Marty, now hearken, this Lady that wants it wants it badly, and, between you and me, you'd better let her have it. 'Twill be bad for you if you don't."

Also, the altercation between Mrs. Charmond's coachman and Giles with a load of oak lumber:

> "You are only going to some trumpery little village or other in the neighbourhood, while we are going straight to Italy."

To which Giles retorts sarcastically:

> "Driving all the way, I suppose?" [69]

Mr. Melbury has an extensive lumber business and has invested the profits in "turnpike bonds and Port Breedy bonds" as well as in houses at Sherton Abbas to secure the future of his only daughter, Grace, whose education in a ladies' finishing school costs him £200 a year, or "enough to take the squeak out of your Sunday shoes," [70] as one of his employees says.

The tragedy of *The Woodlanders* develops from what Marx calls the "Expropriation of the Agricultural Population from the Land," in order to "set free" the agricultural populations as proletarians for the manufacturing industry, which Marty South and Giles are already, as insecure employees of lumberman Melbury. "Giles marvelled," Hardy says, "as many have done since, what could have induced his ancestors at Hintock and other village peoples to exchange their old copyholds for life leases." [71] One suspects that Melbury had something to do with it; possibly it was the price of a road on the property in the interest of enlarging his copse business in return for his promise that Giles should wed Grace. Giles's father, who was the first Mrs. Melbury's lover and who had emigrated with the brother of the lumber-merchant many years before, was "an alliance that was sufficient to place Winterborne, though poor, on an equal footing of social intimacy with the Melburys," who, he did not think would take advantage of him. "Giles looked at the leases again and the letter attached":

> They were ordinary leases for three lives, which a member of the South family, some fifty years before this time, had accepted of the lord of the manor in lieu of certain copyholds and other rights, in consideration of the Lord's having the dilapidated houses rebuilt by said Lord.

Giles had supposed they were copyholders until he investigated the papers in the canvas between the mattress and the sack, "which had remained there unopened ever since his father's death," and he could not understand why his father had not availed himself of "the privilege of adding his life to his son's own life," since they were renewable for three lives. "As in most villages as secluded as this," Hardy comments, "inter-marriages were of Hapsburgian frequency among the inhabitants, and there were hardly two houses in Little Hintock unrelated by some matrimonial tie or other."

The loss of Giles's property relieves Melbury of his promise, "since he had no house to take her to," and he happily encourages Grace to accept the attentions of Dr. Fitzpiers, who feels he "belonged to a different species from the people who are working in that yard," [72] being descended from an aristocratic line, whereas Melbury's own family were yeomen during the Civil Wars. Dr. Fitzpiers is an egocentric Don Juan, who has tried to stabilize his family prestige as Sergeant Troy, whom he resembles, has sunk from the professional class—his father was a doctor—into the military class of the bourgeosie. He has imbibed some philosophy during his medical training at the University of Heidelberg, which boiled down to "Everything is Nothing," and "There's only Me and not Me in the whole world," and "no man's hands could help what they did anymore than the hands of a clock." [73] He proves unfaithful to Grace after their marriage, having an affair with Mrs. Charmond who, it turns out, had known him during his Heidelberg days, and her only regret in having refused to renew Giles's lapsed leaseholds is that in doing so she had foredoomed the revival of her girlhood romance with the doctor. It is her practice, when the leaseholds expire on her tenants' cottages, to have the dwellings torn down. "Then let her pull 'em down," Giles fumes, "and be damned to her," while old Creedle, who did everything that required doing, from making Giles's bed to "catching moles in his field," and who was "a survival from the days when Giles's father held the homestead, when Giles was a playing boy," looks at him "with the face of seven sorrows." Giles, looking out of the window, perceives "that a paralysis had come over Creedle's occupation of manuring the garden, owing, obviously, to a conviction that they might not be living there long enough to profit by next season's crop." [74]

The Woodlanders presents not only the dispossession of the last of the yeomen class by the nouveau riche (Mrs. Charmond) but also their exploitation by the petit bourgeois industrialist (Mr. Melbury). Marty's feelings of insecurity and her father's apprehension of dying are more than an individual's tragedy. This comes out in the converation between Marty and her father and, later, in that between Mr. South and Giles.

"Father," she went on, "can Mrs. Charmond turn us out of our house if she's minded to?"

"Turn us out? No. Nobody can turn us out till my poor soul is turned out of my body. 'Tis lifehold, like Giles Winterborne's. But when my life drops 'twill be hers—not till then.[75]

Marty fetches Giles to see her father, who "was pillowed up in a chair between the bed and the window," outside of which stands the elm tree that exerts a threat to his life:

> "Ah, neighbour Winterborne," he said. "I wouldn't have minded if my life had only been my own to lose; I don't vallie it in much of itself, and can let it go if 'tis required of me. But to think of what 'tis worth to you, a young man rising in life, that do trouble me! It seems a trick of dishonesty toward ye to go off at fifty-five! I could bear up, I know I could, if it were not for the tree—yes, the tree 'tis that's killing me. There he stands, threatening my life every minute that the wind do blow. He'll come down upon us, and squat us dead; and what will ye do when the life on your property is taken away!"
> "Never you mind me—that's of no consequence," said Giles. "Think of yourself alone." [76]

South's life, Hardy explains at the opening of the chapter, "was the last of a group of lives which had been used a measuring-tape of time by law." On his demise, "the small homestead occupied by South himself, the larger one of Giles Winterborne, and half-a-dozen others that had been in the possession of various Hintock village families for the previous hundred years, and were not Winterborne's would fall in and become part of the encompassing estate" of Mrs. Charmond.

Dr. Fitzpiers advises Giles that "the tree must be cut down; or I won't answer for his life." Giles explains " 'Tis Mrs. Charmond's tree . . ."

> "O, never mind whose tree it is—what's a tree beside a life! Cut it down. . . .
> " 'Tis timber," rejoined Giles. "They never fell a stick about here without its being marked first, either by her or the agent."
> "Then we'll inaugurate a new era forthwith . . ." [77]

"As the tree waves South waved his head," Hardy observes, "making it his fugelman with abject obedience."

The tree is cut down, and Mr. South dies. Mr. Melbury, on being informed of South's death, is "sorry" and "grieved" on Winterborne's account. He tells Grace remonstratively, "I told Giles's father when he came into those houses not to spend too much money on lifehold property held neither for his own life nor his son's . . . but he wouldn't listen to me. And now Giles has to suffer for it." To which Grace replies, "Poor Giles." [78] Mr. Melbury continues:

> "Now, Grace, between us two, it is very, very remarkable. It is almost as if I had foreseen this; and I am thankful for your escape, though I am sincerely sorry for Giles. Had we not dismissed him already we could hardly have found it in our hearts to dismiss him now. So I say, be thankful. I'll do all I can for him as a friend; but as a pretender to the position of my son-in-law, that can never be thought of more."

This conversation recalls old Vicar Swancourt's heart-to-heart talk with his daughter Elfride (*A Pair of Blue Eyes*), in which the journalist Knight, his wife's cousin, is described as "no great catch for you, and if she will only bide Providence, she "might mate with a wealthier man" (Lord Luxellian).

The afflictions of "irritated humanity" in *The Woodlanders* derive from social and economic causes, of one class feeling superior to the other because of their hereditary status or professional or educational superiority rather than from "inscrutable fate," and this is true of the other Wessex novels. Dr. Fitzpiers, whom Grace always addresses as "Mr. Fitzpiers," spurns the bucolic Hintock villagers, and almost wishes he had not obtained Mr. Melbury's daughter "so cheap." [79] Mr. Melbury, speaking to Grace of the villagers, remarks, "Oh yes—as yeoman, copyholders and such like. But think how much better this will be for 'ee with allying yourself with such a romantical family, you'll feel as if you stepped into history." [80] Dr. Fitzpiers, descended from aristocratic landowner families that had given their names to the villages of Oakbury and Fitzpiers, disdains his "ramshackle family," but the villagers cherish the memory, and "raise their hats to him." "The House," now occupied by Mrs. Charmond of the *nouveau riche*, had formerly belonged to Melbury's ancestors before the Civil Wars, and though he considers his "girl Grace as well educated as Mrs. Charmond," he uses "the tradesmen's door entrance" when he goes to "The House." [81] Mrs. Melbury, speaking of Mrs. Charmond to her husband, remarks in regard to the tree-felling, "I am afraid 'tis not her regard for you, but her dislike of Hintock that makes her so easy about the trees." [82] Dr. Fitzpiers, likewise, despises Hintock, as much as Eustacia Vye does Egdon Heath, and tells Gammer Oliver, "I was made for higher things," and becomes even more voluble to his father-in-law, whom he does not recognize, being intoxicated, in his outburst, addressing him as "Farmer": [83]

> "I've come all the way from London today. . . . Ah, that's the place to meet your equals. I live at Hintock—worse at Little Hintock!—and I am quite wasted there. There's not a man within ten miles of Hintock who can comprehend me . . . I tell you, Farmer—what's-your-name, that I'm a man of education—the poets and I are familiar friends. . . . There's nobody can match me in the whole of Wessex as a scientist. . . . Yet I am doomed to live with tradespeople in a miserable little hole like Hintock!"

Mr. Melbury's anger at Dr. Fitzpiers' infidelity to his daughter is aggravated by the doctor's addressing him as "Farmer—what's your name?"—and he administers him such a severe beating that on returning home he is afraid that he "may have killed a man." Melbury had also been to London to investigate the new divorce law being enacted by Parliament, but it is a false rumor, to his disappointment. Grace reluctantly takes back Dr. Fitzpiers, though the inference is that she is doomed to spend the rest of her life with an unfaithful husband in a society that had not caught up with the enlightenment of Milton's views on *Discipline and*

Divorce (1648), due to the slowness of the "Imperial will of the realm."

Hardy critically appraises Dr. Fitzpiers:

> The real Dr. Fitzpiers was a man of too many hobbies to show likelihood of rising to any great eminence in the profession he had chosen, or even, to acquire any wide practice in the rural district he had made out as his field of survey for the present.[84]

The dissipation of Fitzpiers' energies is in contrast to the fixed ambition of Clym Yeobright to educate the peasants. He is the opposite of Clym in wanting to raise himself at the expense of the masses; his philosophic reading has turned to German philosophy—Schopenhauer and Schleiermacher[85]—who have stressed individualism—"There is only Me and not Me" in the universe; while Clym's philosophical reading of French philosophy—St. Simon and others— stressed the social prerogatives. Yet Hardy also appraises Clym:

> Was Yeobright's mind well-proportioned? No. A well-proportioned mind is one which shows no particular bias; one of which we may safely say that it will never cause its owner to be confined as a madman, tortured as a heretic, or crucified as a blasphemer. Also, on the other hand, that it will never cause him to be applauded as a prophet, revered as a priest, or exalted as a king. Its usual blessings are happiness and mediocrity. It produces the poetry of Rogers, the paintings of West, the statecraft of North, the spiritual guidance of Tomline; ennobling its possessors to find their way to wealth, to wind up well, to step with dignity off the stage, to die comfortably in their beds. And to get the decent monument which, in many cases, they deserve. It never would have allowed Yeobright to do such a ridiculous thing as throw up his business to benefit his fellow-creatures.[86]

From this aspect Giles has a more practical and better-proportioned mind. Hardy remarks that Giles had, like Hamlet's friend, borne himself "as one in suffering all that suffers nothing." [87] Hardy put something of the character of his own father into that of Giles, as is evident from his writing that "the character of Horatio in *Hamlet* was his father's to a nicety," with his father's name and date of his death opposite the lines in his copy of the play:

> Thou hast been
> As one in suffering all that suffers nothing;
> A man that fortune's buffets and rewards
> Hast ta'en with equal thanks.[88]

The devotion of both Grace and Marty to Giles when he is dying of pneumonia in a shed on Melbury's property is a tribute to womankind, and Marty's visits to his grave a touching reminder of "his having been a good man who did good things;" it recalls Bazarov's parents' grief at loss of their son in Turgenev's *Fathers and Children* (1862), and also Giles's abject thought when he assures Grace that he has not forgotten her voice, as his bitterness indicated.[89] "He could," Hardy writes, "have declared with a contemporary poet"* :

> If I forget,
> The salt creek may forget the ocean;
> If I forget
> The heart whence flowed my heart's bright motion,
> May I sink meanlier than the worst,
> Abandoned, outcast, crushed, accurst—
> If I forget.
>
> Though you forget,
> Nor word of mine shall mar your pleasure;
> Though you forget,—
> You filled my barren life with treasure;
> You may withdraw the gift you gave,
> You still are queen, I still am slave,
> Though you forget.

---

* Edmund Gosse, in his poem "Two Points of View," from *Firdausi in Exile and Other Poems* (1885), third and fourth stanzas, as Carl Weber says in *Hardy of Wessex* (1960), p. 162. He adds *"The Woodlanders* sold well," (*ibid.*, p. 155).

Marty and Grace's love for and devotion to Giles seems to have borne fruit in his own poem "A Poet" (1914), a tribute to both his first and second wife after his second marriage, concluding with the wish:

> Whatever his message—glad or grim—
> Two bright-souled women clave to him;
> Stand and say that while day decays:
> It will be word enough of praise.

It recalls the engraving in Sergeant Troy's watch, given him by his father, who was a physician: *"Amor vincit omnia!"*

Tess of the D'Urbervilles (1891) revolves also, like *The Woodlanders,* around the precariousness of existence for dispossessed lifeholders who like Tess's father, Durbyfield, have tried to prevent falling back into the farmworkers' class so abhorrent to Melbury, and around the problem of getting a divorce,* which was impossible for any other cause than adultery. Tess's father worked in the higgling business, at which he is unable to support his large family, and toward him Tess at times feels "quite a Malthusian." [90] The collision of the Durbyfield's wagon with the mailcar, which kills their horse Prince and demolishes the wagon, leaves them without the means of a livelihood. Tess, who was delivering some crates of beehives to the Casterbridge retailers in time for the Saturday market, blames herself for the tragedy and obtains a job taking care of the poultry of Mrs. D'Urberville, a partially blind well-to-do widow who lives with her son Alec, who seduces Tess following a dance.

* Hardy wrote to J. T. Grein, dramatic critic and founder of the Independent Theater (1891), who had asked for permission to adapt the novel for the theater: "I could not emphasize this strongly in the book by reason of the conventions of the libraries, etc. Since the story was written, however, truth to character is not considered quite such a crime in literature as it was formerly, and it is therefore a question for you whether you will accent this ending, or prefer to obscure it" (July, 1889; *Early Life,* p. 289).

A later attempt by A. H. Evans was performed in Dorchester and London in 1913, and in Weymouth, Jan. 22, 1914 (see R. L. Purdy, *Thomas Hardy, a Bibliographical Study,* p. 352).

Tess is the story of "a pure woman" [91] and her devotion
to her illegitimate child by Alec, whom she refuses to marry
because she does not love him, and her loyalty to Angel
Clare, a minister's son, whom she loves and marries, but
who does not love her enough to forgive her this indiscretion
in her past, which he feels is a man's privilege to make, but
not a woman's. She goes back to her family twice—first to
have her baby by Alec, whom she christens "Sorrow." After
its death she sets out again, finding a job as a dairy-maid at
Marlott, where she meets Angel, returning home again after
Angel deserts her. Angel, disconsolate over having married
a fallen woman, goes to Brazil where, repenting his ill
treatment of her, he returns home to find that she has des-
paired of his ever coming back and married Alec, who had
been kind to her family in their adversity—the illness of
her mother and the death of her father. On seeing Angel
again, she blames Alec for causing her unhappiness a second
time, and stabs him to death; for this crime she is arrested
at Stonehenge, where she had taken flight with Angel. She
is tried, and found guilty of Alec's murder, for which she is
hanged.

Tess's mother comforts her, " 'Tis nater after all and what
do please God," but Angel, in spite of his Comtean belief
expressed to his Vicar father, on the "honour and glory of
man," shows no understanding of Tess's appreciation of the
Sermon on the Mount or her deep love for him: [92]

"O Angel—my mother says that it sometimes happens so—
she knows several cases where they were worse than I . . .
and the husband has forgiven her at least. And yet the woman
has not loved him as I do you."
"Don't, Tess, don't argue. Different societies, different manners. You almost make me say you are an unappreciative
peasant woman, who has never been initiated into the proportions of things. . . .
"I am only a peasant by position, not by nature," she spoke
with an impulse to anger, but it went as it came.
"So much the worse for you. I think that person who un-

earthed your pedigree would have done better if he had held his tongue. I cannot help associating your decline as a family with this other fact—of your want of firmness. Decrepit families imply decrepit wills, decrepit conduct. . . . Here was I thinking you a new-sprung child of Nature; there were you, the exhausted seed of an effete aristocracy!"

"Lots o' families are as bad as mine in that! Retty's family were once large landowners, and so were Dairyman Billet's. And the Debbyhouses, who now be carters, were once the De Bayeux family. You find such as I everywhere; 'tis a feature of our county, and I can't help it."

"So much the worse for the county."[93]

His words might have come out of the mouth of Disraeli's "Young England" group.

The roots of *Tess* go more deeply than the double standard and the death penalty, however; they go to the roots of the Industrial Revolution and the disregard of the industrial capitalist class, as Dr. Kettle states, for the welfare of the yeoman class, which they have destroyed. Marx notes:

Whilst the place of the independent yeoman was taken by tenants at will, small farmers on yearly leases, a servile rabble dependent on the pleasure of the landlords, the systematic robbery of the Communal lands helped especially, next to the theft of the State domains, to swell those large farms, that were called in the 18th century capital farms or merchant farms, and to "set free" the agricultural populations as proletarians for manufacturing industry. (*Capital,* p. 796)

For *Tess* is not only the portrait of a woman "faithfully presented," as Hardy says in the preface, but also of a dispossessed class faithfully presented. The optimism of *Tess* consists of Hardy's showing an event in a woman's experience, one that "has usually been treated as extinguishing her," as the beginning of her ennoblement; the pessimism of *Tess* lies in Hardy's objective depiction of the utter indifference of society to its destruction of a class that had once been the backbone of English village life. There are

descriptions of dispossessed families like Tess's that correspond to those given by Marx. Moreover, in *Tess* we are
shown the effects of the Industrial Revolution on agriculture, which are only hinted at in *The Mayor of Casterbridge*
of the earlier time. The corn-drill was exhibited in Casterbridge only during the early forties, but the steamthresher,
"the *primum mobile* of this world" (p. 415) or "prime mover"
as Marx designates it (p. 458), was in full operation at Flintcomb-Ash in the eighties. The change in harvest methods
within the space of forty years is depicted in Farmer Groby's
placing Tess on the machine platform beside a man to
whom she hands "every sheaf of corn handed on to her by
Izz Huett" from the rick, "so that the feeder could seize it
and spread it over the revolving drum which whisked out
every grain in one moment." Further:

> They were soon in full progress, after a preparatory hitch
> or two, which rejoiced the hearts of those who hated ma-
> chinery. The work sped on till breakfast-time, when the
> thresher was stopped for half an hour; and on starting again
> after the meal the whole supplementary strength of the farm
> was thrown into the labour of constructing the straw-rick,
> which began to grow beside the stack of corn. A hasty lunch
> was eaten as they stood, without leaving their positions, and
> then another couple of hours brought them near to din-
> ner-time; the inexorable wheels continuing to spin and the
> penetrating hum of the thresher to thrill to the very marrow
> all who were near the revolving wire-cage.[94]

The women have become parts of the mechanism; the
donkeyman standing beside "his portable repository of
force" is "in the agricultural world, but not of it":

> The long strap which ran from the driving-wheel of his en-
> gine to the red thresher under the rick was the sole tie-line
> between agriculture and him.

"He travelled with this engine from farm to farm, from
county to county, for as yet the steam-threshing machine

was itinerant in this part of Wessex." In his Dorsetshire Labourer essay Hardy remarks, "Not a woman in the county but hates the threshing machine" (p. 187), and in *An Indiscretion in the Life of an Heiress* he has Egbert save Geraldine's life from "a ghastly death" as she stepped back from the strap, which almost caught her dress (pp. 23–25).

Hardy raises the question on the Durbyfields' plight, "Some people would like to know whence the poet,* whose philosophy is these days deemed as profound and trustworthy as his song is breezy and pure, gets his authority for speaking of 'Nature's holy plan';" and again, in the comment:

> In the ill-judged execution of the well-judged plan of things the call seldom produces the comer, the man to love rarely coincides with the hour for loving. . . . We may wonder whether at the acme and summit of the human progress these anachronisms will be corrected by a finer intuition, a closer interaction of the social machinery than that which now jolts us round and along; but such completeness is not to be prophesied, or even conceived as possible.[95]

This is the major problem posed in *Tess*. The question is raised not only by Hardy but also by his characters. Tess remarks on the number of "has-been landowners' estates" to Angel, whom dairyman Crick has said "you could buy 'em all up for an old song a'most," on their way to deliver Dairy man Crick's milk cans at the railway station, to which Angel replies, "Yes, it is surprising how many present tillers of the soil were once owners of it, and I sometimes wonder that a certain school of politicians don't make capital of the circumstance; but they don't seem to know it." [96] At the milk depot, whither "the railroad had extended its steam-feelers," Tess remarks that "Londoners will drink it at their breakfasts tomorrow, won't they? Strange people that we have never seen." To which Angel replies, ". . . Though not

* William Wordsworth (1770–1850): "Lines Written in Early Spring, 1798."

as we send it. When its strength has been lowered, so that it may not get up into their heads." [97] This reference calls attention to the diluting and adulteration of foods as a form of competition and to the production of a commodity for a blind market. It recalls the lad Egorooska's musing sleepily in Chekhov's story "The Steppe," beside Denisk on the box seat of the long train of baled wool wagons being taken to market, of "the elusive mysterious Varlamov," whom everywhere talked about but no one saw, and "who owned tens of thousands of acres of land" (chapter 4) and also Moshin Bin Sallah, "and a Syed, at that," the Arab merchant and ship owner, owner of the *Vidar* and many other ships in the Far East, who had to employ white men in the shipping part of the business," Conrad says in *The Shadow-Line* (p. 4), "many of whom so employed had never set eyes on him from the first to the last day," and whom "I myself saw but once, quite accidentally, on a wharf—an old, dark little man, blind in one eye, in a snowy robe and yellow slippers."

The psychological effects come through in the conversation about the stars between Tess and her little brother, Abraham, as they take the beehives to Satuday's market:

Abraham asks, "How would it have been if we had pitched on a sound one?" Tess answers, "Well, father wouldn't have coughed and creeped about as he does, and wouldn't have got too tipsy to go on this journey, and mother wouldn't have been always washing, and never getting finished." Abraham interrupts, "And you would have been a rich lady ready-made and not have to be made rich by marrying a gentleman." "Oh, Aby, don't—don't talk of that anymore!"

Tess explains to Angel "how easy it is to escape the misery you are born to by lying on your back and gazing up at the stars at night." [98] *Tess* is the only Wessex novel in which there are several children. It is as if in the other novels, to employ Marx's observation, the children had all been swept up out of the depopulated towns by the great broom of the

Industrial Revolution into industries in large towns; or that, except in the case of Gabriel and Bathsheba (*Far from the Madding Crowd*), they didn't want children.

> When a married woman who has a lover kills her husband, she does not really wish to kill the husband; she wishes to kill the situation. Of course in Clytaemnestra's case it was not exactly so, since there was the added grievance of Iphigenia, which half justified her.[99]

In Tess,° Hardy felt as indignant toward society as Conrad did, and his indignation, like Conrad's toward "the savage aristocracy" and "the Divine Democracy" and Tolstoy's to "*le bien publique*" alike, is there in the epilogue to *Tess* like an unexpressed thought: "Justice was done, and the President of the Immortals (in Aeschylean phrase) had ended his sport with Tess." The words for this purpose could not have been better chosen.

In all the novels sexual love is the magnetic force— natural selection, in Darwin's phrase—man in the aggressive

° Hardy was annoyed at the inane comments on Tess by the Duchess of Abercorn and her set, one of whom said, "They ought all to have been hanged!" (*Later Years*, p. 6).

Marx wrote Engels (Nov. 2, 1867): "The Irish Viceroy Lord Abicorn this is *roughly* his name) has 'cleared' his estate of thousands within recent weeks by forcible executions" (*Correspondence*, p. 228).

Hardy was much pleased with a group of West-End actors from the Garrick Theater, who performed some scenes from *Tess* at Max Gate (Dec. 6, 1925) before the Hardys, their two maids and dog "Wessex," Hardy talking with everyone of Tess, "as if she was some one real whom he had known and liked tremendously" (*Later Years*, pp. 6, 244). "The Russian translation of Tess," Mrs. Hardy states, "appears to have been read and approved by Tolstoi during its twelve-months' career in a Moscow monthly periodical" (*ibid*, p. 45), "exciting great interest there" (*ibid*., p. 7). Mrs. Gertrude Bugler, in a talk before the Corn Exchange, Dorchester, April 7, 1959, recalled Hardy's attending rehearsals of the Dorchester Debating and Dramatic Society of some of his novels, and his asking her to play Tess in a dramatization "which he himself had made in 1895," and which Frederic Harrison would stage in a series of matinees beginning Jan. 8, 1925, at the Haymarket Theater, which he had leased. Mrs. Bugler declined the honor, but did play Tess at the Duke of York's Theater, London, at Mrs. Hardy's request, in the summer of 1929 (see Gertrude Bugler, *Personal Recollections of Thomas Hardy* [Dorchester: The Dorset Natural History and Archaelogical Society, 1964].

role, woman in the passive role, though some of the women, chiefly through their financial independence, like Bathsheba, or trying to acquire it, like Ethelberta, institute and control the courtship, whether it begins with the sending of a valentine, as in Bathsheba's case, or ends in marrying a wealthy octogenarian in Ethelberta's case. Stephen's first impulse is: "I *have* fallen in love and want to get married" (*A Pair of Blue Eyes*), and Tess and Angel's love is at first sight on the May-day festivity.[100] Hardy's males are generally colorful, like male birds, who waylay their mates, who are more plain in house-dresses or workfolk clothes: Sergeant Troy in his blue and red uniform with his flashing sword dance performed in the glen, Farfrae with his Scottish ditties; "the handsome, coercive and irresistible Dr. Fitzpiers," [101] to mention only a few. The woman is the weaker sex, not "the lesser man," in Tennyson's phrase; Grace yields herself to Fitzpiers, Tess to Alec D'Urberville. Even Grace and Giles are said "to have undergone their little experiences." [102]

But social and economic differences alter natural selection. Hardy says:

> It was true: civilization had so far advanced in the soil of Miss Melbury's mind as to lead her to talk of anything save of that she knew well, and had the greatest interest in developing— herself. She had fallen from the good old Hintock ways.

and again:

> No woman is without aspirations, which may be innocent enough within limits; and Grace had been so trained socially, and educated intellectually, as to see clearly enough a pleasure in the position of wife to such a man as Fitzpiers.[103]

A most amusing incident comes out in her conversation with her father, after his showing her the securities he has accumulated and laid aside for her future, when she says, "Don't go on like that, A mere chattel," to which he replies, "A what?" and she answers, "A what, oh, a dictionary word," while "he looked her proudly up and down"; or Giles's caustic remark to Grace's rumination on whether Mrs. Charmond, who is writing her memoirs, should imitate the style of Dumas and Mere and Sterne and others, "Suppose you talk over my head a little longer, Miss Grace Melbury." [104] The social gap exists between Tess, with her sixth-grade education, and Angel's family, who are educated people of staid liturgical belief. The only exceptions are Sue and Jude, who have similar interests and passions, and whose ill-starred union, without benefit of either church or civil ceremony, endures the longest. Grace wants a church wedding; the cynical Fitzpiers reminds her, "that one does not go to church to buy a house or make a will," but she insists, and he gives in, "To holy Church we'll go—and much good may it do us." [105] The second marriage, in Hardy's rendering, turns out better, in most cases, than the first marriage—the glamor of sex having worn off—Bathsheba and Gabriel, Elizabeth-Jane and Farfrae, Sue and Jude.

*The Mayor of Casterbridge** is the only Wessex novel in

° On the physical level, see notably "Casterbridge announced Old Rome in every street, alley and precinct." The Amphitheater, which "might have been called the spittoon of the Jotuns was to Casterbridge what the ruined Coliseum is to modern Rome" (*The Mayor* p. 80). The Market House and Town Hall opposite abutted against its neighbour the church, except in the lower story, where an arched thoroughfare gave admittance to a large square called Bull Stake (the scene of the wagons' mishap). A stone post rose in the midst, to which oxen had formerly been tied for baiting with dogs to make them tender before they were killed in the adjoining shambles. In a corner stood the stocks (p. 219); "a brook divided the moor from the tenements, and to outward view there was no way across it, but under every householder's stairs there was kept a mysterious plank nine inches wide." Even slaughter had not been altogether unknown here. In a block of cottages up the alley there might have been erected an altar to disease in years gone by" (p. 294). On the psychological level in the boys's remark to Creedle, "I s'pose the time when you learnt all these knowing things, Mr. Creedle, was when you was in the militia?" and Creedle's reply, "Well, yes, I seed the world that year somewhat, certainly, and mastered many arts of strange, dashing sort." The boy asks further, "I s'pose your memory can reach a long way back into history, Mr. Creedle?" "Oh yes, Ancient days, when there was battles, and famines, and hang-fairs, and other pomps, seem to me as yesterday. Ah, many's which there is a strong friendship between an older and young man (Henchard and Farfrae) and *Jude* the only London novel in which there is a similar bond between a young boy, Jude, and his teacher, Mr. Phillotson. All Hardy's Wessex novels refute the mercantilists' charge that England could not feed herself and that the Lady Dedlocks and Duke of Argyll's demands for luxuries would supply work for the Hodges and Giles, repudiated in Robert Blatchford's *Merrie England* (1894), in which he proposed a remedy that Hardy had shown his characters already at; Blatchford wrote in the Socialist *Clarion:*

> First of all I would set men to work to grow wheat and fruit and rear cattle and poultry for our own use.[106]

One thinks of Hardy's Gabriel and Bathsheba, Henchard and Farfrae, Giles and Marty, and Tess taking care of Mrs. D'Urberville's poultry, and the great barns "loaded with hay and grain sacks bursting their seams" of *The Mayor,* "with the air of awaiting a famine that would not come," before the repeal of the Corn Laws. Indeed the rain that mars Henchard's outdoor harvest festival has political connotations in the light of Gladstone's historian John Morley's [107] remark on "end of the session of 1845":

> Cobden was aware that, in words used at the time, "three weeks of rain when the wheat was ripening would rain away the corn law."
> Everybody knows how the rain came, and alarming signs of a dreadful famine in Ireland came; how Peel addressed

the patriarch I've seed come and go in this parish!" (*The Woodlanders,* p. 86). And especially in Jude's stream of historical consciousness at the "Four Corners," from the beheading of Charles I and Louis XIV through the American Revolution up to Victoria's middle-time (p. 139) and his admiration for The Tractarians and for the three (Peel, Browning, Newman) during his ruminations in Christminster's quad (*ibid*). Apropos these is Hardy's early remark in the preface of *A Pair of Blue Eyes:* "To restore the grey carcasses of medievalism whose spirit had fled seemed a not less incongruous act than to set about renovating the adjoining crags themselves" (p. vii)—a possible reference to the Oxford Movement, or High Church movement sanctifying the authority of the Apostolic Succession.

his Cabinet to open the ports for a limited period, but without promising them that if the corn duties were ever taken off, they could ever be put on again.

Hardy's novels are rich in "paleontology," to quote Maurer's phrase.

Hardy's short stories are in the same grain—miniature novels—and, perhaps because of that, the economic spectrum is narrowed down to a specific incident characteristic of the short story and not of the digressive, episodic novel. For instance,

"The Three Strangers (1883), in which Timothy Summers, an unemployed watch-maker, who has stolen a sheep to feed his starving family, is given refuge in a shepherd's cottage on Christmas Eve, and eludes the sheriff who has come in search of him, to the pleasure of his host and guests; "The Withered Arm," in which a starving peasant youth is not so fortunate, and is arrested on a charge of arson, of which he is innocent, and hung.

In this respect the short stories are better compared with the narrative ballads, the ballad being a short story in verse —"The Trampwoman's Tragedy" and "The Peasant's Confession," for instance, in which Hardy shows a predilection for peasant subject matter over urban matter; I shall have more to say on this in the chapter on Hardy's poetry.

5

The London Novels

None of Hardy's London novels except *Jude the Obscure* is a tragedy, and it is in a line of direct descent of *The Poor Man and the Lady,* his first novel. The London novels except *Jude* are inferior to the Wessex novels, mainly, I think, because they lack the thick coat of reality of the Wessex ones, which mirror the effects of the Industrial Revolution on the characters and their environment. To begin with, Hardy did not know the London proletariat as George Gissing did, or as Maxim Gorky did the Russian proletariat, and he did not have the interest in or knowledge of the upper classes as did Oscar Wilde. One will find no Lady Windermere, no Pepel, no Carrie in Hardy's London novels. There are no longshoremen waiting on the East India Company's docks at daybreak, as there are unemployed workfolk "waiting on Chance" at the hiring fair and Casterbridge farmers passing up older and experienced men for younger and stronger men. Hardy remarks [1] on "the *miserables*" in Casterbridge:

> if their grief were the grief of oppression they would wish themselves kings; if their grief were poverty, wish themselves millionaires; if sin, they would wish they were saints or angels; if despised in love, that they were some much-courted Adonis of county fame.

Hardy expresses the same thought in Sue's remark to Jude:

> "You are Joseph the dreamer of dreams, dear Jude, and a tragic Don Quixote. And sometimes you are St. Stephen, who, while they were stoning him, could see Heaven opened. O my poor friend and comrade, you'll suffer yet!"

It recalls Jude's sympathy with "the birds' thwarted desires . . . [who] seemed to be living in a world which did not want them . . . whose lives much resembled his own."

Hardy's description of the abutment of poverty and wealth at Gray's Inn, where Knight saw glimpses of "shirtless humanity," good as it is, does not compare with Gissing's description of the piece-workers in the sweatshops of Clerkenwell, adjacent to "a trader in diamonds" and next door to "a den full of children who wait for their day's one meal until their mother has come home with her chance earnings." [2] And it has nothing comparable to Blake's searing observations in his poems "Jerusalem" and "Milton."

> Loud groans Thames beneath the Iron Forge,
> The Surrey hills glow like the clinkers of the furnace;

or to Gissing's later on John Hewett's conversation after he has eaten his supper of "the scraps warmed up from yesterday" by his wife and "laid on a very dirty cloth," and the children have been put to bed, in reply to their boarder Sidney's question whether he "had been to see Corder again":

> "No, I haven't been to Corder—I beg his pardon: Mister Corder—James Corder, Esquire. But where do you think I went this mornin'? Gorbutt in Goswell Road wanted a man to clean windows an' sweep up an' so on;—offered fifteen bob a week. Well, I went. Didn't I, mother? Didn't I go after that job? I got there at half-past eight; an' what do you think I found? If there was one man standin' at Gorbutt's door, there was *five hundred!* Don't you believe me? You go an' ask them as lives about there. If there was one, there was

five hundred! Why, the p'lice had to come an' keep the road clear. Fifteen bob! What was the use o'me standin' there, outside the crowd? What was the use, I say? Such a lot o' poor starvin' devils you never saw brought together in all your life. There they was lookin' ready to fight with one another, for fifteen bob a week.[3]

Hardy refers to an old shepherd for whom "the battle of life had been a hard one," but one will not find the struggle for existence depicted by Gissing in Marxist terms: *omnis contra omnes* in Hardy's novels, except in *Jude*. The heroes of his London novels are architects, musicians, artists, and journalists, who are shown—unlike the Wessex characters at work—at soirées and art exhibits, and in pursuit of matrimony and happiness. They do work, of course; Ethelberta rehearses her stories before her younger brothers and sisters; her older brothers, Sol and Dan, after their day's work for a Pimlico builder, groom themselves; Somerset draws plans for Paula Power's restoration of de Stancy castle, which evokes a newspaper query "Restoration or Demolition?"; Henry Knight performs literary hackwork in Grub Street, and so on. Hardy gives us a caricature of a wealthy libertine, Lord Mountclere, who is obsessed with money-making, and a woman, Paula Power, who indulges herself in the manner of Veblen's leisure class in the restoration of a castle inherited from her railroad-builder father; but he does not go beyond describing their frenetic petty lives spent in the pursuit of pleasure at home and abroad. To be sure, there are a few isolated instances of proletarian coloring, like the soldier, "sullen and reluctant," and his bride, "sad and timid" over her black eye and her pregnancy,[4] who were glimpsed by Sue and Jude in the marriage registry-office, and the two landladies [5]—the unamed one with cheap flats in Charles Square, Hoxton (*Desperate Remedies*), and Mrs. Brooks of Sandbourne (*Tess*). Mrs. Hoxton can't remember the day her tenants the Manstons came together, she tells Owen and Richard, inquiring about them:

We don't notice next door people much here in London—though I remember a very beautiful dream I had that same night—ah, I shall never forget it! Shoals of lodgers coming along the square with angels' wings and bright golden sovereigns in their hands wanting apartments at West-End prices. They would not give any less; no, not if—"

Mrs. Brooks, the householder at the Herons and owner of all the handsome furniture

was not a person of unusually curious turn of mind. She was too deeply materialized, poor woman, by her long and enforced bondage to that arithmetical demon Profit-and-Loss, to retain much curiosity for its own sake, and apart from possible lodgers' pockets.

These belonged to a class of tenants who inhabited the postern end of Bede's Inn (*A Pair of Blue Eyes*), exhibiting "a view of shirtless humanity," and were people who shopped in the gas-lit alley butcher shop for cheap cuts, which Jack London* said "would be fed to dogs in the States."[6] Hardy is ethically disturbed by knocker-and-tanner dealers, who make fortunes out of the manufacture of cat and dog food from the carcasses of horses (*The Hand of Ethelberta*), and to whom Durbyfield refuses to sell Prince's carcass. Hardy is angrier at man's inhumanity to man and the lower animals than he is at food profiteers, unlike Upton Sinclair in his exposure of the malpractice of the Chicago meatpacking industry in *The Jungle* (1906), or Sinclair Lewis in his of the bourgeoisie in *Babbitt* (1922) and *Elmer Gantry* (1927), yet there are notes of his observations of Babbitts and Elmer Gantrys in his journal, such as the following:

January 30, 1879. In Steven's book-shop, Holywell Street. A bustling vigorous young curate comes in—red-faced and full of life—the warm breath puffing from his mouth in a jet into the frosty air, and religion sitting with an ill grace upon him. "Have you *Able to Save?*"

* *People of the Abyss* (New York: Macmillan, 1904) pp. 204–9, 237.

Shopman addressed does not know, and passes on the inquiry to the master standing behind with his hat on: "*Able to Save?*"

"I don't know—hoi!" (to boy at other end). "Got *Able to Save?* Why the devil can't you attend!"

"What, Sir?"

"*Able to Save!*"

Boy's face a blank. Shopman to curate: "Get it by tomorrow afternoon, Sir."

"And please get *Words of Comfort.*"

"*Words of Comfort.* Yes, Sir." Exit curate.

Master: "Why the he--- don't anybody here know what's in stock?" Business proceeds in a subdued manner.

On his trip (August 16, 1884) with his brother Henry to the Channel Islands—Guernsey, Jersey, and Sark, at one of the hotels "every man there except themselves was a commercial traveler." "As they seemed so lonely," Mrs. Hardy says, "they were allowed to dine with these gentlemen, and became very friendly with them." Manners at the dinner-table were highly ceremonious, as put down in Hardy's account:

"Can I send you a cut of this boiled mutton, Mr. President?"

"No thank you, Mr. Vice. May I help you to beef?"

At the end of the dinner: "Gentlemen, you can leave the table."

Chorus of diners: "Thank you, Mr. President."

Possibly this experience entered into Hardy's description of the tradesmen's dinner at the Royal Arms Hotel in *The Mayor of Casterbridge,* but compared with the tensions between the minor tradesmen and the burghers at the dinner presided over by Mayor Henchard, it is so innocuous and corny as to seem valid, and reflects that the anger that Hardy felt toward high society was displaced by amusement at commercial society. It also shows, I think, that Hardy felt uncomfortable in his age, and that his having the Queen of Holland say to Napoleon, "I am reminded too much of my age by having had to live in it" (*The Dynasts,* II, 1, viii) expresses something of his own feelings on the matter. But such instances are few and far between.

He is more concerned with his London characters' anonymity of existence ushered in by the Industrial Revolution and the upper middle-class's avidity for profits. Elfride, quoting Stephen to her father, says,

> Professional men in England don't know anything about their clerks' fathers and mothers. They have assistants who come to their offices and shops for years, and hardly even know where they live. What they can do—what profits they can bring the firm—that's all London men care about. And that is helped by their faculty of being uniformly pleasant.

Similarly, in Wessex, Hardy notes of the "workfolk"—"work people," in Marx's words—that

> the landlord does not know by sight, if even by name, half the men who preserve his acres from the curse of Eden. . . . They come and go yearly like birds of passage, nobody thinks whence or whither.
>
> That in their future there are only the workhouse and the grave is no more and no less true than that in the future of the average well-to-do household there are only the invalid chair and the brick vault.[7]

Hardy emphasizes time and again, disapprovingly, the subdivision of labor, which Marx observes "is the mechanism especially characteristic of the manufacturing period." Stephen's father "was in truth like that clumsy pin-maker," Hardy says, "who made the whole pin, and who was despised by Adam Smith* on that account and respected by Macaul-

---

* Marx notes, "As will be seen more in detail in 'Theories of Surplus-Value,' Adam Smith has not established a single new proposition relating to division of labour. What, however, characterizes him as the political economist par excellence of the period of Manufacture, is the stress he lays on division of Labour (*Capital,* pp. 382–83n). Engels in his letter to Mehring (July 14, 1893) remarks: "Even the victory of the physiocrats and Adam Smith over the merchantilists is accounted as a sheer victory

ay, much more the artist, nevertheless." [8] Christopher Julian
instructs Ethelberta's brothers on seeking employment in
London: "To have any success, Sol, you must be a man
who can thoroughly look at a door to see what ought to be
done to it, but as to looking at a window, that's not your
line; or a person, who to the remotest particular, understands
turning a screw, but who does not profess any knowledge of
how to drive a nail. Dan must know how to paint blue to a
marvel, but must be quite in the dark about painting green.
If you stick to some such principle of speciality as this,
you may be able to get employment in London." [9] Jude
was "a handy man at his trade, an all-round man as
artisans in country-towns are apt to be," Hardy says,
speaking from his own experience, but "in London the man
who carves the boss or knob of leafage declines to cut the
fragment of moulding which merges in that leafage, as if it
were a degradation to do the second half of the whole." [10]
"When there was not much Gothic moulding for Jude to
run or much window tracery on the bankers, he would go
out lettering monuments or tombstones, and take a pleasure
in the change of handiwork." [11] Stephen's father has in common with most rural mechanics too much individuality to be
a typical "working man," Hardy explains, "a resultant of
that beach-pebble attrition with his kind only to be experienced in large towns, which metamorphoses the unit Self
into a fraction of the unit Class." [12] Jude is an example of
the urban proletariat who "labored at a job long or briefly
till it was finished, and then moved on." [13] Despite his trade,
Jude has no more security than the unemployed farm-

of thought, not as the reflection in thought, of changed economic facts but
as the finally achieved correct understanding of actual conditions subsisting
always and everywhere—in fact if Richard Coeur-de-Lion and Philip
Augustus had introduced free trade instead of getting mixed up in the
crusades we should have been spared five hundred years of misery and
stupidity" (*Correspondence*, p. 512). Cf. Hardy's "Had Philip's warlike son
been intellectually so far ahead as to have attempted civilization without
bloodshed, he would have been twice the godlike hero that he seemed
but nobody would have heard of Alexander" (*Return of the Native*, p. 204).

laborers "waiting on Chance" at a hiring-fair, when the farmer's question "Whose farm were you on last?" followed by the worker's answer, " 'My own' . . . invariably operated like a rumour of cholera." [14]

Hardy observes both the psychological and physical effects of London on rural artisans like Sol and Dan. "They quickly obtained good places of work under a Pimlico builder, for though the brothers scarcely showed as yet the light-fingered deftness of London artisans, the want was in a measure compensated by their painstaking, and employers are far from despising country hands who bring with them strength, industry and a desire to please." [15] They became "less spontaneous and more comparative, less genial, but smarter," he notes, "in obedience to the usual law by which the emotion that takes the form of humour in country workmen becomes transmuted to irony among the same order in town." [16] The transformation is most readily seen by a comparison of the talk of Joseph Poorgrass and the rustic peasants (*Far from the Madding Crowd*) with that of Jack Stagg, Tinker Taylor, and the bar habitués (*Jude*). For instance, when the rustics are stupefied by Joseph's reckoning of his age by his turnip-hoeing in the summer and his malting in the winter of the same years—which would make him one hundred and seventeen, according to an old gentleman "given to mental arithmetic"—his son Jacob says, "Ye don't ought to count both halves, father," and Poorgrass replies, "Chok' it all. I lived through the summers, didn't I? That's my question. I suppose ye'll say next I be of no age at all to speak of." Jude retorts, on the other hand, to Tinker Taylor's baiting of him in the tavern with, "Can'st say the creed in Latin, man?" which he proceeds to do. An undergraduate sneers, "That's the Nicene. And we wanted the Apostles'!" Jude exclaims, "You didn't say so! And every fool knows, except you, that the Nicene is the only historic creed!" Egged on by Tinker Taylor, "a decayed church ironmonger," who proffers another glass of liquor to "fetch up and get through it," Jude continues his recital, and several shout "Well done!", enjoying the last word (amen), as being the first and only one they had recognized." Whereupon Jude, shaking "the fumes from his brain . . . stared round upon them" and cried:

> "You pack of fools! Which one of you knows whether I have said it or not? It might have been the Ratcatcher's Daughter in double Dutch for all that your besotted heads can tell! See what I have brought myself to—the crew I have come among!"

The landlord feared a riot, and came outside the counter; however, "Jude, in his sudden flash of reason, had turned in disgust and left the scene, the door slamming with a dull thud behind him."

Both Sue and Jude are offended in the marriage-registry office by the forms they must sign: "Name and Surname of the Parties" [they were to be Parties, not lovers, she thought]. "Condition" [a horrid idea]. "Rank or Occupation" —"Age"—"Dwelling at"—"Length of Residence"—"Church or Building in which the Marriage is to be solemnized"— "District and County in which the Parties respectively dwell." Jude "signed the form of notice."

"It spoils the sentiment, doesn't it," she said, on their way home. "It seems making a more sordid business of it even than signing the contract in a vestry. There is a little poetry in a church. But we'll try to get through with it, dearest, now."

It is seen also in the thwarting of human potentialities by bourgeois society: Marty South's fingers which "might have skillfully guided the pencil or swept the string [of a violin] had they only been set to it in due time," [17] are disfigured by cutting spars for 18 pence a thousand for lumber merchant Melbury. Sol, who tried to prevent his sister Ethelberta from marrying Lord Mountclere, is exas-

perated when she says that "a coronet covers a multitude
of sins." Then he exclaims, "Lord—and you my sister," and,
showing her his hand, "look how my thumb stands out at
the root, as if it were out of joint and that hard place inside there. . . . That comes from the jack-plane, and my
pushing against it day after day and year after year . . .
how can a man branded with work, as I be, be a brother
to a viscountess without something be wrong?" [18] Marx
calls attention to the abnormal development of some
muscles, curvature of bones, and the like, as the result of
manufacture requiring particular workers at specialized jobs
(Capital, p. 383). In Jude, Hardy is angry at society's de-
priving a studious poor boy of a university education, and
his anger is expressed most strongly by Sue. She tells Jude,
"You are one of the very men Christminster was intended
for when the colleges were founded. . . . But you were
elbowed off the pavement by the millionaires' sons." [19] He
describes Angel's two brothers, Felix and Cuthbert, "non-
Evangelical, well-educated, hall-marked young men, correct
to their remotest fibre; such unimpeachable models as are
turned out yearly by the lathe of a systematic tuition"; and
Angel tells Tess: "Darling . . . my brother's fellowship was
won at his college, mine at Talbothay's Dairy." [20] Tess, the
most sensitive and imaginative of Hardy's women, preferred
working in the open air to indoor work: "Society might be
better than she supposed from her slight experience of it,
but she had no proof of this, and her instinct in the circumstances was to avoid it." Similarly Elizabeth-Jane had a
"fieldmouse fear of the coulter of destiny," while Lucetta "in
her poverty . . . had met with repulse from society." Alec, to
get in Tess's good graces, tells her that farmers have no
right to put women at steam-threshing. Elizabeth-Jane and
her mother, Hardy says, "were still in that strait-waistcoat
of poverty from which she had tried so many times to be
delivered for the girl's sake"; Elizabeth-Jane "had learnt the
lessons of renunciation, and was as familiar with the wreck

of each day's wishes as with the diurnal setting of the sun." [21]
One concludes that that coulter of destiny of which she
had still "that field-mouse fear . . . common among the
thoughtful who have suffered early from poverty and oppression," was fabricated by the Industrial Revolution for,
"like Burns's field-mouse, they are overawed and timorous
lest those who can wrong them should be inclined to exercise their power," he remarks in his Dorsetshire Labourer
essay. And further:

> Melancholy among the rural poor arises primarily from a
> sense of their insecurity on the land. . . . The sojourning exist-
> ence of the town masses is more and more the existence of
> the rural masses with its corresponding benefits and disad-
> vantages, and a depopulation is going on that is truly alarm-
> ing.[22]

A table of "Population Movements in some Dorsetshire
Parishes: 1840–1900," is given, by decades, in the appendix
of Mervyn Williams's *Thomas Hardy and Rural England*
(1972). One thinks of Ethelberta's brothers; of the old
shepherd of *The Mayor*, who is brushed aside by farmers
at the hiring-fair for younger and stronger men, and of his
urban counterpart in the old stonemason of the poem "In
the British Museum," an older and disabled Jude, who
hears the voice of Paul in the Areopagus stone and "the Old
Workman" who consoles himself that he has "fixed it firm
up there." [23]

I shall give more attention to Hardy's London novels
than most critics seem to think they are worth. Neither *The
Hand of Ethelberta* nor *A Laodicean* is a "trial balloon," [24]
as Webster calls them, nor are they "feeble satiric
sketches,"[25] as Chew has called parts of them. It is true that
Hardy's London novels are weakened by his having taken
Meredith's advice to write a story with a plot—advice that
Meredith proffered as a publisher's reader but did not himself follow in his own novels. Hardy's *The Poor Man and the*

Lady was rejected partly for its formlessness, being subtitled "A novel with no plot," as well as for its radicalism.
Stephen was always warning Hardy about the "Grundyian
cloud no bigger than his hand" and to "remember the parson's daughter," at his editorial desk at the *Cornhill* office;
but away from it (May 16, 1876) he counseled him differ-
ently:

> I think as a critic, that the less authors read of criticism the
> better. You, *e.g.*, have a perfectly fresh and original vein, and
> I think the less you bother yourself about critical canons the
> less chance there is of your becoming self-conscious and
> cramped. . . . St. Beuve, and Matt Arnold (in a smaller way),
> are the only modern critics who seem to me worth reading.
> . . . We are generally a poor lot, horribly afraid of not being
> in the fashion, and disposed to give ourselves airs on very
> small grounds.

Hardy had admitted to Leslie Stephen in a letter in January
1874:

> The truth is that I am willing, and indeed anxious to give
> up any points which may be desirable in a story when read
> as a whole, for the sake of others which shall please those who
> read it in numbers. Perhaps I may have higher aims some
> day, and be a great stickler for the proper artistic balance
> of the completed work, but for the present circumstances lead
> me to wish merely to be considered a good hand at a serial.[26]

He felt on less firm ground with his London stories than
with his Wessex stories, and made concessions to editors
on the former that he would not make on the latter in
obedience to a literary Gresham's Law, or trade-demands.

In taking their advice "too literally," Mrs. Hardy says,
Hardy contrived more complicated and sensational plots
for *The Hand of Ethelberta* (1876) and *A Laodicean* (1881),
which irretrievably damaged their artistry. He seems to
have paced them after *Desperate Remedies* (1871), his first
published novel, and the only novel not serialized in magazines. It was a murder mystery, with far more scenes in

Wessex than in London, though it contains a few reflections on the malaise of London society like the "usual well-dressed clubbists—rubicund with alcohol" on Pall Mall, and "flocks of house-painters pallid from white lead," and "the growl of Piccadilly," and the menage of an unemployed carpenter and his wife and child in a St. Giles slum-scenes that bear out Crickett's remark that "God sends bread to one house and children without the bread to another—probably remnants of his never-published novel, *The Poor Man and the Lady*." There is also the atheistic and slightly intoxicated postman who sings the song: *

> He flung his mallet against the wall,
> Said, The Lord makes churches and chapels, to fall,
> And there'll be work for tradesmen all!
>> When Joan's ale was new,
>>> My boys,
>> When Joan's ale was new.[27]

Desperate Remedies is important chiefly in showing that "Fate is nothin' compared to a woman's schemin,'" as a character expresses it, and also for its observation on the death of Manston, that "there's a back'ard current in the world," as Edward's father says to his friend Baker, "and we must do our utmost to advance in order just to bide where we be." [28]

Hardy never satirizes the working classes, but both his novels and his journals bristle with animosity toward the upper classes. We are never left in doubt as to how he regarded them: the journalist Knight feels contempt for the fashionably dressed gentleman ticking the Rotten-Row pavement (a corruption of Route de Roi), and Hardy adds his own comment on Knight's looking like a person with "a well-furnished mind instead of the well-finished skin *et praeteria nihil,* which is by rights the Mark of the Row." [29]

* Old English song, "There Were Three Jovial Fellows." See Sears and Phyliss Crawford, *Song Index* (New York: H. W. Wilson, 1926). ed. Annie Early.

Contrast, for instance, the "eating 'normous great dinners and suppers" of Lord Mountclere and his set, described by young Joey to his sister Picotee, "that require physicians to carry 'em off," with the sheepkeeping boy who died of starvation and whose stomach, the autopsy showed, contained ingested bits "of raw turnips only." [30] And compare the unemployed carpenter Higgins and his family living in the third-floor back room of a St. Giles slum, with a baby crying against every chair leg, comparable to that of Marx's family in a Soho slum on Dean Street,[31] with Hardy's journal note (July 19, 1891) on a lady being assisted by her footman from a landau—"the *petite* figure . . . in violet velvet and silver trimming, slim, small; who could be easily carried under a man's arm, and who, if held up by the hair and slipped out of her clothes, carriage, etc. etc., aforesaid, would not be much larger than a skinned rabbit, and of less use." Or Lord and Lady Luxellian in "their liveried chariot," who have been driving by a furrier's window, with their superior expressions of boredom, or Paula Power's cavortings to Monte Carlo—"that negative pole of industry" —and the tourist spots of Europe, with Sue and little Jude's selling Christminster cakes at the railroad station during Jude's unemployment and illness.[32] Or Lord Mountclere, "dressed with all the cunning that could be drawn from the metropolis by money and reiterated dissatisfaction" [33] with his tailor, with Hardy's journal note (Mar. 15, 1890) on Mrs. Jeune's guests: "But these women! If put into rough wrappers in a turnip-field where would their beauty be?"

This bears out Hardy's interest in and empathy with the working classes and his disdain of and hostility toward the upper classes. Class consciousness in Hardy's novels has mostly been ignored by bourgeois critics, who have forgotten that Hardy entitled them studies of "Environment and Character," and his poetry an "application of ideas to life," as he states in the preface to *Late Lyrics and Earlier,* quoting Matthew Arnold in his own defense.

A Pair of Blue Eyes (1873), Hardy's first magazine serial, was a turning point in his life from architecture to literature, for which he drew on his experiences of church restoration with Hicks—"a comic business," he termed it. It is a blighted romance, for which class prudery is to blame and Fate not at all. Vicar Swancourt, "a fossilized old Tory," is at first hospitable to Stephen Smith, a young architect with a London firm, which has sent him to Endelstow at the vicar's request for an estimate of the cost to restore the church in his poor parish. When the Vicar learns, however, of Stephen's lowly class origin—his parents are gardeners and caretakers of Lord and Lady Luxellian's estate—he orders Stephen out of the house and forbids his daughter Elfride to see him again. The Vicar treats Henry Knight, a barrister-journalist, decently because he is the cousin of Mrs. Troyton, a wealthy widow whom he has recently wed; but at the same time he advises Elfride that Knight is really "no great catch" for her, and if she will wait on Providence she can marry "a much wealthier man," [34] meaning Lord Luxellian, whose wife is terminally ill. He tells Elfride, "I am past love, you know, and I honestly confess that I married her for your sake." Elfride is a little piqued at Stephen's admiration for Knight and taunts him with " 'the noblest man in England,' as you told us last night."

Stephen's mother assures her lovelorn son that she does not "read the papers for nothing, and [she knows that] men all move up a stage by marriage." [35] Elfride's stepmother sneers at the working classes usurping "the word 'Sir' and 'Gentlemen', which is still to be heard at Tradesmen's balls"; and the Vicar reviles Stephen to Elfride: [36]

> "He is a villager's son; and we, Swancourts, connections of the Luxellians . . . but now I am to make him my son-in-law . . . are you mad, Elfride?"

The widow Jethway, who blames Elfride for the death of her only son, Felix, a consumptive farmer, condemns Elfride in a letter to Knight as "one who took a man of no birth as a lover, who was forbidden the house by her father," and afterwards secretly left her home and "went with him to London and for some reason or other, returned again unmarried."

Having lost both Stephen and Knight, Elfride marries Lord Luxellian and makes a home for the little motherless girls whom she had often taken care of during their parents' absence in London. Elfride pines away in unhappiness. Stephen and Knight meet accidentally in London and discuss Elfride, Knight not having known that she was the girl whom Stephen had told him about before his leaving for India on an assignment for his firm (salary 350 rupees per month,[37] or £35). They take the same train to Endelstow to make amends to Elfride. On their arrival there they are informed by Elfride's maid, Unity, who has married Martin Cannister, that Elfride has died of a miscarriage in a London hospital. Stephen's father and his workmen are opening the Luxellian vault for the interment of Elfride's remains, which, ironically, were in the baggage car of their train.

This class psychology is presented at the commencement of the romance. Elfride's learning from Stephen that his father is "the master mason" of Lord Luxellian's estate, and not a member of the fraternal order of Masons, elicits more than a lover's quarrel when he proudly reminds her that his parents had planted the trees and built the park at Endelstow. Knight's failure to introduce Elfride to Stephen at the embarrassing meeting at the Luxellian vault evokes a sarcastic reply from Stephen, "You should have said that I seemed still the rural builder's son I am, and hence an unfit subject for the ceremony of introductions." Elfride had come to like Knight better than Stephen during Stephen's absence in India on account of their literary interests, Knight having reviewed her not-very-good novel *The Court of Kellyon Castle* in a magazine called *The Present*. These literary proclivities anticipate Mrs. Charmond's of *The Wood-*

landers in her wanting Grace to collaborate with her on the writing of a new *Sentimental Journey*, for which she hasn't the energy to do alone," and Elfride's misconstruing Stephen's reference to masonry is echoed in Melbury's remark on Mrs. Charmond's hospitality to Grace:

> " 'Twas wonderful how she took to Grace in a few minutes; that free masonry of education—made 'em close at once." [38]

The sophisticated Knight suffers from a possessiveness toward Elfride after learning that she has had two previous lovers, Felix and Stephen. Stephen's color "changed like a chameleon when the company he was with assumed a higher or lower tone"; he is embarrassed by the crude speech of William Worm and Robert Lickpan, his father's workmen, about "many's the rum-tempered pig I've knowed." "Never mind," he tells his mother after supper, "I'll put up with it now," and she assures him, "When we leave my lord's service, and get further up the country—as I hope we shall soon—it will be different." [39]

The widow Jethway casts a psychological spell on Elfride to the point of hallucinations, Elfride imagining that she is following her on the boat from her London holiday with her parents. And a gothic element is introduced when the church tower falls on Mrs. Jethway and kills her during her nightly vigil at her son's tomb.

The most exciting incident is Elfride's rescue of Knight, who has lost his footing on the Cliff without a Name, where they had gone on a hike. While Elfride* goes for help where none appears to be, Knight, "a fair geologist," feels himself "in the presence of a personalized loneliness," staring

---

* The following insight into feminine nature is surprising: "Decisive action is seen by appreciative minds to be frequently objectless, and sometimes fatal; but decision, however suicidal, has more charm for a woman than the most unequivocal Fabian success" (p. 140), when the Fabian Society was not organized until 1884. The name was taken from *Fabius Cunctator* (Fabius the Delayer), dictator at the time of the Second Punic War (218 B.C. to 201 B.C.).

at the fossilized remains of extinct crustacean life imbedded in the scarp, "separated by millions of years," reflecting in a fraction of a moment on the palimpsest before him:

> The immense lapses of time each formation represented had known nothing of the dignity of man. They were grand times, but they were mean times, too, and mean were their relics. He was to be with the small in his death.[40]

It recalls Marx's observation to Engels in his letter of March 25, 1868, on Maurer's books,* that "human history is like paleontology," and that

> his [Maurer's] books are exceptionally important. Not only primitive times but the whole later development of the free imperial cities, of the immunity of landowners, of public authority and of the struggle between free peasantry and serfdom is given an entirely new form.[41]

This passage in *A Pair of Blue Eyes* shows the early direction of Hardy's scientific mind, which he was to develop with deeper insight** in *The Mayor of Casterbridge*, *The Woodlanders*, and *The Return of the Native* and *Tess*.

There are numerous insights on this subject in Hardy's biography: "At Tintern (July 1, 1872), where he repeated some of Wordsworth's lines thereon," he noted, 'silence is part of the pile. Destroy that, and you take a limb from an organism. A wooded slope visible from every mullioned window. But compare the age of the building with that of the marble hills from which it was drawn!' . . . This shortcoming of the most ancient architecture by comparison with

---

* *Geschichte der Fronhöfe* (1862): *Einleitung sur Geschichte der Markverfassung* (1854).

** Again in Ethelberta's reflection that "the yacht changed its character in her eyes; losing the indefinite interest of the unknown, it acquired the charm of a riddle on motives, of which the alternatives were, had Lord Mountclere's journey anything to do with her own, or had it not?" (*The Hand of Ethelberta*, p. 281).

geology was a consideration," Mrs. Hardy continues, "that frequently troubled Hardy's mind when measuring and drawing up old Norman and other early buildings," and "the thought that Greek literature had been at the mercy of dialects." In Rome (1887) Hardy began to feel, he said, "its measureless layers of history to lie upon him like a physical weight," and "the peeling of the Colosseum and other ruins of their vast accumulations of parasitic growth made the ruins of the ancient city—the *'altae moenia Romae,'* as he called them, from the *Aeneid,* more gaunt to the vision and more depressing to the mind than they had been to visitors when covered with greenery," and account for the adjectives in his poems on Rome written after his return, "as exhibiting 'ochreous gauntness, umbered walls,' and so forth." There was a great spurt of building going on at the time, on which he remarks:

> I wonder how anybody can have any zest to erect a new building in Rome in the overpowering presence of decay on the mangy and rotting walls of old erections, originally fifty times the strength of the new.

Of Genoa and the Mediterranean, he noted, "everything marble, even little doorways in slums . . . nobly redeemed its character when they visited its palaces during their stay." Lodging at the Villa Trollope in the Piazza dell' Indipendenza in Florence, they were "fortunately able to see the old Market just before its destruction." Then they had gone on to Rome, "their first glimpse of it being of the Dome of St. Peters across the stagnant flats of the Campagna." At Hereford (Aug. 1893) they stopped to see the Cathedral with Lady Catherine and her daughter, who had met them at the station, and "were interested to find that their bedroom was in the Norman part of the building, Hardy saying that he felt quite mouldy at sleeping within walls of such high antiquity."

These random notes show not only Hardy's interest in what Maurer goes into more deeply in his books, but how they enriched his imagination. *A Pair of Blue Eyes* is significant in another way: a woman rescuing a man is a startling reversal of the chivalric tradition in Western literature. It offers a piquancy to Elfride's remark to Stephen that "the difference between me and you and men and women generally, perhaps, is that I am content to build my happiness on any accidental basis that may lie near at hand; you are for making a world to suit your happiness" (p. 64). In Tennyson's code "woman is the lesser man," and that thought prevailed in Victorian society. Hardy's observation that "Elfride's capacity for being wounded was only surpassed by her capacity for healing, which rightly or wrongly is by some considered an index of transientness of feeling in general" shows a nice insight into the woman of that day. Hardy was fond of *A Pair of Blue Eyes*. The wild landscape on the Cornwall coast, or Lyonnesse as he preferred to call the place, had been the scene of his courtship of Emma Gifford. It was a novel "that he did not wish to let die," even "at the expense of profit" [42] to himself. Both Tennyson and Coventry Patmore admired the novel, but Tinsley thought it "by far the weakest of the three books I published of his." [43]

The story in the *St. Launce's Gazette* treats ironically Stephen's being acclaimed as "a local boy who has made good" (pp. 396, 415), when actually he has lost the one person whom he loved. The class differences are set forth in the rustic Martin's comment on Lady Luxellian's death: "I suppose my lord will write to all the other lords anointed in the nation to let 'em know that she that was is now no more," and his companion replies: "It's done and past," describing the letters with one-half inch wide black borders, to which Martin replies: "I'm sure people don't feel more than a very narrow border when they feels most of all," and in Stephen and Knight's looking at the metal coronet,* which the smith has yet to fix on Elfride's tomb, "beautifully finished isn't it. Ah, that cost some money!"[44]

Hardy notes that "never could there be a greater contrast between two places of like purpose than that between this graveyard and that of the further village:

> Here the grass was carefully tended, and formed virtually a part of the manor-house lawn; flowers and shrubs being planted indiscriminately over both, whilst the few graves visible were mathematically exact in shape and smoothness, appearing in the daytime like chins newly shaven. There was no wall, the division between God's Acre and Lord Luxellians's being marked only by a few square stones set at equidistant points. Among those persons who have romantic sentiments on the subject of their last dwelling-place, probably the greater number would have chosen such a spot as this in preference to any other: a few would have fancied a constraint in its trim neatness, and would have preferred the wild hill-top of the neighbouring site, with Nature in her most negligent attire.[45]

Incidentally, Hardy proved himself to be "a good hand at a serial" in *A Pair of Blue Eyes,* his first magazine story, but no installment endings quite come up to the one in which Knight is left dangling on the side of the cliff (instalment 6, chaps. 19–21) and is rescued by Elfride (instalment 7, chaps. 22–24).

The Hand of Ethelberta (1876) had "nothing in common with anything he had written before," Mrs. Hardy says. The heroine Ethelberta Petherwin, the fifth of ten children,

---

* It recalls Springrove's saying to Baker on Manston's "rough elm" coffin: "Well, death's all the less insult to him. I have often thought how much smaller the richer class are made to look than the poor at last pinches like this. Perhaps the greatest of all the reconcilers of a thoughtful man to poverty—and I speak from experience—is the grand and quiet it fill him with when the uncertainty of his life shows itself more than usual" (*Desperate Remedies,* p. 431).

in her problem of "how they might be decently maintained," illustrates Marx's refutation of Malthus that "the pressure of population is not upon the means of subsistence but upon the means of employment" (Engels's letter to F. A. Lange Mar. 29, 1865). She wishes she were a man, and is "going to talk De Foe on a subject of my own," making her first public appearance the second week of February after the opening of Parliament." Its suspense depends on her keeping the secret of her and her family's identity "right in the heart of the aristocracy," which, if revealed, she says, "would kill me and ruin us all." [46] She defends her brothers, Sol and Dan, who, she says, "represent the respectable British workman in his entirety, and a touchy individual he is after imbibing a few town ideas from his leaders." Sol and Dan show some standards of craft in their remark "what a rum staircase," and assert that they "know nothing besides our trades." [47] Ethelberta's father, Mr. Chickerel, is a serving man to the Doncastles and is "growing ashamed of his company—so different as they are to the servants of old times." Ethelberta would rather have "a crust of bread and her liberty" than remain in the Petherwin household; she seems to prefer the musician Christopher Julian, who had composed the music to one of her poems, to her other suitors, but confides to her sister Picotee, "I am not going to marry until he gets rich." Disillusioned with her success as a raconteur to high society, she finally marries Lord Mountclere, a septuagenarian and the wealthiest of her suitors, who "sighed like a poet over a ledger." There is an amusing scene between Lord Mountclere, who insists, "I am not an old man," and his butler, who replies, "Old in knowledge of the world, I meant, my lord, not in years," and a still more amusing scene when Doncastle confronts Chickerel:

> "Do you mean to say that the lady who sat here at dinner at the same time that Lord Mountclere was present, is your daughter?"

"Yes, sir," said Chickerel respectfully.
"How did she come to be your daughter?"
"I—well, she is my daughter, sir."[48]

Ethelberta confesses to Christopher, "I too am compelled to follow a course I did not originally mean to take," and puts a question to him: "Have you considered whether the relations between us which have lately prevailed are—are the best for you—and for me?" To which Christopher replies, after thanking her for the opportunity of speaking upon that subject "as an object to exist for and strive for":

> In short, Ethelberta, I am not in a position to marry, nor can I discern when I shall be, and I feel it would be an injustice to ask you to be bound in any way to one lower and less talented than you. You cannot, from what you say, think it desirable that the engagement should continue. I have no right to ask you to be my betrothed, without having a near prospect of making you my wife.[49]

"A second meaning was written in Christopher's look," Hardy continues, "though he scarcely uttered it":

> A woman so delicately poised upon the social globe could not in honour be asked to wait for a lover who was unable to set bounds to the waiting period.

Her father and her brothers try, but fail to prevent her marriage to Lord Mountclere. Though Sol had called Lord Mountclere "a bad man," and warned Ethelberta of "a creeping up among the useless lumber of our nation that'll be the first to burn if there comes a flare,"[50] both he and Dan soon become reconciled to their brother-in-law. Lord Mountclere represents the aristocracy, and bankrocracy, or "*haute finance*," as Marx termed it (*Capital*, p. 795); when Ethelberta asks Mountclere, "But my father, and friends?" he replies: "It would take fifty alliances with fifty families as little disreputable as yours is, darling, to drag mine down," and he reminds her brother-in-law that "modern developments have shaken up the classes like peas in a hopper" and that "Manufacture is the single vocation in which a man's prospects may be said to be illimitable," which bears out Sweezy's statement, "The aristocracy has become thoroughly capitalist" (p. 230). Mrs. Belmaine remarks to Ethelberta at Milton's tomb (and she comes from "one of the good old families"):

> "People of that sort push on, and get into business, and get great warehouses, until at last, without ancestors, or family, or name or estate . . . they are thought as much of as if their forefathers had glided unobtrusively through the peerage."

One recalls also Dan's remark to Christopher: "Why down in these parts just as you try a man's soul by the Ten Commandments, you try his head by that there sum—hey, Sol?" and proceeds to give an example in which he brings in Parson Malthus[*] without naming him (p. 112):

[*] Marx had scant respect for Malthus, whose "Essay on Population" (1798) he declared "a libel on the human race," and nothing more than "a schoolboyish, superficial plagiarism of De Foe, Sir James Steuart, Townsend, Franklin, Wallace, & c.," (*Capital*, pp. 675–76n). Nor for Bentham, whom he called "a plagiarist in a dull way of Helvetius," and declared to be "among philosophers, what Martin Tupper is among poets. Both could only have been manufactured in England" (*ibid*, p. 668). Malthus, Marx notes, did not approve of families the size of the Chickerels' of course, but he did "preach high rents, heavy taxes, so that the pressure of the spur may constantly be kept on the industrious by unproductive consumers" (*ibid.*, p. 653) which "prevented him from from seeing that an unlimited prolongation of the working-day, combined with an extraordinary development of machinery, and the exploitation of women and children (which Ethelberta so dreads) have made a great portion of the working class 'supernumerary,' particularly when the war should have ceased, and the monopoly of England in the markets of the world should have come to an end" (*ibid.*, p. 580). Mrs. Belmaine asks Ethelberta. "And have you any theory on the vexed question of servant-government?" to which Ethelberta replies in a Swiftean vein: "I think the best plan would be for somebody to write a pamphlet, 'The Shortest Way with Servants,' just as there was once written a terribly stinging one, 'The Shortest Way with Dissenters,' which had great effect" (p. 78). Hardy, likewise in a Swiftean vein, replied to the Rev. S. Whittel Key, who had inquired of him concerning "sport": "In the present state of affairs there would appear to be no logical reason why the smaller children, say, of overcrowded families,

"A herring and a half for three-half pence, how many can you get for 'levenpence: that's the feller; and a mortal teaser he is, I assure 'ee. Our parson, that's not altogether without sense o' week days, said one afternoon, 'If cunning can be found in the multiplication table at all, Chickerel, 'tis in connection with that sum.' " *

Ethelberta, according to her brothers, is a whiz at calculating "the sum," and Ethelberta complains to Julian that Mrs. Petherwin "was the absolute mistress of her wealth" and had left her "nothing but her house and furniture in London." Lady Petherwin, also a widow, Hardy heard the hostler say that she "married a gentleman who was a man of valour in the Lord Mayor's Show" (pp. 101, 4). Hardy reiterates in *The Hand of Ethelberta* what he had said earlier in *A Pair of Blue Eyes*, that "man's case is always that of the prodigal's favourite or the miser's pensioner" (p. 243). Ethelberta confides to her sister Picotee that "marriage is the only way for a poetess to prevent herself from becoming what Dryden called himself when he got old and poor: a rent-charge on Providence." Hardy says that Ethelberta

had begun as poet of the Satanic school in sweetened form; she was ending as a *pseudo*-utilitarian. Was there ever such a transmutation effected before by the action of a hard environment? . . . in other words from soft and playful Romanticism to distorted Benthamism. Was the moral incline up or down?[51]

Her admirers thought that "she lives what paper poets only

should not be used for sporting purposes. Darwin has revealed that there would be no difference in principles; moreover, these children would often escape lives intrinsically less happy than those of wild birds and other animals" (*Later Years,* pp. 106–7).

* It may have been suggested by Hardy's reading David Urquart's *Portfolio* (new series) in the papers (1858), in which Marx says, "interesting details on the fish trade will be found," of which "the brave Gaels caused the smell of the fish (to rise) to the noses of the great men. They scented some profit in it and let the seashore to the great fishmongers of London" (*Capital,* p. 802 and 802n) and the practice in herring-fishing (*ibid.*, p. 360).

write." Hardy's journal note (May 29, 1889) reads like a comment on the novel:

> In London anew: "One difference between the manners of the intellectual middle class and the nobility is that the latter have more flexibility, almost a dependence on their encompassment, as if they were waiting upon future events; while the former are direct and energetic, and crude, as if they were manufacturing a future to please them."

Ethelberta's brothers end up by aspiring to rise from the working class into the money-making class in spite of Ethelberta's efforts at educating them—"Catalogue in hand" and her Milton in her coat—at Milton's tomb and the art exhibit, on Saturday, "the only day and hour at which they could attend without 'losing a half.'" [52] The brothers are less interested in the paintings than in

> the gilding of the frames, the construction of the skylights overhead, or admiration for the bracelets, lockets, and lofty eloquence of persons around them.

They had done "most of the actual work on Ethelberta's mantelpiece," though she says she "drew the outlines and designed the tile round the fire." The artist Neigh, a nephew of the Doncastles, and Ethelberta's suitor until he learns that she is the daughter of a butler, is said by a man with a wheelbarrow to be "a terrible hater of women, I hear, particularly the lower class." [53] This may have been suggested to Hardy by Gladstone's characterizing the Tory Robert Lowe as "a remarkable man, especially remarkable for his power of spontaneous aversion" with which "he hates the working classes of England." [54] Neigh comes of a family "that have made a very large fortune by the knacker-business and tanning, though they be only sleeping partners in it now, and live like lords." Neigh remarks to the artist Mr. Ladywell, "My heart is in the happy position of a country which has no history or debt." [55] Lord Mountclere sets Sol and Dan up in business, and we learn, finally, that "they have signed a contract to build a hospital for twenty thousand pounds." The novel bears out Robinson Jeffers's opinion that it is "no use our turning to the factory-workers, as Tolstoy did to the peasant and Rousseau to the primitive, for what the factory-workers want is exactly what the middle-classes want, and if they get it," he believed (May 17, 1933), "they would have all the middle-class fatuities; only more so because they have less security," [56] which recalls Hardy's remark that "young men would rather wear a black coat and starve than wear fustian and do well" (p. 418). In this respect *The Hand of Ethelberta* is a pessimistic novel compared with Hardy's great novels. The corruption of the working classes by materialism following World War II, however, is worse than that of Ethelberta's kind before World War I.

A Laodicean, subtitled "A Story of To-day" (1881), "in neo-Pagan days" presents a wider purview of the past than *The Hand of Ethelberta,* as *Tess* does also, in depicting the nouveau riche as they ape the feudal aristocracy. A decadent aristocrat, Captain de Stancy tries to regain his family's castle and glorious past by marrying Paula Power, who has inherited the castle from her father. He was "a great railway contractor," an eminent Baptist and nonconformist, and an M.P., who was opposed to dancing. Paula, "a medieval flower in a modern flower pot," has two suitors—George Somerset, a poor architect who has been drawn to her on account of "her sketches for City planning corresponding with nothing he had seen in the country," and Captain de Stancy, who has been "continuously absent from home in India or elsewhere" and "lacks advancement," and whose health had "somewhat suffered in India." [57] His sister, Charlotte, lives with Paula in the castle. Paula is thinking of leasing part of her land for the development of Hellenic pottery and pottery manufacture, yet she never speaks of the pottery workers who, Marx notes, were "underpaid,

prematurely old and short-lived" and the victims of potter's
asthma (*Capital,* pp. 269–70; Jack London, p. 258). Paula
favors Captain de Stancy; when she wishes nostalgically
that she had "a well-known line of ancestors," Somerset
replies:

> "I mean that you represent the march of mind—the steam-
> ship and the railway and the thoughts that shake mankind"—
> reminding her, "You have Archimedes, Newcomen, Watt, Tel-
> ford, Stephenson—those are your father's direct ancestors.
> . . . Have you forgotten them? Have you forgotten your
> father, and the railways he made over half of Europe, and his
> great energy and skill, and all connected with him as if he
> had never lived?" [58]

She replies, "No, I have not forgotten it. But I have a
prédilection d'artiste for ancestors of the other sort like the
de Stancys," but she does not reply to his question, "You
are one of the largest shareholders in the railway, are you
not, Paula?"

Paula, however, abandons her socially minded projects
and capriciously invites bids for the restoration of the
castle. William Dare, the illegitimate son of Captain de
Stancy, who has a "Book of Chances as well thumbed as a
minister's Bible," [59] resorts to a conspiracy with Havill, an
older architect, to steal Somerset's drawings and to blackmail
Somerset by trick photography, in order to further his
father's romance with Paula. Finally, when the truth of
Dare's crimes is ferreted out and his identity made known,
Paula rejects Captain de Stancy, whom she was about to
marry "for pity's sake, in spite of Uncle Abner," [60] and weds
Somerset. From their honeymoon suite in the Markton village hotel, they see the castle in flames, Dare presumably
the arsonist. The "fear of the chateau" is said to have
"haunted the imagination of the French peasant," Arnold
says in his essay on "Eugénie de Guérin," "well into the
nineteenth century," and the conflagration seems to repre-

sent the English fear of French Jacobism. Uncle Abner is the inventor of a portable explosive, more effective than the assassin's dagger, and he "is *wanted* by certain European governments as badly as ever" (p. 413); he blackmails Dare into joining him in South America for some nefarious purpose, and is a hired *agent provacateur,* a different type from Verloc in Conrad's *Secret Agent* (1907).

A *Laodicean* abounds in examples of primitive accumulation—from the private wire that brings, "with the hum of a night bee," stock-market quotations to Sir William de Stancy, who had lost his money in stock, "in racing speculations," and in "a useless silver mine" suggestive of Charles Gould's San Tomé mine later in Conrad's *Nostromo,* to a modern chronometer and private gymnasium in which Paula is observed clandestinely by Captain de Stancy and Dare, "clad in pink flannel costume . . . going through her gymnastics in the air like a goldfish in its globe." [61] Somerset questions Sir William on how Paula and the Captain will live happily, when "she is a Dissenter and a Radical [she refuses to go through with the baptismal ceremony] and a New Light and a Neo-Greek and a person of red blood, when Captain de Stancy is the reverse of them all!" The Baronet replies, "I anticipate no difficulty on that score . . . You have skill in architecture, therefore you follow it. My son has skill in gallantry, and now he is about to exercise it profitably," adding "the favourable Bank-returns have made the money-market much better to-day, I learn," to which Somerset replies, "O have they? I suppose they have." [62]

The anomaly of the situation is heightened by Hardy's contrasting "the living people in the Chapel belonging to the vast majority of society [who] are denied the art of articulating their higher emotions," and the de Stancy forebears' portraits in the castle gallery, which evoke Captain de Stancy's question to his son: "Why was a line so antiquated and out-of-date prolonged till now?" to which Dare replies:

"The truth is, captain, we aristocrats must not take too high a tone. Our days as an independent division of society, which holds aloof from other sections, are past. . . . The case is even more pressing than ordinary cases—owing to the odd fact that the representative of the new blood who has come in our way actually lives in your old house, and owns your old lands. The ordinary reason for such alliances is quintupled in our case. . . . Beggars mustn't be choosers." [63]

In fact, Somerset in surveying the castle discovers among "these antique inscriptions" two recently bright and clear ones—"de Stancy and W. Dare" (p. 84), and de Stancy admonishes Paula, whom he had privately told his sister, Charlotte, "ought to be called Miss Steam Power" (p. 171):

"Well, you will allow me to say this, since I say it without reference to your personality or to mine—that the Power and de Stancy families are the complements to each other; and that, abstractedly, they call earnestly to one another: 'How neat and fit a thing for us to join hands!'"

These lines are prophetic of the Industrial Feudalism that Rudolph Hilferding (1877–1941), leader of German socialist democrats, saw taking shape in 1912.

Hardy describes the Castle, in which there is a dungeon, as "a fossil of feudalism" and as "such a masterpiece of fortification that it was believed before the invention of gunpowder, it could not be taken by any forces than divine." He refers to the Castle's having entertained guests of old Cavalier families who still believed in the Apostolic Succession." [64] This may have been suggested by Hardy's having read Newman's *Apologia,* in which Newman quoted with opprobrium Bishop Blomfield's* remark that ". . . Apostolical

---

* "Blomfield, the Bishop of London of the day, an active and open-hearted man, has been for years engaged in diluting the high orthodoxy of the Church by the introduction of members of the Evangelical body into places of influence and trust. He had deeply offended men who agreed in opinion with myself, by an offhand saying (as it was reported) to the effect that belief in the Apostolical succession had gone out with the Non-jurors. 'We can count you,' he said to some of the gravest and most venerated

Succession had gone out with the Non-jurors";[65] Hardy re-quoted it to his employer, the Bishop's son, Arthur Blomfield (later knighted), to the amusement of both.

The tragedy underneath the comedy—and Hardy agreed with Ruskin that "comedy is tragedy if you only look deep enough," [66] is that young architect George Somerset is forced to degrade his talents by restoring Paula Power's castle when he would rather have employed them on socially minded projects. One does not know whether to censure Hardy or compliment him for his use of such sensational intrigues as the Third Estate was making capital of.

There is an excellent description of the Casino at Monte Carlo, where Somerset finds the library empty and the gaming-hall full:

> The people gathered at this negative pole of industry had come from all civilized countries; their tongues were familiar with many forms of utterances, that of each racial group or type being unintelligible in its subtler variations, if not entirely, to the rest. But the language of *meum* and *teum* they collectively comprehended without translation.[67]

He describes Dare seated at a gaming-table "like one turned into a computing machine which no longer had the power of feeling." Dare remarks to Havill on the R.I.B.A's (Royal Institute of British Architects) finding his and Somerset's plans for the castle resortation "singularly equal and singularly good": "It is as if I had spun a sovereign in the air and it had lighted on its edge." The antithesis of Monte Carlo is found in Hardy's description of the Pimlico plant of Messrs. Nockett & Co's. yard, where Lord Mountclere's younger brother has gone to look up Ethelberta's brother, Sol, to prevent her marriage to the Viscount; on inquiry a clerk "signified the foot of a flemish ladder on the other side

persons of the old school. . . . I thought the Evangelicals played into the hands of the Liberals" (Newman, *Apologia Pro Vita Sua;* J. W. Bowyer and J. L. Brooks, *The Victorian Age* [New York, 1941], p. 236).

of the yard, with, 'You will find him, sir, there in the joiners shops.' " [68] Hardy relates the incident:

> When the man in the black coat reached the top he found himself at the end of a long apartment as large as a chapel and as low as a malt-room, across which ran parallel carpenters' benches to the number of twenty or more, a gangway being left at the side for access throughout. Behind every bench there stood a man or two, planing, fitting, or chiselling, as the case might be. . . . He waited ten seconds, he waited twenty; but, beyond that a quick look had been thrown upon him by every pair of eyes, the muscular performances were in no way interrupted: every one seemed oblivious of his presence, and absolutely regardless of his wish. In truth, the texture of his salmon-coloured skin could be seen to be aristocratic without a microscope, and the exceptious artizan has an off-hand way when contrasts are made painfully strong by an idler of this kind coming, gloved and brushed, into the very den where he is sweating and muddling in his shirt-sleeves.
>
> The gentleman from the carriage then proceeded down the workshop, wading up to his knees in a sea of shavings, and bruising his ankles against corners of board and sawn-off blocks, that lay hidden like reefs beneath. At the ninth bench he made another venture. . . .
>
> "Damn it all, can't one of you show me?" the visitor angrily observed. . . . "Here, point him out." He handed the man a shilling.
>
> "No trouble to do that," said the workman; and he turned and signified Sol by a nod without moving from his place.

Jude the Obscure (1896) was, in Hardy's own words, "concerned first the labours of a poor student to get a University degree, and secondly with the tragic issues of two bad marriages, owing in the main to a doom or curse of hereditary temperament peculiar to the family of the parties," as he wrote Swinburne on November 10, 1895. The conflict between the intellectual and the biological urges provides the dialectic of the novel. Jude's thirst for knowledge runs through the story from his boyhood at the age of eleven, when he is bidding goodbye to his teacher, Mr.

Phillotson, whose night-pupil he had been, and from his studying Latin grammars, obtained from Physician Vilbert, an itinerant quack, while driving his aunt's bakery cart, until his marriage to Arabella, the butcher's daughter, who seduced him one Sunday afternoon when her parents were away at church, and who despises his "dear ancient classics."

They separate on Arabella's finding that she is not pregnant after all, and Jude, with his tools on his back, goes to London, where he finds work as a stonemason in a yard near Christminster College. "He was a species of Dick Whittington whose spirit was touched to finer issues than mere material gain," Hardy says, and who says himself, "Let me only get there," with the fatuousness of Crusoe* over his big boat, "and the rest is but a matter of time and energy"; but he soon discovers that there was "a wall which divided him from those happy contemporaries of his—men who had nothing to do from morning till night but to read, mark, learn and inwardly digest—"only a wall but what a wall!" [69] To some whom he overhears he is irresistibly drawn because of sharing similar dreams, but they see in him only "a young workman in a white blouse . . . with stone dust in the creases of his clothes." He reacts to the rejection of his application to Christminster by Dean Tetuphenay, who advised him to "stick to his trade" without ever having seen him, by writing in chalk on the college wall:

> "I have understanding as well as you; I am not inferior to you: yea, who knoweth not such things as these?"—Job. xii, 3.

Giving up his work as "a cathedral mason," he and Sue go to Aldbrickham, where it is said of him by the poor people in his own neighbourhood:

---

* Marx notes that "Robinson Crusoe's experiences are a favourite theme with political economists," and remarks that "even Ricardo has his stories à la Robinson. For example: He makes the primitive hunter and the primitive fisher straightway as owners of commonplace exchange fish and game in the proportion in which labour-time is incorporated in these exchanges values . . . (*Capital* p. 88). Jude, of course, fits Marx's definition of a worker in having nothing but his labor to sell.

"What a cheap man this 'Jude Fawley: Monumental Mason'
[as he called himself on his front door] was to employ for the
simple memorial they required for their dead. But he seemed
more independent than before, and it was the only arrangement under which Sue, who particularly wished to be no
burden on him, could render any assistance.[70]

Jude had first met his cousin, Sue Bridehead, in an art
store, where she was employed, and they shared the same
intellectual and artistic interests. Sue, who had married
Jude's old teacher Mr. Phillotson, leaves him on account of
a physical repulsion to him, and returns to Jude to live on
"a Shelleyean plane." Their relationship is complicated by
the arrival of "Little Jude," "with the face of Melpomene,"
from Australia—Arabella had been pregnant after all—and
Jude loses his job because of gossip about Sue and their
unwed state. During a spell of illness Sue and "Little Jude"
sell Christminster cakes at the railway station until Jude
recovers, when they return to London. On account of the
children and Sue's advanced pregnancy, they are turned
down by landlords and have to take separate lodgings
temporarily. While Sue goes to see Jude, "Little Jude"
hangs the small children in the closet and then himself—
"Done because we are too menney." * Sue, overcome with
grief and guilt, suffers a miscarriage and goes back to Phillotson. Jude seeks release in drink and is snared into a second
marriage by Arabella, who is working as a barmaid. Jude,
wrought up emotionally, and in weakened condition, goes

* The Malthusian reference here is obvious. In it Chew finds "prophecies
of the future generations, foretold by von Hartmann . . ." (*Thomas Hardy*,
p. 72). Hardy's description of Little Jude, "like an enslaved and dwarfed
Divinity," on the down-train to Albrickham (p. 326) may represent "a
children's opiate" who "shrank up into a little old man" or "wizzened little
monkeys", on which Marx comments, "We here see how India and China
avenged themselves on England" (*Capital*, p. 436n2). Engels says "the
workers have neither time nor money to procure proper food for their
children, and they often give them brandy, even opium" (*Condition of
the Working Class in England in 1844*, p. 114). Anne Seaway of *Desperate
Remedies* suspects Manston of trying to poison her when she sees him
pour some drops from a small phial labeled "Battley's Solution of Opium"
(p. 408).

to see Sue and, on his return to Arabella in London, suffers a relapse. He dies within the shadows of Christminster, where the hurrahs from the boat races interrupt his anguished words from the Book of Job. Arabella, supposing him asleep, had slipped out to attend the boat races with Dr. Vilbert.

Jude, Hardy tells us, is a sensitive, frail boy, who "is doomed to ache a good deal"; Jude himself comes to realize, when it is too late, that he wasn't cut out for the stone-mason's trade, which "began the mischief inside." [71] Jude clings to his dream of Christminster as "the City of Light and the spiritual granary" even after he has burned his books. Sue has "no respect for Christminster, except . . . on its intellectual side." [72]

> "My friend I spoke of, took that out of me. He was the most irreligious man I ever knew, and the most moral. And intellect at Christminster is new wine in old bottles. The medievalism of Christminster must go, be sloughed off, or Christminster itself will have to go. To be sure, at times one couldn't help have a sneaking liking for the traditions of the old faith, as preserved by a section of the thinkers there in touching and simple sincerity; but when I was in my maddest, rightest mind I always felt, 'O ghastly glories of saints, dead limbs of gibbeted Gods!' "

Jude says defensively, "I still think Christminster has much that is glorious, though I was resentful because I couldn't get there." She retorts:

> "It is an ignorant place, except as to the townspeople, artisans, drunkards and paupers. . . . *They* see life as it is, of course, but few of the people in the colleges do."

Sue resents Jude's calling her "a creature of civilization, or something," because she affirms, "I am a sort of negation of it." Jude replies, " 'A negation' is profound thinking," which is connotative of Marx's Hegelian negation of the negation.*

---

* See Robert Freedman, *Marxist Social Thought* (New York: Harcourt, Brace & World, 1968), p. 48.

Both show further insight into their situation when they sit down "to tea in the familiar home" after Aunt Drusilla's funeral, and recall that she had opposed their marriage on account of "a curse or doom on the families."

"We are rather a sad family, don't you think, Jude," she said. "She said we made bad husbands and wives. Certainly we make unhappy ones. At all events, I do, for one!"

Sue was silent. "Is it wrong, Jude," she said, with a tentative tremor, "for a husband or wife to tell a third person that they are unhappy in their marriage? If a marriage ceremony is a religious thing, it is possibly wrong; but if it is only a sordid contract, based on material convenience in householding, children, making it necesssary that the male parent should be known—which it seems to be—why surely a person may say, even proclaim upon the housetops, that it hurts and grieves him or her?"

"I have said so, anyhow, to you."

Presently she went on; "Are there many couples, do you think, where one dislikes the other for no definite fault?"

"Yes, I suppose. If either cares for another person, for instance."

"But even apart from that? Wouldn't the woman, for example, be very bad-natured if she didn't like to live with her husband; merely—her voice undulated, and he guessed things merely—because she had a personal feeling against it—a physical objection—a fastidiousness, or whatever it may be called—although she might respect and be grateful to him? I am merely putting a case. Ought she try to overcome her pruderies?"

Jude threw a troubled look at her. He said, looking away: "It would be just one of those cases in which my experiences go contrary to my dogmas. Speaking as an order-loving man —which I hope I am, though I fear I am not—I should say yes. Speaking from experience and unbiassed nature, I should say no. . . . Sue, I believe you are not happy." [73]

There is a flare-up between them when each, a little jealous of the other's mate by a previous marriage, disappears from their earlier closeness to each other:

He laughed. "Never mind!" he said. "So that I am near you, I am comparatively happy. It is more than this earthly wretch

called Me deserves—you spirit, you disembodied creature, you
dear, sweet, tantalizing phantom—hardly flesh at all; so that
when I put my arms round you, I almost expect them to pass
through you as through air! Forgive me for being gross, as
you call it! Remember that our calling ourselves cousins when
really strangers was a snare. The enmity of our parents gave
a piquancy to you in my eyes that was intenser even than
the novelty of ordinary new acquaintances."

"Say those pretty lines, then, from Shelley's 'Epipsychidion'
as if they meant me," she solicited, slanting up closer to him
as they stood. "Don't you know them?"

"I know hardly any poetry," he replied, mournfully.

> "There was a Being whom my spirit oft
> Met on its visioned wanderings far aloft.
>
> .   .   .   .
>
> A seraph of Heaven, too gentle to be human,
> Veiling beneath that radiant form of a woman . . ."

"Oh, it is too flattering, so I won't go on! But say it's me.—
say it's me!"

"It *is* you, dear; exactly like you!" [74]

The conversation between Jude and Arabella, who is
anti-intellectual and scornful of Jude's tender sensibilities,
is the basis of Jude's complaint "that of having based a
permanent contract on a temporary feeling which had no
necessary connection with affinities that alone render a lifelong comradeship tolerable." They butcher their pig themselves on account of the butcher Challow's failure to show
up, Jude having shoveled the snow away for the space of a
couple yards:

"Upon my soul, I would sooner have gone without the pig
than have had this to do!" said Jude. "A creature I have fed
with my own hands."

"Don't be such a tender-hearted fool! There's the sticking
knife—the one with the point. Now whatever you do, don't
stick un too deep."

"I'll stick him effectually, so as to make short work of it.
That's the chief thing."

"You must not!" she cried. "The meat must be well bled,

and to do that he must die slow. We shall lose a shilling a score if the meat is red and bloody! . . .

"He shall not be half a minute if I can help it, however the meat may look," said Jude, determinedly. . . .

" 'Od damn it all!" she cried, "that ever I should say it. You've over-stuck un! And I telling you all the time—"

"Do be quiet, Arabella, and have a little pity on the creature!"

However unworkmanlike the deed, it had been mercifully done. The blood flowed out in a torrent instead of in the trickling stream she had desired. The dying animal's cry assumed its third and final tone, the shriek of agony; his glazing eyes rivetting themselves on Arabella with the eloquently keen reproach of a creature recognizing at last the treachery of those who had seemed his only friends.[75]

Hardy felt an inner compulsion to write *Jude,* as is shown in his journal note (April 28, 1888): "A short story of a young man—'who could not go to Oxford'—his struggles and ultimate failure. Suicide. There is something [in this] the world ought to be shown, and I am the one to show it to them—though I was not altogether hindered going, at least to Cambridge, and could have gone up easily at five-and-twenty." His quarrel with society in the larger sense of the word, suppressed since the rejection of *The Poor Man and the Lady,* breaks out again and again in the novels, and "finally explodes," [76] Quiller-Couch observes, "in *Jude the Obscure.*"

While awaiting the publication of *Jude* (Nov. 1, 1895), Hardy had written in his journal: "Never retract. Never explain. Get it done and let them howl. Words said to Jowett by a very practical friend." In London, in December 1896, he and Mrs. Hardy went to see Forbes-Robertson and Mrs. Patrick Campbell as Romeo and Juliet, and supped with them afterwards "at Willis's Rooms," finding the ballroom there "unaltered since the days in 1862, when he had used to dance on its floor." Hardy must have thought of William Morris, who had died that fall on October 3, as well as of Jude, as R. B. Cunninghame Graham must have thought of Jude as well as of Morris when he described how Morris's friends carried his body from London to Lachlade station for Kelmscott Manor, where he was buried, to judge from his little essay "With the North West Wind," which Hardy might have written himself:

> The train rolled on through Oxford, but no undergraduates thronged the station, silently standing to watch the poet's funeral. True, it was the Long Vacation; but had the body of some Buluwayo* Burglar happened to pass, they had all been there. The ancient seat of pedantry, where they manufacture prigs as fast as butchers in Chicago handle hogs, was all unmoved. . . .
>
> Sleeping but sterterous, the city lay girt in its throng of jerry buildings, quite out of touch with all mankind, keeping its sympathy for piffling commentators on Menander.[77]*

At home Hardy had plenty of time to read the reviews of *Jude*, which were "unequalled in violence since the publication of Swinburne's *Poems and Ballads* written thirty years before." [78] Indeed, Mrs. Hardy had gone to London to try to get Dr. Richard Garnett at the British Museum "to help her persuade Hardy not to publish his 'vicious manuscript of *Jude*,'" [79] but to no avail; and Miss Jeannette Gilder in the *New York World* (Dec. 8, 1898) was "shocked, appalled by this story!" and declared that there "was not a newspaper in England or America that would print this story of Thomas Hardy's as it stands in the book." "The outcry in America against it was only an echo of its misrepresentation here," Hardy wrote on July 26, 1896, "by one or two scurrilous papers. . . ." The Reverend W. W. How, Bishop of Wakefield, not only wrote a letter to the paper that he had thrown Hardy's godless book into the fire," but also to W. F. D. Smith, Esq. M.P., which resulted in "the withdrawal of the book from the library, and an assurance that any

---

* The reference to Buluwayo Burglar and to "piffling commentators on Menander," Eshelman says "would seem to refer to Cecil Rhodes and Matthew Arnold" (*A Victorian Rebel*, p. 346n).

other books by the some author would be carefully examined before they were allowed to be circulated." [80]

Swinburne, however, wrote Hardy that "the tragedy—if I may venture an opinion—is equally beautiful and terrible in its pathos. The beauty, the terror and the truth, are all yours. . . . But if you prefer to be—or to remain—the most tragic of authors no doubt you may; for Balzac is dead, and there has been no tragedy in fiction—on anything like the same lines—since he died." [81] Hardy replied appreciatively that "as for the story itself, it is really sent out to those into whose soul the iron has entered, and has entered deeply at some time of their lives"; he added in a postscript that the " 'grimy' features of the story go to show the contrast between the ideal life a man wished to lead and the squalid real life he was fated to lead. . . . It is fact to be discovered in everybody's life, though it lies less on the surface perhaps than it does in my poor puppet's. He "used Jude's difficulties of study as he would have used war, fire, or shipwreck for bringing about a catastrophe." [82]

The reviews "were producing phenomena among his country friends which were extensive and peculiar, they having a pathetic reverence for press opinions." On some of these Hardy observed:

> Tragedy may be created by an opposing environment either of things inherent in the universe, or of human institutions. If the former be the means exhibited and deplored, the writer is regarded as impious; if the latter, as subversive and dangerous; when all the while he may never have questioned the necessity or non-necessity of either. [83]

This he had learned between writing *The Poor Man and the Lady* and *Jude the Obscure*.

In May 1896, Hardy received a request from the members of the Glasgow University Liberal Club to stand as their candidate in the election of a Lord Rector for the University, the objection to Mr. Joseph Chamberlain, who had been nominated, being that he was "not a man of letters." Replying from Brighton (May 16, 1896), "where I am staying for a few days for change of air after an illness," he wrote, "I am deeply sensible of the honour . . . [and] in other circumstances I might have rejoiced at the opportunity." But he was obliged to decline it for "personal reasons which would be tedious to detail," and he concluded with his sincere thanks for their "generous opinion of my worthiness."

To comment a little more on Hardy's frank treatment of marital and love matters for his era. Hardy is concerned foremost with love in all his novels—the love of man and woman for each other beginning in courtship and ending in marriage. His lovers are mostly young people who feel first a physical attraction for each other (Sergeant Troy, Fanny Robin; Eustacia Vye, Clym Yeobright; Thomasin, Venn; Tess, Angel, and so on. It is in most instances a case of love at first sight, whereby they see more and more of each other and a maturation of physical emotions, under Victorian inhibitions, that arouse reciprocal passion—the desires of male and female. Love is stronger in some of Hardy's characters than in others—notably in Sergeant Troy, Eustacia, Damon Wildeve, Lucetta Templeman, Dr. Fitzpiers, Suke Damsun, Michael Henchard, Alec D'Urberville, Arabella Donn, and weaker in those such as Thomasin Wildeve, Diggory Venn, Grace Melbury, Giles Winterborne, Elizabeth-Jane and her mother, St. Swithin. It is quiescent in Tess and sublimated unsuccessfully in Jude, but it is a call of youth to youth, corresponding to when the bud bursts into bloom.

Younger women in Hardy's novels feel pity and compassion for older men—Bathsheba for the lonely, puritanical Boldwood oftener than older men feel the same emotion for younger women—Boldwood for Fanny, for instance, of which I think of no other example; but they seldom encourage their attentions or marry them. To be sure, there is the exception of Ethelberta and Lord Mountclere and, to some extent, of Sue and Mr. Phillotson, but for the most part they are drawn to those of about their own age and their own generation. Michael Henchard, after his wife Susan's death, seeks out Lucetta Templeman, whom he had known previously and who is nearer his own age.

It is the romance that attracts the reader, both old and young, to Hardy's novels, along with their verisimilitude and the disappointments of hope, either before or after marriage, that lead to the altar or to the grave. In no instance does Hardy begin a novel with an already married couple, except in *The Mayor of Casterbridge,* and they go their separate ways after the transaction in the furmity-woman's tent and come together in chapter two eighteen years afterwards. Since Hardy's novels are predominantly courtships, there is considerable love play between male and female, with the object of sexual intercourse and marriage, in which frequently the female deploys to gain her end. One thinks particularly of the coquettish Bathsheba watching Sergeant Troy in his brilliant cavalry uniform performing a sword dance in the ferny glade for her alone, and of Eustacia Vye disguising herself as the Turkish Knight in the mummers' "well-known play of 'St. George,'" at Mrs. Yeobright's Christmas party for her son Clym, returned from Paris, and of Mrs. Charmond enticing Dr. Fitzpiers to her château on the pretext of an injured leg, and of Dr. Fitzpiers libidinal experience at the Midsummer Eve celebrations at which he seduces Suke Damsun. Hardy's males are very susceptible to feminine charms, and appear as their protectors—Diggory Venn watches over Thomasin and Giles is loyal to Marty South, Shepherd Oak warns Bathsheba about Sergeant Troy (which she resents and fires him for), Henchard risks his life to save Lucetta from an angry bull. They exhibit the normal emotions and jealousies toward their rivals, and often their character comes out under these stresses of assignations and elopements—Bathsheba sends Boldwood an anonymous valentine; Fanny and Sergeant Troy have a mix-up on whether they were to meet at All Saints or All Souls Church; Thomasin and Wildeve return unwed from Anglebury; after eighteen years of separation Henchard meets clandestinely with Susan at Dorchester's Roman amphitheater, "The Ring"; Arabella returns from Australia with Jude's son by her, 'Little Father Time'; and many more. These situations create the suspense in the story and caused Hardy's friend Mrs. Proctor (Nov. 1874) to write him: "You would be gratified to know what a shock the marriage of Bathsheba was . . . and to deceive such an old novel-reader as myself is a triumph."

In fact, it is the triangle of the marital relationship both before and after marriage that Hardy portrays naturally and without any moralizing in the conduct of his characters. He does not condemn any of them for their premarital relationships (Fanny and Sergeant Troy; Tess and Alec D'Urberville; Arabella and Jude), nor does he censure the unfaithfulness of Eustacia Vye or Sue Bridehead any more than he does that of his men. One would say from Hardy's novels that couples did not marry primarily to have children, and, of course, they did not in those days have automobiles or contraceptives to prevent having an unwanted child. The women show themselves to be friendlier to children than the men—Eustacia gives Johnny Nunsuch "a crooked sixpence" to tend her fire on Egdon heath, and allows Charlie, three years younger that she, to hold her hand at the summers' rehearsal of "St. George" in the shed, with "Well, 'tis over and now I'll home along." Sue accepts Jude and Arabella's child, "Little Father Time," and tries to make him feel that he belongs with them. Above all, Tess takes her illegitimate infant, "Sorrow," into the harvest field with her and bestows on it maternal love and anxiety, even in death.

Hardy exhibits the equality of the sexes and some of his greatest scenes are of men and women sharing physical work: Oak and Bathsheba wash the sheep, or deliver the ewes of their lambs; Giles and Marty plant the young trees in the orchard; Jude and Sue collaborate on a replica of Christminster, which is exhibited at the Fair and causes Arabella, glimpsing their looking at it, to say enviously, "Still admiring their own work, I see." If Hardy is saying anything, he is saying that a marriage based on mutual helpfulness and similarity of interests has a greater chance of success than one based on purely physical passion, such as Fitz-piers's for Grace, or Alec's for Tess, or Jude and Arabella's. Hardy's portrayal of Tess does not suffer from Hawthorne's puritanical attitude toward Hester Prynne, but each novel is, of course, a study of a particular milieu, and one is neither greater nor less than the other. Eustacia Vye belongs in the literary gallery along with Flaubert's Madame Bovary, and both depict realistically the fate of the romantic bour-geoisie after the Napoleonic Wars. To Hardy sex is a fact of life, not a venial sin, and, moreover, he is always aware of the economic uncertainties and vicissitudes that put a strain on his men and women's lives: Gabriel's loss of his unin-sured sheep; and, with only a few shillings to his name, Henchard's rise and fall from affluence to bankruptcy; Giles's loss of his lifehold property and his intended bride; the Souths' indigence and sickness; Jude's insecurity. These are all those things that resulted from the instability of society and that are the cause of "irritated humanity," add-ing economic discord to domestic life, and conjugal in-fidelity on account of the rigor of the marriage vow. Hardy approved of a freer divorce law on other grounds than adultery, and thought the marriage vow should be dissoluble when the marriage became intolerable to either party, a subject especially treated in *The Woodlanders*. In his atti-tude toward sex and marriage Hardy offended not only the Puritan moralists but also the feudal and legal institution of the church, which brought down the crash of broken com-mandments to the accompaniment of cymbals upon his head, or words to that effect, a complaint he made after seeing Ib-sen's *Hedda Gabler* and *Rosmersholm* in June 1893, with:

I could not understand the attitude of the English press towards these tragic productions—the culminating evidence of our blinkered insular taste being offended by the nickname of the "Ibscene" drama which they received.

This was the price one had to pay for writing in the English language, and sometimes it made him feel that a person must be a fool to stand up as he had done and deliberately allow himself to be shot at. Charles Morgan of the London *Times,* who interviewed him on the subject at Max Gate in 1922 after a performance at Dorchester of *Desperate Remedies,* his first published novel, was surprised at "the bitterness," with which Hardy spoke, and noted that "there was in him something timid as well as something fierce, as if the world had hurt him and he expected it to hurt him again." Hardy's poem "Spectres that Grieve," which appeared in the *Saturday Review* (Jan. 3, 1914), reveals something of the same impression, in the fourth and fifth stanzas.

> We are among the few death sets not free,
> The hurt, misrepresented names who come
> At each year's brink, and cry to History
> To do them justice, or go past them dumb.

> We are stript of rights; our shames lie unredressed,
> Our deeds in full anatomy are not shown,
> Our words in morsels merely are expressed
> On the scriptured page, our motives blurred, unknown.

The futility of the protest, voiced in the poem, developed twenty-four years after his protest in his essay "Candour in English Fiction" (1890), in which he stated:

Life being a physiological fact, its honest portrayal must be largely concerned with, for one thing, the relations of the sexes, and the substitution for such catastrophes as favour the false colouring best expressed by regulation finish that "they married and were happy ever after," of catastrophes based upon sexual relations [sic] as it is. To this expansion English society opposes a well-nigh insuperable bar.

It is significant that Hardy equated Art with Truth*
after Thackeray and Dickens rather than with Beauty after
Keats, whom he admired, and the romantic novelist Scott,
whom he soon outgrew, and, more important, that Darwin
trimphed over Newman, whom his friend Moule "liked so
much." "About Thackeray," Hardy wrote his sister Mary
(Dec. 19, 1863): "You must read something of his. He is
considered to be the greatest novelist of the day—looking
at novel writing of the highest kind as a perfect and truthful
representation of actual life—which is no doubt the proper
view to take. . . . *Vanity Fair* is considered one of his best."
This was, of course, only a young man's opinion—Hardy
was twenty-three—and probably should be discounted somewhat. One conjectures that Hardy's admiration for *Vanity
Fair* (1847–48), which was "a novel without a hero," and
also for *The Newcomes* (1853–1855), which was "a novel
without a plot," influenced him to subtitle his own first novel
The Poor Man and the Lady (1868) "a novel with no plot."
He had prefaced a chapter to it with a quotation from
Thackeray's *Book of Snobs* ("Come forward some great marshall and organize equality in society") that had appeared
in *Punch* magazine, from which Thackeray had resigned in
1854 on account of "a forthcoming article 'so wicked by
poor—' that I don't think I ought to pull any longer in the
same boat with such a savage little Robespierre." [84]

Hardy's youthful years in London opened his eyes to the
plight of the urban proletariat as portrayed by Dickens and
later by George Gissing, and enabled him to see that it was
even worse than that of the agricultural proletariat. In *The
Poor Man and the Lady* and in *Jude,* Hardy, like Dickens,
sided with the lower classes against the upper classes—unlike Thackeray, who paid scant attention to the lower
classes. Dickens had lived through the disillusionment and

---

* Hardy entered in his notebook (Aug. 1925): " 'Truth is what will work',
said William James. A worse corruption of language was never perpetrated"
(*Later Years,* p. 242).

perfidy of the First Reform Bill (1832) and exerted his literary talents with great energy toward attacking bad institutions—the workhouse and the debtors' prisons—which he and his father had firsthand knowledge of. Dickens knew better, as J. S. Mill did not, from experience than to expect Parliament "to make good laws for a state of society which had never existed in the world before," which Hardy had looked forward to envisioning in his poem "1967" (1867). In fact, by 1856, Dickens had become "quite an Infidel" in regard to political reform, whereas Hardy, in the disillusion-ment after the Second Reform Bill (1867), became an agnostic.[85] Moreover, Hardy had a background in nature that is lacking in Dickens's novels, and he was more influenced by Darwin's thought in a cosmic way. Hardy was greatly sad-dened to read the news of Dickens's death as he crossed Hyde Park on the morning of June 9, 1870.

The world of Dickens is larger than Hardy's, as London was larger than Wessex, and one has the feeling of a mass of humanity, in a physicist's terms, in Dickens as one does in Gissing's *The Nether World* (1889) and Gorki's* *The Lower Depths* (1903). In Hardy the emphasis is on the individual and the family—two people fighting alone against society as in *Jude,* not with masses of people on an epic scale, except in *The Dynasts,* who are ground down in the daily warfare of life. Yet there is not a novel of Hardy's in which one will not find criticism of bourgeois society and the marks of insecurity and poverty on human lives created by the Industrial Revolution and the emergence of the predatory bourgeoisie. There are fragments of naturalism in both Hardy's London and Wessex novels—flashes suggestive later of Gissing, Dreiser, Farrell, Remarque, Barbusse,

* Mr. Nevinson encountered Hardy arriving at Terry's Theater to attend a play by Gorky (Blunden, p. 120). In May 1907, at a dinner given by his friend Dr. Hagberg Wright, they met "M. and Mme. Maxim Gorky," having arrived late "after driving two hours about London, including the purlieus of Whitechapel, which he had mistaken for 'Westminster,' " Wells, Shaw, Conrad, Richard Whiteing, and others were there (*Later Years,* p. 124).

Masters, and others—Mixen Lane, "the *pis-aller* of Caster-bridge domiciliation" (*The Mayor*), Arabella's throwing "the pizzle" at Jude, the carnage of war in the prose descriptions following battles in *The Dynasts.*

Hardy's novels bear a closer affinity with George Crabbe (1754–1832) in his humanity toward the agricultural proletariat than with George Eliot (1819–1880). Indeed, Hardy's distinction between George Eliot's work and his own states the difference very well: "she had never touched the life of the fields; her country-people having seemed to him, too, more like small townsfolk than rustics; and as evidencing a woman's wit cast in country dialogue rather than real country humour, which he regarded as rather of the Shakespeare and Fielding sort." [86] Hardy declared that "Fielding as a local novelist has never been clearly regarded, to my mind: and his aristocratic, even feudal, attitude toward the peasantry (*e.g.*, his view of Molly as a "slut" to be ridiculed, not as a simple girl, as worthy a creation of Nature as the lovely Sophia) should be exhibited strongly. But," he went on, "the writer could not well be a working novelist without his bringing upon himself a charge of invidiousness." [87]

One feels Hardy's deep love for the peasants—particularly the women—"Fanny, Marty, Tess, Marian," in the novels, and his affectionate memory for the field-women of his childhood, "in curtained bonnets and light array," commemorated in his poem "At Middlefield Gate in February" (Bockhampton Lane), "a bevy now underground." They had been "young women about twenty when he was a child," and years afterward he recalled to his wife that their names "were Unity Sargent, Susan Chamberlain, Esther Oliver, Emma Shipton, Anna Barrett, Ann West, Elizabeth Hurden, Eliza Trevis and others." [88] Hardy's liking for unlettered rustics and his fondness for their homely humor transcends Sandburg's in *The People Yes* (1936).

Hardy had little patience with the sophisticated humor of the Comic Spirit of George Meredith, agreeing with

Ruskin that "humour always reveals a blind spot," and disliked the superficial refinement—"the minutiae of manners" —of Henry James, whose subjects, he wrote, "are those one could be interested in at moments when there is nothing larger to think of." [89] "Yet, I can read James," he added on May 14, 1915, "when I cannot look at Meredith." Walter Pater, whom he met in July 1886, he described as one "whose manner is that of one carrying weighty ideas without spilling them." He criticized "Howells and those of his school" (Oct. 30, 1891), for forgetting "that a story *must* be striking enough to be worth telling," or, as he said, "to hold the Wedding Guest . . . for we are all Ancient Mariners." Hardy "adhered to a dialectical aesthetic that 'the aim [of the artist] should be contrast,' and that ' a story should be an organism.' " [90]

The predominance of tragedy in Hardy's novels differentiates him from George Eliot, Thackeray, and Trollope among his contemporaries. His diary note following his observation of the differences between "church people and chapel people" (July 1876) expresses some misgivings on shortcomings that Thackeray came to have: " 'All is vanity' saith the Preacher. But if all were only vanity, who would mind. Alas, it is too often worse than vanity—agony, darkness, death also." Hardy's denial of an "all purposive Will" and "an eternally changeless moral law" inclines him toward Naturalism and "Fatalism: world of malignant chance," as Parrington classifies it. [91] But in portraying man's condition in bourgeois society, Hardy does not descend into the sewer as does Victor Hugo (1802–1885) in *Les Miserables* (1862), whose memory he thought "must endure," and to whose funeral "he and Browning sent cards attached to a wreath." [92]

Literature from the time of Sophocles through the Middle Ages down to Shakespeare had presented Kings and Queens, royalty, feudal lords, prelates, chivalry—"periwigged charioteers riding cock-horse to parade" in Masefield's words—but had paid no attention to slaves, serfs, peasants, or to "the men with the broken heads and the

blood running into their eyes." honored in Masefield's "Con-
secration" to *Salt Water Ballads*." Not until "the revolution
of 1789," Lukacs notes, quoting Father Brosette in Balzac's
The Peasants (1844), did they have "possession of the soil
from which the feudal laws had barred them for twelve
hundred years." [93] The former, it might be conceived, had
a self-originating will and their tragedy result from some
transgression of a moral law or an act of hubris punishable
by poetic justice, but hardly the latter, who were no more
than human chattel. This raises the questions, What is the
hubris of the poor? and whether we have learned anything
much except about bourgeois man? It was not until the
time of Defoe (1659–1731) that an English novelist regarded the poor as a worthy subject, and it is in Hardy's
rejection of the Aristotelian concept that partly lie his sub-
versiveness and impiety.

Hardy is, of course, a consummate artist. He can create
a feeling of oppressive heat (as he does in Mrs. Yeobright's
exhausting trip across the heath in *The Return of the
Native* and in the storm-breeding pre-harvest weather of
The Mayor of Casterbridge) as well as Keats does a feeling
of cold in his poem "On the Eve of St. Agnes," and sustains
it better than Hilda Doolittle does in her compressed
imagistic poem "Heat," or than Eli Siegel does in his
lengthy poem "Hot Summers Have Been in Montana." And
he can give us a portrait as colorful as a Van Gogh in Bathsheba's sitting on the front seat of the gig amid her bird-
cage and household effects, or a Rembrandt in Clym in
the shade of the settle at his mother's Christmas party for
him. Hardy can describe the stillness of a morning in the
country without dragging in Wordsworth's espistemologi-
cal beginning, "Dear God, the very houses seem asleep,
and all that mighty heart is lying still" ("Sonnet Composed
Upon Westminster Bridge"), as he does in Tess's awakening
the other dairymaids first and finally Angel for their day's
work at Dairyman Crick's at "a little past three":

The gray half-tones of daybreak are not the gray half-tones of the day's close, though the degree of their shade may be the same. In the twilight of the morning light seems active, darkness passive; in the twilight of evening it is the darkness which is active and crescent, and the light which is the drowsy reverse. . . .

At these non-human hours they could get quite close to the waterfowl. Herons came, with a great bold noise as of opening doors and shutters, out of the boughs of a plantation which they frequented at the side of the mead; or, if already on the spot hardily maintained their standing in the water as the pair walked by, watching them by moving their heads round in a slow, horizontal, passionless wheel, like the turn of puppets by clockwork.

They could see the faint summer fogs in layers, wooly, level, and apparently no thicker than counter-panes spread about the meadows in detached remnants of small extent. On the gray moisture of the grass were marks where the cows had lain through the night—dark-green islands of dry herbage the size of their carcasses in the general sea of dew. From each island proceeded a serpentine trail by which the cow had rambled away to feed after getting up, at the end of which trail they found her; the snoring puff from her nostrils, when she recognized them, making an intenser little fog of her own amid the prevailing one. Then they drove the animals back to the barton, or sat down to milk them on the spot, as the case might require. . . .

About this time they would hear Dairyman Crick's voice lecturing the non-resident milkers for arriving late, and speaking sharply to Deborah Fyander for not washing her hands.

"For Heaven's sake, pop thy hands under the pump, Deb! Upon my soul, if the London folk only knowed of thee and thy slovenly ways, they'd swaller their milk and butter more mincing than they do a'ready, and that's saying a good deal." [94]

D. H. Lawrence, probably thinking of Tess, criticized Hardy for his tendency "to make calamity fall on those who represent the principle of love," but granted when Hardy forgets his metaphysic, which must always obtrude when he thinks of people, and "turning [*sic*] to the earth, to landscape, then he is true to himself." [95]

Why are Hardy's novels great works of art? Was it be-

cause he "had mostly aimed at keeping his narratives close
to natural life and as near to poetry in their subject as the
conditions would allow," as he says, "and had often regretted that these conditions would not let him keep them
nearer still?" [96] There is much poetry in his novels, it is
true. Or is it because he depicted the individual in Wessex
and London well in his relation to other individuals in the
society of his time, which was suffering "a sea change" as
the result of expanding industrialism and world trade? Or
is it because he created a world of Wessex out of his native
Dorset and the Heptarchy surviving from Alfred's ancient
kingdom, and a world of Christminster, or Oxford, and its
environs, pointing up the still unsolved problems of bourgeois society in which "alas poor Theology" and the Code
Napoleon were irreconcilable dogmas.

Hardy was, of course, a product of his age. He had
strong feelings against bourgeois materialism and against
Capitalism's vested interest in Christianity. What interested
him in the personality of Christ was not Christ's mystic
origin, nor His promise of eternal reward for misery on
this earth in return for faith, nor Christ's "masochistic"
suffering. What interested him was Christ's zeal as "a
young reformer," which is evident in his poem "Panthera"
and his diary note (Nov. 10, 1905) on Zionism, in a letter to
Israel Zangwill, about "an autonomous Jewish state or
colony":

> So that if I were a Jew I should be a rabid Zionist no doubt.
> . . . "like unto them that dream"—as one of you said in a
> lyric which is among the finest in any tongue, to judge from
> its power in a translation.

One feels that fervor in his great tragic Wessex novels and
his still greater tragic London novel, *Jude the Obscure.*
Hardy depicts real people in their struggle, with all the
foibles that flesh is heir to, against inequalities of opportunity, insecurity of employment, deprivation of education,

the legal *rigor mortis* of inheritance, and the like, under a bourgeois system of society that resembled predatory Nature. Perhaps no one among his contemporaries shows quite so well as Hardy the human condition in rural England and in London in its transition from an agricultural to a mercantilist society. In a summation of his Wessex and London novels one is reminded of Marx's comment: [97]

> The foundation of every division of labour that is well developed, and brought about by the exchange of commodities, is the separation between town and country. It may be said, that the whole economical history of society is summed up in the movement of this antithesis.

and of William Morris's lines in "The Dream of John Ball":

> When Adam delved
> And Eve span,
> Who was then
> The gentleman?

Angel says to Tess:

> "I should have been glad to know you were descended exclusively from the long-suffering, dumb, unrecorded rank and file of the English nation and not from the self-seeking few who made themselves powerful at the expense of the rest." [98]

6

Constancy and Change

There are certain traits of constancy in Hardy's London and Wessex novels, and of change in his transitional novels, that will be considered in this chapter, foreshadowing his epic of the Napoleonic Wars, *The Dynasts* (1903–1906–1908).

One common denominator of all Hardy's novels is that they are about poor boys falling in love with girls in a class above them. The involvement in the story presents the deciduous-evergreen tree relationship of Hardy's early poem "Postponement" (1866), in which "being born to an evergreen tree," he explained to Vere Collins, "meant simply and solely having money," [1] and the deciduous tree not having it. Physical attraction, one grants, is the basis of natural selection in Hardy's romances, but the heroine's objection, or her parents', to the hero's not being good enough for her, follows class lines and provides the dilemma and suspense in the story's unfolding that derive from the displacement of "natural love by 'sordid ambition,'" [2] of bourgeois society, described in Hardy's short story "On the Western Circuit."

Will Strong of *The Poor Man and the Lady* (1868), re-named Egbert Mayne in *An Indiscretion in the Life of an*

Heiress (*New Quarterly Magazine*, July 1878), feels that Miss Allamont, renamed Geraldine Allenville, looks down on him because "he has never dressed for dinner or made use of a carriage in his life." "The feeling that she gave him that he was not worthy to marry a woman whose instinct said that he was worthy was a great anomaly he thought with some rebelliousness." [3] Geraldine acknowledges to him that she is not marrying for love. Egbert reflects:

> The only natural drift of love was towards marriage. But how could he picture her in a cottage as his wife or himself in a mansion as her husband? Both were alike painfully incredible.[4]

Egbert's grandfather advises him that "nothing you can ever do will root out the notion of people that where the man is poor, and the woman high-born he's a scamp and she's an angel." [5] Egbert tells Geraldine that his "grandfather's mind is disturbed on account of his having to leave the farm," due to her father's having "decided to enlarge the park," and he asks her: "Don't you think it would be possible to enlarge the park without taking my grandfather's farm? Greenman has already five hundred acres." To this she replies, "I—I will do all I can that things may remain as they are." [6] There are other examples of this sort:

> Edward Springrove's hope of marrying Cytherea Graye (*Desperate Remedies*) is not only ended by the destruction of his father's cottage by fire, on which the insurance had lapsed— an adversity which Miss Aldclyffe, the lady of the Manor, seized on to promote a match between her illegitimate son Aeneas and Cytherea—but Edward is also rejected by his cousin, Miss Minton, who married a well-to-do farmer, "old enough to be her father," who "has business in every bank, and measures his money in half-pint cups." Elfride of *A Pair of Blue Eyes* is disappointed to learn that Stephen's father is not "a Free-mason," as she had supposed, but only "a cottager and working class master-mason," and that his mother, though her people "had been well-to-do yeomen for centuries, was only a dairy-woman, having been left an orphan." [7]

Stephen's mother tries to comfort him, after Elfride has turned him down, with a derogatory remark about Vicar Swancourt: "You might go higher than a bankrupt pa'son's girl then." [8] Elfride's father is provoked at her for liking Stephen:

> "I have been deluded by having him here,—the son of one of my village peasants,—but now I am to make him my son-in-law! Heavens above, are you mad Elfride?"

Elfride reminds her father that Stephen's father "is better off than we are, they say, or he couldn't have put his son to such an expensive profession." The Vicar shakes his head scripturally, "Let a beast be lord of beasts, and his crib shall stand at the king's mess," to which Elfride bursts out, "You insult me, papa!" [9] He tells Elfride that he married Mrs. Troyton "for your sake," and that she has "three thousand five hundred a year . . . and a fair-sized mansion in town. Yes, Elfride, she is wealthy in comparison with us," and "you'll find she is not much to look at, though a good deal to listen to. . . . With your good looks, if you now play your cards well, you may marry anybody." Mrs. Swancourt runs Stephen down "in the tones of arch concern that so well became her ugliness":

> "My dear, you mustn't say 'gentlemen' nowadays. We have handed over 'gentlemen' to the lower middle class—where the word is still to be heard at tradesmen's balls and provincial tea-parties, I believe. It is done with here." [10]

"What must I say, then?" Elfride asks; Mrs. Swancourt replies " 'Ladies and *men*' always." When the Swancourts accidentally passed the Luxellians in London, "Lord Luxellian had looked long at Elfride"—one of the most natural "plants," to use a short-story analyst's term, to be found in literature. Mrs. Swancourt is a woman of more irascible temperament than Mrs. Melbury of *The Woodlanders*, who is "a placid woman, who had been nurse to his child Grace after her mother's death." To Ethelberta, as to Paula Power, and Elfride,

> there lay open to her two directions in which to move. She might annex herself to the easy-going high by wedding an old nobleman, or she might join for good and all the easy-going low, by plunging back to the level of her family, giving up her ambitions for them, settling as the wife of a provincial music-master named Julian, with a little shop of fiddles and flutes, a couple of old pianos, a few sheets of stale music pinned on a string and a narrow back parlour, wherein she would wait for the phenomenon of a customer.[11]

Bathsheba Everdene (*Far from the Madding Crowd*), a poor girl living with her aunt, advises Gabriel Oak, a shepherd, "to marry a woman with money who would stock a larger farm" than he now has; Gabriel, after losing his uninsured sheep, reflects: "Thank God I am not married; what would *she* [Hardy's italics] have done with the poverty now coming upon me." She inherits her uncle's sheepfarm; a bystander remarks to the unemployed Gabriel:

> "She've business in every bank in Casterbridge, and thinks no more of playing pitch-and-toss sovereign than you and I do pitch-half penny—not a bit in the world, shepherd." [12]

The lumber merchant Melbury (*The Woodlanders*) spends two hundred pounds a year on his daughter Grace's education at a genteel girls' finishing school and thinks, " 'Tis wasting her to give her to a man of no higher standing than he" (Giles Winterborne). His respect for Dr. Fitzpiers was "based less on his professional position, which was not much," Hardy says, "than on the standing of his family in bygone days." [13] Ethelberta, who wishes she were a man, rejects the poor musician Christopher Julian, who has composed music to her poem "When Tapers Tall," and surrenders to the wealthy Lord Mountclere, who has just pocketed a document, Hardy says,

in which romance, rashness, law and gospel are so happily
made to work together that it may safely be regarded as the
neatest compromise which has ever been invented since Adam
sinned.[14]

Picotee asks Ethelberta, "How much longer will the house be
yours?" and on Ethelberta's reply of two years, adds, "You
ought to marry before the house is gone if you mean to marry
high." Mrs. Yeobright, a vicar's daughter, does not consider
the dairy-farmer-reddleman, Diggory Venn, good enough for
her niece Thomasin, or Eustacia Vye, good enough for her son
Clym. She remarks, "She hasn't a farthing." When Clym reminds her that Captain Vye was in the Royal Navy, she replies, "No doubt he has been to sea in some old tub or other."[15]
Clym, a poor boy by choice, considers that his needs on the
heath are so few that he does not require much money, whereas Grace Melbury, on losing her purse that she valued more
than its contents because it was a gift, assures Dr. Fitzpiers,
who hoped "there was not much money in it":

> "Scarcely any. . . . Indeed money is as of little more use at
> Hintock than on Crusoe's island: there's hardly any way of
> spending it."[16]

Farfrae thinks Lucetta must be living on "capital" because
of her fine furniture. Somerset, brooding over Paula's rejection of him, recalls an earlier time "when poetry, theology,
and the reorganization of society had seemed matters of
more importance to him that a profession which should
help him to a big house and income, a fair Deïopeia and a
lovely progeny."[17] Owen asks his sister, Faith, "How many
thousands of women like you marry every year to secure
a home and mere ordinary, material comforts?" and Hardy
comments, "Marrying for a home—what a mockery it was!"
Similarly Somerset of A Laodicean "could not see himself
as the husband of Paula in any likely future," and Swithin
St. Cleve of Two on a Tower, the son of a curate and a
farmer's daughter, is said to have "two stations of life in

his blood." [13] Lucetta, as a young girl, "would hardly have looked at a tradesman," and recalling the past, reminds Henchard, "I was a poor girl then, and now my circumstances have altered [her aunt's bequest], so I am hardly the same person," and tells Elizabeth-Jane, "I wish I was richer, and your stepfather had not been offended." [19] Somerset cannot broach the subject of matrimony to Paula on account of "lack of social dexterity"; Paula tells him:

> "Delicacy is a gift, and you should thank God for it; but in some cases it is not so precious as we would persuade ourselves," to which he replies, "Not when the woman is rich, and the man is poor." [20]

Referring to Paula, Havill exclaims to Dare, "A girl with fifty thousand and more a year to throw herself away upon a fellow like that, she ought to be whipped," and Hardy says, "All the reasoning of political and social economists would not have convinced Christopher that he had a better chance in London than in Sandbourne by making a decent income by reasonable and likely labour," where "mediocrity stamped 'London' fetches more than talent marked 'provincial,'" as Faith tells Christopher.[21]

These instances recall Egbert Mayne's dejection over "what a vast gulf lay between that Lady [Geraldine] and himself . . . and how painful was the evil when a man of his unequal history was possessed of a keen susceptibility." [22] Angel Clare comes from a Low Church Evangelical family —a picture of his sister, who married a missionary in Africa, hangs on the parlor wall—yet Angel prefers Tess, who "can milk cows, churn butter, set hens," to Dr. Chant's daughter, Mercy, who plays the church organ and "glories in her protestantism," despite his father's objections, in his conviction "that a knowledge of a farmer's wife's duties came second to a Pauline view of humanity." [23] Similarly, Clym considers that Eustacia will make an excellent matron of his projected boarding school for farmers' sons in Bud-mouth. Egbert Mayne is bitterly aware that, "much as he loved her [Geraldine] his liking for the peasantry about him—his mother's ancestors—caused him at times a twinge of self-reproach for thinking of her so exclusively, and nearly forgetting his old acquaintances, neighbours, and his grand-father's familiar friends, with their rough but honest ways." [24]

The "poor boy" and "high-born maiden" are not found in *Tess*, nor in *Jude*. Yet they exist in Tess by a kind of complementary power in the spell that falls on Tess's father when the antiquarian, Parson Tringham, greets him as "Sir John" and tells him that he is descended from Sir Pagan D'Urberville, "who came with William the Con-queror as appears by Battle Abbey Roll." [25] "And where do we raise our smoke now . . . I mean, and where do we D'Urbervilles live now?" he asks. The parson replies: "You don't live anywhere. You are extinct—as a county family . . . gone down, gone down under." He declines Durbyfield's invitation to have a quart of beer "on the strength o't," and the old man, who has insisted that he "be just plain Jack Durbyfield," sits down alone with his reveries and sends a boy to the Pure Drop Inn for a horse and carriage. Tess's mother repeats the story of the family greatness "long back before Oliver Grumble's time—to the days of the Pagan Turks—with monuments and vaults and crests and 'scut-cheons and the Lord knows what all," concluding, "Don't that make your bosom plim?" Tess, stupefied, asks, "Will it do us any good, mother?" The Stoke-D'Urbervilles are not really "D'Urbervilles" at all, as Hardy explains:

Simon Stoke, who had made his fortune as an honest merchant (some said money-lender) in the North, conning . . . in the British Museum the works devoted to extinct, half-extinct obscured, and lost families . . . considered that *d'Urberville* looked and sounded as well as any of them, and annexed [it] to his own name for himself and his heirs eternally—never inserting a single title above the rank of strict moderation.[26]

Yet Tess's mother thinks that they may be their "wealthy kinsman," her father hoping that "D'Urberville blood will be her trump card," and her mother replying, "No, stupid; her face, as 'twas mine," and the children wailing, "I wish poor Tess wasn't gone away to be a lady." [27] Later, Alec tells Tess, "You *must* spell your name correctly—d'Urberville. . . . Good heavens, why dozens of mushroom millionaires would jump at such a possession!" [28] But Tess likes her father's spelling, Durbyfield, "rather best."

Marty's trump card is her note of warning to Giles, "written in charcoal":

> "O Giles, you've lost your dwelling-place,
> And therefore, Giles, you'll lose your Grace."

The meaning of the evergreen-deciduous tree is not only developed in the elm tree outside Mr. South's bedroom window, but also in Tess's impression of the D'Urbervilles' property on her arrival there:

> Everything on this snug property was bright, thriving, and well kept; acres of glass-houses stretched down the inclines to the copses at their feet. Everything looked like money— like the last coin issued from the Mint. The stables, partly screened by Austrian pines and evergreen oaks, and fitted with every late appliance, were as dignified as Chapels-of-Ease. On the extensive lawn stood an ornamental tent, its door being open toward her.[29]

Ethelberta declares, "I must get a Herald to invent an escutcheon of my family and throw a genealogical tree into the bargain in consideration of my taking a few second-hand heirlooms of a pawnbroking friend of his. It would be considered far more credible to make good my descent from Satan in the age when he went to and fro on the earth than from a ministering angel under Victoria," and at another point, gowned "in a dress sloped about as high over the shoulder as would have drawn approval from Reynolds and expostulation from Lely," she appeared at a country house that reminded her of a hotel for an entertainment of the Imperial Association. Hardy writes of her reactions:

> Not a single clergyman was there. A tendency to talk Walpolean scandal about foreign courts was particularly manifest. And although tropical travellers, Indian officers and their wives, courteous exiles and descendants of Irish kings, were infinitely more pleasant than Lord Mountclere's landed neighbours would probably have been, to such a cosmopolite as Ethelberta, a calm Tory or old Whig company would have given a greater treat. They would have struck as gratefully upon her senses as sylvan scenery after crags and cliffs, or silence after the roar of a cataract.[30]

In *Jude the Obscure* Jude's passion for an education has become a form of sublimated love, but because of the obstacles encountered in bourgeois society, it is as unattainable as the young woman "born to on evergreen-nesting tree" is to the young man of the poem "Postponement," who is "born to a leafless tree." Hardy's poem "To a Tree in London" has a particular application to Jude's tragedy and to the Negro's plight in American society today:

> Thus, black, blind
> You have opined
> Nothing of your brightest kind.

The stigmata produced by the blind struggle in the forest were "as obvious as a city slum" (*The Woodlanders*), and the parasitism of "the ivy that slowly strangled to death the promising sapling" [31] has its parallel in Christminster's *coup de grâce* to Jude's intellectual aspirations. Hardy knew from experience what Lady Ritchie, Thackeray's daughter, meant when she wrote him (Nov. 1874): "I hear that you are coming to live in stony-hearted London. . . . Our great fault is that we are all alike. . . . We press so closely against each other that any small shoots are cut off at once and the young tree grows in shape like the old one."

The economic disparities are depicted on a mass scale in the comparison of the shopping habits of the riding world and the pedestrian world in *The Mayor of Caster-bridge:*

> Together they [Lucetta and Elizabeth-Jane] saw the market thicken, and in course of time thin away with the slow decline of the sun towards the upper end of the town, its rays taking the street endways and enfilading the long thorough-fare from top to bottom. The gigs and vans disappeared one by one till there was not a vehicle in the street. The time of the riding world was over; the pedestrian world held sway. Field labourers and their wives and children trooped in from the villages for their weekly shopping, and instead of a rattle of wheels and a tramp of horses ruling the sound as earlier, there was nothing but the shuffle of many feet. All the implements were gone; all the farmers, all the moneyed class. The character of the town's trading had changed from bulk to multiplicity, and pence were handled now as pounds had been earlier in the day.[32]

"The farmer, in his ride, who could smile at artificial grasses," Hardy says, "look with solicitude at the coming corn, and sigh with sadness at the fly-eaten turnips, bestowed upon the distant upland of heath nothing better than a frown" (*Return of the Native,* p. 205). Wildeve, a civil engineer who has perforce retrogressed to bartender, tells Eustacia, "It seems impossible to do well here, unless one were a wild fowl or a landscape painter," and suggests that they go to Wisconsin (p. 98). Casterbridge, "as a representative centre of husbandry," closed its shops on the visit of King George IV, "to express its sense of the great services he had rendered to agricultural science and economics by his zealous promotions and designs for placing the art of farming on a more scientific footing"; the guests at the Royal Reception for the King are said to "fall apart 'by a process of natural selection.' "[33]

There are examples of sumptuousness and conspicuous consumption in Hardy's London novels that would have amused Veblen and that relate to F. Scott Fitzgerald's descriptions of the American parvenus: "the devils of indigestion," "the splitting headaches, and inward cusses of high society," and Ethelberta's "far from having the thoroughbred London woman's knowledge of sets, grades, coteries, cliques, forms, glosses, niceties," [34] and so on. Other instances are Paula's spending £100,000 on castle restoration and £6 a mile for her private telegraph line" (A Laodicean)[35]—"indulgent hobbies or things that people do since the family got rich," as they acquire "raked-up pedigrees" and "a mansion in town," or "as they build ruins on maiden estates and cast antiques at Birmingham," which are "made to look old" and are sometimes shipped to India for the tourist market* (A Pair of Blue Eyes); or as they collect "man-traps, spring-guns, etc.," [36] as Mrs. Charmond's husband did (The Woodlanders). Hardy observes in The Hand of Ethelberta:

> What was honest in Enckworth Court was that portion of the original edifice which still remained, now degraded to subservient uses. Where the untitled Mountclere of the White Rose faction had spread his knees over the brands, when the place was a castle and not a court, the still-room maid now simmered her preserves, and where Elizabethan mothers and daughters of that sturdy line had tapestried the love-scenes of Isaac and Jacob, boots and shoes were now cleaned and coals stowed away. (Pp. 330–31).

Blatchford in his book Merrie England has a word to say on how our " 'Noble' families got possession of their estates"

---

* Stephen writes Elfride from India: "One day I bought some small native idols to send home to you as curiosities, but afterwards finding they had been cast in England, made to look old, and shipped over, I threw them away in disgust. Speaking of this reminds me that we are obliged to import all our house building ironwork from England. Never was such foresight required to be exercised in building houses as here. Before we begin, we have to order every column, lock hinge, and screw that will be required. We cannot go into the next street, as in London and get them cast at a minute's notice. Mr. L. says somebody will have to go to England very soon and superintend the selection of a large order of this kind. I only wish I may be the man" (A Pair of Blue Eyes, pp. 223–24).

from Charles II's profligacy with Crown Lands, confiscated
by Henry VIII from the Church, by giving them to his
favorites—Henry Bennett, the Earl of Arlington, from whom
the Fitzroys were descended, and the Duke of Grafton, to
whom he gave a hereditary pension of £9,000 and a lucrative sinecure, which he "surrendered in 1795 for an annuity
of £870 a year—an arrangement ratified by the Act 46 Geo.
III., Cap. 89" (pp. 66ff).

Hardy at times appears to look back nostalgically to a
more communal society, which now existed only in a threat
to the harvest as depicted in *The Mayor of Casterbridge:*

> Nearly the whole town had gone into the fields. The Caster-
> bridge populace still retained the primitive habit of helping
> one another in time of need, and though the corn belonged
> to the farming section of the little community—that inhabiting
> the Durnover quarter—the remainder was no less interested
> in the labour of getting it home.[37]

Or he looks forward in *Jude* to an enlightened society, in
which we will consider that "all the little ones of our times
are collectively the children of us adults of the time, and
entitled to general care," and when, as he has Jude say,
"the father of a woman's child will be such a private matter
of hers as the cut of her under-linen, on whom nobody will
have any right to conjecture . . . ," and the right of divorce
will be available to either partner of a marriage when the
marriage has become intolerable.

These ideas are similar to those Marx expressed to Engels in his letter of March 25, 1868, "with regard to Maurer":

> Owing to a certain judicial blindness even the best intelli-
> gences absolutely fail to see the things which lie in front of
> their noses. Later, when the moment has arrived, we are
> surprised to find traces everywhere of what we failed to see.
> The first reaction against the French Revolution and the
> period of Enlightenment bound up with it was naturally to
> see everything as medieval and romantic, even people like

Grimm are not free from this. The second reaction is to look beyond the Middle Ages into the primitive age of each nation, and that corresponds to the socialist tendency, although these learned men have no idea that the two have any connection. They are therefore surprised to find what is newest in what is oldest—even equalitarians, to a degree which would have made Proudhon shudder.

Hardy finds them. The contrast is brought out not only in the communal harvest scene in *The Mayor of Casterbridge,* but also in Jude's collectivist attitude toward children, and conversely in Henchard's brooding rejection of Elizabeth-Jane when he learns from his dying wife's confessional letter that Elizabeth-Jane is not his own flesh and blood but sailor Newson's: "O you fool! All this about a daughter who is no daughter of thine!" [38]

One must attribute the difference in attitudes to education and to socioeconomic change: [39] the steam-engine in the threshing field, which has revolutionized agriculture, and the corn-drill in *The Mayor,* which is to revolutionize corn-planting, but has not been adapted to tree-felling in *The Woodlanders,* in which the handicraft system still persists. Contrast the curtailment of social intercourse accompanying work, for instance: Mr. Melbury "told ancient timber stories, as he sat, relating them directly to Fitzpiers, and obliquely to the men, who had often heard them before." The division of labor is more pronounced in *Tess* as the result of the introduction of "the primum mobile."

The old men on the rising straw-rick talked of the past days when they had been accustomed to thresh with flails on the oaken barn floor; when everything, even to winnowing . . . was effected by hand-labour, which to their thinking, though slow, produced better results. Those, too, talked a little. . . . The women on the cornrick—Marian, who was one of them, in particular—could stop to drink ale or cold tea from the flagon now and then, or to exchange a few gossiping remarks while they wiped their faces or cleared the fragments of straw and husk from their clothing.

These people were beyond the reach of the steam-engine and lightened their duties with social intercourse, "but the perspiring ones at the machine, including Tess, could not lighten their duties by the exchange of many words." For Tess there was no respite,

> for, as the drum never stopped, the man who fed it could not stop, and she who had to supply the man with untied sheaves, could not stop either.

It is in the Wessex novels that one finds the effect of the Industrial revolution, which was replacing men with machines, driving them off the land and depopulating the villages. Weydon Priors, to which Michael Henchard comes "travelling for employment," is such a place. A man tells him that

> "Pulling down is more the nater of Weydon. There were five houses clared away last year and three this; and the volk nowhere to go."

Likewise of Lady Constantine of the village of Welland, (*Two on a Tower*) which is without a parish, and Little Hintock of Mrs. Charmond, who assents to old man South's cottage being torn down after his death—a practice of land-lords, Marx notes, to reduce labourers' dwellings on their estates and thus reduce by half their responsibility to the poor" (*Capital,* p. 750). A notable example of moral and physical decay is the village of Shaston, to which Jude gravitates in search of work, of which Hardy writes :

> It was a place where the churchyard lay nearer heaven than the church-steeple, where beer was more plentiful than water, and where there were more wanton women than honest wives and maids. It is also said that after the Middle Ages the inhabitants were too poor to pay their priest, and hence were compelled to pull down their churches and refrain altogether from the public worship of God; a necessity they bemoaned over their cups in the settles of their inns on Sunday afternoons.

The question of the relationship of the individual in society to the family of man is raised again by Jude toward the end of the book. Running into his old friends—Jack Stagg, who had dubbed him "the Tutor of St. Slums," when they had "worked in repairing the college masonry," and Tinker Taylor, the bartender, who remembered his reciting the Apostles' Creed in Latin at his place, Jude is asked, "You don't seem to have done any great things for yourself by going away?" Jude, to Sue's dismay, insists on answering the cutting remark without personal rancor:

> It is a difficult question, my friends, for any young man— that question I had to grapple with, and which thousands are weighing at the present moment in these uprising times— whether to follow uncritically the track he finds himself in, without considering his aptness for it, or to consider what his aptness or bent may be, and re-shape his course accordingly. I tried to do the latter, and I failed. . . .
> However, it was my poverty and not my will that con- sented to be beaten. It takes two or three generations to do what I tried to do in one; and my impulses—affections—vices perhaps they should be called—were too strong not to hamper a man without advantages, who should be as cold-blooded as a fish and as selfish as a pig to have a really good chance of being one of his country's worthies.[40]

From this speech one can see how far Jude has developed socially from the ivory towerism of scholasticism on his arrival at Christminster, when he recited the Nicene creed in Latin to the habitués of Tinker Taylor's tavern. In fact, this social insight is what *Jude the Obscure* is mainly about.

The disappointment is all the sharper because Jude and Sue and the children are waiting for the academic procession to begin, waiting in the same spot by the circulatory theater where his meditation many years before had "convinced him at last of the futility of his attempt to be a son of the University." The "red-and-black gowned forms" of the academic community of Christminster seemed "like inacces- sible planets across an object-glass." [41] This emphasizes, in retrospect, the earlier experience at Christminster with his contemporaries, who looked at him in his workclothes, when he felt, "as far apart from them as if he had been at the antipodes," and, "in passing him they did not even see him, or hear him, rather saw through him as through a pane of glass at their familiars beyond." [42]

The London and Wessex novels are alike in this respect, that the situation was tragic "when the woman was rich and the man was poor." In the London novels, however, natural selection is modified by social and economic factors, although Hardy says that "when the heart was hot with a dream Pall Mall had much the same aspect as Wessex" (p. 224). Ethelberta's suitors seem, by comparison with those of Bathsheba, Eustacia, Grace, and Tess, sexless men. As Hardy says in his story "On the Western Circuit," "Sordid ambition has taken the place of time-honoured love," and bear out, as Marx said, "You can exchange love only for love" (*A Marxist Dictionary*, compiled by Morris Stockhammer, [New York: The Philosophical Library, 1965], p. 141).

Moreover, the Wessex novels bring out strongly England's capacity to feed her own population, contrary to the propaganda of industrialists in Parliament for legislation favoring themselves at the expense of the agricultural proletariat, beginning with the repeal of the Corn Laws in 1846, which Hardy recognized as a mere panacea. He was well aware from experience of the ruin wrought on agriculture without reading the statistics in the *Quarterly Review*, cited by Robert Blatchford.* Indeed, the Wessex

* Blatchford's table of the relative proportions of home-grown and foreign-grown wheat:

	Home-grown wheat	Foreign-grown		Home-grown wheat	Foreign-grown
1821	18,800,000	600,000	1861	21,500,000	6,706,000
1831	21,850,000	700,000	1871	19,278,000	11,661,000
1841	24,280,000	1,200,000	1880	12,152,000	22,352,000
1851	23,550,000	3,930,000		*Merrie England,* p. 248	

novels, from *Far from the Madding Crowd*, through *The Mayor of Casterbridge*, to *Tess*, establish the fact that the workfolk, on a subsistence wage, supplied not only rural England with mutton, corn, and milk but also London and lesser urban centers. The main reason for the pessimism of the Wessex novels is the farmworkers' loss of their freeholds that they had enjoyed as yeomen, and in their plight of not having any voice in Parliament. The urban workers, on the other hand, had the right to vote since 1867, and also the right to form labor unions, which was denied the farmworkers till Joseph Arch's union activities in the early seventies. Before then the farmworkers were kept in ignorance and subjection, which stifled their lives and reduced them to pauperism. That a haytrusser like Michael Henchard became a corn merchant was the exception. One finds him, in his ignorance, consulting a conjuror on the weather, or imagining that an enemy has cursed a waxen image of him, yet at the same time uttering that "a man must be a fool to mind the common risks of trade"; or he may condemn himself and view his adversities as God's punishment for his badness. But not so London tradesmen, like Ethelberta's brothers and Jude, who have been awakened by agitators of a Will Strong of *The Poor Man and the Lady* or a Jude, and have come to know that something was wrong with the social system and, like Jude, joined artisans' societies to improve themselves and their society. In *Tess* and *Jude*, Hardy most fully depicts the effect of the Industrial Revolution in Wessex and London, and both bear out the historical change.

Three of Hardy's serialized novels—*The Trumpet-Major* (1880), *Two on a Tower* (1882), and *The Well-Beloved* (1897)—represent a departure from the subject matter of the other novels—as a result on the one hand of his appraisal of his novel writing,[43] and on the other hand, of his desire to do something with his Napoleonic materials ever since reading Thackeray's *Vanity Fair*. He laid aside his unfinished poem "The Battle of the Nile" [44] (1868), and repeatedly visiting the Napoleonic veterans on Waterloo Day at Chelsea Hospital, where he learned that the father of James Gillray (1757–1815), the caricaturist, had been an outpatient, having lost one arm at the battle of Fonteney, and that the sexton at the Moravian burial grounds had been there for forty years, and that his son was born there.

Before we go into this matter, however, it is necessary to consider the dilemma in which Hardy found himself in 1880. Neither *The Hand of Ethelberta* (1876) nor *The Return of the Native* (1878) was the success that *Far from the Madding Crowd* (1874) had been, many copies of both novels having been left to the printer to be remaindered. In his return to his grandfather's time in *The Trumpet-Major*, Hardy seems to have been repeating his course following the rejection of *The Poor Man and the Lady*, when he had written *Under the Greenwood Tree* (1872), "the story of humble life" of the earlier time. One wonders why he did not write the story of "the 6 farm labourers at Tolpuddle in Dorset" or "the Tolpuddle Martyrs," [45] as Marx named them. It would have taken less research than he was to spend even on *Two on a Tower*, for which he is to be commended, however, for showing a young man interested in plotting the stars of the southern hemisphere rather than shooting big game, marrying an African princess, or dying a hero's death in a war against the Boers or the Zulus in the race for empire, as so many of the novelists from Kipling down were doing. Instead, Hardy "copied passages from the contemporary newspapers, drawings of costumes, details from Gillray caricatures &C.," [46] for the *Trumpet-Major*, at the British Museum, to supplement the hearsay of his grandfather's time, prompted by the same desire for accuracy that led him to visit the Royal Observatory at Greenwich and to correspond with W. C. Unwin about lenses for the writing of *Two on a Tower*, in which he wanted "to make science," as he wrote his friend Edmund Gosse, "not the mere padding of a romance but the actual vehicle of romance."

Neither novel "took hold," however, and he turned back to Casterbridge during "the hungry forties" for *The Mayor* (1886) and to Little Hintock forest for *The Woodlanders* (1887), the novel he had laid aside after finishing *Far from the Madding Crowd.* He called *The Mayor* "mere journeywork, and cared little about it as art," Mrs. Hardy says, "though he admitted [of the plot] that it was quite coherent and organic." [47] In *The Woodlanders* we see the emergence of the household system into home industry—seasonal piecework "where loss of time in one part of the day or week can be made good by subsequent overtime, or by night work" (*Capital,* p. 523), as with Marty's fabricating spars, and exhibiting "anarchy of production that in its turn pre-supposes unbridled exploitation of labour-power by the capitalist." "The completion of *The Woodlanders,*" Hardy wrote (Dec. 31, 1887) has "enabled me to hold my own in fiction, whatever that may be worth." He fancied he "had damaged [*The Mayor*] more recklessly than any other of his novels as an artistic whole" by his "aiming to get an incident into almost every part . . . ," a self-criticism that bears out J. W. Beach's critique:

> Plot was, for Hardy, the one thing needful. . . . He seems to have read life in terms of action. And he craved moreover complication of incident, a web of action crossing and re-crossing.[48]

Hardy's dissatisfaction with "the novel of physical sensation," in which *The Mayor* abounds, is revealed in a journal note of January 14, 1888:

> A "sensation novel" is possible in which the sensationalism is not casualty, but evolution; not physical but psychical. . . . The difference between the latter kind of novel and the novel of physical sensationalism—*i.e.* personal adventure, etc., is this: that whereas in the physical the adventure itself is the

subject of interest, the psychical results being passed over as commonplace, in the psychical the casualty or adventure is held to be of no intrinsic interest, but the effect upon the faculties is the most important matter to be depicted.

In this note Hardy seems to have been looking forward to the psychosomatic experiences he had touched on in old Mr. South's illness in *The Woodlanders,* in Rhoda Brook's inexplicably blighted "left arm" in his short story "The Withered Arm," and in the kiss in "The Marchioness of Stonehenge." He recognized that

what has been written cannot be blotted," and that "Each new style of novel must be the old with added ideas, not an ignoring and avoidance of the old." Looking around on a well-selected shelf of fiction or history [Easter Sunday, 1885], he noted: "how few stories of any length does one recognize as well told from beginning to end! The first half of this story, the last half of that, the middle of another."[49]

It seemed to him that "the modern art of narration was in its infancy." He had considered his novel-writing "mere journeywork" up to this time (May 1886) and "cared little about it as an art." He had been troubled with having something to say of "a real literary message" ever since finishing *Far from the Madding Crowd;* and in *Tess* and *Jude* he concentrated on it in artistic terms. In fact, he had written Swinburne (Nov. 10, 1893) that "it required an artist to see that the plot (of *Jude*) is almost geometrically constructed— I ought not to say *constructed,* for beyond a certain point, the characters necessitated it, and I simply let it come."

Some insight into his literary predicament is revealed in his conversation in 1919 with Charles Morgan, later literary editor of the London *Times,* who asked him why he did not write any more stories? Hardy explained that his stories "were all written, and that if he wrote a story now, they would want it to be what the old ones were."

The Well-Beloved (1897) was not like the old ones. It

was entirely different from anything he had written before, and it is related to the development of the supernatural part of *The Dynasts* as *The Trumpet-Major* is to the historical part and as *Two on a Tower* is to *The Dynasts* setting. The dramalike shape of *The Dynasts* is evident in some of the chapter titles of the historical novel: "Later in the Evening of the Same Day" (chapter 14) and "A Sailor Enters" (chapter 35). One can hardly agree with Michael Millgate's opinion (quoting Michael Edwards's thesis) that "*The Trumpet-Major* falls outside the category of historical fiction as practiced by Scott and analysed by Georg Lukacs." [50] This judgment overlooks Lukacs's commendation of Scott and Balzac, who he said, "tolerate the appearance of great historical figures only as secondary characters." [51] This is Hardy's method of presenting George III in *The Trumpet-Major;* moreover, it neglects the impressment of sailors in the Royal Navy, the drilling of recruits on the church grounds and the storage of pikes in the church vestibule, and makes no mention of the novel's importance in the development of *The Dynasts.*

On finishing *The Trumpet-Major* (1880), Hardy found himself in the tantalizing position of having touched the fringe of a vast international tragedy, he says in the preface to *The Dynasts*, "without being able to find the cosmic perspective and a philosophic mode." He found "the stellar universe" and the "larger canvas" in *Two on a Tower*, and in *The Well-Beloved* "the spectral tone"—"the deeper reality," or "abstract realisms" that he had been searching for since 1880 "as a framework to enclose the historical part." [52]

Leslie Stephen regretted that Hardy had not offered his historical novel to him for *The Cornhill*, but Hardy had been led to believe, from Stephen's reply (June 1879), that he would not be interested in it:

> I can only tell you what is my own taste, but I rather think that my taste is in this case the common one. I think that a historical character in a novel is almost always a nuisance;

but I like to have a bit of history in the background, so to speak; to feel that George III is just around the corner, though he does not present himself in full front.

This lively romance depends on the villagers' anxiety over Napoleon's being "just around the corner," and also on who is to win the widow Garland's daughter, Anne—the squire's son, Festus Derriman; or Miller Loveday's son, John, the trumpet-major of the cavalry company, dispatched to defend the coast; or his younger brother Bob, a sailor on Nelson's flagship *Victory*. The story, because the invasion did not come off, takes on a mock-heroic quality that is barely saved by the Press Gang's rounding up able-bodied seamen for His Majesty's fleet, and by Bob's reenlisting and coming home, after Trafalgar, with a scar on his face and a hole in his head. The threat is treated with a mixture of humor and irony in the disappointment of miller Loveday and in the Garlands' not being able to celebrate their delivery by Providence, because the miller's man, David, on hearing that "The French have landed!" had turned the spigots on the cider casks. This was, Hardy told William Archer, "a literal fact." [53] The scenes around the old flour and grist mill give a reality to the life of the Overcombe inhabitants and emphasize, by contrast, their peaceful existence disrupted by war in the manner of the stage directions and the Pities' speeches before and after battles in *The Dynasts*.

The Trumpet-Major, which Hardy's wife Em thought "nice," [54] was devoid of that serious, deeper quality in his nonhistorical novels and particularly of *The Dynasts* in his attitude toward and criticism of war. There is none of the class consciousness or class antagonism that he was to put into *The Dynasts*, since everyone is feeling one hundred percent patriotic and nationalistic, like the widow Garland, who exclaims at the Weymouth water-games, "Thank God, I have seen my King!" [55] One is reminded of Mrs. Penny (*Under the Greenwood Tree*) who, Hardy says, "like all good wives, however much she was inclined to play the Tory to her husband's Whiggism and *vice versa*, in times of peace, she coalesced with him heartily enough in times of war," [56] and of The Prince of Wales's remark to the royal Spanish refugees in *The Dynasts:* "Señor Viscount: When Government and opposition do agree, their unanimity is wonderful!" [57] The only exceptions to this are the fine scene of the village men being drilled on the churchyard grounds, which precedes the rumor of invasion, and Hardy's caustic comment that "the religion of the country had, in fact, changed from love of God to hatred of Napoleon Bonaparte, and as if to remind the devout of this alteration, the pikes for the pikemen (All those accepted men who were not otherwise armed) were kept in the church of each parish." [58]

Some of the characters in the novel appear in *The Dynasts* at the Weymouth water-games of "single-stick" and "grinning through horse-collars," honoring the King, who tells Fox, "I am interested in whatever entertains my subjects," and invites him to lay aside affairs of state and join the royal party, which includes "Mr. Phipps the oculist—not the least important to me," and later some of the enlisted men at Mrs. Loveday's party honoring the miller's son John, the trumpet-major, and a local boy.[59] The description of Anne's watching Bob's ship *Victory* shrink to the size of a feather, till it finally is no more than "a dead fly's wing on a sheet of spider's web" [60] shows that Hardy was beginning to view his drama, if not from a great height, at least from a great distance, and with some insight into the intrigue of "the international tragedy." One of the most memorable and Hardyan passages in the novel is the description of sailor Bob Loveday, who, although he "had been all over the world from Cape Horn to Pekin, and from India's coral strand to the White Sea, the most conspicuous of all the marks that he had brought back with him was an increased resemblance to his mother, who had lain all the time beneath Overcombe church wall." [61] There is no reference to his part in extending the daylight in the British Empire, but there is to his bringing back some souvenirs for his family and for Anne. Nor does Hardy have anything to say about the sanguinary exploits as did the voluble old crippled veterans at Chelsea Hospital, whom he and his wife listened to on Waterloo Day anniversaries.

In the novel *Two on a Tower*—"his story moving in an astronomical direction"—Hardy employs astronomy as he had geology in *A Pair of Blue Eyes*. Knight's reflection on the fossil-imbedded cliff, that "he was to be with the small in his death," [62] is a transient fear lasting a few paragraphs, whereas Swithin and Lady Constantine's agoraphobia that "whatever the stars were made for, they were not made to please our eyes," [63] permeates the whole book. Hardy remarks that "it is just the same in everything; nothing is made for man," and that "until a person has thought out the stars and their interspaces, he has hardly learned that there are things much more terrible than monsters of shape—namely, monsters of magnitude, without known shape." [64] This statement is like a paraphrase of the passage in *The Dynasts*, except that the prose in the novel is transformed into poetry:

> *Yet but one flimsy riband of Its web*
> *Have we here watched in weaving—Web Enorme,*
> *Whose furthest hem and selvage may extend*
> *To where the roars and plashings of the flames*
> *Of earth-invisible suns swell noisily,*
> *And onwards into ghastly gulfs of sky,*
> *Where hideous presences churn through the dark—*
> *Monsters of magnitude without a shape,*
> *Hanging amid deep wells of nothingness.*
>
> *Yet seems this vast and singular confection*
> *Wherein our scenery glints of scantest size,*
> *Inutile all—so far as reasonings tell.*[65]

And:

> *Christianity . . . a local thing. . . .*

The stars—instead of being companionable personifications of God's watchfulness over humanity as in *Far from the Madding Crowd,* or places that one can escape to where life is happier than on earth as Tess imagines them to be— are the anatomy of the Immanent Will, the unconscious, unteleological force of *The Dynasts,* in a subhuman form that has not yet developed consciousness but is in the process of doing so. "Astronomy of all the sciences," Hardy declares, "alone deserves the character of the terrible" (*Two on a Tower*) and he adds, "There is something in the inexorably simple logic of such men which partakes of the cruelty of the natural laws that are their study." [66]

The gist of *Two on a Tower* is given in an advertisement Hardy drew up for the publisher: "the story of the unforeseen relations into which a lady and a youth many years her junior were drawn by studying the stars together; of her desperate situation through generosity to him, and of the reckless *coup d'audace* by which she effected her deliverance." [67] The student-patron relationship between Lady Constantine and Swithin, who is looking at "a cyclone in the sun" through his telescope when she comes upon him in a crow's-nest of a column on her estate (chapter 1), develops into love and they are married secretly, she supposing her husband on safari in Africa is dead, and knowing nothing of Swithin's disregarding his uncle's bequest of £600 a year for life provided that he remained single until he was twenty-five.[68] On learning this, Lady Constantine, or Viviette, releases him from his marriage vow so that he can pursue his study of the southern stars. Then, discovering her pregnancy after he has sailed, she marries Bishop Torkingham, who had apologized for proposing to her before confirmation of the death of her husband, Sir Blount, who had married a tribal princess. The Bishop dies, and Stephen, returning home, although repulsed at first by Viviette's wasted physical condition, recalls that her devotion to him had transcended mere physical beauty. The joy of their reunion is too much for her weak heart and she dies, leaving him to comfort their little son.

Her asking him early in their courtship, "Without the Church to cling to what have we?" and his reply "Each other," recall Matthew Arnold's lovers "on the receding sea of Faith" in the poem "Dover Beach":

> Ah, Love let us be true
> To one another! . . .

Swithin's "wild wish for annihilation" during his illness arises from his disappointment that another astronomer has beaten him to the publication of his research—possibly a reference to the Darwin-Wallace research carried on independently. There is a scene where Swithin is roused by old Hannah's mentioning a comet during his delirium: "Well, tell me, tell me . . . Is it Gambart's? Is it Charles the Fifth's, or Halley's or Faye's or whose?"[*] The faithful Hannah replies "Hush," thinking him delirious again," and in the tones of Milton's "Sonnet on his Blindness," replies, " 'Tis God A'Mighty's, of course." [69] There is a detachment from life that seems to envelop the actors in the story in a sort of nebulous haze that anticipates the use of clouds and mists in *The Dynasts*.

The Well-Beloved (1897), which Hardy says he had sketched "when comparatively a young man, and interested in the Platonic idea," describes the quest for the Platonic ideal.[70] and its earlier title *The Pursuit of the Well-Beloved* better describes that quest. It seems to have been suggested by Shelley's lines "In many mortal forms I rashly sought the shadow of that idol of my thought," [71] as exemplified also by Proust many years later," Mrs. Hardy says. "The novel is entirely modern in date and subject," Hardy informed his publisher, and it "embraces both extremes of society, from

[*] See Hardy's poem "The Comet at Yell'ham" (*Collected Poems*, p. 138), of which he wrote "The comet appeared I think, in 1858 or 1859—a very large one—and I remember standing and looking at it as described" (Purdy, p. 115).

peers, peeresses and other persons of rank and culture, to villagers," [72] of which it may be noted there are a great number in *The Dynasts*.

Considering the personae of the novel and the slightness of the theme, it is surprising that Hardy, by his economy of style, made it as good a novel as it is. The characters are not people of flesh and blood that the reader can believe in, yet this is the very effect that Hardy consciously tried to achieve. The incorporeality of the characters and the abstractions of the quarriers' world are combined to give an insubstantial dreamlike quality that is found to a lesser extent in the setting of *A Pair of Blue Eyes*, with Lyonnesse: "a region of dream and mystery," in which the landscape and "the eternal soliloquy of the waters . . . lent . . . an atmosphere like the twilight of a night vision." [73] The sculptor Pierston frequently becomes a spirit: "Pierston was as he had sometimes seemed to be in a dream," Hardy writes, "unable to advance toward the object of pursuit unless he could have gathered up his feet into the air." [74] The spirits in *The Dynasts* have this power of levitation.

One of the extraordinary features of the novel is the way in which Hardy keeps the balance between the tangible and abstract, achieving the willing suspension of disbelief, in Coleridge's phrase, that gives credence to the fantasy. By studied performance Hardy has reduced the material world and the lives of his characters to abstractions and essences—"abstract realisms—to be the Realities hitherto called abstractions"—which he was coming to believe were "the true realities of life." [75] Hardy never takes Pierston to the quarries, but only to the "Top-o'Hill-as the summit is mostly called," where we view through his eyes "the busy doings in the quarries beyond, where the numerous black hoisting-cranes scattered over the central plateau had the appearance of a swarm of crane-flies resting there." [76] This is all the more phenomenal considering that Hardy's father was a builder and contractor and that Hardy himself was an architect with an expert's knowledge of stone and brick. One recalls Hardy having Lord Mountclere show the external walls of Enckworth Court, "veneered with massive and solid freestone," to King George, who exclaims, "Brick, brick, brick" (*The Hand of Ethelberta*, p. 330). Hardy had great admiration for Portland stone and Purbeck marble, and a romantic interest in the Isle of Slingers. Many times he and Mrs. Hardy had walked around "the Triangle," as they called it—"down the lane by the side of our house, and along the cinder-path beside the railway line," stopping to watch "a goods train carrying away huge blocks of Portland stone." [77]

Moreover, in the Wessex novels Hardy had faithfully portrayed the occupations of his characters in earning their livelihood, as Chew has observed[78]—the shepherds' world (*Far from the Madding Crowd*), the grain merchants world (*The Mayor of Casterbridge*), the lumber business (*The Woodlanders*), the dairy industry (*Tess of the D'Urbervilles*), the stone-mason's trade (*Jude*); but in *The Well-Beloved* the physical and economic aspect is conspicuously absent, or very rarely alluded to. The rivalry between the two quarry owners, Pierston's father and Marcia's father, who hate each other as do Shakespeare's Montagues and Capulets,* is suggested in Bencomb's objecting to Marcia's marriage to a "hated Pierston," he having found Jocelyn's sire "a trifle too big to digest" compared to the "small stone-merchants" [79] in amassing his fortune. One is constantly reminded in the Wessex novels of the workaday lives of the characters to whom "labour suggests nothing worse than a wrestle with gravitation, and pleasure nothing better than a renunciation of the same," and that "the defense and salvation of the body by daily bread is still a study, a religion, and a desire." [80] The descriptive passage of Knollsea in *The Hand*

---

* "Jocelyn [Pierston] thought it strange that he should be thrown by fate into a position to play the son of the Montagues to this daughter of the Capulets" (p. 24).

of Ethelberta anticipates a fuller development in *The Well-Beloved:*

> The knowledge of the inhabitants was of the same special sort as their pursuits. The quarrymen in white fustian understood practical geology, the laws and accidents of dip, faults, and cleavage, far better than the ways of the world and mammon; the seafaring men in Guernsey frocks had a clearer notion of Alexandria, Constantinople, the Cape, and the Indies than of any inland town in their own country. This, for them, consisted of a busy portion, the Channel, where they lived and laboured, and a dull portion, the vague unexplored miles of interior at the back of the ports, which they seldom thought of.[81]

But in *The Well-Beloved* there is only a fleeting instance of the occupational hazards in the quarries in Avis II's letter to Pierston referring to her husband's accidental death in connection with the sculptor Pierston's pursuit of Avis I, his Platonic ideal, though the Aristotelian world.

In the postscript of a letter to Swinburne in 1897 Hardy wrote:

> *The Well-Beloved* is a fanciful exhibition of the artistic nature, and has, I think, some little foundation in fact.

Indeed, Hardy has given a kind of ecology to his species of Platonism, and states that the Isle of Slingers* is "a spot to generate a type of personage" that he has sketched. On the "peninsula carved by Time out of a single stone . . . standing out so far into midsea that touches of the Gulf Stream soften the air till February . . . and Fancies, like certain soft-

---

* Hardy may have read *Climate and Vegetable World throughout the Ages: A History of Both* (1847), by Fraas, whom Marx called "a Darwinist before Darwin," as well as "an agricultural expert" in showing that as a result of cultivation and in proportion to its degree the 'damp' so much beloved by the peasant is lost (hence too plants emigrate from south to north) and eventually the formation of steppes begins. The first effects of cultivation are useful, later devastating owing to deforestation" (D. Torr, *Marx-Engels Correspondence,* p. 237).

wooded plants which cannot bear the silent inland frosts,
but thrive by the sea in the roughest of weather, seem to
grow up naturally here, in particular, amongst those natives
who have no actual concern in the labours of the 'Isle.' " [82]

There is an instance of this bionomics in *The Dynasts*
(after Austerlitz): A spirit allays a woman's anxiety about
England's vulnerability ("She's lost her Nelson now"), with:

> *Sweet Lady . . .*
> > *We'll let seemings be.—*
> *But know, these English take to liquid life*
> *Right patly—nursed therefor in infancy*
> *By rimes and rains which creep into their blood,*
> *Till like seeks like. The sea is their dry land,*
> *And, as on cobbles you, they wayfare there.*[83]

She replies:

> > > I'd call you ghost
> > Had not the Goddess Reason laid all such
> > Past Mother Church's cunning to restore,

and bids him "Adieu, I'll not be yours to-night. I'd starve
first!"

The comparison of the Isle to "a great snail" or "the
head of a bird" [84] uses particularly well-chosen images to
express the corporeal and aerial correlatives of the theme
and to anticipate imagistically the truest treatment of the
idealistic spirits in *The Dynasts*, the one embodying the
concept of Time, the other the Spirit of the Pities.

The Well-Beloved is a kind of Odyssey of the artist as
Ulysses. Hardy speaks of Pierston's seeing "the rejuvenated
Spirit of the Past in Avis II," and remarks on Pierston's
thinking of his laundress as Odysseus did of Nausicaa that
"as the scientific might say, 'Nature was working her plans'
for the next generation under the cloak of a dialogue on
linen." [85] One can imagine what restraint Hardy exercised
in the selection of his material and to what reducing pro-

cesses of his imagination he subjected it in order to achieve the draughtman's symmetry, the Platonic impression of *The Well-Beloved. The Trumpet-Major* and *Two on a Tower* seem, in comparison, simple exercises in plot and narration. "The exact truth as to material fact ceases to be important in Art," Hardy wrote (1885); "it is a student's style."

The Well-Beloved was an experiment in which Hardy tried expressing some of his philosophical observations recorded in his journal note (March 4 1886):

> Novel-writing as an art cannot go backward. Having reached the analytical stage it must transcend it by going still further in the same direction. Why not by rendering as visible essences, spectres, etc. the abstract thoughts of the analytic-school?

"This notion was approximately carried out," Mrs. Hardy says, "not in a novel, but through the much more appropriate medium of poetry in the supernatural framework of *The Dynasts* as also in smaller poems." [86]

The transition novels served as a bridge between Hardy's novel-writing and his preparation to write his epic, *The Dynasts*. Their importance lies in that they helped to bring Hardy's Napoleonic materials into focus and to exert a coalescing influence on the historical and supernatural parts of the drama, without which they had been static and inert. But for these, *The Dynasts* might have been a ballad sequence, or a historical drama, or another novel like Thackeray's *Vanity Fair* or Tolstoy's *War and Peace* (which Hardy had not read, according to Macdowall,[87] and which he had read, according to Wright)* instead of the epic poem it is.

---

* Wright examined "The Hardy Memorial Library" in the Dorset County Museum, which included Nathan H. Dole's translation of *War and Peace* (4 vols., London, n.d.) and found annotations, *W. & P., in* Hardy's handwriting in these volumes (p. 223). He cites Emma Clifford's article "War and Peace and *The Dynasts*" (*Modern Philology* 54, no. 1 [1956]: 41–42) for his statement that "Hardy had now a source perhaps more significant for interpretation than for facts—*War and Peace*" (pp. 195, 222), but he notes that "Tolstoy's reliance on Christian theology was not acceptable to Hardy" (p. 226).

Hardy was not particularly pleased with *The Well-Beloved;* he was "much surprised, and even grieved by a ferocious review attributing immorality to the tale," of which he wrote to Swinburne, that "the writer's meaning is beyond me," and to an editor's inquiry on the subject, he replied, "No: I do not intend to answer the article on *The Well-Beloved.* Personal abuse best answers itself." [88]

"Such were the odd effects of Hardy's introduction of the subjective theory of love into modern fiction," Mrs. Hardy says, "and so ended his prose contributions to literature (beyond two or three short sketches to fulfill engagements), his experiences of the few preceding years having killed all his interest in this form of imaginative work, which had ever been secondary to his interest in verse." [89]

"Pale Beech
and Pine So Blue"

Hardy began writing poems at about the same age as the late Pablo Neruda, Chilean Nobel winner and defender of Allende's overthrown Marxist government in 1973—that is, at the age of fifteen or sixteen, and for the same reason "because he liked doing them." [1] He wrote some nine hundred poems* in all (918, Weber says, p. 280), between 1856, the date of his first poem "Domicilium," and 1928, the date of his late poem "He Resolves to Say No More, A Philosophical Fantasy,"published in his posthumous volume *Winter Words*** (1928).

---

* Mrs. Hardy states: "There is more autobiography in a hundred lines of Mr. Hardy's poetry than in all the novels." This was in reply to a letter (Oct. 30, 1919) inquiring "if *Jude the Obscure* is autobiographical" (*Later Years*, p. 196).

** This volume contains a curious poem, "How Dora Went to Ireland," written at the request of Clement Shorter, in memory of his wife Dora Sigerman Shorter, a passionate Irish patriot, who died 6 Jan. 1918, and was taken to Dublin for burial. It reflects Hardy's irony over the struggle for Home Rule, and he may have thought that ironically, D.O.R.A. had come to stand for the Defense of the Realm Act (1914–16), which was forced against Ireland during the bloody Easter Monday uprising (1916) by Lloyd George. Shorter was editor of the *London Illustrated News*, in which Hardy's novel *The Well-Beloved* was serialized (Oct. 1–Dec. 17, 1897) and

The necessity of earning a living delayed his becoming a poet. His classical studies during his apprenticeship years (1856–1862), with Mr. Hicks of Dorchester, precluded the writing of poetry, and his first three years in London working at Blomfield's architectural office left him little time for the Muse. London and the Great Exhibition absorbed his cultural interests and his night classes in shorthand (1862–63) and in French (1865–66), under Professor Stièvenard,[2] "the most charming Frenchman I ever met," occupied most of his spare time. Moreover, Nature, as he had known it in Wessex, was nonexistent in the City to stimulate his poetic expression in the old way, and the multiplicity of experiences in London was still too fresh and bewildering to stimulate it in the new way.

He read a good deal of English poetry in his lodgings— evenings—Byron's *"Childe Harold* and [Moore's] *Lallah Rookh*, till ½ past 12," on July 2, 1865," and he also wrote between 1865 and 1867, some seventeen poems, many of them adumbrated with date and the address of Westbourne Park Villas. Some of these he had planned to use in his first novel, *The Poor Man and the Lady* (1868), "a story with no plot, containing some original verses"; "others were dissolved into prose" in his first published novel, *Desperate Remedies* (1871), "it having been unanticipated at that time that they might see the light."[3] Poetry "he had just been able to keep alive from his early years, half in secrecy, under the pressure of magazine writing."[4] "He had always "wanted to write poetry in the beginning," he told Charles Morgan, an undergraduate at Oxford who had asked him in 1920 why he didn't write any more stories; "now I can."[5] At first "he had found an awkwardness in getting back to an expression in numbers," Mrs. Hardy* says, "but that soon wore off."[6] Be-

---

later of *The Sphere* and *The Tatler.* He also published some of Hardy's anti-war poems and essays. (See R. Purdy, *Thomas Hardy, a Bibliographical Study*, pp. 349–50.)

* Mrs. Hardy says further that he "shaped his poetry accordingly, introducing metrical pauses, and reversed beats; and found for his trouble that some particular line of a poem exemplifying this principle was

tween the writing of *Tess* and *Jude*, Hardy began getting together some poems and making some sketches for *Wessex Poems* (1898), which he offered to take "the risk of producing . . . so that, if nobody bought it they (Harper & Brothers) should not be out of pocket." [7] They were willing, however, on the face value of Hardy's reputation as a novelist, to undertake the volume of poetry.

The criticism of *Wessex Poems* was typical of bourgeois critics, that "he had 'at the eleventh hour,' as they untruly put it, taken up a hitherto uncared for art," and later that he was "a realistic novelist who has . . .a grim determination to go down to posterity wearing the laurels of a poet," Mrs. Hardy says, but the fact of the matter was that "a sense of the truth of poetry . . . had awakened itself in him." [8] One might say that he had found Kant's "thing-in-itself" in poetry.

Hardy's poems have a certain quietude and composure, like his temperament that is his and his alone. How much of this was the result of his loneliness as a boy on the heath or in London as a youth, and how much of it was the result of his training as an architect, it is difficult to say. He does not exult in physical sensation for its own sake as Browning so often does, nor does he rise into the realms of abstract thought as Shelley does. Hardy dwells closer to the earth and to common experience, yet there is always some reflection on his observations—some "neutralization of experience," [9] as I. A. Richards calls it—that indicates that they

---

greeted with a would-be jocular remark that such a line 'did not make for immortality.'" Yet the same critic, he pointed out, might have discovered in one of our cathedrals "that the carved leafage of some capital or spandrel in the best of Gothic art strayed freakishly out of its bounds over the moulding, where by rule it had no business to be . . . or that there was a sudden blank in a wall where a window was to be expected from formal measurement [and] have declared with equal merry conviction, 'This does not make for immortality,'" (*Later Years*, p. 79). He was well aware that "few critics discern the solidarity of the arts, and indeed dwelt upon it in a little known poem, "Rome: The Vatican: Sala delle Muse,' in which a sort of composite Muse addresses him, 'Be not disturbed . . . I and my sisters are one'" *ibid*, p. 77).

passed through his mind and emerged with some meaning for himself that he would like to share with others. There is a "sad music" in much of his poetry that for want of a better word one would call pessimism, like the poem "Let Me Enjoy (Minor Key)," [10] from the group "A Set of Country Songs":

> Let me enjoy the earth no less
> Because the all-enacting Might
> That fashioned forth its loveliness
> Had other aims than my delight.
>
> About my path there flits a Fair,
> Who throws me not a word or sign;
> I'll charm me with her ignoring air,
> And laud the lips not meant for mine.
>
> From manuscripts of moving song,
> Inspired by scenes and souls unknown,
> I'll pour out raptures that belong
> To others, as they were my own.
>
> And some day hence, toward Paradise
> And all its blest—if such should be—
> I will lift glad, afar-off eyes,
> Though it contain no place for me.

A similar mood persists half way through the poem "For Life I Had Never Cared Greatly," [11] with the repetitive despondency of Poe's "Ulalume," but in the second half of the poem the depression is dispelled by Hardy's having discovered someone and something—(Love, Art), which fill him with joyous resolution.

> For Life I had never cared greatly,
>   As worth a man's while;
>   Peradventures unsought,
> Peradventures that finished in nought,
> Had kept me from youth and through manhood till lately
>   Unwon by its style.

In earliest years—why I known not—
    I viewed it askance;
    Conditions of doubt,
Conditions that leaked slowly out,
May haply have bent me to stand to show not
        Much zest for its dance.

With symphonies soft and sweet colour
    It courted me then,
    Till evasions seemed wrong,
Till evasions gave in to its song,
And I warmed, until living aloofly loomed duller
        Than life among men.

Anew I found nought to set eyes on,
    When, lifting its hand,
    It uncloaked a star,
Uncloaked it from fog-damps afar,
And showed its beams burning from pole to horizon
        As bright as a brand.

And so, the rough highway forgetting,
    I pace hill and dale
    Regarding the sky,
Regarding the vision on high,
And thus re-illumed have no humour for letting
        My pilgrimage fail.

This poem recalls the lines in his poem "When I Set Out For Lyonesse (1870)," about his meeting Miss Gifford: "A starlight lit my lonesomeness," and "My radiance rare and fathomless," when he came back, leading to their early married life at Sturminster-Newton, "our happiest time," [12] he wrote on March 18, 1877.

The cameo-colloquy, "Waiting Both" (p. 665), is a curious blend of the personal and the cosmic, the finite and the infinite:

A star looks down at me,
And says, "Here I and you
Stand, each in our degree.

What do you mean to do—
Mean to do?

I say: "For all I know,
Wait, and let Time go by,
Till my change come,"—"Just so.
The star says; "So mean I—
So mean I."

In the poem "A Sign-Seeker," [13] one feels Hardy's deep feeling for the earth and humankind, and a confrontation also with a pensive thought on personal extinction:

I view the evening bonfires of the sun
    On hills which morning rains have hissed;
    The eyeless countenance of the mist
Pallidly rising when the summer droughts are done.

I witness fellow earth-men surge and strive;
    Assemblies meet, and throb, and part;
    Death's sudden finger, sorrow's smart,
—All the various moils that mean a world alive.

. . . .

I have lain in dead men's beds, have walked
    The tombs of those with whom I had talked,
Called many a gone and goodly one to shape a sign,

And panted for response. But none replies,
    No warnings loom, nor whisperings,
    To open out my limitings,
And Nescience mutely muses: when a man falls he lies.

This feeling is expressed with joyous sadness in the poem "The Bullfinches," [14] which shows the keenness of Hardy's observation and his ability to translate a rhythmic flight into a verbal flow:

BROTHER Bulleys, let us sing
From the dawn till evening!—
For we know not that we go not
When to-day's pale pinions fold
Where they be that sang of old.

. . . .

Come then, brethren, let us sing,
From the dawn till evening!—
For we know not that we go not
When the day's pale pinions fold
Where those be that sang of old.

The greatness of this poem lies in Hardy's expressing a visual image in the exactly right auditory tones, describing the finches oscillating rhythm at times as one who has watched their soundless flight movement. The intervening stanzas are weighted down with heavy fantasy and heavier metaphysic, which spoil the poem; it is too bad that Hardy, with his fine eye and ear, did not detect the flaw and revise the poem.

Hardy's narrative sense is especially good, and his ballads have to do with common people who had never been deemed worthy subject matter by the anonymous folk balladists or their refined imitators. "The Slow Nature," [15] subtitled "An Incident of Froom Valley" (1894), is a Dorset tragedy, not elegant, of the quick and the dead.

"Thy husband—poor, poor Heart!—is dead—
Dead, out by Moreford Rise;
A bull escaped the barton-shed,
Gored him, and there he lies!"

—"Ha, ha—go away! 'Tis a tale, methink,
Thou joker Kit!" laughed she.
"I've known thee many a year, Kit Twink,
And ever has thou fooled me!"

—"But, Mistress Damon—I can swear
   Thy goodman John is dead!
And soon th'lt hear their feet who bear
   His body to his bed."

So unwontedly sad was the merry man's face—
   That face which had long deceived—
That she gazed and gazed; and then could trace
   The truth there; and she believed.

She laid a hand on the dresser-ledge,
   And scanned far Egdon-side;
And stood; and you heard the wind-swept sedge
   And the rippling Froom; till she cried:

" O my chamber's untidied, unmade my bed,
   Though the day has begun to wear!
'What a slovenly hussif!' it will be said,
   When they all go up my stair!"

She disappeared; and the joker stood
   Depressed by his neighbour's doom,
And amazed that a wife struck to widowhood
   Thought first of her unkempt room.

But a fortnight thence she could take no food,
   And she pined in a slow decay;
While Kit soon lost his mournful mood
   And laughed in his ancient way.

"A Trampwoman's Tragedy" [16] (rejected by the English periodical *The Cornhill* as unprintable "in a family magazine," and published in *The North American Review* [Nov. 1903]) Hardy "considered, upon the whole, his most successful poem." [17] It was based on incidents that occurred in 1827, and is narrated by a woman, a principal in the tragedy of a group of migratory folk. Too long to quote in its entirety, I give only three stanzas.

     Full twenty miles we jaunted on,
       We jaunted on,—

My fancy-man, and jeering John,
    And Mother Lee, and I.
And, as the sun drew down to west,
We climbed the toilsome Poldon crest,
And saw, of landskip sights the best,
    The inn that beamed thereby.

. . . .

Lone inns we loved, my man and I,
    My man and I;
"King's Stag," "Windwhistle" high and dry,
    "The Horse" on Hintock Green,
The cosy house at Wynyard's Gap,
"The Hut" renowned on Bredy Knap,
And many another wayside tap
    Where folk may sit unseen.

. . . .

Inside the settle all a-row—
    All four a-row
We sat, I next to John, to show
    That he had wooed and won.
And then he took me on his knee,
And swore it was his turn to be
My favourite mate, and Mother Lee
    Passed to my former one.

Then "her only love," asked her, "Whose is the child you are
like to bear?—*His*?" and though "God knows 'twas not!"
in despair she "nodded—still to tease." The fancy-man then
sprang up and stabbed jeering John "with his knife,"

    Ere scarcely Mother Lee and I
    Knew that the deed was done.

. . . . ,

> Thereaft I walked the world alone,
>   Alone, alone!
> On his death-day I gave my groan
>   And dropt his dead-born child.
> 'Twas nigh the jail, beneath a tree,
> None tending me; for Mother Lee
> Had died at Glaston, leaving me
>   Unfriended on the wild.

Johnny's ghost "rose up" and asked her, "was the child mine
. . . or was it his?" so that he "may rest in peace," and she
continues:

> O doubt not but I told him then,
>   I told him then,
> That I had kept me from all men
>   Since we joined lips and swore.
> Whereat he smiled, and thinned away
> As the wind stirred to call up day . . .
>   —'Tis past! And here alone I stray
>   Haunting the Western Moor.

The incremental repetition contributes a haunting effect to
the whole poem; it reminds one of Bret Harte's story "The
Outcasts of Poker Flat," but Hardy's treatment of his subject is not marred by Harte's sentimentality.

There are countless notes in Hardy's journal on county
history and observations of people and nature. Some of
these he made into poems like the one quoted above, or
like the one on the itinerant young musicians—sisters—in
the poem "Music in a Snowy Street," "who were," he wrote
on April 26, 1884, "what Nature made them before the smear
of 'civilization' had sullied their existences." There are still
others that show his poetic impulse, like his seeing, when
"coming back from Talbothays by West Stafford Cross, [he
saw] Orion upside down in a pool of water under an oak,"* [18]

* This recalls Heine's lines:
      The stars are at their loveliest in Paris

and like "his prose of a poetic kind," of which he did not designate his intent to make a poem. Every experience that becomes a poem has something to recommend it over an experience that does not become a poem. It is impossible to consider in one chapter all of Hardy's poems (to which J. O. Bailey has recently devoted a whole book, *The Poetry of Thomas Hardy: A Handbook and Commentary* [1970]), and I shall limit myself to a representative sampling to show the range of his poetic gift, which too often critics have narrowed down to a preconceived estimate of their own. I shall first consider Hardy's love poems, relating them to his aesthetic, and next take up other carefully selected and related poems that show both the range of his poetry and the coherence of his thought.

By far the greatest number of Hardy's poems are love poems. These may be classified chronologically into two main groups: the youthful love poems written in London lodgings and the mature love poems—particularly the "Poems of 1912–13," which relive his courtship of Mrs. Hardy after her death (Nov. 27, 1912), and to which he referred as "an expiation." [19]

These poems together form a close-knit body of verse. One can not fully realize Hardy's loss until he has read the poem "The Voice," [20] beginning, "Woman much missed, how you call to me, call to me," with its haunting, anguished tones, or the poem "The Walk" [21] on his returning from a walk to "the hill-top tree," which they used frequently to

> When, on a winter evening,
> They are mirrored in its puddles.
> (Atta Toll, verse 14, trans. Yvonne Kapp)

These lines Hardy doubtless knew, since he visited Heine's grave in the Montmarte in August 1890, and Engels quoted them to Marx's daughter, Laura Lafargue, in his letter dated 22 July, 1884 (*Engels-Lafargue Correspondence*, p. 217). Hardy glimpsed Heine's grave at Montmartre (*The Early Life*, p. 300), and had two volumes of Heine's poems in his library (R. Purdy, p. 117). In the eighteen-thirties Heine became a member of "Young Germany," an organization of youthful writers" against reaction and for a liberal German government (see Buckner B. Trawick, *World Literature* [New York: Barnes & Noble, 1955], 2:231).

take together. He is confronted by "the look of a room on returning thence." One may gather something of the collapse from which his second wife, Florence Emily Dugdale Hardy, rescued him in his poem to her: "I Sometimes Think (For F.E.H.)," [22] which ends

> For one did care,
> And, spiriting into my house, to, fro
> Like wind on the stair,
> Cares still, heeds all, and will, even though
> I may despair.

To understand Hardy's love poems one must go back to his journal notes during his youthful years in London:

> April 1865—There is not that regular gradation among woman-kind that there is among men. You may meet 999 exactly alike and then the thousandth—not a little better, but far above them. Practically, therefore, it is useless for a man to seek after this thousandth to make her his,

and the second note describing his loneliness:

> June 2 (1865) My 25th birthday. Not very cheerful. Feel as if I had lived a long time and done very little.
> Walked about by moonlight in the evening. Wondered what woman, if any, I should be thinking about in five years' time.

In his poem "In Vision I Roamed" [23] (1866) he describes his feelings as he "roamed the flashing Firmament . . . where stars the brightest here are lost to the eye," concluding that the beloved person—the one in a thousand—"though far away," is on this planet and "not on some foreign Sphere," while the poem "At a Bridal" (1866) expresses, with its church setting, the dilemma of the rejected suitor:

> When you paced forth, to await maternity,
> A dream of other offspring held my mind,

and condemns society's laws and false standards:

> Should I, too, wed as slave to Mode's decree,

> Each mourn the double-waste; and question dare
> To the Great Dame whence incarnation flows,
> Why these high-purposed children never were:
> What will she answer? That she does not care,
> If the race all such sovereign types unknows.

In a little-known poem "Discouragement" (1863–1867), he speaks of "a whole life's circumstance" being dependent "on hap of birth," which "is frost to flower of heroism and worth." [24] These lines remind one in another sense of his objections to speaking of a fine winter day, rather than of a criticism of the callousness of Nature. In his short story "On the Western Circuit," he describes "a gentlemanly young fellow, one of the *species* [italics mine] found in large towns only and London particularly not altogether typical of the middle class male of a century wherein sordid ambition is the master passion that seems to be taking the place of time-honoured love." [25] In the poem "A Poor Man and a Lady," [26] intended to preserve an episode in the novel by that name, the speaker is "a striver with deeds to do and little enough to do them with," and the person addressed is "a comely woman of noble kith, with a courtly match to make were you," in which he reflects at their parting:

> I saw you no more. The track of a high,
> Sweet, liberal lady, you've doubtless trod.
> All's past! No heart was burst thereby,
> And no one knew, unless it was God.

These poems throw light on the young man of the poem "Postponement" (1866), who has built a nest in "a leafless tree" for his betrothed, but she grows tired of waiting for him and marries someone else, "born to an evergreen-nesting tree." [27] She leaves him, meditating:

"Ah, had I been like some I see,
Born to an evergreen nesting-tree,
None had eyed and twitted me,
    Cheerily mating!"

and possibly refers to the misogynistic resolve in the poem "Revulsion" [28] (1866), after he rationalizes:

For winning love we win the risk of losing
And losing love is as one's life were riven;
It cuts like contumely and keen ill-using
To cede what was superfluously given

. . . .
So may I live no junctive law fulfilling,
And my heart's table bear no woman's name.

It will be recalled that Hardy told Vere Collins, who had asked him about the image of "the evergreen tree," that it "meant simply and solely having money," [29] and the deciduous tree, of course, the opposite. It is possible that this image was suggested by a tree designated as the "Reformer's Tree"* in Hyde Park, on a spot formerly known as "the Mound," where the Reform Leaguers held their meetings during the sixties.

This identification of the image not only sheds light on the impecunious situation of the youth in the love poem and on old man South's making the tree "his fugelman with abject obedience" (*The Woodlanders*, p. 108), but also provides Darwinian insight into the poem "In a Wood" [30] (1887–1896), in which Hardy describes the natural struggle in the forest in terms of the competitive struggle among men in London:

* Hardy was read in Adam Smith, Ricardo, and Mill, and Marx's censure of Mill's explanation of the cause of profit would have amused him, because food, clothing, materials and tools last longer than the time . . . required to produce them: "He here confounds the duration of labour-time with the duration of its products. Of course, it is very true, that if birds nests did not last longer than the time it takes in building, birds would have to do without nests" (*Capital*, p. 566).

But, having entered in,
    Great growths and small
Show them to men akin—
    Combatants all!

The different species of trees described in stanza 1 take on class meanings and reflect class antagonisms:

Pale beech and pine so blue,
    Set in one clay,
Bough to bough cannot you
    Live out your day?
When the rains skim and skip,
Why mar sweet comradeship,
Blighting with poison-drip
    Neighbourly spray?

Touches from ash, O wych,
    Sting you like scorn!
You, too, brave hollies, twitch
    Sidelong from thorn.
Even the rank poplars bear
Lothly a rival's air,
Cankering in black despair
    If overborne.

as they do also in Hardy's description of the human condition in Mixen Lane, "the less picturesque side to the parish":

Yet this mildewed leaf in the sturdy and flourishing Caster-bridge plant lay close to the open country; not a hundred yards from a row of noble elms, and commanding a view across the moor of airy uplands and corn-fields, and mansions of the great.

Its "inn [which was] called Peter's Finger was the church of Mixen Lane," with "a mere slit dividing it from the next building," and "[it had] a narrow door" into which a pedestrian "would vanish, causing the gazer to blink like Ashton at the disappearance of Ravenswood" (pp. 295–96).

The poem "In Tenebris" [31] (I, II, III, 1895–96)—in the shadows or gloom—suggests the forest of "In a Wood," and expresses more personally Hardy's anger at society during his youthful years at Blomfield's when his co-workers had criticized him for his lack of worldly ambition and also expresses his disgust at the rewards of a competitive society as managed by Tories and Liberals alike:

> The stout upstandars say, All's well with us; ruers have nought to rue!
> And what the potent say so oft, can it fail to be somewhat true?
> Breezily go they, breezily come, their dust smokes around their career,
> Till I think I am one born out of due time, who has no calling here.
>
> Their dawns bring lusty joy, it seems; their evenings all that is sweet;
> Our times are blessed times, they cry: Life shapes it as is most meet,
> And nothing is much the matter; there are many smiles to a tear;
> Then what is the matter is I, I say. Why should such an one be here? . . .
>
> Let him in whose ears the low-voiced Best is killed by the clash of the First,
> Who holds that if way to the Better there be, it exacts a full look at the Worst,
> Who feels that delight is a delicate growth cramped by crookedness, custom, and fear,
> Get him up and be gone as one shaped awry; he disturbs the order here.

Moreover, Hardy's images of deciduous and evergreen trees are curiously connected with his gambling images and his images of chance, which also derive from his youthful years in London and his feelings of anonymity there. His diary entry of April 1865—"The world does not despise us;

it only neglects us"—contains the emotional response to "the purblind Doomsters" addressed in his early poem "Hap" (1866):

> —Crass Casualty obstructs the sun and rain,
> And dicing Time for gladness casts a moan. . . .

One is reminded of Engels's observations on London where "everything is done by guess-work and at the mercy of accident";[32] also of London smog, which Hardy described in his letter to his sister as "having the colour of brown paper or of pea-soup," and as "rayless rime" in his poem "The Dream of the City Shopwoman" (1866). This explains Hardy's preference for Turner's later paintings such as *Rain, Steam and Speed* and *Snowstorm on a Steamboat*,[33] and his choice in setting on the heath [34] the gambling game in which Wildeve entices the simple-minded peasant Christian Cantle into gambling with the box of spade-guineas "that had lain there many a year (a hundred in all)," which Mrs. Yeobright entrusted him with delivering to Clym and Thomasin. Christian is fascinated by the wooden dice and even more by Wildeve's success stories of how to win money and influence people: "an Italian who sat down at a gaming-table with only a louie (that's a foreign sovereign) in his pocket . . . and won ten thousand pounds," to which Christian exclaims, "Ha—ha, splendid! Go on—go on!" Wildeve continues:

> "Then there was a man of London,* who was only a waiter at White's Club-house. He began playing first half-crown

* They recall Elfride's remark on Stephen: "It has become a normal thing that millionaires commence by going up to London with their tools at their back; and a half-a-crown in their pockets. That sort of origin is getting so respected, that it is acquiring some of the odour of Norman ancestry" (*A Pair of Blue Eyes*, p. 79;) and Hardy's comment: "So much for Norman blood, unaided by Victorian lucre"; and yet again on the stone house, "the old fashioned stranger instinctively said, 'Blood built it, and Wealth enjoys it,' however vague his opinions of those accessories might be" (*The Mayor of Casterbridge*, p. 160).

stakes, and then higher and higher, till he became very rich, got an appointment in India, and rose to be Governor of Madras. His daughter married a member of parliament, and the Biship of Carlisle stood godfather to one of the children."

The reddleman Venn° mimics Wildeve, whom he has overheard from a "neighbouring bush," as he wins back in the lantern light what Christian had lost:

"Won back his coat," said Venn slily. Another throw, and the money went the same way.
"Won back his hat," continued Venn.
"Oh, oh!" said Wildeve.
"Won back his watch, won back his money, and went out of the door a rich man," added Venn, sentence by sentence, as stake after stake passed over to him.

The peasant Hodge "thinks Lunnon a place paved with gold," Hardy remarks in the Dorsetshire Labourer essay (p. 169).

Worthy of note is a singular description of a soot-covered deciduous tree under which a "placid porter" is seated on a park bench in front of Bede's Inn.[35] It is obviously more than a bit of descriptive padding in that some meaning is given to the imagery by Marx's commentary on the sophistry of the legal argument of a lawsuit in 1862 when the juryman had "to decide whether soot is genuine

---

° Venn's exclamation "I've thrown nothing at all!" connotes "the hind" (a name for the agricultural labourer, inherited from the time of serfdom) and "fixed at the lowest possible amount on which he can live—the supplies of wages and shelter are not calculated on the profit to be derived from him. He is a zero in farming calculations" (Marx, *Capital* p. 745) Engels's observation in a letter to Bloch (Sept. 21, 1890) "because of the 'conflicting wills' in bourgeois society, they do not attain what they want, but are merged into a collective mean, a common resultant. it must be concluded that their value=zero" (*Correspondence*, pp. 476–77). Neither Venn or Wildeve gets what he wants, and poor Christian, of course, seems the example *par excellence.* This recalls Hardy's comment that "Stephen's father has in common with most rural mechanics too much individuality to be a typical 'working man'—a resultant of that beach-pebble attrition with his kind only to be experienced in large towns, which metamorphoses the unit Self into a fraction of the unit Class" (*A Pair of Blue Eyes*, p. 96).

soot in the commercial sense or adulterated soot in the legal sense," and "The *'amis du commerce'* decided it to be genuine commercial soot," Marx notes, "and non-suited the plaintiff farmer, who had in addition to pay the costs of the suit" (*Capital*, 274n). One may be sure that Hardy followed the case in *The Times* because of his description of the sycamore tree in the book:

> We notice the thick coat of soot upon the branches, hanging underneath them in flakes, as in a chimney. The blackness of these boughs does not at present improve the tree—nearly forsaken by its leaves as it is—but in the spring their green fresh beauty is made doubly beautiful by the contrast.

Hardy employs his tree imagery also in describing a particular gambler whom he met in a Parisian hotel at Dinant on September 23, 1896, after the fact of the novel. He glimpsed him the following morning outside the hotel entrance "without a hat" and "looking 'wild' like a tree that has suddenly lost its leaves."

The novels are full of gambling images.* The "oft-repeated noise of switches [of a deciduous tree] outside Cytherea's bedroom window scraping against the wall during a silver thaw" (*Desperate Remedies*) is likened to "the rattling of dice," and the workfolk are redistributed

---

* The most notable is the gambling with Widow Yeobright's inheritance of "spade guineas," already referred to. Venn's exclamation "I've thrown nothing at all!" when the wooden dice splits in two and lands with the cleft sides upright, presents what might be described in T. S. Eliot's phrase as an "objective correlative," it seems to me, when compared to 1) Dr. Julian's Public Health Report (1864): "That the 'hind' (a name for the agricultural labourer inherited from the time of serfdom) is fixed at the lowest possible amount on which he can live—the supplies of wages and shelter are not calculated on the profit to be derived from him. He is a zero in farming calculations" (*Capital*, p. 745), and 2) to Engel's observation letter to J. Bloch: Sept. 21, 1890) "because of the 'conflicting wills' in bourgeois society, they do not attain what they want, but are merged into a collective mean, a common resultant, it must be concluded that their value=zero" (*Correspondence*, pp. 476–77). Neither Venn nor Wildeve get what they want, and poor Christian Cantle, of course, is "the hind" par excellence.

every spring "like a shuffled pack of cards." [36] (*The Mayor*). Henchard recognizes that one can as "readily gamble on the square green areas of a field as upon those of a card room," following his visit to Conjuror Mintern ". . . one evening when it was raining so heavily that willow and laurel resounded like distant musketry." [37] Hardy writes of Giles Winterborne's deceased grandmother's stained pack of playing-cards that "the kings and queens wore a decayed expression of feature, as if they were a rather impecunious dethroned dynasty hiding in obscure slums rather than real regal characters" [38] (*The Woodlanders*). The deciduous tree image is found again in *The Dynasts* in Marshall Berthier's description to Napoleon of Colonel Toll's finding the Emperor Alexander after the battle of Austerlitz:

> . . . seated on a stone
> Beneath a leafless roadside apple tree,
> His coal-black uniform and snowy plume
> Unmarked, his face disconsolate, his grey eyes
> Mourning in tears the fate of his brave troops—

and in the Third Servant's remark to his companion on hearing the alarm beat after Fontainebleu:

> I stay here. . . .
>   The storm which roots—Dost
> Know what a metaphor is, comrade? . . .
> . . . The storm which roots the pine spares
> the p--b--d.[39] [Prince Bourbon Dynasty?]

There is a curious juxtaposition of imagery with stage business at Lord Malmesbury's on a Sunday morning in the same autumn [1804] before the battle of Ulm. Pitt enters and is greeted by Lord Mulgrave:

> Good day, Pitt. Ay, these leaves that skim the ground
> With withered voices, hint that sunshine-time
> Is well-nigh past.—And so the game's begun,
> Between him and the Austro-Russian force. . . .
> What has been heard on't? Have they clashed as yet? [40]

The poem "Embarcation" (Southampton Docks, October 1899) describes the troops being shipped off to the Boer War, "yellow as autumn leaves, alive as spring," and in the companion poem "Departure" [41] (same scene) the two images are fused together in the question:

"How long, O striving Teutons, Slavs, and Gaels
   Must your wroth reasonings trade on lives like these,
   That are as puppets in a playing hand?—

The scene is given a Turner coloration in the poem "The Going of the Battery" (November 2, 1899):

Great guns were gleaming there, living things seeming there,
Cloaked in their tar-cloths, upmouthed to the night;
Wheels wet and yellow from axle to felloe,
Throats blank of sound, but prophetic to sight.

Hardy's poem "The Master and the Leaves" [42] (1917), one of his strongest and most beautiful protests against war, employs the same imagery:

We are budding, Master, budding,
   We of your favourite tree;
March drought and April flooding
   Arouse us meerily,
Our stemlets newly studding;
   And yet you do not see!

We are fully woven for summer
   In stuff of limpest green,
The twitterer and the hummer
   Here rest of nights, unseen,
While like a long-roll drummer
   The nightjar thrills the treen.

We are turning yellow, Master,
   And next we are turning red,
And faster then and faster
   Shall seek our rooty bed,

All wasted in disaster!
But you lift not your head.

—"I mark your early going,
And that you'll soon be clay,
I have seen your summer showing
As in my youthful day;
But why I seem unknowing
Is too sunk in to say!"

The images of flowers in Hardy's poems are another thing: the problem of identifying and interpreting them is immeasurably increased by the lack of any explanation by Hardy of their meaning, so that one is without a key. On the whole, the transient plants do not struggle among themselves for supremacy, as the trees do in the poem "In a Wood," but against their general environment—Nature—consequently the images do not conceal a perpetual class struggle under the guise of a natural struggle for existence. Certainly the more permanent plants, whose stalks survive their seeds, have greater validity as class-conscious images than do transient plants whose stalks do not, particularly in the case of trees, with their connotations of "roof-tree," "family tree," and the like, and their associations with property rights, hereditary position, and inheritance.

These images are an instance of Hardy's skill in his choice of images that embody his meaning. Possibly the selection explains the difference between the flower images in his early and his later poems. Those in the Westbourne Park Villas poems (1865–1869), instead of presenting a single imaged-symbol relationship as in the conifer and deciduous tree image in the poem "Postponement," are composite images: "rose gown" in the poem "Amabel," the carving of "the wormy poppy-head" on the church pew in the poem "Her Dilemma," and the "once peony eyes" of the beloved in the poem "The Revisitation" [43] (1904). The lover of Amabel laments not only the change in her dress, "once rose, now earthen brown," as the result of "her custom-straitened views," but also the loss of spontaneity in her gait, which has become mechanical, and the listlessness of her personality generally. He mourns over the grievous change wrought in her and muses on who may love her now, finally resolving to shut her out of his memory "till the last Trump." The "millinery image" of "Amabel" offers a sharp contrast with the young man and woman in the poem "At a Bridal," who wed according to "Mode's decree."

"Amabel" seems to have been suggested by Hardy's observation of a saleslady "like an automaton" in a fashionable Regent Street apparel shop in October 1880, who "acts as by clockwork . . . and has a machine-made answer promptly ready for each." The saleslady can never expect to own the fineries or to move in the circles of those to whom she displays the gowns, any more than can Amabel. The observation of Hardy's sister Mary "that face expressions have their fashions like clothes," and "that women of the past generation have faces that are now out of fashion" (Nov. 16, 1884), is very freshly put, and suggests that Hardy's sister may have stimulated his poetic imagination as Dorothy did Wordsworth's.

Most of the flower images in the later poems do not reflect class lines or social disparities in the narrower sense of the word as they do in the early, youthful poems. In the poem "A Backward Spring" [44] (April 1917), for instance, anxiety is felt about the weather by trees and grass as well as by bushes and flowers. The trees are described as being "afraid," the grass "timid," the barberry "fretful," not because of any lesson learned from the previous winter, but because of the unfavorable aspect of Nature in winter's hindrance of spring. On the other hand, there is implicit

° "The hobby of her life had been portrait painting, but she had been doomed to school-teaching and organ-playing." The two poems "Logs on the Hearth" and "In the Garden" in *Moments of Vision* refer to her and also the Fourth person in "Looking Across." Mary died on Dec. 23, 1915, after a week's illness at their brother Henry's house at Talbothay (*Later Years*, p. 170). Their father died on Jan. 20, 1892, and their mother on Easter Sunday, April 3, 1904 (*ibid.*, pp. 10 and 106).

in this poem, considering the date of its composition—during World War I—the anxiety expressed by the flora and fauna on the eve of the battle of Waterloo in *The Dynasts:* [45]

> *The trees seem opprest, and the Plain afraid*
> *Of a Something to come, whereof these are the proofs,—*
> *Neither earthquake, nor storm, nor eclipse's shade!*

In the poem, however, the snowdrop "betrays no gloom," nor does the primrose, which "pants aggressively," yet the myrtle asks "if it's worthwhile?" The poem "A Backward Spring" expresses Nature's plea against war in behalf of the flowers as the Chorus of the Years in *The Dynasts* does in behalf of Nature, but the Years, speaking with the experiences of the past—History—have a foreknowledge of the tragedy, which to the Pities is only a terrible apprehension :

> *Yea, the coneys are scared by the thud of hoofs,*
> *And their white scuts flash at their vanishing heels,*
> *And swallows abandon the hamlet-roofs.*
>
> *The mole's tunnelled chambers are crushed by wheels,*
> *The lark's eggs scattered, their owners fled,*
> *And the hare's hid litter the sapper unseals.*
>
> *The snail draws in at the terrible tread,*
> *But in vain; he is crushed by the felloe-rim;*
> *The worm asks what can be overhead,*
>
> *And wriggles deep from a scene so grim,*
> *And guesses him safe; for he does not know*
> *What a foul red flood will soak down to him!*
>
> *Beaten about by the heel and the toe*
> *Are butterflies, sick of the day's long rheum,*
> *To die of a worse than the weather-foe.*
>
> *Trodden and bruised to a miry tomb*

Are ears that have greened but will never be gold,
And flowers in the bud that will never bloom.

The Pities chorus:

So the season's intent, ere its fruit unfold,
Is frustrate, and mangled, and made succumb
Like a youth of promise struck stark and cold! . . .

Hardy wrote to his friend Edward Clodd (Feb. 20, 1908) "that in the many treatments of Waterloo in literature, those particularly personages who were present have never been alluded to before." (*Later Years,* p. 276).

Hardy was fond of Nature, especially its wilder aspects[46] as captured in his poems "Beeny Cliff," "Comet at Yell'ham," and "Wessex Heights,"—"Mind chains do not clank where one's next neighbour is the sky." But one will not find anything in the poems on the heath or in Little Hintock wood to equal his descriptions of nature in his novels. For one who enjoyed hiking as a boy, swimming as a young man, and bicycling till he was eighty-two, this is surprising. There are poems like "The Spring Call," [47] in which he reproduces the song of the blackbird in faithful onomatopeia, according to the dialect of the listener's region, and like "Weathers," [48] in which he identifies himself with cuckoos, nightingales, rooks and shepherds, sharing the same likes and dislikes for weather as they do in the twice-repeated refrain: "And so do I." He sometimes seems to have found a therapist in Nature, in the poem "The Wound," [49] for instance:

> I climbed to the crest,
>   And, fog-festooned,
> The sun lay west
>   Like a crimson wound:
>
> Like that wound of mine
>   Of which none knew,
> For I'd given no sign
>   That it pierced me through.

As he grew older he showed less interest in Nature as "Beauty" and more interest in Nature as "Mystery": [50] poems like "The Mother Mourns," "The Lacking Sense" (suggested by "A sad-coloured landscape, Waddon Vale"), and "The Subalterns." The last poem is a kind of colloquy between the poet and the forces of Nature—"the leaden sky," "The North," "Sickness," and finally "Death," each of whom sorrowfully admits, "But I, too, am a slave!" and the poet reflects:

> We smiled upon each other then,
>   And life to me had less
> Of that fell look it wore ere when
>   They owned their passiveness.

Hardy's first poem "Domicilium," [51] about his birthplace on the heath, was a nature poem:

> It faces west, and round the back and sides
> High beeches, bending, hang a veil of boughs,
> And sweep against the roof. Wild honeysucks
> Climb on the walls, and seem to sprout a wish
> (If we may fancy wish of trees and plants)
> To overtop the apple-trees hard by.
>
> Red roses, lilacs, variegated box
> Are there in plenty, and such hardy flowers
> As flourish best untrained. Adjoining these
> Are herbs and esculents; and farther still
> A field; then cottages with trees, and last
> The distant hills and sky.
>
> Behind, the scene is wilder. Heath and furze
> Are everything that seems to grow and thrive
> Upon the uneven ground. A stunted thorn
> Stands here and there, indeed; and from a pit
> An oak uprises, springing from a seed
> Dropped by some bird a hundred years ago.

Mrs. Hardy refers to these lines as "post-Wordsworthian," but are they not rather pre-Darwinian? Darwin describes the favorable effects of insectivorous birds and the unfavorable ones of grazing cattle on the growth of Scotch pine seedlings on a barren heath in Staffordshire, whose survival is dependent upon chance in his essay "Struggle for Existence":

> As we here and there see a thin, straggling branch springing from a fork low down in a tree, and which by some chance has been favored and is still alive on the summit.

And "the place where the hollies grew," Hardy observes in *The Return of the Native*, "was in a conical pit so that the tops of the trees were not much above the general level of the ground,"[52] so that Mrs. Yeobright and Thomasin easily obtained branches for decorations for Clym's Christmas party. And there is the poem to "The Statue of Liberty,"[53] reminiscent of the tragedy in Wordsworth's poem "Michael," in which Hardy sees a scrubwoman washing down a statue with "motherly care," for which her daughter was the sculptor's model. The sculptor on hearing her story, identifies himself as "the carver and her child my model . . . [who] in the dens of vice had died."

Hardy's poems show that he valued people more than Nature. He wrote in his journal on September 28, 1877:

> An object or mark raised by Man on a scene is worth ten times any such formed by unconscious Nature.—Hence clouds, mists and mountains are unimportant beside the wear of a threshold, or the print of a hand.

An instance is his poem "by the Barrows,"[54] suggested by a story a Mrs. Cross told him of a woman, "Not far from Mellstock . . . on the Upland called the He'th," whose example won his admiration and impressed him as being one of the first glimmers of woman's enfranchisement:

> Here once a woman, in our modern age,
> Fought singlehandedly to shield a child—

One not her own—from a man's senseless rage.
And to my mind no patriots' bones there piled
So consecrate the silence as her deed
Of stoic and devoted self-unheed.

Other such poems [55] are "To My Father's Violin"; "Heiress and Architect (for A. W. Blomfield)"; "The Last Signal," on his poet friend William Barnes's funeral; "After the Last Breath," on his mother's death; "George Meredith"—"His note was trenchant turning kind"; "To Shakespeare after Three-Hundred Years," in which a Stratford man says, "I' faith, few knew him much here, save by word . . . Though to be sure he left with us his wife." The other replies:

—"Ah, one of the tradesmen's sons, I now recall. . . .
    Witty, I've heard. . . .
We did not know him. . . . Well, good-day. Death comes to all."

Hardy also wrote several occasional poems: [56] "Zermatt: to the Matterhorn," commemorating the terrible accident of July 14, 1865, which he read of at the time, and later, in May 1894, when at Edward Clodd's, he had heard Edward Whymper, the sole survivor of the five, tell of his ascent. Whymper "marked for Hardy on a sketch the track of the adventures to the top and the spot of the accident," Mrs. Hardy says, "a sketch which is still at Max Gate." Hardy wrote his poem soon after viewing the Matterhorn on June 28, 1897. Other such poems are "The Convergence of the Twain"—lines on the loss of the *Titanic* (April 15, 1912)—"A Singer Asleep" to Swinburne (1910) and a valedictory, "Ancient to Ancients" (1912), concluding:

> Much is there waits you we have missed;
> Much lore we leave you worth the knowing.
> Much, much more has lain outside our ken,
> Nay, rush not; time serves: We are going,
>   Gentlemen.

Later he wrote "And There Was a Great Calm," on the signing of the Armistice (Nov. 11, 1918).

Aye; all was hushed. The about-to-fire fired not,
The aimed-at moved away in trance-lipped song.
One checkless regiment slung a clinching shot
And turned . . .
Thenceforth, no flying fires inflamed the gray,
No hurtlings shook the dewdrop from the thorn,
No moan perplexed the mute bird on the spray;
Worn horses mused: "We are not whipped to-day";°
No weft-winged engines blurred the moon's thin horn.

Hardy's anti-war poems constitute a large proportion of his poetry, and he inspired a whole generation of anti-war poets from Siegfried Sassoon and Wilfred Owen to Michael Hamburger in England and from Edgar Lee Masters to Muriel Rukeyser and Robert Bly in America. Hardy lost a cousin in World War I, Second Lieutenant Frank William George of the 5th Dorset Regiment, killed at the battle of Gallipoli (Aug. 22, 1915), whom he memoralized in his poem "Before Marching and After," [57] "in that game overseas Where death stood to win." Sassoon says that both he and Owen, while hospitalized at Craiglockhart War Hospital, London, "vowed our confederacy to unmask the ugly face of Mars and—in the words of Thomas Hardy 'war's apology wholly stultify' " [58] ("Often When Warring").

"Drummer Hodge," [59] in Hardy's poem by that name, who falls in the Boer War, a sacrifice to British imperialism, had never been outside his native Dorset, where he had lived in a mud-and-thatched cottage like those in *The Mayor of Casterbridge* "built with the occupier's own hands" (p. 213) and had been what Marx called "the hind, the soldier of peace" (*Capital*, p. 762):

They throw in Drummer Hodge, to rest
Uncoffined—just as found.

° In July 1894 Hardy had "an interesting conversation with Dr. W. H. Russell, a *Times* correspondent during the Franco-Prussian War, who told Hardy a distressing story of a horse with no under jaw, laying its head upon his thigh in a dumb appeal for sympathy, two or three days after the battle of Gravelotte, when he was riding over the field, and other such sickening experiences" (*Later Years*, p. 33).

His landmark is a kopje-crest
  That breaks the veldt around;
And foreign constellations west
  Each night above his mound.

Young Hodge the Drummer never knew—
  Fresh from his Wessex home—
The meaning of the broad Karoo,
  The Bush, the dusty loam,
And why uprose to nightly view
  Strange stars amid the gloam.

The lines from *The Dynasts* describe the burial at night of
John Moore, in a shallow grave of the Jardin de San Carlos,
Coruña, with the chaplain reciting the Recessional from the
Book of Job, the diggers of the Ninth hastily filling in the
grave as the French guns on the heights, at dawn, open fire,
and the "ships in the harbour take in their riding-lights." [60]
   The conversation between Pitt and Wiltshire on art in
Wiltshire's private gallery does not have the psychological
finesse of Browning's "The Last Duchess" as a dramatic
monologue, but it has something else that is entirely lacking
in the monologue between the Italian aristocrat and the
count's emissary on his matrimonial mission. Wiltshire is
showing Quin's portrait of a woman to Pitt,[61] "who looks
emaciated and walks feebly":

Wiltshire:
    Now here you have the lady we discussed:
    A fine example of his manner, sir?
Pitt:
    It is a fine example, sir, indeed,—
    With that transparency amid the shades,
    And those thin blue-green-greyish leafages
    Behind the pillar in the background there,
    Which seem the leaves themselves,—Ah, this is Quin.
Wiltshire:
    Yes, Quin. A man of varied parts, though rough
    And choleric at times. Yet at his best,
    As Falstaff, never matched, they say. But I
    Had not the fate to see him in the flesh.

Pitt:

Churchill well carves him* in his "Characters":—
"His eyes, in gloomy socket taught to roll,
Proclaimed the sullen habit of his soul.
In fancied scenes, as in Life's real plan,
He could not for a moment sink the man:
Nature, in spite of all his skill, crept in;
Horatio, Dorax, Falstaff—still 'twas Quin."
—He was at Bath when Gainsborough settled there
In that house in the Circus which we know.—
I like the portrait much.—The brilliancy
Of Gainsborough lies in this his double sway:
Sovereign of landscape he; of portraiture
Joint monarch with Sir Joshua.—Ah?—that's—hark!

Their conversation is suddenly interrupted by a courier,
bringing news of General Mack's defeat at Austerlitz. He
is "splashed with mud from hard riding," and Pitt, on gloomily
reading "the heavy news," departs to pressing matters of state.
Hardy never panders to the chaplain's "but for the Grace of
God" doctrine of survival, or the nationalistic myth *Dulce et
decorum est pro patria mori* of the Sir Walter Scott-Rupert
Brooke school of poetry. In "The Man He Killed," [62] the survivor realizes that he might as easily have been the victim,
and in trying to rationalize his act only becomes confounded,
yet dimly perceives the political-economic causes of war:

"I shot him dead because—
Because he was my foe,
Just so: my foe of course he was,
That's clear enough, although

"He thought he'd 'list, perhaps,
Off-hand like—just as I—

* James Quin (1683–1766), Irish actor, born in London; rival to Garrick
in Shakespearean roles as Richard III and Falstaff, he retired to Bath in
1751. See *The Life of Mr. James Quin Comedian* (London: Reader, 1887),
in which Hardy's reference to Churchill is found in "the occasion of Mr.
Churchill's introducing him into the *Rosciad*, in which the lines appear
"His eyes, in gloomy sockets taught to roll, etc." (pp. 92–93).

Was out of work—had sold his traps,
No other reason why.

Similarly, Gabriel Oak and Giles Winterborne nearly en-
list in the army when they are penniless and unemployed;
Sergeant Troy is going to get out of the army "because war
is a barbarous way of settling a quarrel." The survivor in
"The Man He Killed" feels a natural revulsion to killing a
person and sadly reflects that in a peaceful world they might
have become friends:

> "Yes; quaint and curious war is!
> You shoot a fellow down
> You'd treat if met where any bar is,
> Or help to half-a-crown."*

Hardy depicts how the survivors feel after the war, disillusioned and embittered, as does Siegfried Sassoon, who
asks " 'Does It Matter . . . losing your legs?" and "there's
such splendid work for the blind! "; and Edgar Lee Masters,
in "Knowlt Hoeheimer," a casualty of Missionary Ridge, who
wishes he had gone to jail for stealing hogs instead of to
war, and who asks, sarcastically, what the graven words
"Pro Patria" on his tombstone "mean anyway?" [63] Hardy was
no recruiting sergeant like Kipling in his poetry for the
British Empire, and unlike Kipling he does not give us static
recollections of individual soldiers** and camp life (*Barrack*

---

* What frets Rostov, who is awarded the St. George's Cross for his
gallantry at Ostravna, was something he could not make out at all. "So
they are even more afraid than we are!" he thought. "Is this, then, all
that is meant by what is called heroism? And did I do it for my country's
sake? And where was he to blame, with his dimple and his blue eyes?
And how frightened he was! He thought I was going to kill him. Why
should I kill him? My hand trembled. But they have given me the St.
George's Cross. I can't make it out. I can't make is out at all" (*War and
Peace,* p. 611).

** Tolstoy has Rostopchin, "who was quoted everywhere," make an
interesting generalization on soldiers and soldiering: "The French soldier,"
pronounced Rostopchin, "has to be incited to battle by high-sounding
phrases; the German must have it logically proved to him that it is more
dangerous to thin away then to advance, but the Russian soldier has to
be held back and urged to go slowly!" (*War and Peace,* p. 279).

Room Ballads), but he shows them *en masse,* in a dramatic situation, like the regiment marching coastwards to defend their country against Napoleon's invasion, as in the "Marching Song" [64] of Part I of *The Dynasts:*

> We be the King's men, hale and hearty,
> Marching to meet one Buonaparty;
> If he won't sail, lest the wind should blow,
> We shall have marched for nothing, O!
> Right, fol-lol!

This song comes alive from the dramatic situation. It swells in the ears of the passengers of the stagecoach that overtakes them, and fades in the distance as it leaves them behind.

There is a healthy cynicism in "The Sergeant's Song," [65] sung by Sergeant Stanner at miller Loveday's party for his trumpet-major son, John:

> When lawyers strive to heal a breach,
> And Parsons practice what they preach;
> Then Boney he'll come pouncing down
> And march his men on London town!
> Rollicum-rorum, tol-lol-lorum
> Rollicum rorum, tol-lol-lay!

and a mixture of hostility and nostalgia in the song "The Budmouth Dears," [66] sung on the eve of the battle of Vitoria, by Sgt. Young, of the King's Hussars:

> Do they miss us much, I wonder
> Now the war has swept us sunder,
> And we roam from where the faces smile
> To where the faces frown?
> And no more behold the features
> Of the fair fantastic creatures,
> And no more *Clink! Clink!* past the parlours
> Of the town?

The girls back home in the poem "Sitting on the Bridge" [67] (Grey's Bridge, Dorchester) wonder about them:

> Perhaps that soldier's fighting
>> In a land that's far away,
> Or he may be idly plighting
>> Some foreign hussy gay;
> Or perhaps his bones are whiting
>> In the wind to their decay! . . .

and sing "at the time of curfew-ringing, "Take me, Paddy; will you now? . . . Paddy, will you now?" This poem, subtitled, "Echo of an old song," is a compound of gaiety, sunset, dream, and somberness.

"The Woman's Song," [68] sung on Durnover Green at the burning of Napoleon in effigy to the tune of Wellington's Hornpipe, expresses the anachronism of war and the irony that Might makes Right:

> My Love's gone a-fighting
>> Where war-trumpets call,
> The wrongs o' men righting
>> Wi' carbine and ball,
> And sabre for smiting,
>> And charger, and all!

So does the Pities' observation of Ney's cavalry charge at the battle of Waterloo: [69]

> *Behold the gorgeous coming of those horse,*
> *Accoutred in kaleidoscopic hues*
> *That would persuade us war has beauty in it!—*
> *A lingering-on, to late in Christendom,*
> *Of the barbaric trick to terrorize*
> *The foe by aspect!*

Hardy's philosophical poems, from the early, much-anthologized poem "Hap" (1866) to the late, posthumously published poem "He Resolves to Say No More" (1928), are chiefly of interest in showing the development of *The Dynasts*. These agnostic poems* aroused almost as much

---

* There are numerous references in the official biography: Apr. 29, 1867: "Had the teachings of experience grown cumulatively with the

age of the world we should have been ere now as great as God" (*Early Life*, p. 73). At an evening service at St. George's Hanover Square (May, 1890): "everything looks like the Modern World: the electric light and the old theology seem strange companions; and the sermon was addressed to Native tribes of primitive simplicity, and not to the Nineteenth Century English" (*ibid.*, p. 295). May 9, 1890: "In the streets I see patient hundreds, labouring on, and boxes on wheels packed with men and women. There are charcoal trees in the squares. A man says, 'When one is half-drunk, London seems a wonderfully enjoyable place, with its lamps and cabs moving like fire-flies. Yes, man has done more with his materials than God has done with his'" (*ibid.*, p. 295). At St. James, Picadilly, Sunday (Apr. 1891)—"the church his mother had been accustomed to go to when as a young woman she was living for some months in London"—Hardy notes: "The preacher said that only five per cent of the inhabitants entered a church, according to the Bishop of London. On coming out there was a drizzle across the electric lights, and the paper boys were shouting, not 'Go to Church!' but, 'Wee-naw of the French Oaks!'" (*ibid.*, p. 309), The note for an article "The Hard case of the Would-be-Religious. By Sinceritas" (1907), in which he says, "The days of creeds are as dead and done with as the days of Pterodactyls," and continues: "We enter church, we have to say, 'We have erred and strayed from Thy ways like lost sheep,' when what we want to say is, 'Why are we made to err and stray like lost sheep?' Then we have to sing, 'My Soul doth magnify the Lord,' when what we want to sing is. 'O that my soul could find some Lord that it could magnify? Till it can, let us magnify good works, and develop all means of easing mortals' progress through a world not worthy of them'" (*Later Years*, pp. 121–22). And the very curious experience of May 12, 1889: (Sunday evening): "To St. James's, Westmoreland Street, with Em. Heard Haweis—a small lame figure who could with difficulty climb into the pulpit. His black hair, black beard, hollow cheeks and black gown, made him look like one of the skeletons in the church of the Capuchins, Rome. The subject of his discourse was Cain and Abel, his first proposition being that Cain had excellent qualities, and was the larger character of the twain, though Abel might have been the better man in some things. Yet, he reminded us, good people are very irritating sometimes, and the occasion was probably one of agricultural depression like the present, so that Cain said to himself: ' 'Tis this year as it was last year, and all my labour wasted!' (titter from the congregation). Altogether the effect was comical. But one sympathized with the preacher, he was so weak, and quite in a perspiration when he had finished" (*Early Life*, pp. 286–87).

It is also seen in the character of "the weather-caster (*The Mayor of Casterbridge*) who "behind his back," Hardy says, "was called 'Wide-oh,' on account of his reputation," and "to his face 'Mr.' Fall." Hardy notes: "people supported him with their backs turned," and "He was sometimes astonished that men could profess so little and believe so much at his house, when at church they professed so much and believed so little" (p. 213).

Also, see the letter of the Rev. A. B. Grosart to Hardy (Feb. 1888) enumerating "some of the horrors of human and animal life, particularly parasitic," and inquiring about the problem of "how to reconcile these with the absolute goodness and non-limitation of God," to which Hardy replied: "Mr. Hardy regrets that he is unable to suggest any hypothesis animosity as Shelley's essay "on the Necessity of Atheism" (1811), which led to his expulsion from Oxford. The critics were mainly Catholic, like Chesterton, who called Hardy "a sort of village atheist brooding and blaspheming over the village idiot," and Alfred Noyes, who accused Hardy of caricaturing God as "an imbecile jester" in the poem "Nature's Questioning," [70]—"a poem," Hardy declared, "often quoted against me." [71] And in "God's Funeral" (1908–1910), he viewed the "man-projected figure, of late, imaged by me" through Comtean eyes, and wondered "who or what shall fill his place" glimpsing "a pale yet positive gleam low down behind,"* which is seen by only "a certain few who stood aloof." The poem concludes:

> And they composed a crowd of whom
> Some were right good, and many nigh the best. . . .
> Thus dazed and puzzled 'twixt the gleam and gloom
> Mechanically I followed with the rest.

His loss of faith is not even restored by an elder's retelling the story of "The Oxen" [72] kneeling on Christmas Eve at "twelve of the clock" in "the lonely barton by yonder coomb our childhood used to know."

which would reconcile the existence of such evils as Dr. Grosart describes with the idea of omnipotent goodness. Perhaps Dr. Grosart might be helped to a provisional view of the universe by the recently published Life of Darwin [*The Life & Letters of Charles Darwin*, ed. F. Darwin, 3 vols., London, 1887] and the works of Herbert Spencer and other agnostics" (*Early Life*, p. 269).

Hardy had been inclined to the scientific view ever since July 2, 1865, when he had weighed Darwin and Newman in his mind and found Newman, whom his friend Moule "likes so much," wanting: "style charming and his logic really human, being based not on syllogisms but on converging probabilities. Only—and here comes the fatal catastrophe—there is no first link to his excellent chain of reasoning, and down you come headlong" (*ibid.*, pp. 63–64).

* Very different from the streak of light on the horizon described by Disraeli in his letter to Lady Bradford (Oct. 28, 1876): "Whether it be the victory of the Turks, or whether it be that the Russians commence to comprehend that England will stand no nonsense," he hoped it was "not a mirage" (Monypenny & Buckle, *Life of Disraeli*, 2 : 957). It recalls Kaiser Wilhelm's threat to American ambassador James Gerard that he

In the poem "God-Forgotten," [73] a messenger from Earth reminds God, "Lord, it existeth still!" and in "Panthera" [74] it is related that a Roman soldier by that name, stationed in Palestine, was the father of Christ. The story is narrated by a disabled veteran and friend of Panthera, who had told him of seeing a weeping woman on Calvaria, "though I betrayed some qualms, she marked me not, and I was scarce of mood to comrade her," or

> To claim a malefactor as my son—*
> (For so I guessed him). And inquiry made
> Brought rumour how at Nazareth long before
> An old man wedded her for pity's sake
> On finding she had grown pregnant, none knew how,
> Cared for her child, and loved her till he died.

Panthera, the narrator says, brooded "upon the fate of those he had known":

> Even of that one he always called his own—
> Either in morbid dream or memory. . . .

and he concludes that

> He died at no great age, untroublously,
> An exit rare for ardent soldiers such as he.

In the poem "The Wood Fire (A Fragment)" Hardy relates what became of the wood. Though it "outwardly refers to the Crucifixion," Edmund Blunden notes that it was "in reality inspired by the news of the clearance of the wooden crosses on the old Western Front" (p. 167), but it really forms an epilogue to the "Panthera" poem and a comment-

"would stand no nonsense from America after the war" (see *My Four Years in Germany* [1917]).

    * By contrast "the two wretched parents" of the innocent poor starved lad hanged for arson, "come themselves for the body . . . with a wagon and sheet for its conveyance," under a law allowing the relatives of an executed convict "the privilege of claiming the body for burial, if they chose to do so" (see Hardy's short-story "The Withered Arm," near the end).

ary on his remarks on Zionism as well as to Erich Remarque's notable anti-war novel *All Quiet on the Western Front* (1929), the showing of which caused the Nazis to let loose white mice in the theater and Remarque to flee for his life to Switzerland and Rudolph Hilferding, editor of the *Social Democrat,* to France, where he hanged himself in a Paris cell on Pétain's surrender to Hitler in the museum railway coach at Compiègne. Hardy's poem (pp. 585–86) follows:

"This is a brightsome blaze you've lit, good friend, to-night!"
"—Aye, it has been the bleakest spring I have felt for years,
And nought compares with cloven logs to keep alight;
I buy them bargain-cheap of the executioners,
As I dwell near; and they wanted the crosses out of sight
By Passover, not to affront the eyes of visitors.

"Yes, they're from the crucifixions last week-ending
At Kranion. We can sometimes use the poles again,
But they get split by the nails, and 'tis quicker work than mending
To knock together new; though the uprights now and then
Serve twice when they're let stand. But if a feast's impending,
As lately, you've to tidy up for the comers' ken.

"Though only three were impaled, you may know it didn't pass off
So quietly as was wont? That Galilee carpenter's son
Who boasted he was king, incensed the rabble to scoff;
I heard the noise from my garden. This piece is the one he was on. . . .
Yes, it blazes up well if lit with a few dry chips and shroff;
And it's worthless for much else, what with cuts and stains thereon."

Hardy's composer's ear developed from his early love of and participation in music, and he is especially successful at extracting the inherent music from his experiences in such poems as "Voices from Things Growing in a Country Church-yard"; his astonishing "Drinking Song," which Duffin calls "a real drinking song":[75] "Dead 'Wessex' the Dog to the

Household." In the last there is, in Mark van Doren's words, "sheer music." The dog, Hardy entered in his diary, "Dec. 28 (1926) sleeps outside the house the first time for thirteen years":

> Do you think of me at all?
> Wistful ones?
> Do you think of me at all,
> As if nigh?
> Do you think of me at all,
> At the creep of evenfall,
> Or when the sky-birds call,
> As they fly?

His poem "Last Words to a Dumb Friend," [76] on one of Mrs. Hardy's cats, is pedestrian and undistinguished, except for the last stanza:

> Housemate, I can think you still
> Bounding to the window-sill,
> Over which I vaguely see
> Your small mound beneath the tree,
> Showing in the autumn shade
> That you moulder where you played.

There is music as to a dance-step with a letting-go of hands in the love poem "First or Last" (Song),[77] of which I quote the first and last stanzas:

> If grief comes early
> Joy comes late.
> If joy come early
> Grief will wait;
>   Aye, my dear and tender!
>
> . . . .
>
> And joy being ours
> Ere youth has flown,
> The later hours
> May find us gone;
>   Aye, my dear and tender!

Hardy had a sense of humor—the "Swiftian rather than the Dickensian kind," that is evident in poems[78] like "Ah, Are you Digging on My Grave?", "The Bride-Night Fire at Tranter Sweatley's" (his first published poem), and the delightfully subtle "The Garden Seat,"* with a materialist's sense of humour:

> Its former green is blue and thin,
> And its once firm legs sink in and in;
> Soon it will break down unaware,
> Soon it will break down anaware.

> At night when reddest flowers are black
> Those who once sat thereon come back;
> Quite a row of them sitting there,
> Quite a row of them sitting there.

> With them the seat does not break down,
> Nor winter freeze them, nor floods drown,
> For they are as light as upper air,
> They are as light as upper air!

Hardy adhered to the principle that the "ultimate aim of the poet should be to touch our hearts by showing his own, and not to exhibit his learning, or his fine taste, or his skill in mimicking the notes of his predecessors." [79] He practiced "perhaps unconsciously the Gothic art-principle . . . of spontaneity—that of stress rather than syllable, poetic texture rather than poetic veneer." [80] He owned Walker's *Rhyming Dictionary*,[81] but one doubts that he used it very

---

* "The Garden Seat" recalls Wellington's order in the thick of the artillery fire at Waterloo: "To hold out unto the last, / As long as one man stands on one lame leg / With one ball in his pouch!—then end as I" (III,7,vii), and the Spirit Sinister's exclamation: *"One needs must be a ghost / To move here in the midst 'twixt host and host! / Their balls scream brisk and breezy tunes through me / As I were an organ-stop. It's merry so; / What damage mortal flesh must undergo!"* Hardy had some fun at playing at being a ghost in June–July 1887, writing whimsically: ". . . when I enter into a room to pay a simple morning call I have unconsciously the habit of regarding the scene as if I were a spectre not solid enough to influence my environment; only fit to behold and say, as another spectre said: 'Peace unto you!'" (*Early Life*, p. 275).

much, except possibly in his poem "The Alarm," in which Blunden—probably punning—finds "a Teniers in every stanza" (p. 252). "When one considers," Mrs. Hardy says,

> that he might have made himself a man of affluence in a few years by taking the current of popularity as it served, writing "best-sellers," and ringing changes upon the novels he had already written, his bias toward poetry must have been instinctive and disinterested.[82]

And Marx said that "a poet is not a capitalist."

Poetry has a way of outlasting prose, and after the lapse of time Hardy may be remembered longer for his poetry than for his novels.

His poems show a deep love for Nature and Humanity, a hatred of cruelty of all kinds, and of war, especially, a rational rather than a mystical temperament, a well-balanced personality, with a wide range of interests, receptive to new ideas and to change. He feels consistently that Nature is better than Society, and consequently the irony of life subdues the gaiety, and the somber view of life prevails in his poetry as in his novels.

Hardy wrote a few political poems—important poems—not many—like "The Rejected Member's Wife"[83] (Jan. 1906)* on the decisive defeat of the Conservative Party:

---

* It was not until 1906 that any "significant change" occurred in the House of Commons. K. B. Smellie states (p. 192). The Conservatives were reduced from 369 to 157 while the Liberals totalled 381, which, with the Labour-Liberal men came to 400 (see S. Maccoby's *English Radicalism: The End*, p. 26)). A. L. Morton notes that it was then that "a group of twenty-nine Labour members was returned to the House of Commons" (*A People's History of England*, p. 454). Atherley Jones, radical of North-West Durham since 1885, addressed his constituents in the General Election of Jan. 1906: "To the great satisfaction of the Country the Tory Government has come to an ignominious end; it has taken the extraordinary course of resigning while it still possessed a Parliamentary majority. . . . Since 1895 . . . all that it could perform was to pass the Workmen's Compensation Act, in many respects an inadequate and unsatisfactory measure. But it has been active in looking after the interests of the Church, the Liquor Trade and the Landowners; it has passed an Education Act which has compelled Nonconformists to pay for the support of Schools managed by Teachers belonging to the Established Church. Their evil work

does not end here; they have increased the National Debt . . . they have violated the noblest tradition of the Country by establishing slavery under the British flag at the bidding of a few foreign capitalists. . . . Now at length the Liberal Party is in power. The task before them is indeed heavy" (Simon Maccoby, *English Radical Tradition*, 5:219–20).

On February 8 (1907), Hardy noted of Mrs. Hardy in his journal: "E. goes to London to walk in the suffragist procession to-morrow" (*Later Years*, p. 123).

Hardy was interested in the history of the transition from feudalism to capitalism, as is shown in the scene of Ethelberta's taking her brothers to Milton's tomb (referred to earlier) and in the following passage from *A Laodicean*: "There was a certain unexpectedness in the fact that the hoary memorial of a stolid antagonism to the interchange of ideas, the monument of hard distinctions in blood and race, of deadly misrtust of one's neighbour in spite of the Church's teaching, and of a sublime unconsciousness of any other force than a brute one, should be the goal of a machine (the telegraph) and the intellectual and moral kinship of all mankind" (p. 22).

Scott's novels and his pale imitator Kenelm Digby's *The Broadstone of Honour* (1882) fostered a romanitc interest in medievalism, and a revival of medieval notions was carried out in a medieval tournament at Eglinton in the summer of 1830, which was spoiled by rain (Woodard, *Age of Reform*, p. 109).

"We cannot turn our people back into Catholic English peasants and guild-craftsmen," said William Morris, "or into Heathen Norse-bonders, much as may be said for such conditions of life" (Eshelman, *Victorian Rebel*, p. 230). Or, as Hardy says, Jude "did not at that time (1860–1870) see that medievalism was as dead as a fern leaf in a lump of coal . . ." (*Jude* p. 99; *Later Years*, p. 249).

Among the guests at Paula's garden party (*A Laodicean*) is "the Radical member for Tonebrough who had succeeded to the seat rendered vacant by the death of Paula's father" (p. 13). Pierston (*The Well-Beloved*) perceives that "the small and early reception had resolved itself into something very like a great and late . . . remembers that there had just been a political crisis which accounted for the enlargement of the Countess of Channelcliffe's assembly; for hers was one of the neutral or non-political, houses at which party politics are more freely agitated than at the professedly party gatherings" (p. 561). Also Lord Mountclere's guests of the archaeological society in *The Hand of Ethelberta*, among whom were "Mr. and Mrs. Tynn, member and member's mainspring for North Wessex; Sir Cyril and Lady Blandsbury; Lady Jane Joy; and the Honourable Edgar Mountclere, the viscount's brother . . . the learned Doctor Yore, Mr. Small, a profound writer, who never printed his works; the Reverend Mr. Brook, rector: the very Reverend Dr. Taylor, dean; and the moderately Reverend Mr. Tinkleton, Nonconformist, who had slipped into the fold by chance" (pp. 263–64).

We shall see her no more
On the balcony,
Smiling, while hurt, at the roar
As of surging sea
From the stormy sturdy band,
Who have doomed her lord's cause
Though she waves her little hand
As it were applause . . .

and "The Peace Peal" [84] (1918), about a wistful daw that, on hearing St. Peter's bells (Dorchester) after four years' silence, flies from "his louvred niche to take up life in a damp dark ditch." Hardy noted:

—So mortal motives are misread,
And false designs attributed,
In upper spheres of straws and sticks,
Or lower, of pens and politics.

The poem "Lausanne: In Gibbon's Old Garden (June 27, 1897)," [85] on "the 110th anniversary of the completion of the 'Decline and Fall,'" in which he addresses the Spirit of Gibbon in the dimly lit grove of acacia trees, reveals much about them both:

How fares the Truth now?—Ill?
—Do pens but slily further her advance?
May one not speed her but in phrase askance?
Do scribes aver the Comic to be Reverend still?

Still rule those minds on earth
At whom sage Milton's wormwood words were hurled:
*'Truth like a bastard comes into the world
Never without ill-fame to him who gives her birth'* ?*

* The quotation is from *"The Doctrine of Discipline of Divorce."* Mrs. Hardy says (*Later Years*, p. 69): "Truth is as impossible to be soiled by any outward touch as the sunbeam; though this ill hap wait on her nativity, that she never comes into the world, but like a bastard to the ignominy of him that brought her forth; till Time, the midwife rather than the mother of truth, have washed and salted the infant and declared her legitimate" (*ibid*, p. 69n).

8

The Dynasts

It is not my intention here to trace the literary history of *The Dynasts* from Hardy's outlining a poem "The Battle of the Nile" (never finished) following Palmerston's death in 1865 to his settling down at home "on a belated day in 1897" [1] to his outlining and writing his epic of the Napoleonic wars, *The Dynasts* (1903–1906–1908). Nor is it necessary to enumerate his many trips to Chelsea Hospital with Mrs. Hardy on the anniversary of Waterloo Day (June 18), nor his trips alone to the actual scenes of battles on the Continent,* nor his extensive research in historical books, some

---

* In 1876, 1880, 1887 and 1896. Hardy made the following notes, which may be of some value here: "From their lodgings in Yeovil they set out at the end of May (1876) for Holland and the Rhine—the first thing that struck them being that 'the Dutch seemed like police perpetually keeping back an unruly crowd composed of waves.'" "Heidelberg they loved, and looking west one evening from the top of the tower on the Königsstuhl, Hardy remarks on a singular optical effect that was almost tragic: Owing to mist the wide landscape itself was not visible, but 'the Rhine glared like a riband of blood, as if it serpentined through the atmosphere above the earth's surface.'" August 5, 1880: "They went on to Trouville . . . and thence to Honfleur, a place more to Hardy's mind, after the fast life of Trouville. On a gloomy gusty afternoon, going up the steep incline through the trees behind the town they came upon a Calvary tottering to its fall . . . with a crudely painted figure of Christ which seemed to writhe and cry in the twilight: 'Yes, Yes! I agree that this travesty of me and my doctrines should totter and overturn in the modern

of which "were very long and not very good," [2] as he told his friend Vere Collins, nor in the Parliamentary records of *Hansard* in the British Museum. There is no purpose, either, in repeating the influences of Hardy's earlier scientific or later philosophical reading, considerable as that of Darwin and Spencer was, as other critics have already shown, or of the Greek dramatists and English poets from Aeschylus to Shelley, which influence has been treated exhaustively by classical and literary scholars to the point of diminishing returns.

It was to be expected that a novelist and poet with a strong narrative sense in his poetry would turn first to the narrative form for his historical materials, "forming altogether an Iliad of Europe from 1789 to 1815"; then "a ballad sequence" (1875), and "a grand drama" [3] (1877), as it was also to be expected that a poet who had shown a sensitive response to the tragedy of life in his novels should have become dissatisfied with depicting a historical epoch without "a larger canvas" and "a spectral tone" [4]—and should choose to interpret it through drama by which history becomes literature and art. On March 4, 1886, he noted further:

world. . . .'" Hardy was more interested in Pagan than in Christian Rome (p. 249); of the latter preferring churches in which he could detect columns from ancient temples. Christian Rome, he said in 1887, "was so rambling and stratified that to comprehend it in a single visit was like trying to read Gibbon at a single sitting." "At dinner at the Grand Hôtel de Milan, Hardy met a young Scotch officer of Foot ('a sort of Farfrae') returning from India," who had never heard of 'The Bridge of Lodi' (song) or the battle, and together, the next morning they went to the historic spot and over the quiet-flowing of the Adda, the two re-enacted the fight and the 'Little Corporal's' dramatic victory over the Austrians" (*Early Life,* p. 257; *Collected Poems,* pp. 97ff).

"In London (Jan. 1891) a part of the month where he saw 'what is called sunshine up here—a red-hot bullet hanging in a livid atmosphere reflected from window-panes in the form of bleared copper eyes, and inflaming the sheets of plate-glass with smears of gory light. A drab snow mingled itself with liquid horsedung, and in the river puddings of ice moved slowly on. The steamers were moored, with snow on their gangways. A captain, in sad solitude, smoked his pipe against the bulk-head of the cabin stairs. The lack of traffic made the water like a stream through a deserted metropolis'" (*Early Life,* p. 304).

The human race to be shown as one great network or tissue which quivers in every part when one point is shaken, like a spider's web if touched.

The Realities to be the true realities of life, hitherto called abstractions. The old material realities to be placed behind the former as shadowy accessories.

It is enlightening to compare Hardy's note on "Abstract Realism" with a Russian critic's review of Marx's *Capital* in the *European Messenger* (St. Petersburg, May 1872) in which the reviewer remarked:

Marx treats the social phenomena as a process of natural history, governed by laws not only independent of human will, consciousness, and intelligence, but rather on the contrary determining that will, consciousness, and intelligence. . . . That is to say, that not the idea, but the material phenomenon alone can serve as a starting point. (*Capital*, p. 22)

In March–April (1890), reflecting on "Altruism or the Golden Rule, or whatever 'Love your Neighbour as Yourself' may be called," Hardy thought [it] would be brought about . . . by the pain we see in others reacting on ourselves, as if we and they were a part of one body," because finally "mankind, in fact, may be and possibly will be viewed as members of one coporeal frame."

There are two earlier experiences of particular importance that brought the history of the Napoleonic period alive for Hardy. One was the outbreak of the Franco-Prussian War (July 15, 1870), when the coup of Louis Napoleon to restore the empire by the bloody suppression of the Paris Commune made it appear as if the history of Hardy's grandparent's time was going to repeat itself. At this time Hardy was in London, assisting his friend Raphael Brandon, a sixty-one year old architect, "who would go into the Strand for every edition of the afternoon papers as they came out and read them to Hardy, who grew as excited as he," Mrs. Hardy says, not realizing "that should England become involved in the Continental strife, he might have been among the first to be called to serve, outside the regular army." "The London *Standard* [July 13, 1870] gave a long analysis of the routes which Napoleon might take," Howard says, but "did not even consider an invasion of France," and "Friedrich Engels pointed out in the *Pall Mall Gazette* [July 29], if the French had not planned an offensive, their declaration of war did not make sense."[5] All Hardy seems to have done, Mrs. Hardy says,

> was to go to a service at Chelsea Hospital and look at the tattered banners mended with netting, and talk to the old asthmatic and crippled men, many of whom in the hospital at that date had fought at Waterloo, and some in the Peninsula.[6]

These men he honors in *The Dynasts:*

> The young sleep sound; but the weather awakes
> In the veteran, pains from the past that numb;
> Old stabs of Ind., old Peninsular aches,
> Old Friedland chills, haunt his moist mud bed,
> Cramps from Austerlitz; till his slumber breaks.[7]

Hardy may very well have read Engels's articles on the Franco-Prussian War in *The Pall Mall Gazette*, a leading literary and political magazine of the day. There were sixty in all, and they attracted great attention. In his article of August 8, 1870, Engels wrote:

> The French army has lost all initiative. Its movements are dictated less by military considerations than by political necessities. Here are 30,000 men almost within sight of the enemy. If their movements are to be ruled, not by what is done in the enemy's camp, but by what may happen in Paris, they are half beaten already. Nobody, of course, can foretell with certainty the result of the general battle which is now impending, if not going on; but this much we say, that another week of such strategy as Napoleon III has shown since Thursday is alone sufficient to destroy the best and largest army in the world. (*Correspondence*, p. 294)

Hardy may have projected some of this psychology in *The Dynasts* in Decrès's remark at Boulogne on Napoleon's invasion maneuvers, "The Emperor can be sanguine. Scarce can I" (I, 2, iv) and in Napoleon's at Fontainebleau, asking Caulaincourt, after Marmont's defection, for maps, paper, and ink, "to schedule all my generals and my means!" who replies, "Sire, you have not the generals you suppose" (III, v. iv).

The other was a serious illness from a cerebral hemorrhage during the winter of 1880–81 when, confined to his bed, he must have wondered like Tolstoy, "If I live . . . , whether he would ever get to *The Dynasts*. He noted in his journal (Feb. 7, 1881) on Carlyle's death, "Both he and George Eliot have vanished into nescience while I have been lying here," and reflected on history:

> Discover for how many years, and on how many occasions, the organism, Society, has been standing, lying, etc., in various positions, as if it were a tree or a man hit by vicissitudes. There would be found these periods:
> 1. Upright, normal, or healthy periods.
> 2. Oblique or cramped periods.
> 3. Prostrate periods (intellect counterpoised by ignorance or narrowness, producing stagnation).
> 4. Drooping periods.
> 5. Inverted periods.[8]

The import of this note does not appear as "irrelative" or "vague," [9] as Mrs. Hardy describes it when one considers his description of Europe in the forescene of Part I of *The Dynasts:*

> The nether sky opens, and Europe is disclosed as a prone and emaciated figure, the Alps shaping like a backbone, and the branching mountain-chains like ribs, the peninsular plateau of Spain forming a head. Broad and lengthy lowlands stretch from the north of France across Russia like a grey green garment hemmed by the Ural mountains and the glistening Arctic Ocean.

He already had, of course, his cosmic perspective in both his early poems "At a Lunar Eclipse" [10] (1866) ending:

> Is such the stellar guage of earthy show,
> Nation at war with nation, brains that teem,
> Heroes, and women fairer than the skies?

and "To the Matterhorn (Zermatt)," [11] ending:

> Yet ages 'ere men topped thee, late and soon
> Thou didst behold the planets lift and lower;
> Saw'st, maybe, Joshua's pausing sun and moon,
> And the betokening sky when Caesar's power
> Approached its bloody end; yea, even that Noon
> When darkness filled the earth till the ninth hour.

Moreover, it should be remembered that history and nature had become inextricably associated in Hardy's imagination as a boy on field trips with his parents to Napoleonic relics on Rainbarrow Heath, which related the struggle in nature to man's history. This is seen, as has been mentioned, in his comparison of the movements of armies "to a silent insect-creep," or to "caterpillars" or "ants in an ant-hill." [12] The Lisbon defense workers are "like cheese-mites," and the "three reddish-grey streams of marching men"—"the English army entering them for shelter—" whose "motion seems peristaltic and vermicular, like that of three caterpillars," and even Napoleon himself, "like meanest insects on obscurest leaves." [13]

This material remained static, however, until Hardy's discovery of a "mode," or coalescing medium, as given in his diary entry of March 27, 1881:

> Mode for a historical Drama, Action mostly automatic; reflex movement, etc. Not the result of what is called *motive,* though always ostensibly so, even to the actors' own consciousness. Apply an enlargement of these theories to, say, "The Hundred Days"!

The exclamation point is Hardy's, and it curiously reveals his excitement over his idea. "This note," Mrs. Hardy says, "is apparently Hardy's first written idea of a philosophic scheme or framework as the larger feature of *The Dynasts* enclosing the historical scenes." Another important diary note is that of July 14 (1889): "Sunday. Centenary of the fall of the Bastille. Went to Newton Hall to hear Frederic Harrison lecture on the French Revolution. The audience sang 'The Marseillaise.' Very impressive."

His inventory of the "Books read or pieces looked at" (1887) of two years before is more revealing as a guide to what he should avoid imitating than anything else. It somewhat refutes Walter F. Wright's [14] statement that "We cannot, of course, perfectly establish the chronology of his reading, but the evidence does permit certain conclusions." On the list were:

Milton, Dante, Calderon, Goethe.
Homer, Virgil, Molière, Scott.
The Cid, Nibelungen, Crusoe, Don Quixote.
Aristophanes, Theocritus, Boccaccio.
Canterbury Tales, Shakespeare's Sonnets, Lycidas,
Malory, Vicar of Wakefield, Ode to West Wind, Ode
    to Grecian Urn.
Christabel, Wye above Tintern.
Chapman's Iliad, Lord Derby's ditto, Worsley's Odyssey.

This is evident from his conversation on religion with Leslie Stephen (May 11, 1901), who said, "The old ideas have become obsolete, and the new are not yet constructed. . . . We cannot write living poetry on the ancient model. The gods and heroes are too dead, and we cannot sympathize with the idealized prizefighter."* Whether this was a reference

---

* William James refers to the "famous international prize fight between Tom Sayers and Heenan the Benicia Boy in 1857 (1860?)" to which "the *Times* devoted a couple pages of report and one or more eulogistic editorials to the English champion, and the latter, brimming over with emotion, wrote a letter to the *Times*, in which he touchingly said that he would live in future as one who had been once deemed worthy of commemoration in its leaders" (*Letters*, 2:65 [letter to F. C. S. Schiller, Oct 23, 1897]).

to the Jeffries-Corbett fight at Coney Island (1900) for the world's championship, which had been initiated with the Sullivan-Kilrain fight in Richburg, Mississippi (1889), is a matter for conjecture. It will be recalled that Hardy, on his shortcuts to Blomfield's office "passed daily the liquor saloons" of ex-prize fighters, whom he saw behind their respective bars in Seven Dials, and he may have reflected on Thackeray and the Bible, "All is vanity," or with Lucretius, *Sic transit gloria mundi.*

He seems to have been cogitating further on his tentative dialectic for *The Dynasts* alluded to in his journal note of April 26, 1890: "View the Prime Cause or Invariable Antecedent as 'It' and recount its doings. This was done in *The Dynasts*," Mrs. Hardy adds. But his conversation with Stephen[*] had helped him to settle the question in his mind, as is shown in his preface to *The Dynasts:*

> The wide prevalence of the Monistic theory of the Universe forbade, in this twentieth century, the importation of Divine personages from antique Mythology as ready-made sources of channels of Causation, even in verse, and excluded the celestial machinery of, say, *Paradise Lost*, as peremptorily as that of the *Iliad* or the *Eddas*. And the abandonment of

[*] On March 23, 1875, Hardy was summoned by Leslie Stephen "to witness his signature, to what, for a moment, I thought was his will; but it turned out to be a deed renunciatory of holy-orders under the act of 1870. He said grimly that he was really a reverend gentleman still, little as he might look it, and that he thought it was as well to cut himself adrift of a calling for which, to say the least, he had always been utterly unfit. The deed was executed with due formality. Our conversation then turned upon theologies decayed and defunct, the origin of things, the constitution of matter, the unreality of time, and kindred subjects. He told me that he had 'wasted' much time on systems of religion and metaphysics, and that the new theory of vortex rings had 'a staggering fascination' for him" (*Early Life*, p. 139).

There may be a reference to this theory in Engels's letter to Marx (May 28, 1876) in which he writes: "I hope Wilhelm (Wilhlm Liebknecht) will publish Most's article in the *Neue Welt*, for which it was obviously written. As usual Most cannot even copy right and so makes Dühring responsible for the most comic imbecilities in the field of natural science, e.g., the detachment of *rings* (according to Kant's theory) from *fixed stars!* (see *Marx and Engels Selected Correspondence* (Moscow, USSR: Progress Publishers, 1955).

the masculine pronoun in allusions to the First or Fundamental Energy seemed a necessary and logical consequence of the long abandonment by thinkers of the anthropomorphic conception of the same.

"I believe, too," Hardy said, "that the Prime Cause, this Will, has never before been called 'It' in any poetical literature, English or foreign?" [15] It is Hardy's conception of the Prime Cause as a force of neuter gender, gradually progressing from unconsciousness to consciousness, that gives the time essence to his epic drama, in which human history becomes but a stage in the maturation of the human race, and the Napoleonic Wars but a footnote in the autobiography of the Immanent Will, or God.

Besides the Will there are the Spirit of the Years, "the best human intelligences of their time in a sort of quintessential form," as Hardy described them, and the Spirit of the Pities, "Humanity, with all its weaknesses," [16] which comprise the collective dualism and present the dialectic of the drama. These spirits are the kind of "those rare forms that might have been" of the poem "Her Dilemma" (1866), which are thwarted from being by the class restrictions of bourgeois society, yet the mutual effect of the spirits on each other is seen in the Pities' looking to the intelligence of the Years for guidance, at Albuera, "Speak more materially, and less in dream" (II, 6, iv), and the Years' developing an artistic instinct, as the result of the Pities' humanizing influence, in their admonishing the Pities:

> *Abide the event, young Shade:*
> *Soon stars will shut and show a spring-eyed dawn,*
> *and sunbeams fountain forth, that will arouse*
> *Those forming bands to full activity.*
> (I, 1, iii)

In a journal entry of April 1890, Hardy thought that "by the pain we see in others reacting on ourselves . . . as if we and they were a part of one body . . . mankind . . . possibly will be viewed as members of one corporeal frame." These dualistic spirits and their choruses, as stated above, embody the theme of the drama:

But O, the intolerable antilogy of making figments feel! [17]

and express, tentatively, the Comtean hope of human perfectibility,

> *Consciousness the Will informing, till It fashion all things fair!* [18]

"Their doctrines," Hardy explained, "are but tentative and are advanced with little eye to a systematized philosophy warranted to lift 'the burthen of the mystery' of this unintelligible world." [19]

The seriousness of the drama is lightened by the Spirits Ironic and Sinister and their choruses, who indulge in cynical quips on human foibles and supernatural idealisms in the manner of Gilbert and Sullivan and Henry Mencken. The Spirit Ironic and the Spirit Sinister, disguised as ordinary strangers, enter the Gallery of the House of Commons, where they sit in on the debate on Pitt's Defense Bill, the one remarking that it nauseates him *"to hear this Pitt sung so strenuously,"* and the other commenting, *"There's sure to be something in my line toward, where politicians are gathered together!"* [20] The Spirit Ironic interrupts the Spirit of the Pities' comment on *"this terrestrial tragedy,"* with, *"Nay, comedy."* [21] The Spirit Sinister is rebuked by the Spirit of the Years for having called him *"Father Years"* in the presence of the Shade of the Earth, with, *"Thou Iago of the Incorporeal World, 'as they would say below there.'"* [22]

The spirit Sinister undoubtedly owes something to Mephistopheles in Goethe's *Faust*, as Rutland [23] has observed, and to Hardy's "macabre experiences" of grave exhumation at Blomfield's, as Blunden [24] has observed, but more, I think, to Byron's *Don Juan* [25] (1814–1824). Hardy read

widely in English poetry between 1863 and 1865, and these
spirits display much the same barbed tone as Byron's
acerbities; Byron says of Pitt,

> . . . as a high soul'd minister of state is
> Renowned for ruining Great Britain gratis.

and:

> . . . I shall be delighted to learn who,
> Save you and yours, have gained by Waterloo?

and especially:

> Behold the world! and curse your victories.

They owe something also to Swift's *Gulliver's Travels* and to
Twain's *Connecticut Yankee at King Arthur's Court* and his
sharper fantasies.

Hardy's statement that in *The Dynasts* he "tried to
spread over art the latest illumination of the time," which
he later feared, "has darkened counsel in respect of me," [26]
should have reminded critics that *The Dynasts* was a contemporary epic and that they should have focused their
minds, not on the productions of the past, but on "the
thought of the age," which Hardy believed a poet should
express: the discoveries of science and the beginnings of
social science and experimental psychology. *The Dynasts*
belongs to the age of Darwin and Marx and likewise to the
age of Wundt's perceptual psychology and Einstein's fourth
dimension, as well as to the age of Krupp's cannon, Enfield
rifles, Nobel's dynamite, Roentgen's discovery of x-rays, and
aerial photography, and a host of other contradictions in
bourgeois society represented by lives as far apart as those
of General Booth and Florence Nightingale, which Shaw
satirizes in *Major Barbara* (1905). The anatomy of the Will,
for instance, whose "sum is like the lobule of a brain," is
shown "enduing men and things with a seeming transparen-

cy," or "like winds grown visible," or "a beating brain lit by phosphorescene," [27] whose "urging becomes visualized." A surgeon at the Women's Camp near Mont Saint-Jean delivers a woman of a child, "which a second woman is holding," and other women "are dressing the slighter wounds of the soldiers," while "a camp-follower is playing a fiddle near," [28] all of them taking "hardly any notice of the thundering cannon" at Waterloo. The very foundations of society and its superstructure appear to Pitt to be crumbling after Austerlitz. After looking at a map of Europe brought in at his request by a servant of Lord Wiltshire [29] at Shockerwick House, Bath, Pitt declares:

> Roll up that map. 'Twill not be needed now
> These ten years! Realms, laws, peoples, dynasties,
> Are churning to a pulp within the maw
> Of empire-making Lust and personal Gain!

Hardy himself described *The Dynasts* as "the Clash of Peoples artificially brought about," and his recent critic Wright notes that "far more than any of his other major works, the epic-drama is concerned with actual fact." [30]

The catalysts of Hardy's art in *The Dynasts* were not so much Homer and Virgil as they were Turner (1775–1851), in whose later paintings he found the material world atomized into the spiritual, and Tchaikovsky (1840–1893), whose "impetuous march in the third movement of the *Symphony Pathetique*," which he heard in London while working on Part III of the drama, "was the only music he knew that was able to make him feel exactly as if he were in a battle." [31]

The Dynasts, which was published in three parts (1903, 1906, 1908) respectively and consists of nineteen acts and one hundred and thirty scenes, depicts in cinematographic manner the political intrigue and the sanguinary events of the Napoleonic Wars (1805–1815). Hardy described the work as "a series of historical 'ordinates' (to use a term in geometry): the subject is familiar to all; and foreknowledge is assumed to fill in the curves to combine the whole gaunt framework into an artistic unity." [32] It opens with a scene from the Overworld, with the spirits looking down on the globe "where peoples, distressed by events which they did not cause, are seen writhing, crawling, heaving and vibrating in their various cities and nationalities";[33] and it closes in the Overworld with the Spirit of the Years and the Spirit of the Pities looking down again on the corpus delicti of Europe "prone and emaciated," the sea "a disturbed bed [34] on which the figure lies," with the Years dubious about the future of mankind and the Pities voicing their paean of hope.[*] One of the remarkable things about the *The Dynasts* is that the spectator-reader views the calamity through the eyes of the spirits, who partake of the alienated individual, uncorrupted by party lines or nationalistic prejudices.

Hardy begins *The Dynasts in medias res,* although he had studied the entire historical epoch (1789–1815) from the commencement of the French Revolution and Napoleon's seizure of power in 1799 to the end of the Napoleonic Wars (June 15, 1815). We see almost simultaneously the English preparations in the House of Commons and on the Wessex downs against Napoleon's invasion, and Napoleon's massing his troops and armada across the Channel at Boulogne.

The "foreknowledge," which Hardy assumes in his reader, is given in retrospective comments of the various spirits as the drama progresses, and it illuminates, in lightning flashes, the career of Napoleon in consolidating his position by subjugating Austria at the battle of Marengo (July 14, 1800) and securing the support of the temporary world by his treaty with Alexander I and that of the apostolic world by his concordat with Pope Pius VII (formerly Count Chiaramonti), before he felt ready to attack England.

[*] The perspective recalls that of Blake in his poem "The French Revolution" (1791): "The dead brood over Europe, the clouds and vision descend[s] over cheerful France" (Book I).

For instance, the Recording Angel reads "from a book in recitative" to the Spirit of the Years:

> *The easternmost ruler sits wistful,*
> *And tense he is to midward;*
> *The King to the west mans his borders*
> *In front and in rear.*[35]

And the Spirit of the Pities, on seeing Napoleon take the Crown of Lombardy from the Pope and placing it on his own head, declares:

> *That vulgar stroke of vauntery he displayed*
> *In planting on his brow the Lombard crown,*
> *Means sheer erasure of the Luneville* pacts,*
> *And lets confusion loose on Europe's peace*
> *For many an undawned year! . . .*[36]

At other times, the "foreknowledge" is given by the characters themselves, as in the case of the Old Grenadier, who says optimistically to Napoleon before Austerlitz:

> We'll bring thee Russian guns and flags galore
> To celebrate thy coronation-day! [37]

and Old Augereau, before Leipzig: "the Augereau of Castiglione days, unless you give the boys of Italy back again to me!" There is also the case of the English stragglers after Coruña, recalling Sir John Moore's leading them on with " 'Remember Egypt!' in the very eye of that French battery playing through us." And "the skeletoned men" at Walcheren, "who are kept moving because it is dangerous to stay

---

* The Lunéville Pacts (Feb. 9, 1801) "gave Napoleon everything he wanted from Austria: the final separation from Austria of the whole of Belgium; the cession of Luxembourg; all the German possessions on the left bank of the Rhine; the recognition of the 'Batavian Republic' (Holland), the 'Helvetian Republic' (Switzerland), the 'Cessalpine Republic' (Geneva) and the 'Ligurian Republic' (Lombardy) . . . and the treaty with Tsar Paul, confirmed by Alexander I, the pact directed his thoughts to new wars and distant conquests" (Tarlé, Bonaparte, pp. 118, 121).

still"; and in the stage directions at Boulogne, with the soldiers singing *Le Chant du Depart* and the babble of repeating the days of Italy, Egypt, Marengo, and Hohenlinden.[38]

i. EUROPE IN THROES

Part I of *The Dynasts* reaches its climax in the battle of Trafalgar, which redeems the English allies' defeat at Ulm, and ends with Napoleon's Berlin decree, "Ships can be wrecked by land!" [39] following his victory at Austerlitz.

Part II depicts the great land battles—Jena, Tilsit, Wagram, Walcheren, and the Peninsular campaign, Coruña, Talavera, Vimiero, Torrès Vedras, and Albuera, with the vicissitudes on both sides. It also relates Napoleon's divorcing Josephine ("'Tis the Empire dictates this divorce")[40] and his marriage to Maria Louisa, of which the Shade of the Earth owns: *"When France and Austria wed . . . I have reason for a passing dread!"* [41]

Part III chronicles Napoleon's Russian campaign from Borodino to Moscow—Leipzig, which "magnifies a failure into a catastrophe," of which the Spirits observe, *"Neither is the victor,"* and Moscow, which he finds deserted and in flames ("This, then, is how Muskovy fights!") followed by his abdication at Fontainebleau, his imprisonment on the Isle of Elba, and his escape therefrom to Paris to recruit another army—"Men of the Fifth"—against the Bourbon "usurpers," leading from the battle of Ligny, Quatre Bras, to Waterloo.[42]

The Dynasts is fairly well summed up politically by Whitbread's quotation of Sheridan in the Old House of Commons in submitting his amendment "to limit ministers' aggressiveness," which is defeated 37 to 220:

> The wittiest man who ever sat here* said
> That half our nation's debt has been incurred

* Sheridan.

> In efforts to suppress the Bourbon power,
> The other half in efforts to restore it (laughter)
> And I deprecate a further plunge
> For ends so futile! [43]

and historically in terms with which Marx categorized the later Franco-Prussian War (1870–71): "the highest heroic effort of which the old society is capable . . . which is now proved to be a mere government humbug, intended to defer the struggle of classes, and to be thrown aside as soon as the class struggle bursts out into civil war. The national governments are as *one* against the proletariat. The national class rule is no longer able to disguise itself in a national uniform." [44] For instance, George III turns down Pitt's request to lift the onerous shackles in respect to his Home Defense Bill, with, "Rather than Fox, why, give me civil war!" [45] Pitt hated Fox for speaking against his Bill:

> It sets a harmful and unequal tax
> Capriciously on our communities.—
> Though held as shaped for English bulwarking,
> Breathes in its heart the perverse schemes of party,
> And instincts toward oligarchic power,
> Galling the many to relieve the few! (Cheers).[46]

The matter is recalled in Pitt's bedchamber by Bishop Tomline and Pitt's physician Sir Walter Farquhar, Tomline diagnosing his disease as "Austerlitz," and Farquhar blaming the King for it:

> And yet he might have borne it, had the weight
> Of governmental shackles been unclasped . . .
>   But relief the King refused,
> "Why want you Fox? What—Grenville and his friends?"
> He harped. "You are sufficient without these—
> Rather than Fox, why, give me civil war!"

The same dilemma on the other side is given a personal and domestic turn in the conquered King Francis, who has misgivings about having Napoleon for a son-in-law and voices them to Metternich:

> In state affairs, sire, as in private life
> Times will arise when the faithfullest squire
> Finds him unfit to jog his chieftan's choice . . .[47]

and his daughter Maria Louisa, who had, up till then, hated Napoleon. She replies to Metternich's tidings of Napoleon's proposal for her hand:

> My wish is what my duty bids me wish.
> Where a wide Empire's welfare is in poise.
> That welfare must be pondered, not my will.[48]

Contemporary historian Eugene Tarlé states that Napoleon "did not so much 'complete' the Revolution as 'liquidate' it." [49] Tolstoy had no more respect for *le bien publique* than Conrad had for either "the Savage Autocracy" or "the Divine Democracy"; Hardy was skeptical of both. Marx observed that any system of government based on the enrichment of the few and the enslavement of the many carried its own seeds of destruction within it (feudalism, capitalism, fascism).[50]

In Milan cathedral, at the coronation rites of Napoleon,* who shouts angrily, "Where are the Cardinals?", the Pities censure the Church's handing the Italian sceptre to one who

---

* The Recording Angel recites the names of the celebrated guests to the Spirit of the Pities, who has observed the "pompous train . . . with faces speaking a sense of adventure" beginning with "the Emperor's brother Louis, Holland's King," etc., and ending with Lords and Ladies-in-waiting "and others called by office, rang, or fame," to which the Spirit of Rumour comments: "New, many, to Imperial dignities; / Which, won by character an quality / In those who now enjoy them, will become / The birthright of their sons in aftertime" (II,v,viii). During the ceremony, Marie Louise says "sadly" to Napoleon, "I know not why, I love not this day's doing half so well / As our quaint meeting-time at Compiègne," and he tries to recover from his black humour produced by the absence of "those Devils of Italian Cardinals," and tells her, "Now I'll be bright as ever—you must, too."

> *Professed at first to flout antiquity,*
> *Scorn limp conventions, smile at mouldy thrones*
> *And level dynasts down to journeymen!—*
> *Yet he, advancing swiftly on that track*
> *Whereby his active soul, fair Freedom's child,*
> *Makes strange decline, now labours to achieve*
> *The thing it overthrew.*[51]

and at La Haye Sainte, Waterloo, seeing its defenders, the King's German Legion, "nearly all cut or shot down," by Ney and Donzelot's division, reflects:

> *O Farm of sad vicissitudes and strange!*
> *Farm of the Holy Hedge, yet fool of change!*
> *Whence lit so sanct a name on thy now violate grange?*

which an Aide reports is "now one pool of blood." [52] The Pities' earlier intuition is confirmed by the Years' "whispering to Napoleon" at the birth of his and Marie Louise's son and heir:

> *At this high hour, there broods a woman nigh,*
> *Ay, here in Paris, with her child and thine,*
> *Who might have played this part with truer eye*
> *To thee and to thy contemplated line!*

And Napoleon says anxiously to the obstetrician, Dubois:

> Fancy that you are merely standing by
> A shop-wife's couch, say, in the Rue Saint Denis;
> Show the aplomb and phlegm that you would show
> Did such a bed receive your ministry.

Napoleon, startled by the Spirit of the Years' whisper, muses:

> Strange that just now there flashes on my soul
> That little one I loved in Warsaw days,
> Marie Walewska, and my boy by her!—
> She was shown faithless by a foul intrigue
> Till fate sealed up her opporunity. . . .
> But what's one woman's fortunes more or less
> Beside the schemes of kings!—ah, there's the news! [53]

A gun from the Invalides fires twenty-two shots, and amidst the ringing of bells and huzzas of the crowd, "a balloon ascends from the Champ de Mars . . . from which the tidings are scattered in hand-bills as it floats away across France."

At the scene in the Tuilleries, Napoleon tells his step-daughter Hortense and the Queen of Holland, "You must stay with me . . . and your mother, too, must keep her royal state . . . Equal magnificence will orb her round in after-times as now." [54] This recalls the coronation cermony at the start of which the Spirit Sinister had remarked:

> *It may be seasonable to muse on*
> *the sixteenth Louis and the bride's great aunt,*
> *as the nearing procession is, I see, appositely cross-*
> *ing the track of the tumbril which was the last*
> *coach of that respected lady. . . . It is now*
> *passing over the site of the scaffold, on which she*
> *lost her head. . . . Now it will soon be here.*[55]

The Pities observe on Napoleon's abdication at Fontaine-bleau:

> *Yet is it but Napoleon who has failed.*
> *The pale pathetic peoples still plod on*
> *Through hoodwinkings to light!*

The "hoodwinkings" of these lines go back to "the blinkered time" of 1867 in Hardy's poem "1967" (*Time's Laughing-stocks*), in which the failure of political reform has blighted his hope and the threat of rival imperialisms set it farther back. Napoleon, on his escape incognito from the Isle of Elba, makes, as the destroyer of feudalism and the emanci-pator of the bourgeoisie, the same appeal to his soldiers that he had made to them in 1799:

> Soldiers, I come with these few faithful ones
> To save you from the Bourbons—treasons, tricks,
> Ancient abuses, feudal tyranny—
> From which I once of old delivered you.

> The Bourbon throne is illegitimate
> Because not founded on the nation's will,
> But propped up for the profit of a few.
> Comrades, is this not so? [56]

The soldiers huzza "The Emperor forever," and an old grena-
dier exclaims, "Yes verily, sire. You are the Angel of the
Lord to us: We'll march with you to death or victory!" The
Years noted Napoleon's "suasive pull."

They march, of course, to death. On the field of Waterloo, Napoleon has a false sense of victory when he observes
Wellington calling up reinforcements for Baring's Germans
(imagining "a darkly crawling sluglike shape" to be
Grouchy's vanguard) and he orders Ney, before they join,
to charge:

> All prospers marvelously! Goumont is hemmed;
> La Haye Sainte too; their centre jeopardized;
> Travers and d'Erlon dominate the crest,
> And infantry in strength is following close.
> Their troops are raw; the flower of England's force
> That fought in Spain, America now holds.—
> To-night we sleep in Brussels! [57]

The troops are not Grouchy's but Blucher's; in a last shout
to his shattered Imperial Guard, which rallies feebly at his
voice, "They are crushed! So it has ever been since Crécy!"
he falls off his horse and mounts another steed brought
him by a page.

Several scenes later, Napoleon, in the wood of Bossu,
soliloquizes:

> If but a Kremlin cannon-shot had met me
> My greatness would have stood . . .
> —Yes, a good death, to have died on yonder field;
> But never a ball came passing down my way!
> So, as it is, a miss-mark they will dub me.

and reflects commiseratingly, albeit with faith in bourgeois
historians:

And yet—I found the crown of France in the mire
And with the point of my prevailing sword
I picked it up! But for all this and this
I shall be nothing. . . .
Great men are meteors that consume themselves
To light the earth. This is my burnt-out hour.

The Spirit of the Years replies:

Thou sayest well. Thy full meridian shine
Was in the glory of the Dresden days,
When well-nigh every monarch throned in Europe
Bent at thy footstool. [58]

Their observation at the end bears out the Pities' suspicion
at the beginning:

The more that he, turned man of mere traditions,
Now profits naught. For the large potencies
Instilled into his idiosyncracy—
To throne fair Liberty in Privilege' room—
Are taking taint, and sink to common plots
For his own gain.[59]

The Spirit Ironic jibes Napoleon for blaming England solely
for his defeat:

Yea, the dull peoples and the Dynasts both,
These counter-castes not oft adjustable,
Interests antagonistic, proud and poor,
Have for the nonce been bonded by a wish
To overthrow thee. . . .[60]

to which Napoleon, still brooding on Marshall Soult's defection to "Bourbonry," makes no reply.

These "counter-castes" are exhibited before Madrid in
the tête-à-tête between Godoy, the Prince of Peace, and
Queen Maria Louisa, who want to escape the rabble at the
gates, and the Prince who, in behalf of King Carlos, "lauds
the French as true deliverers"; they were likewise exhibited

earlier, before Ulm, in General Mack's advising the Archduke Ferdinand, who wants to escape through Bosnia, that
he has had orders

> That none of your Imperial Highness' line
> Be pounded prisoner by this vulgar foe,
> Who is not France, but an adventurer
> Imposing on that country for his gain—[61]

and in the Archduke's reply:

> I amply recognize the drear disgrace
> Involving Austria if this upstart chief
> Should of his cunning seize and hold in pawn
> A royal-lineaged son, whose ancestors
> Root on the primal rocks of history.[62]

The Ironic Spirit nudges a fellow-spirit: "Note that! Five
years and legal brethren they!—this feudal treasure and the
upstart man!" The Empress Josephine complains to Napoleon, who wants her to consent to a divorce:

> Were I as coarse a wife
> As I am limned in English caricature—
> (Those cruel effigies they draw of me!)—
> You could not speak more aridly.

to which Napoleon* replies:

---

* After Jena, Napoleon receives the vanquished King of Prussia and
his wife, Queen Louisa, who are reconciled to the loss of "half" of the
realm, "but Dear Magdeburg *that* I would retain!" Napoleon takes a rose
from a vase and offers it to the Queen, who pleads, "Let Magdeburg come
with it, sire!", to which Napoleon replies, "It is for you to take what I can
give. And I give this—no more" (II, 1, viii). Hardy has General Mack say
on surrendering to Napoleon, "Behold me, Mack the unfortunate!" (I, 4, v);
Tolstoy has him say, "You see the unfortunate Mack" (*War and Peace*,
p. 109), but in Tolstoy, Mack surrenders to General Kutuzov, who ushers
him into his study.

Interesting in this connection is Johnann von Thunen's *Der Isolierte
Staadt* (*The Isolated State*, 1863), in which he asks from his personal
farming experience on his estate at Tellow, in the province of Mecklenberg,
following the Napoleonic Wars, "how will the farming system of the various
districts be effected by their distance from the Town." The place was 5 miles

There's not a bourgeois couple in the land
Who, should dire duty rule their severance,
Could part with scanter scandal than could we.[63]

She revives his infatuation with Marie Waleska, who, he
says, "was a week's adventure—not worth words," and she
sobs, "It hurts me so,/it cuts me like a sword." The Mother
of all the Russias tells her Tsar-son Alexander on his disappointment over Napoleon's choosing "one of Austrian
blood" instead of his sister Anne,

> . . . But an affront
> There is, no less, in his evasion on't,
> Wherein the bourgeois quality of him
> Veraciously peeps out.

north northwest of the small market town of Teterow, 130 feet above sea level
in a country of glacial ground moraine, small lakes, and alluvial marsh, without a railroad until 1880; Mecklenberg agriculture had been retarded by the
Thirty Years War (1618–1648), then by the Seven Years War (1756–1763).
Part I starts out with a beautiful exposition of the Isolated State: "Imagine
a very large town, at the centre of a fertile plain, which is crossed by no
navigable river or canal. Throughout the plain the soil is capable of cultivation and of the same fertility. Far from the town, the plain turns into
an uncultivated wilderness which cuts off all communication between the
state and the outside world. There are no other towns on the plain. The
central town must therefore supply the rural areas with all manufactured
products, and in return it will obtain all its provisions from the surrounding
countrywide" (p. xxi). Von Thunen's treatise offers quite a contrast to Plato's
Myth of the Cave.

In 1848 von Thunen was elected representative to the German National
Assembly, the 'ill-fated 'Professors Parliament,' " at Frankfurt am Main,
but could not take his seat. He was born June 24, 1783, and died Sept.
22, 1850, "quickly and in autumn when the leaves fall," as he had wished.
He evolved a formula for "natural wage: $A = \sqrt{ap}$," which he had engraved
on his tombstone in the village churchyard at Belitz, the state next to
Tellow. (See Carlo M. Wartenberg's translation of von Thunen's *Isolated
State* (New York: Pergamon Press, 1966).

There is something touching about Thunen, "Marx wrote to Kugelmann
(London, March 6, 1868), a Mecklenburg *junker* (true, with a *German*
training in thinking) who treats his estate at Tellow as the land and
Mecklenburg-Schwerin as the *town*, and who proceeding from premises,
with the help of observation, the differential calculus, practical accounting,
etc., constructs for himself the Ricardian theory of rent. It is at once
worthy of respect and at the same time ridiculous" (*Correspondence*, p. 233).
In Schumpter's words, von Thunen was "one of the patron-saints of econo-
metrics" (p. xvii). Marx wrote Engels (May 20, 1865): I am doing some
Differential calculus   . I have no patience to read anything else. Any
other reading drives me back to my writing desk" (*Correspondence*, p. 202).

and explains, "I am a Romanoff by marriage merely." [64] The
Austrian Marie Louisa remarks to a Lady-in-Waiting, "I am
sure that the Empress her mother will never allow one of the
house of Romanoff to marry with a bourgeois Corsican. I
wouldn't if I were she." The Prince Regent, on being informed at the Carlton House banquet by the Duchess of
Angoulême "that Buonaparte's child, 'the King of Rome' is
dead, and not your royal father, sire," replies:

> Call him a king—that pompous upstart's son
> Beside us scions of the ancient lines! [65]

and informs the royal Spanish refugees at the Marchioness
of Salisbury's, "We are going to vote fifty millions, I hear
. . . and preserve your noble country for 'ee, Señor Viscount,"
and the debate

> thereon is to come off to-morrow. It will be the finest thing
> the Commons have had since Pitt's time. Sheridan, who is to
> open it, says He and Canning are to be absolutely unanimous;
> and, by God, like the parties in his "Critic," when Government
> and Opposition do agree, their unanimity is wonderful!

A Lord remarks, "I'd lay a guinea there will be a war between Russia and France before another year has flown" (II,
6, vii). In London, at the Liberal Club in St. James,[66] a member declares: "How is the debate going? Still braying the
Government in a mortar?" He is answered:

> Well, the war must go on. And that being the general con-
> viction this censure and that censure are only as so many
> blank-cartridges.

Another member, who favors "A revolution, because Ministers are not impeached and hanged," says of the defection
of their allies:

> The Lord look down! Our late respected crony Austria! Why,
> in this very night's debate they have been talking about the

laudable principles we have been acting upon in affording
assistance to the Emperor Francis in his struggle against the
violence and ambition of France!

Another jibes, "O House of Hapsburg, how hast thou fallen!" The debate in the House of Commons on the final
phase of the war is highlighted by Burdett's stinging reply
to Castlereagh:

> Sir, I am old enough to call to mind
> The first fierce frenzies for the selfsame end,
> The fruit of which was to endow this man,
> The object of your apprehension now,
> With such a might as could not be withstood
> By all of banded Europe, till he roamed
> And wrecked it wantonly on Russian plains.
> Shall, then, another scourging score of years
> Distract this land to make a Bourbon king? [67]

A servant in Paris opines, "I think I'll turn Englishman in
my older years, where there's not these trying changes in the
Constitution!"; the Shade of the Earth puts the question[63]
to the Spirit of the Years on the futility:

> *What boots it, Sire,*
> *To down this dynasty, set that one up,*
> *Goad panting people to the throes thereof,*
> *Make wither here my fruit, maintain it there,*
> *And hold me travailing through fineless years*
> *In vain and objectless monotony,*
> *When all such tedious conjuring could be shunned*
> *By uncreation? Howsoever wise*
> *The governance of these massed mortalities,*
> *A juster wisdom his who should have ruled*
> *They had not been*

The economic and geopolitical aspects of war, under
Hardy's treatment, add emphasis to the beginning stage of
rival imperialisms. Before Austerlitz, Napoleon exclaims to
Marshall Soult, "God, yes! Even here Pitt's guineas are the

foes," [69] and after it he admonishes Tsar Alexander that England's fleet

> . . . at any minute can encoop
> Yours in the Baltic; in the Black sea, too;
> And keep you snug as minnows in a glass! [70]

and, promoting their partnership, he continues:

> . . . Nothing can greaten you
> Like this alliance. Providence has flung
> My good friend Sultan Selim from his throne,
> Leaving me free in dealings with the Porte. . . .

In Gilbert and Sullivan fashion "the twain" toast "the freedom of the seas," at which the Spirit Ironic chides, "Another hit at England and her tubs!"

> Hence, we fast-fellowed by our mutual foes,
> Seaward the British, Germany by land,
> And having compassed, for our common good,
> The Turkish Empire's due partitioning,
> As comrades can conjunctly rule the world
> To its own gain and our eternal fame!

Alexander, "stirred and flushed," replies: "I see vast prospect opened!" Napoleon flatters Alexander further:

> Prussia's a shuffer, England a self-seeker,
> Nobility has shown in you alone,[71]

and he tells Francis, after Tilnitz: "One country sows these mischiefs Europe through by her insidious chink of luring ore," and he boasts to his staff after Astorga, tearing open the dispatches:

> Nor Pitt nor Fox displayed such blundering
> As glares in this campaign! It is indeed
> Enlarging Folly to Foolhardiness
> To combat France by land! But how expect

Aught that can claim the name of government
From Canning, Castlereagh, and Perceval,
Caballers all—poor sorry politicians—
To whom has fallen the luck of reaping in
The harvestings of Pitt's bold husbandry.[72]

At a fete in Vauxhall Gardens an attaché says, "Of course,
an enormous subsidy is to be paid to Francis by Great
Britain for this face-about?", and the First Attaché gains the
ear of the Second Attaché, "Yes, as Bonaparte says, English
guineas are at the bottom of everything!—Ah, here comes
Caroline." [73]

The Spirit of Rumour ridicules Napoleon's *"renowned
'Berlin Decree'"*—*"To bar from commerce with the Continent all keels of English frame"*—as if he had forgotten Trafalgar; and the Spirit Ironic comments on England's re-
taliatory *"Orders of Council—to impound the marine of
France and her allies"*—on which the Spirit of the Pities
observes sadly: *"And peoples are enmeshed in new calamity!"* [74] The price of his Berlin Decree is conveyed to him in
Darwinian terms by the President of the Senate who, after
congratulating Napoleon on the birth of a son, answers his
question:

Nothing in Europe, sire, that can compare
In magnitude therewith to more effect
Than with an eagle some frail finch or wren.
To wit: the ban on English trade prevailing,
Subjects our merchant-houses to such strain
That many of the best see bankruptcy
Like a grim ghost ahead. Next week, they say
In secret here, six of the largest close.

Napoleon replies:

It shall not be! Our burst of natal joy
Must not be sullied by so mean a thing:
Aid shall be rendered. Much as we may suffer,
England must suffer more, and I am content.
What has come in from Spain and Portugal? [75]

The news of Massena's retreat before Lord Wellington, which Berthier says was "for prudence' sake," angers Napoleon:

> Ever retreating . . .
> When Lisbon could be marched on without strain?
> Why has he dallied by the Tagus bank . . .
> And shunned the obvious course? I gave him Ney,
> Soult, and Junot, and eighty thousand men,
> And he does nothing. (II, 6, iii).

After the battle of Salamanca and before Borodino, Napoleon, harassed by a cold, boasts nasally:

> Behoves it me,
> Someday, to face this Wellington myself!

an echo of Austerlitz, " 'Tis all a duel between this Pitt and me" (II, 6, i), and:

> I'll see how I can treat this Russian horde
> Which English gold* has brought together here
> From the four corners of the universe. . . .[76]

At Kowno he says to his soldiers:

> Then let us forthwith span the Niemen's flood.
> Let us bear war into her great gaunt land.[77]

This is met by Russian counter-proclamations:

> Rankmen! officers!
> You fend your lives, your land, your liberty.
> . . . Heaven frowns on the aggressor,

---

* Massena and Foy, coming upon Wellington's impregnable fortress near Calendrix "in foul weather," decide on a withdrawal action rather than to "heap corpses hereabout" (II,6,ii). After Ulm, Tolstoy has Prince Andrey recollect Napoleon's words with "a wounded pride and the hope of glory": "As for that Russian Army which English gold has brought from the ends of the universe—we shall see that it meets the same fate" (the fate of the army at Ulm) (*War and Peace* trans. by Constance Garnett (Modern Library, New York, n.d.), p. 147.

the Spirit Ironic chiding, *"Ha! 'Liberty' is quaint and pleases me, Sounding from such a soil!"* [78]

The Empress-Mother, geopolitically minded, counsels her son Alexander:

> A backward answer is our country's card—
> The special style and mode of Muscovy.
> We have grown great upon it, my dear son . . .

and recalls Napoleon's reply to his foreign minister Champagny:

>   No—not I.
> My sense of my own dignity forbids
> My watching the slow clocks of Muscovy! [79]

On Campagny's advice that he give up the Arch-duchess Anne in favor of Marie Louise, Napoleon reminds him that the gynecologist "Caulaincourt says [that Anne] will be incapable of motherhood for six months yet or more—a grave delay."

The Russians burn Smolensk, "the peacock of Russian cities to western eyes," and Rostopchin, the Mayor of Moscow, instead of handing over the keys of the city to Napoleon as the Mayor of Berlin had done, sets fire to the city and demolishes the fire-fighting equipment following Kutuzof's withdrawal. The Spirit of Rumour comments on Napoleon's ghastly surprise: "Moscow deserted? What a monstrous thing!" [80]

Napoleon* finds his retreat blocked by Kutuzof's cavalry

---

* Napoleon wrote his stepson, Eugene Beaucharnais, whom he had left as a rear guard in Moscow, "that it might be well to arouse the peasantry to revolt," as the Cossack Pugachev had done in 1773–74 during Catherine II's reign. Tarlé explains "There is little need to surmise [why he didn't] he explained it himself." "He subsequently asserted that he had feared to let loose the elements of national revolt, that he had been disinclined to create a situation in which there 'would be no one with whom' he might conclude a peace" (*Bonaparte*, p. 291). There is no reference in *The Dynasts* to Pugachev, unless it be in the Years' observation following the battle of Leipzig: "Now every neighbouring realm is France's warder /

under the Cossack Platoff at the Smolensk road; Partonneau is defeated, and seven thousand soldiers are separated from the demoralized, retreating Grand Army, whose haggard remnants cross the Beresina river and seek shelter in Lithuania. Napoleon deserts his men, flees back to Paris, is hardly recognized by his wife, who asks "Where is the Grand Army 'That cheered me deaf at Dresden?'" He explains, "Not Russia, but God's sky has conquered me!"[81] "Fishes as good swim in the sea as have come out of it," he remarks; he "will guild the dome of the Invalides in the best gold leaf and on a novel pattern." "Guild the dome, dear? Why?"

> To give them things
> To think about. They'll take to it like children,
> And argue in the cafés right and left
> On its artistic points.—So they'll forget
> The woes of Moscow.[82]

A woman hearing of his civic enterprise, comments: "Rodomontade is cheap!"

His idea is symptomatic of the pre-Raphaelites of the *fin de siècle* (the Rosettis, Holman Hunt, Wilde, Théophile Gautier [in France], and others of the "Art for Art's Sake" school in England, against whom both Ruskin and Morris inveighed, and Hardy, also, who agreed with them that "Art was for everybody." * One recalls Hardy's comment on Clym's being ahead of his time for a successful propagandist:

And smirking satisfaction will be feigned: / The which is seemlier?—so-called ancient order, Or that the red-breath'd war-house prance unreined?" (III,3,v). The seeds of revolution are suggested by Tolstoy, after Smolensk, in Karp's shouting to Old Dron, the Rostovs' steward: "How many years have you been fattening on the village? What is it to you if our homes are ruined or not," and a little old man bursts out, "It was your son's turn to be conscripted, but no . . . they took my Vanka to be shaved for a soldier," to which old Dron replies, "I'm not one to go against the mir (the commune). You've grown fat off it. . . ." (*War and Peace*, p. 687).

* Letter (Dec. 19, 1863) to his sister Mary: "You have no right to say you are not connected with art. Everybody is to a certain extent: the only difference between a professor and an amateur being that the former has (the often disagreeable) necessity of making it his means of earning bread and cheese and thus rendering what is a pleasure to other people

A man who advocates aesthetic effort and deprecates social effort is only likely to be understood by a class to which social effort has become a stale matter.[83]

Napoleon raises a second army and attempts to subdue the vassals of his already-rebelling confederates before he again sets out to attack England, "setting free," as he had said to Decrès in 1804 at Boulogne, "from bondage to a cold manorial caste, a people who await it." At Leipzig, "the combat of Napoleon's hope," of which the Pities observes, *"Neither the victor is,"* the Rumours retort:

> But, for France and him,
> *Half-won is losing!* [84]

Before the battle, Napoleon complains to his old Grenadier Augereau, of "an atmosphere of scopeless apathy, in which I do not share," to which the Old Grenadier replies

> There are reasons, sire,
> Good reasons, for despondence! As I came
> I learnt, past question, that Bavaria
> Swerves on the very pivot of desertion.
> This adds some three score thousand to our foes.[85]

At the Thonberg Windmill bivouac, Napoleon, dozing in front of the fireplace, wakens, and is astonished that his

a 'bore' to himself" (*Early Life*, pp. 52–53). This is a very different view from that of Dickens's Miss Mollflathers, proprietor of a young ladies' seminary, who feels that the lower classes were made only "to toil unremittingly in factories and on farms," and who censures Little Nell's delivering handbills advertising Mrs. Jarley's waxworks: "Don't you feel how naughty it is of you to be a wayward child, when you might have the proud consciousness of assisting to the extent of your infant powers, the manufactures of your country; of improving your mind for the constant contemplation of the steam engine and of earning a comfortable and independent subsistence of from two and nine pence to three shillings per week. Dr. Watt's poem about the little busy bee . . . is only for genteel children for whom the work means painting on velvet and fancy needlework; for poor people's children there should be nothing but toil" (Edgar Johnson, *Dickens: His Tragedy and Triumph* [New York: Simon & Schuster, 1952], p. 328).

marshals look with gloomy faces at the flaming logs, and asks:

> Am I awake
> Or is this all a dream?—Ah, no. Too real!
> And yet I have seen ere now a time like this.

Bidding them adieu, he rides with Berthier and Caulaincourt to Leipzig. Pursued by Macdonald and Poniatowski's Poles, the French blow up the bridge of Lindenau in their retreat; Macdonald swims to safety, Poniatowski is drowned, and the Pities, in chorus, mourn:

> *And every current ripples red*
> *With marshals' blood and men's.*

In the general rout, Wellington shouts "Where are the Emperor's headquarters now?" to a fleeing commandant, who replies, "My Lord, there are no headquarters . . . how could we fight today with our hearts in our shoes?" The Chorus of the Years recites a requiem:

> *The Battle of the Nations now is closing,*
> *And all is lost to One, to many gained;*
> *The old dynastic routine reimposing*
> *The new dynastic structure unsustained.*
> (III. 3. v).

This vicissitude recalls the Years' comment on Napoleon's turning back from Astorga to "leave to you the destinies of Spain," that he *"suggests one turning from his apogee!"*[86] and the Windsor Castle scene in which the stricken monarch, King George, complains of the loss of the Princess Amelia to his doctors, "My friends, don't bleed me—pray don't!" [a treatment for all ailments by the medical profession from the Middle Ages to the death of Byron] and asks quixotically, on being told he has won a victory at Albuera, "far in harried Spain":[87]

But I thought
I was a poor afflicted captive here,
In darkness lingering out my lonely days,
Beset with terror of these myrmidons
That suck my blood like vampires! . . .
And yet he says
That I have won a battle! O God, curse, damn!
When will the speech of the world accord with truth,
And men's tongues roll sincerely?

There is caustic comment on both the temporal and spiritual institutions, and their collaboration on "holy wars" of unholy nature. On the eve of Moscow, General Kutuzof has displayed to his peasant army the icon of Smolensk—the Holy Synod having, in solemn congress, pronounced Napoleon the anti-Christ (1804). Napoleon, observing the ritual through field glasses, declares to his officers and men:

Ay! Not content to trust in their own strength,
They try to hire the enginry of Heaven.
I am no theologian, but I laugh
That men can be so grossly logicless,
When war, defensive or aggressive either,
Is in its essence Pagan and opposed
To the gist of Christianity! [88]

Napoleon, incidentally, salutes the sunrise on the morning of the battle of Borodino as "the sun of Austerlitz"—the battle-field of which the Ironic spirits

Beheld the rarest wrecked amain,
Whole nigh-perfected species slain
By those that scarce could boast a brain;

and again, following Napoleon's imprisonment at Elba:

The Congress of Vienna sits,
And war becomes a war of wits,
Where every Power perpends withal
Its dues as large, its friends' as small;
Till Priests of Peace prepare once more
To fight as they have fought before.[89]

The Pities ask, following Waterloo, *"Is this the Esdraelon of moil for mortal man's effacement?"*, to which the Spirit Ironic retorts in a Marxian vein:

> *Warfare mere,**
> *Plied by the Managed for the Managers;*
> *To wit: by fellow folks who profit nought*
> *For those who profit all!* [90]

England's advantage as a sea-power ("that curst Oligarch of the Sea," in Napoleon's words) in the conquest of the world market is given philosophical overtones (in the Spirit of the Years' reply (III, 7, vii) to the Spirit of the Pities at Waterloo) in its important trade sailing-ship image:

> *Knowest not at this stale time*
> *That shaken and unshaken are alike*
> *But demonstrations from the Back of Things?*
> *Must I again reveal It as It hauls*
> *The halyards of the world?*

The contrast in *The Dynasts* between the resplendence of the ruling classes and the menial existence of the ruled and exploited is appalling.[91] The Spirit Ironic observes of the *"douced and diamonded"* royal guests at the Carlton House ball: *"The gloom upon their faces is due rather to their having borrowed those diamonds at eleven per cent than to their loyalty to a suffering monarch!"* On the lavish spectacle of Napoleon and Marie Louise's wedding in the Grand Gallery of the Louvre, the Spirit of the Years observes to the Pities, *"Yet see it pass, as by a conjuror's wand,"* and describes the exodus following the Battle of Vitoria as *"a Noah's Ark procession—wives, mistresses, actresses, dancers, nuns and prostitutes, which struggle through*

---

* Marx, refuting Clausewitz in a letter to Engels (Jan. 7, 1857), says that war is neither an art nor a science but "most like trade," and adds that "fighting is to war what cash-payment is to trade, for however rarely it may be necessary for it actually to occur, everything is directed towards it and eventually it must take place all the same and be decisive" (p. 100).

droves of oxen, sheep, goats, horses, asses, and mules—laden with pictures, treasures, flour, vegetables, furniture, finery, parrots, monkeys, etc." King Joseph Buonaparte remarks:

> The Englishry are a pursuing army,
> And we a flying brothel! See our men—
> They leave their guns to save their mistresses! [92]

At the glittering coronation spectacle in the Milan Cathedral, Napoleon on taking the Crown of Lombardy says: " 'Tis God has given it to me. So be it. Let any who shall touch it now beware!" The English deserters in a cellar at Astorga—ragged men, women, and children—lie half buried and intoxicated in grime and straw. The First Deserter, who has recognized the Duke of Dalmatia in their pursuit, is answered by the Second Deserter, "The Duke of Damnation for our poor rears by the look on't!" A Cheapside lad blames Pitt for the death of his Uncle John's parrott, "which talked itself to death," and Napoleon's little son asks his Empress-mother, "What did we get up so early for?" Cambacérès, Arch Chancellor to Napoleon, advises the Empress, "there's not a thrice to lose." [93]

At the Royal Pavilion, Brighton, celebrating the English victories in the Peninsula, the Prince Regent and Castlereagh announce the sending of an expedition to the Walcheren, and amid the ballroom gaiety, the Pities already hear the dying moans of Moore's seasoned veterans in the Scheldt. This scene reminds one of Poe's stories "The Cask of Amontillado" and "The Masque of the Red Death," in the first of which Montresor leads Fortunato to die in his family catacombs, and the second of which Prince Prospero and his select guests are reveling in the castle in the disease-ravaged*

---

*"The cholera is still the great topic" Paul Lafargue wrote Engels from Paris (July 10, 1884). "It *is* a question of the Asian cholera coming straight from Tong-King [a war of conquest: 1883–1885], which has not yet sent any nuggets," and earlier, July 4, "The cholera has not yet reached Paris: it will certainly do so," and again on July 12, "The cholera has reached Paris; several deaths are announced this morning" (*Engels-La* swamp. One remembers that the American South contributed considerably to feudalism while the outside world perished of cholera. The bad times following the Napoleonic Wars (1815) and the instability of the western nations affected the tobacco industry in Virginia and figured in the failure of Poe's stepfather, John Allan, and his partner, Ellis, tobacco exporters. The ruin of the South was chronicled earlier in the novels of Ellen Glasgow and later in those of William Faulkner. Marx noted that "whilst the cotton industry introduced child slavery in England, it gave in the United States a stimulus to the transformation of the earlier, more or less patriarchal slavery into a system of commercial

Fargue Correspondence (Moscow, USSR: Foreign Languages Publishing House, 1959), pp. 214–15, 213, 216). Lafargue's first son, nicknamed Schnaps," had died in Spain from the after-effects of cholera in 1872 (*ibid.*, p. 156n).

Hardy's wife's Uncle Holder, as a young curate in Bristol during the terrible cholera visitation, "conducted many funerals of cholera victims"— among them that of a charming young widow, met at a friend's house a few days before, "who invited him to call on her. With pleasant anticipations he went at tea-time a day or two later and duly inquired if she was at home. The servant said with a strange face: 'Why sir, you buried her this morning'" (*Early Life*, p. 202). Cholera had taken a toll of 20,000 in England and Wales during the summer of 1864 (see Edgar Johnson, *Charles Dickens*, 2:285). See Allan's letter (Sept. 21, 1815) from Greenock, Scotland to his partner Charles Ellis: "I arrived here about a half an hour ago . . . finding some American vessels on the eve of sailing I avail myself of the chance to write a few lines, though I cannot say much about our business. . . . I flatter myself from the small quantity in London & the Postieur of affairs on the Continent that our sales will be profitable.

It would appear that France and the Allies have concluded a Treaty but it has not been promulgated—the Allies will hold the strong posts for a while until the refractory spirit of some of the old adherents of Bonaparte has subsided. France is far from being settled. Louis is too lenient and too peaceable the French delight in War I believe they care but little who rules them provided that ruler indulges them in their Habit which 25 years of war has so strongly fixed upon them, etc." (Hervey Allen's *Israfel*, p. 55). Also see William Bittner's *Poe*, p. 33. ". . . Ellis and Allan went into receivership (1822–23) and John Allan retained posession of his property only on the sufferance of his creditors."

Hervey Allen notes in his *Israfel* (p. 51) "an interesting letter in the *Ellis & Allan Papers* which throws considerable light on the state of culture among the poorer up-country whites at this time, in which one of the Ellises depicts their incredulity over his prediction of an eclipse of the sun, and their superstitious astonishment at its fulfillment. The mental condition of these 'poor whites' seems to have approached that of the medieval peasant during the early Renaissance."

exploitation. In fact," he says, "the veiled slavery of the wage-earners in Europe needed, for its pedestal, slavery pure and simple in the New World." Dickens observed that America was "not the republic of his imagination," and Hardy, in his poem "On an Invitation to the United States," wrote:

> My ardours for emprize nigh lost
> Since Life has bared its bones to me,
> I shrink to see a modern coast
> Whose riper times have yet to be;
> Where the new regions claim them free
> From that long drip of human tears
> Which peoples old in tragedy
> Have left upon the centuried years.
>
> For, wonning in these ancient lands,
> Enchased and lettered as a tomb,
> And scored with prints of perished hands,
> And chronicled with dates of doom,
> Though my own Being bear no bloom
> I trace the lives such scenes enshrine,
> Give past exemplars present room,
> And their experience count as mine.

Hardy thought (in Jan. 1909), however, that Poe's "qualities, which would have been extraordinary anywhere, are much more extraordinary for the America of his date."

The Dynasts abounds in carnage on sea and on land, from Trafalgar to Waterloo, with the groans of the dying and the stench of the dead until the Shade of the Earth is nauseated by *"The fumes of nitre and reek of gore";* the Spirit of the Years cries *"Enough, and more, of inventories and names!"* [94] The barbarity of war is everywhere contrasted with the peacefulness of Nature, and Hardy is unsparing in his criticism of the contradiction between Christianity and "this Christ of War" (III, 3, i). At Albuera "the birds, in the wood, unaware that this is to be different from every other day there known, are heard singing their over-

tures with their usual serenity," and "the green slopes behind and around the hill are untrodden—though in a few
hours to be the sanguinary scene of the most murderous
struggle of the whole war." [95] We hear Pitt's God-speeding
"Amen, Amen" to Nelson; the chaplain's inanity on Nelson's
death: "He has homed to where there's no more sea"; and
the Chaplain, with a lantern and book, in the Jardin de la
Carlos after the battle of Coruña, within the sound of
French guns, reciting, to the impatience of General Hope
and Captain Hardinge: ". . . not to be sorry as men without
hope, for them that sleep in Him," and the officers' and
men's "Amens," as they "hastily fill in the grave." [96] The
Army called "the Grand [500,000]" a Recording Angel observes, . . . "Israel-like, moved by some master-sway,/Is made
to wander on and waste away!" (III, 1, ix). A woman exclaims, "Give me back my two sons, murderer!" which is
augmented by cries of the same kind from the Populace; a
mad soldier sings, "So foolish Life adieu and ingrate Leader
too," and the Spirit Sinister says, "*Good. It is the selfish and
unconscionable characters who are so much regretted.*"* [97]
An officer points out some sleeping French bivouackers to
Kutuzof, who says, "Go stir them up! We slay not sleeping
men." On being told "Prince, they are dead," he replies:

> We shall be stumbling on such frost-baked meats
> Most of the way to Wilna.[98]

The Spirit Ironic, after Astorga, remarks, "Quaint poesy and
real romance of war," and the Pities replies:

---

* Elfride and Knight, while playing chess in the library, bring up the
matter of whether an inexperienced player playing with an experienced
player is "a vanity" or "a virtue," and Elfride declares, "O yes [vanity]
in battle." "Nelson's bravery lay in his vanity," to which Knight replies,
"Indeed! Then so did his death," and she retorts, "O no, no! For it is
written in the book of the prophet Shakespeare":
    Fear and be slain? No worse can come to fight,
    And fight and die is death destroying death!
                                    (*Pair of Blue Eyes*, p. 190).

Mock on, Shade, if thou wilt! But others find
Poesy ever lurk where pit-pats poor mankind![99]

One recalls Siegfried Sassoon's observation as a World War I combatant in the battle of the Somme in which he was wounded, that "It wasn't easy to be a poet and a platoon commander at the same time," and that "the Somme battle was, to put it mildly, an inhuman and beastly business." He felt that no explanation of his "could ever reach his elders," because of "their patriotic suppression of those aspects of war that never got into the newspapers." [100]

The one consistent note voiced again and again by the Pities is that Might does not make Right, and that the people are being "hoodwinked" by their rulers. The Shade of the Earth asks the Pities, "*And who, then, Cordial One,/Wouldst substitute for this Intractable?*", and on being told ". . . *those of kindlier build,/In fair Compassions skilled,*" remarks:

> *They may come, will they. I am not averse.*
> *Yet know I am but the ineffectual Shade*
> *Of her the Travailler, herself a thrall*
> *To It; in all her labourings curbed and kinged!* [101]

In the After Scene of Part III, the Years reply:

> *In the Foregone I knew what dreaming was,*
> *And could let raptures rule! But not so now.*
> *Yea, I psalmed thus and thus. . . . But not so now!*

In the beginning the Years remind the Pities that "*old Laws operate yet; and phase and phase/Of men's dynastic and imperial moils/Shape on accustomed lines. Though, as for me,/I care not how they shape, or what they be.*" The Pities, censuring the Years for their "small sense of mercy," remind the Years: "*They are shapes that bleed, mere marionettes or no, and each has parcel in the total Will.*" (I, Fore Scene)

> *So the Will heaves through Space, and moulds the times,*
> *With mortals for Its fingers! We shall see*
> *Again men's passions, virtues, visions, crimes,*
>> *Obey resistlessly*
> *The purposive, unmotived, dominant Thing*
> *Which sways in brooding dark their wayfaring!* [102]

After Napoleon's abdication at Fontainebleau, the Years opine, *"How heavily grinds the Will upon his brain,/His halting hand, and his unlighted eyes,"* to which the Spirit Ironic remarks: *"A picture this for kings and subjects too!"*; the Pities cannot take *"this tale of Life's impulsion by Incognizance,"* and argue with the Years on the Will's "inadvertent Mind":

> *Men gained cognition with the flux of time,*
> *And wherefore not the Force informing them?* [103]

At the battle of Austerlitz, the Pities pray to the *"Great Necessitator,"* who, the Years asks them to *"note anew"*, is *"the Eternal Urger, pressing change on change,"* [104] and the Ironic Spirits, addressing the Pities as "O Innocents," advance a deterministic theory:

> *Stand ye apostrophizing That*
> *Which, working all, works but thereat*
> *Like some sublime fermenting-vat*

and:

> *Could ye have seen its early deeds*
> *Ye would not cry, as one who pleads*
> *For quarter, when a Europe bleeds!* [105]

At Waterloo, the Pities, who imagine they have seen some change wrought in Wellington, again address the Will in chorus:

> *To thee, whose eye all Nature owns,*
> *Who hurlest Dynasts from their thrones,*
> *And liftest those of low estate,*
> *We sing, with Her men consecrate!*

Yea, Great and Good, Thee, Thee we hail,
Who shak'st the strong, who shield'st the frail,
Who had'st not shaped such souls as we
If tendermercy lacked in Thee![106]

Neither the Pities nor the Years have anything good to say about warfare and military leaders, but the Years are less naive and hopeful than the Pities. The movement of both opposing armies converging in Bavaria is compared to that "of molluscs on a leaf," and the Years, after Waterloo, speak with dispassionate contempt of Napoleon:

Such men as thou, who wade across the world
To make an epoch, bless, confuse, appal,
Are in the elemental ages' chart
Like meanest insects on obscurest leaves
But incidents and tools of Earth's unfolding;
Or as the brazen rod that stirs the fire
Because it must.[107]

ii. "THE PALACE AND THE COTTAGE"

Indeed, Hardy had as little respect for politicians as did Dickens.* It is enlightening to compare Dickens's view, given in his letter to Forster (Apr. 27, 1855), of the situation

---

* Dickens reported Parliamentary proceedings for the *Morning Chronicle* (1835–1844), whose editor John Black was considered by J. S. Mill "the first journalist who carried criticism and reform into the details of English institutions, which Dickens was attacking in his novel" (see T. A. Jackson, *Charles Dickens*, (New York: Simon & Schuster, 1952), p. 54).

In 1852, "Powerful Chartist elements, also, were busy forcing Whitehall on to war with Russia before the Preston 'lockout' had commenced. Thus, at the crowded and enthusiastic London tavern meeting of Oct. 7th, William Newton, the leader of the engineers strike of 1852, had demanded in the name of the working men of London a costly war rather than dishonour. At the Finsburg meeting of Oct. 18 such Chartist leaders as Bronterre O'Brien, Julian Harney and Dobson Collett went farther and attacked the British Government as well as the Russian," declaring, "that the system of secret diplomacy is calculated to mislead the people of this country, and has enabled the British Cabinet to assist Continental despotism while professing a zeal for Constitutional Government" (see S. Maccoby, *English Radicalism*, 4:20).

during the Crimean War, before the time of the bread-riots in Liverpool and London and the fall of Sebastapol, for it recalls Blake's lines, "To cut off bread from the city that the remnant may learn to obey." It is also enlightening to contrast the Poet Laureate's "Charge of the Light Brigade" (1854) at the time of the Crimean War with Hardy's poems of *The Dynasts* at the time of the Boer War. Dickens seethed in anger:

> A country which is discovered to be in this tremendous condition as to its war affairs; with an enormous black cloud of poverty in every town which is spreading and deepening every hour; and not one man in two thousand knowing anything about, or even believing in, its existence; with a non-working aristocracy and a silent parliament; and everybody for himself and nobody for the rest; this is the prospect, and I think it a very deplorable one.[1]

Hardy has the Spirit of the Pities say in *The Dynasts:*[2]

> *Each for himself, his family, his heirs;*
> *For the wan weltering nations, who concerns,*
> *Who cares?*

During the years that Hardy was gathering material for his drama, he saw plenty of examples of the indifference of politicians to the people's welfare. Throughout the prolonged agricultural depression (1875–1896), Disraeli and the Conservative Party had shown not only an abysmal ignorance of the condition but a heartless selfishness to correct it, as is disclosed in his letter (Dec. 27, 1876) to Lady Bradford:

> What is the cause of this distress? And, if permanent, is there to be a permanent Committee of Relief? And the property of the nation to support the numbers of unemployed labour? —Worse than Socialism. To hoist the flag of distress, when there has been no visible calamity to account for it, like a cotton famine, no bread and meat famine, no convulsion of nature, is difficult and may not be wise.[3]

It is also observable in his speech in Parliament (Mar. 28, 1879) on the same subject:

> No one can deny that the depression of the agricultural interest is excessive. Though I can recall several periods of suffering none of them have ever equalled the present in its intenseness. . . . The remarkable feature of the present agricultural depression is this—that the agricultural interest is suffering from a succession of bad harvests and that these bad harvests are accompanied for the first time by extremely low prices. . . . In old days, when we had a bad harvest. we had also the somewhat dismal compensation of higher prices. That is not the condition at the present; on the contrary, the harvests are bad, and the prices are lower.[4]*

The plight of the agricultural interest, as Disraeli called it, had stimulated some reformers to alleviate their condition in 1879—"the blackest year"—and Disraeli harangued against them at the Agricultural Association meeting at Aylesworth (Sept. 2, 1879): "Beware of Cockney agitators sent out by the party, which always viewed the agricultural interests with hostility. But a year ago they were setting the agricultural labourers against the farmers; now they are attempting to set the farmers against the landlords."[5] John Bright had reported (Dec. 10, 1858) Lord Derby's saying "that if anyone would tell him what were the politics of three or four of the great landed proprietors of any county, he could tell at once what were the politics of the Members for that county . . . the Members are the representatives of those great proprietors."[6] It recalls Balzac's statement in *The Peasants:* "Tell me what you possess, and I will tell you what you think."[7]

Disraeli appears to have been somewhat premature in his self-congratulatory letter (Oct. 30, 1870) to John Manners, the head of his Young England organization: "How well

* "This was because of the foreign competition, which was the inevitable result of Peel's action in 1846 in the repeal of the Corn Laws" (Monypenny and Buckle, p. 1368).

for the country that we settled the suffrage question! The trading agitators have nothing to say, or if they open their mouths, are obliged to have recourse to European Jacobism." [8] William Pitt in 1803 had recognized Napoleon's threat to England's supremacy, yet believed that there was "no longer that Jacobin propaganda—'Revolutionary poison' —which in former days had undermined even his Britannic Majesty's fleet, not to speak of the working populations of the industries and coal-mining centres." Pitt "vividly remembered the sailors' mutinies of 1797" (Nore and Spithead), declares contemporary historian Eugene Tarlé;* these arose from the low wages, irregular payments, bad food, and brutal conditions prevailing in the fleet.[9]

In the seventies agitation for the extension of the suffrage to male farm workers, Disraeli admonished Parliament:

> Now I say when you come to this question of the suffrage for the boroughs, there is a principle in saying a man shall have a vote who has, by his residence and his contribution to local taxation, proved that he is interested in the welfare of his community. That man is a man whom you may trust in preference to a migratory pauper.[10]

Hardy, in his essay "The Dorsetshire Labourer" (1883), refers to an article by a lady on the peasants of Auvergne and their sordid habitats, remarking,

> When we know that the Damocles' sword of the poor is the fear of being turned out of their houses by the farmer or squire, we may wonder how many scrupulously clean English labourers would not be glad with half-an-acre of the complaint that afflicts these unhappy freeholders of Auvergne.[11]

His diary entry of February 28, 1883—the year of Marx's death—describes how some of the agriculturalists were dealing with their depressed situation, at an auction of turn-

* p. 137.

pike bonds.* He attended it with Walter Fletcher, County Surveyor to Corfe Mullen (a town 18 miles ESE of Dorchester, famed for the manufacture of ornamental Purbeck marble such as that from which the ancestral vaults of the D'Urbervilles had been made), and it was held at an inn, with the auctioneer and the trustees at one end of the room and at the other

> a crowd of strange beings, looking as not worth sixpence among them. Yet the biddings for the "Poole Trust" would sometimes reach £1400. Sometimes the bidders would say "Beg yer pardon, gentlemen, but will you wait to let us step outside a minute or two?" Perhaps the trustees would say they could not. The men would say, "then we'll step out without your letting us." On their return only one or two would bid, and the peremptory trustees be nettled.

Hardy was interested in foreign affairs also. In December 1876 he attended a conference on the Eastern Question at St. James Hall, and heard Mr. Gladstone, Lord Shaftesbury, Hon. E. Ashley, Anthony Trollope, and the Duke of Westminster, at which Trollope was irritated because the Duke, who was chairman, pulled at his coattails because he had exceeded "the five or seven minutes allowed" and, exclaiming "parenthetically 'Please leave my coat alone,' went on speaking." Hardy's attending the debate on Gladstone's Home Rule Bill for Ireland in the House of Commons—"a motley assembly nowadays," he wrote, "April 8, 9, 10, 11 [1886] and a critical time politically"—proved especially valuable to him when he came to writing *The Dynasts:*

* The Fenians, organised in 1879, fought eviction by means of boycotts and pledged themselves "never to bid for, take or hold the farm from which our neighbor has been evicted for the non-payment of an unjust rent, and never to take any hand, act or part in sowing or saving the crops thereon and to hold the man who will do so as a public enemy" (A. L. Morton, *A People's History of England*, p. 416). American farmers in the Dust Bowl during the depression of the nineteen-thirties protected their interests in a similar way. Marx gives a list of the wages paid in three villages in the neighbourhood of Blanford, Wimbourne, and Poole "showing the weekly income of the whole family, and their expenses for the necessities of life, taken from the London *Economist*" (March 29, 1845) *Capital*, pp. 290, 743–44).

Saw the dandy party enter in evening dress, eye-glasses, diamond rings, etc. They were a great contrast to Joseph Arch* and the Irish members in their plain, simple, ill-fitting clothes. Gladstone's frock-coat dangled and swung as he went in and out with a white flower in his button-hole and open waistcoat. Lord Randolph's manner in turning to Dillon, the Irish member, was arrogant. Sir R. Cross was sturdy, like T.B., the Dorchester butcher, when he used to stand at the chopping block on market days. The earnestness of the Irish members who spoke was very impressive; Lord G. Hamilton was entirely wanting in earnestness; Sir H. James quite the reverse; E. Clarke direct, firm and incisive, but inhuman.

To realize the difficulty of the Irish question it is necessary to *see* the Irish phalanx sitting tight: it then seems as if one must go with Morley, and get rid of them at any cost. . . .

Morley kept trying to look used to it all, and not as if he were a consummate man of letters there by mistake. Gladstone was quite distinct from all others in the House, though he sits low in his seat from age. When he smiled one could see benevolence on his face. Large-heartedness versus small-heartedness is a distinct attitude which the House . . . takes up to an observer's eye.**

* In 1885 Joseph Arch secured a 600-vote majority over the Duke of Portland's brother (Smellie, *A Hundred Years of English Government*, p. 198).

** "Though he did not enter it here," Mrs. Hardy says, "Hardy often wrote elsewhere, and said of Home Rule that it was a staring dilemma, of which good policy and good philanthropy were the huge horns. Policy for England required that it should not be granted; humanity to Ireland that it should. Neither Liberals nor Conservatives would honestly own up to this opposition between two moralities, but speciously insisted that humanity and policy were both on one side—of course, their own" (*Early Life*, p. 234). "In May 1905 he saw Ben Jonson's play, *The Silent Woman*, and Shaw's *John Bull's Other Island* and *Man and Superman*" (*Later Years*, p. 111).

"Of Ireland" Marx said "that the cause of English labour was inextricably bound up with the liberation of Ireland, whose cheap labour was a continual threat to the English unions, her economic subjection as in the analagous case of serfs in Russia and slavery in the United States. Marx attacked Lord Russell as "a pseudo-radical" and Palmerston as "a disguised Russian agent" (Berlin, pp. 201, 203).

Hardy was pro-Gladstone and inclined toward Home-Rule; Tennyson anti-Gladstone and anti-Home-Rule (see Charles Tennyson, *Tennyson* [New York: Macmillan, 1949], pp. 480–81). Charles Bradlaugh, editor of the *National Reformer*, was elected from North Hampton but denied his seat on account of his atheism. Arnold thought Gladstone "no more than an

Hardy met Disraeli in May 1875 as "one of a deputation ... in support of a motion for a Select Committee to inquire into the state of Copywright Law," and found him unexpectedly urbane, he recalled on Disraeli's death on April 19, 1881 (*Early Life,* pp. 139, 192).

In 1890 at a society gathering, Hardy "chanced to converse with the then Dowager Duchess of Marlborough, Lord Randolph Churchill's mother," and noted: "She is a nice warm-feeling woman"; she "deplored that young men like ——should stand in the forefront of the Tory party, and her son be nowhere." "Poor woman," Hardy wrote, "I was sorry for her. . . . Parnell, however, was the main thing talked about, and not Randolph" (*Early Life,* p. 301).

The incident recalls the two society ladies' conversation on Ethelberta:

"A very anomalous woman. . . ."
"Like the British Constitution she owes her success in prac-

eloquent manager," and Bright "a man with a foot in both world, the world of middle-class liberalism and the world of democracy . . . a shallow person" (see *Culture and Anarchy,* ed. J. Dover Wilson, p. xxvii). Arnold, according to Hardy, who met him in Feb. 1880, "had a manner of having made up his mind upon everything years ago, so that it was a pleasing futility for his interlocutor to begin thinking new ideas different from his own, at that time of day" (*Early Life,* p. 175).

Some light is thrown on the political situation under Disraeli, who wrote Lady Bradford (Nov. 2, 1876): "As I have often told you there is no gambling like politics" (Monypenny and Buckle, 2:958), and is reflected in Mrs. Pine-Avon's comment to Pierston (*The Well-Beloved*) that she "wouldn't trade her position for anything with her cousin who is quite wild for fear her husband will be turned out at the next election," and in her observation:

"Yes, it is mostly the women who are the gamesters; the men only the cards. The pity is that politics are looked on as being a game for polticians, just as cricket is a game for cricketers; not as the serious duties of political trustees" (p. 63).

"How few of us ever think or feel that 'the nation of every country dwells in the cottage' as somebody says!" (A paraphrase of Disraeli's "The palace is not safe when the cottage is not happy" [2: 709]).

"Yes, though I wonder to hear you quote that."

"O—I am of no party, though my relations are. There can be only one best course at all times, and the wisdom of the nation should be directed to finding it instead of zigzagging in two courses, according to the will of the party which happens to have the upper hand" (p. 64).

tice to her inconsistencies in principle" (*The Hand of Ethelberta,* p. 77).

It also recalls Captain de Stancy's remark to his sister Charlotte:

> "My sedulous avoidance hitherto of all relating to our family vicissitudes has been, I own, stupid conduct for an intelligent being; but impossible grapes are always sour, and I have unconsciously adopted Radical notions to obliterate disappointed hereditary instincts. But these have a trick of re-establishing themselves as one gets older, and the castle and what it contains have a keen interest for me now" (*A Laodicean,* p. 204).

The Conservatives had repeatedly used the threat of war abroad to try to prevent unrest at home. Disraeli wrote Lady Bradford (Nov. 11, 1874) on the success of their strategy: "Saturday was a great, I believe I might say a complete success. The Party is what is called on its legs again, and jingoism is triumphant!" [12] He had termed the revolt in Bosnia and Herzegovina (1875) "stock-jobbing" for this purpose. The Bulgarian atrocities appeared in the *Daily News** (July 23, 1874) and evoked Gladstone's protest. The Music Halls were vibrating with chauvinistic gibberish, that disturbed Conrad as well as Hardy:

> We don't want to fight, but, by Jingo, if we do,
> We've got the ships, we've got the men, we've got
> The money too.[13]

These words were not lost on Hardy, who complained later (Aug. 1914) about "the noisy crew of music-hall Jingoes."

---

* It was to "be kept free from personal influence or party bias," the prospectus said, to be "devoted to the advocacy of all rational and honest means by which wrong may be redressed just rights maintained, and the happiness and welfare of society promoted" (see F. T. Marzials, *Life of Charles Dickens* [London: W. Scott, 1887], pp. 99-100). First number came out on morning of Jan. 21, 1846. Dickens's salary was to be £2,000 a year; he held the post of editor for three weeks.

They are heard earlier in *The Dynasts* (1903–1908), in the
Ironic and Sinister Spirits' burlesques * of bourgeois society
in doggerel like the one quoted above in their gossip on
Napoleon's divorcing Josephine to marry Maria Louise, who
is *enceinte* (II, 5, vl):

> *First 'twas a finished coquette,*
> *And now it's a raw ingénue.—*
> *Blonde instead of brunette.*
> *An old wife doffed for a new.*
> > *She'll bring him a baby*
> > *As quickly as maybe,*
> *And that's what he wants her to do,*
> > > *Hoo-hoo!*
> *And that's what he wants her to do!*

In 1877 the Queen wrote Disraeli (April 25) that

she wishes no general war—God knows! for no one abhors
it more than she does; but then there ought to be an understanding that we cannot allow the Russians to occupy Constantinople and that we must see that this is promised, or
the consequences may be serious.

One recalls Hardy's having Napoleon say after his victory at
Astorga (*The Dynasts*, II, 3, ii).

> Now eastward. So!—
> The Orient likewise looms full sombrely. . . .
> The Turk declines pacifically to yield
> What I have promised Alexander. Ah! . . .
> As for Constantinople being his prize
> I'll see him frozen first. . . .

Morris had written in 1877: "As to the Russians, all I say is

* Mr. Ladywell one of Ethelberta's suitors, exclaims, "I would have
burlesque quotation put down by Act of Parliament, and all who dabbled
in it placed with him who can cite scripture for his purposes" (*The Hand
of Ethelberta*, p. 59).

this: we *might* have acted so that they could have had no pretext for interfering with Turkey except in accordance with the unanimous wish of Europe: We *have* so acted as to drive them into separate interference whatever may come: and to go to war with them for this would be a piece of outrageous injustice." [14]

Disraeli had written Lady Chesterfield at the same time (May 29, 1876): "We shall certainly not drift into a war, but go to war, if we do, because we intend it, and have a purpose to accomplish." [15] A year before, following the murder in Hong Kong of a British Consular official, A. R. Margay, Disraeli* confided to Lady Bradford (Sept. 27, 1875): "I have taken a step in diplomacy, wh. I am sure never was taken before. I have induced the Japanese Minister in England to telegraph to his Government, urging them to offer their mediation in the event of a serious difficulty arising between China and England, and to declare that

* Oct. 17, 1874, Disraeli to the Queen: "The telegrams I received from China this morning are very menacing; and I more than fear that war between that country and Japan is inevitable. This will increase your difficulties, for the East hangs together and is wonderfully mesmeric" (Monypenny and Buckle, 2:767).

The Queen to Disraeli (Apr. 25, 1877): "To let it be thought that we shall never fight and that England will submit to Egypt being under Russia would be to abdicate the position of Great Britain as one of the Great Powers to which she never will submit, and another must wear the Crown if this is intended" (*ibid.*, 2:1005).

Disraeli to the Queen (Nov. 1, 1877): ". . . so far as a march on Constantinople is concerned there is now no fear of a *coupe de main*. Constantinople is itself now strongly fortified; both peninsulas Gallipoli and Durkos, being in a state of defense which, with sufficient troops, would render them impregnable, and, with insufficient troops, would offer a long resistance. Adrianople, too, which was an open town, is now as strong as Plevna" (2:1065). Again (New Year's Day, 1879): "The authority of yr. Majesty's throne stands high in Europe . . . and yr. Majesty's arms have achieved, in Asia, a brilliant and enduring success" (ibid., p. 1277). And yet again (Feb. 9, 1878): "The country is greatly stirring at last; if we had only a *corp d'armée* at Gallipoli, the crown of Great Britain and India would not be unworthy of the imperial brow which they adorn" (*ibid.*, p. 1116).

Tolstoy has Napoleon say to Alexander's emissary Prince Balashev, "I hear you have concluded a peace with the Turks?" and interrupts the bowing Balashev to continue with irritable vehemence, "Yes, I know you have made peace with the Turks without obtaining Moldavia and Wallachia if China will not accept that mediation and act upon it, Japan will join England against her, and place a Japanese contingent under the orders of any British forces employed by us gainst the Celestial Empire. I know not why Japan shd. not become the Sardinia of the Mongolian East. They are by far the cleverest of the Mongol race. Now you know one of the greatest secrets of State going!" [16] Dobson Collet, a Chartist earlier, had introduced a resolution in Parliament declaring "that the system of secret diplomacy is calculated to mislead the people of this country and has enabled the British Cabinet to assist Continental despotism while professing a zeal for constitutional government." [17] One recalls Sheridan's attack on this devious diplomacy in his speech against Pitt, the minister

> Whose circumventions never circumvent,
> Whose coalitions fail to coalesce;
> This dab at secret treaties known to all,
> This darling of the aristocracy—
> (Laughter, "Oh, oh," cheers, and cries of "Divide")
> Has brought the millions to the verge of ruin,
> By pledging them to Continental quarrels
> Of which we see no end!

"It was Palmerston, who hastened to recognize Napoleon III after his *coup d'état* in December 1851," declares Morton, "and Palmerston who bears the heaviest responsibility for the predatory wars upon China [18] in 1840 and

—while I would have given your Sovereign those just as I presented him with Finland . . . and he might have united them to his Empire and in a single reign would have extended Russia from the Gulf of Bothnia to the mouth of the Danube." concluding with a greedy sniff from his gold snuffbox, "What a glorious reign the Emperor Alexander's *might have been!*" (*War and Peace*, p. 580).

"Over and over again," Northcote tells us, "did we curse Gladstone for having given up Corfu, which would have been invaluable to us" (*Life of Disraeli*, 2:1163); and Disraeli wrote the Queen (May 5, 1878): "Cyprus is the key of Western Asia. One of Jerusalem's gossips remarks in Disraeli's *Tancred:* "The English want Cyprus, and they will take it as compensation" (*ibid.*, p. 1171).

1860." Professor Lattimore in our own time has observed of this period in history that "all that prevented foreign imperialism from mastering China outright was rivalry between the imperial powers." [19] Hardy was impressed in 1865 by a cartoon entitled "The Giant and the Dwarf," which he found in an old issue of *Punch* (Feb. 23, 1859) eight months after the Tientsin Treaty, and which he copied at the end of his letter to his sister Mary (Oct. 28, 1865) following his description of Palmerston's funeral. He signed his initials in tall letters as if he were the Giant in the cartoon, and it shows his political awareness of the economic aspect of the political situation:

> A tall man went to see Chang the Chinese Giant, and on his offering to pay, the doorkeeper said "Not at all Sir, we don't take money from the *profession!*" at least so *Punch* says.

This awareness is shown again in Hardy's having Napoleon say, "But Asia waits a man, and—who can tell?" [20]—takes on additional significance in the light of the post-Napoleonic age, in which the successors to Napoleon and Wellington had dreams of empire similar in grandioseness to Napoleon's dream of world conquest when, at Tilsit, he had proposed to Alexander that they divide the world between them. This comes out after Waterloo, when "stung by spectral questionings," he is commiserating:

> Why did the death-drops fail to bite me close
> I took at Fontainebleau? Had I then ceased,
> This deep had been unplumbed; had they but worked,
> I had thrown three-fold the glow of Hannibal
> Down History's dusky lanes! Is it too late? . . .
> Yea. Self-sought death would smoke but damply here!

Erdman observes in *William Blake: Prophet Against Empire* that even during the Napoleonic wars, in *The Four Zoas* (1797) "Blake spells out the sinister relationship between war and commerce." Erdman quotes Geoffrey Keynes on Blake's lines depicting the development of the British textile industry "before the hounds of Nimrod," in lightning voyages "Across Europe & Asia to China & Japan" (2: 267–75) as follows:

> China and Japan are apt symbols. During the Napoleonic wars the British navy did move belligerently in Far Eastern waters—in an unsuccessful attempt to break the Dutch monopoly of Japanese trade and in a show of naval and military force against Portugal's China port of Macao, fore-stalled by the Peace of Amiens. The British were not desperate for markets, but opportunity seemed to beckon.[21]

Disraeli had warned his constituents at the Wynward Agricultural Show at Aylesworth in 1848, a year of revolution in Europe and one of unrest and Chartist agitation at home, that "the palace is not safe when the cottage is not happy,"[22] and between 1860 and 1870, he did his best as prime minister to put the brakes on reform. In 1870 he declared in Parliament:

> Let me impress upon the attendance of the House the character of this war between France and Germany [one wonders who wrote his speech for him]. It is no common war, like the war between Prussia and Austria, or like the Italian war in which France was engaged some years ago; nor is it like the Crimean War. This war represents the German Revolution a greater political event than the French revolution of the last century. I don't say greater, or as great a social event. What its social consequences may be are in the future.

He went on in a gravely disturbed analytical vein:

> Not a single principle in the management of our foreign affairs, accepted by all the statesmen for guidance up to six months ago, any longer exists. There is not a diplomatic tradition which has not been swept away. You have a new world, new influences at work, new and unknown objects and dangers with which to cope. . . . We used to have discussions in this

House about the balance of power. Ld. Palmerston,* eminently a practical man[,] trimmed the Ship of State and shaped
its policy with a view to preserve an equilibrium in Europe.

"But what has really come to pass?" he declaimed. "The
balance of power has been entirely destroyed, and the country which suffers most, and feels the effect of this great
change most, is England." [23]

Those "who suffered most" were the English proletariat.
They protested in 1866 at a meeting presided over by Professor Edward Beesly**—Hardy's friend at a later date,
against the excessive military expenditures compared to
those on education, the treatment of the poor in the workhouse, the operation of the game-laws and other problems,
in which Hardy was interested.

Marx described the Franco-Prussian War as "the most
tremendous war of modern times," and observed cynically
that after the "chastisement of godless and debauched
France by pious and moral Germany . . . the conquering and
conquered hosts should fraternize for the common massacre
of the proletariat. This unparalleled event does indicate, not
as Bismarck thinks, the final repression of a new society up-
heaving but the crumbling into dust of bourgeois society;"
and Conrad as a war "characterized by especial intensity of
hatred, to confine examples only to illustrious persons." [24]

* John Bright, the Quaker free-trade advocate, wrote to his friend
Charles Sturge on Palmerston's death (1865): "The old Minister is gone
at last. I wish there were more to be said in his praise. We are breaking
with the old generation and I hope we shall see new and better principles
and policy in the ascendant. I think the present Cabinet with merely a new
chief cannot go on doing nothing: It cannot be provided with another
chief who can keep so many people quiet as Lord Palmerston was able
to do" (B. M. Trevelyan, *Life of John Bright*, p. 344).
** Edward Spencer Beesly was born at Feckenham, Worcestershire,
January 23, 1831, and died at St. Leonards, Sussex, July 7, 1915. He was
Professor of Latin at Bedford College, London (1860–1889), and of history
at University College (1889–1893). With Frederic Harrison and John
Henry Bridges, he led the positivist movement in England, and was editor of
Positivist Review (1893–1900), and translator of Comte's *Discourse in the
Positive Spirit* (1903).

In 1875 Lord Derby admonished Disraeli, "No doubt the Continent is arming but with Germany and France watching one another, both are likely to be more civil to us than if they were on good terms," and doubted from the Cabinet discussions "that an increase of £300,000 or £400,000 is justifiable because inevitable—I mean taking Army and Navy together. Beyond that we must not go." [25] Their attitude is somewhat like the beekeeper Enoch in Hardy's *Under the Greenwood Tree* (1872), who says, "But 'tis the money, for without money man is a shadder!", asking Geoffrey, who is shaking the bees off his clothes and neck, "Have the craters stung ye?", who replies, "on'y a little here and there," "while the rest looked on," Hardy observes, "with a complacent sense of being out of it, much as a European nation in a state of internal commotion is watched by its neighbours." [26] *

Lord Derby regretted to Queen Victoria (Jan. 14, 1875): "There must be an increase probably between £500,000 to £600,000" during a conservative ministry, "and Mr. Disraeli will be satisfied if the expenditure, though increased, is not accompanied by fresh taxation." Disraeli questioned how long these enormous armaments would be endured by "the masses who are compelled to serve." [27] That winter, an expenditure of £60,000 alone was made on the Prince of Wales's visit to India, described by the Press as "eminently successful," while poor clerks were paid eight cents an hour for copying official documents, and William Morris was advocating a "Revolutionary Socialism that would effect a change in economic power." [28] In his address to workingmen (1876) Morris said: "Will anyone here tell me that a Russian moujik is in a worse state than a sweating tailor's slave?", and added that both the leaders and the led are incapable of

---

* Possibly a reference to Schleswig-Holstein, Disraeli said "Nobody in England wanted to interfere in the internecine quarrels of the German powers, who had robbed Denmark" (see Monypenny and Buckle, *Life of Disraeli*, 2:200).

saving so much as a half-dozen commons from the grasp of inexcusable commerce." [29]

Hardy's buoyant poem "In the Seventies" must have been written before the long agricultural depression and the conservatives' return to power with the annexation of the Fiji Islands, which Bright said in a speech at Manchester (Oct. 25, 1879) "may lend a seeming glory to the Crown and may give scope for patronage and promotion . . . to a limited few, but to you, the people, it brings expenditures of blood and treasure, increased debt and taxes,* and added risks of war in every quarter of the globe." [30] Hardy was constantly annoyed by the mediocrity and banality of political talk: "Of when the next election would be—of Lord This and the Duke of That—everything, he noted" (July 19, 1891) "except the people for whose existence these politicians alone exist. Their welfare is never once thought of." The travesty of bourgeois government is well described by the Years in *The Dynasts*:[31]

> *The ritual of each party is rehearsed,*
> *Dislodging not one vote or prejudice;*
> *The ministers their ministries retain,*
> *And Ins as Ins and Outs as Outs, remain.*

and in the Chorus of Ironic Spirits in their comment:

> *'Tis enough to make half*
> *Yonder zodiac laugh*
> *When rulers begin to allude*
> *To their lack of ambition,*
> *And strong opposition*
> *To all but the general good!*

and the Years retort, "*Hush levities. Events press on.*"

In this connection Hardy's observation of "a lot of poli-

---

* A national debt and subsidies totaling £50,000,000 to European powers against Napoleon, states A. L. Morton (*A People's History of England*, p. 320), who estimates that "a labourer earning 10 shillings a week paid half of it in indirect taxes."

ticians whom he met during the summer of 1886" is trenchant: "Plenty of form in their handling of politics, but no
matter, originality," and likewise his comment on Lord
and Lady Carnarvon's "nominally social but really political
parties" in the spring of 1885, "amid a simmer of political
excitement" over the murder of General Gordon climaxing
British expansion in the Sudan.* A conservative peeress remarked to Hardy, "I'm ashamed of my party! They are
all hoping that it may ruin Gladstone." Auberon Herbert
told Hardy at Lady Portsmouth's (June 29, 1886) that "the
clue to Gladstone's faults was personal vanity," and his
niece, Lady Winifred Herbert, said "politics had revealed
themselves to her as a horror of late." Hardy's comment
written before Gladstone's resignation in June and the Conservatives return to power is indicative of his contempt:

> The offhand decision of some commonplace mind high in
> office at a critical moment influences the course of events for
> a hundred years. Consider the evenings at Lord Carnarvon's,
> and the intensely average conversation on politics held there
> by average men who two or three weeks later were members
> of the Cabinet. A row of shopkeepers in Oxford Street taken
> just as they came would conduct the affairs of the nation as
> ably as these.[32]

A similar criticism was made by free-trade advocate John
Bright, who called the House of Commons "a sort of deputy
House of Lords . . . utterly unworthy of popular confidence,"
and who declared: "If the clerk of the House were placed
at Temple Bar and had orders to lay his hand on the
shoulder of every well-dressed and apparently clean-washed
man who passed through the ancient bar until he numbered
658, and if the Crown summoned these 658 men . . . my

---

* Gladstone was evasive on General Gordon's failure to follow his
instructions in a manner that reminds one of some of the supporters of
the United States' bipartisan foreign policy in respect to Cuba who criticized
the Bay of Pigs invasion only because it was a failure. (See Morley's *Life
of Gladstone*, 2:167–69; also, Charles Tennyson's *Tennyson*, p. 480, and
Haynes Johnson, *The Bay of Pigs*, prefaces.)

honest conviction is that you would have a better Parliament than now exists." [33]

Other observations by Hardy are symptomatic of the general malaise he found in the society of his time.[*] At a soirée (June 1883) "Lord Houghton hastened forward to prevent Browning from introducing him to Rhoda Broughton with the manner of a man who means to see things properly done in his own house . . . and then like one who having set a machinery in motion has now only to wait and observe how it goes." At the annual dinner of the Royal Academy (Apr. 1887) he observed the Raja of Kapurthala "in his mass of parently unknown to a good many more I knew. At these times men do not want to talk to their equals but to their superiors." At a reception during the Jubilee year (June 1887) he observed the Raja of Kapurthala in his mass of jewels and white turban and tunic . . . amid the babble and gaiety . . . feeling himself *alone* and having too much character to pretend to belong and throw himself into a thoughtless world of chit-chat and pleasure which he understood nothing of." Hardy noted (July 1, 1892): "The art of observation (during travel, etc.) consists in this: the seeing of great things in little things, the whole in the part—even the infinitesimal part. For instance, you are abroad; you see an English flag or a ship-mast from the window of your hotel: you realize the English navy. Or, at home, in a soldier you see the British Army; in a bishop at your club, the Church of England; and in a steam-hooter you hear Industry." He describes the pandemonium at the horse-races at Long-

[*] As Marx observed, "To delude others, and by deluding them to delude yourself—this is: *parliamentary wisdom* in a nut-shell! *Tant-mieux!*" (*Correspondence*, p. 386). Engels wrote Bebel (Oct. 28, 1885) on "the chronic depression in all decisive branches of industry in England, France, and America, 'especially in iron and cotton' resulting from such colossal overproduction that it cannot even bring things to a crisis! The fools want to reform society to suit themselves and not themselves to the development of society" (*Correspondence.*, pp. 441–42). Maccoby observes of the Peace at the end of the Crimean War: "there was truculent mourning over the spectacle of 'a great nation,' ruled, thwarted, flouted, plundered and dishonoured, by a man, not naturally of a capacity superior to the average church-warden" (3:50n, quoted from *Reynolds* newspaper [May 11, 1856]).

champ and the Grand Prix de Paris (June 10, 1888) where "the horses passed in a volley, so close together that it seemed they must be striking each other . . . and the cries of 'Vive la France!' a French horse having won." And the following morning (June 14), they went to l'Etoile in twilight where under the enormous arch he and Em "read some names of victories which were never won," and in the afternoon went to the Archives Nationales where, he says,

I seemed close to those keys from the Bastille, those letters of the Kings of France, those edicts, and those corridors of white boxes, each containing one year's shady document of a past monarchy.

The next day "coming out of the Bourse, he learnt of the death of the Emperor of Germany," of whom Dr. Quain had said to Hardy on April 21, 1887, "it was a mistake for anyone to have as many doctors as the German Emperor has, because neither feels responsible." On a trip to Bray, Ireland, with Trevelyan the historian, they

found the Chief Secretary (John Morley) and the Lord Chancellor at the Grey hotel by the shore "making magistrates by the dozen," as Morley said.

In June 1890 Hardy "met H. M. Stanley, the explorer, at a dinner given by the publishers," and was more impressed by DuChaille, asking him,

"Why didn't you claim more credit for finding those dwarfs?" to which Du Chaille said with a twinkle, 'Noh, noh, it is *his* dinner.' "

Leaving Lady Yarborough's evening party on a wet May evening (1894) Hardy had to return to South Kensington on the top of a "bus, as there were no cabs to be got on account of a strike," sharing his umbrella with a young girl who had been to "The Pav" and whose affectionate nature "was a

strange contrast to the scene I had just left." In the middle
of June the Hardys went to the Continent to escape "the
racket" of the Sixtieth Jubilee, which Jack London, in his
book *The People of the Abyss,* called

> a lot of pomp, vanity, show, and mumble-jumbo foolery—a
> performance from fairyland rather than the performance of
> sane and sensible people who have mastered matter and
> solved the secret of the stars. (p. 146)

Hardy spread out the copy of the London *Times* on the
coronation, which he had taken with him, and read it "in the
snowy presence of the maiden monarch (the Jungfrau) that
dominated the place"—an aspect of the Will of *The Dynasts,*
"impassible as glacial snow . . ." (*The Dynasts,* I, 4, v).

At the time of the Sudan disaster (1885) Morris was
saying in his *Manifesto to the Workingmen of England:*

> Who are they that are leading us into war? Greedy gamblers
> on the stock exchange, idle officers of the army and navy,
> desperate purveyors of exciting war-news for the comfortable
> breakfast table of those who have nothing to lose by war;
> and lastly in the place of honour, the Tory Rump that we
> fools, weary of peace, reason, and justice chose at the last
> election." [34]

The "Cheap Press," whose journalists Carlyle had eulogized
as "the true kings and clergy," was now behaving more in
the manner of the bourgeois press. As Hardy in *The Dynasts* [35] has Pitt say to Lord Mulgrave while handing him a
Dutch paper:

> These foreign prints are trustless as Cheap Jack
> Dumbfounding yokels at a country fair . . .

and Lord Mulgrave calls in Lord Malmesbury, who "is great
at Dutch . . . having learned it at Leyden years ago."

Morris was exhorting the working-classes to a collective
stand against the ruling classes and their imperialistic wars:
In 1886 he wrote:

We have but one weapon against that terrible organization of selfishness which we attack, and that weapon is Union . . . organized brotherhood to break the spell of anarchical Plutocracy. One man with an idea in his head is in danger of being considered a madman; two men with the same idea may be foolish, but can hardly be mad; ten men sharing an idea begin to act; a hundred draw attention as fanatics; a thousand and society begins to tremble; a hundred thousand and there is war abroad, and the cause is victorious, tangible and real; and why only a hundred thousand? Why not a hundred million and peace upon earth? You and I who agree together, it is we who have to answer this question.[36]

Marx defended the Workingmen's Association against the slanders of Disraeli and his Young England group and "the attacks of the police-tinged bourgeois mind," declaring (May 30, 1871): "Our association is, in fact, nothing but the international bond between the most advanced workingmen in the various countries of the civilized world. . . . To stamp it out," he declared, "the governments would have to stamp out the despotism of capital over labour—the condition of their own parasitical existence." [37]

Hardy had recognized that "the question of the Dorset cottager here merges in that of all the houseless and landless poor and the vast topic of the Rights of Man";[38] and he continued: "they might often be postulated in the words addressed to King Henry the Fourth by his fallen subject":

Our house, my sovereign liege, little deserves
The scourge of greatness to be used on it;
And that same greatness, too, which our own hands
Have holp to make so portly.
("*Dorsetshire Labourer,* July 1883)

The subject was "beyond the scope of a merely descriptive article," but in *The Dynasts* he found the epic scope to project the masses of the most enlightened and Christian nations of the earth groaning under the yoke of oppression and subjected to blind obedience by their governments in the historical transition from feudalism to capitalism. Hardy's picture of oppression recalls Lenin's plea at the Versailles Conference (1919) for "Land, Peace and Bread," and Marx's recognition that the "true character" of the Franco-Prussian War "was the crumbling into dust of the old bourgeois society." [39] There was only a generation between the end of the Napoleonic Wars and the outbreak of the Franco-Prussian War. Hardy's account of the Napoleonic Wars was considerably colored by the Franco-Prussian War, which he viewed neither through the eyes of Homer nor Virgil, nor through the sensational bourgeois press and the bourgeois historians (caricatured by his Spirit Sinister in *War makes rattling good history, but Peace is poor reading* [40]), but through the eyes of pity and experience of the alienated poet turned historian. It finds a meaningful expression in the reddleman Diggory Venn (*The Return of the Native*), a counsellor of warning against the triumph of the Code Napoleon and of the bourgeosie, who might have taken for his text Gabriel's dog, Young George, "standing dark and motionless, like Napoleon at St. Helena" after driving his master's uninsured sheep (stocked by a cattle dealer) over the cliff, "as if he expected to be rewarded," but he is shot instead.

iii. THE PEASANTS

One may well ask why Hardy got so absorbed in the Napoleonic Wars that he wrote *The Dynasts*.

He says in the Preface, characteristically, that "the choice of such a subject was mainly due to three accidents of locality": [1] his familiarity with that part of England, it being the "favourite summer residence" of George III during "that stressful time," and its happening "to include the village which was the birthplace of Nelson's flag-captain at Trafalgar" (Admiral Thomas Hardy, descended from another bianch of the Dorset Hardys), and also "the provokingly slight regard paid to the English influence and action by Continental writers seemed to leave room for a new handling of the theme which should re-embody the features of this influence in their true proportion." [2]

The reasons, however, go deeper than that; the drama itself belies its preface. One does not question Hardy's veracity, but such information is intended for the hasty reviewer, the compiler of literature textbooks for the secondary schools, and the obituary eulogist,* and it belongs to the legerdemain of bibliography.

The true reasons go back to Hardy's recognition that the question of the Dorset cottager "merges in that of all the houseless and landless poor and the vast topic of the Rights of Man," [3] which he stated was beyond the scope of an essay. His concern for the peasants in Wessex was like Tolstoy's concern for the peasants in Russia and Balzac's** concern for the *bonhomme misère* (nickname for the French peasant) in France, and Victor Hugo's also. Hardy had read both Balzac and Hugo*** earlier, as Wright [4] has recently shown, and Tolstoy's *War and Peace* later. Tolstoy, who had first contemplated writing a novel about the 1825 Decembrist officers' uprising, found that he had to go back and study the impact of Napoleon's invasion of Russia on the nobility and peasantry. The leaders of the Decembrist Revolt, who had absorbed some emancipating ideas, were either exiled or executed, as Monmouth's followers had been

* The day after Hardy's death, the leading article of *The Times* (Jan. 12, 1928) epitomized *The Dynasts* as "a national epic for English" (W. R. *Rutland*, p. 269).

** "By the bye I have been reading scarcely anything but Balzac while laid up," wrote Laura Lafargue, Marx's daughter, to Engels (Dec. 13, 1883) "and enjoyed the grand old fellow thoroughly. *There* is the history of France from 1815 to 1848. . . . What a revolutionary dialectic in his poetical justice" (Engels-Lafargue *Correspondence*, p. 160).

*** W. R. Rutland says that Hardy could never have forgotten Hugo's epic description of Waterloo in *Les Miserables* (p. 272); Samuel C. Chew has mentioned Hardy's debt among others to Hugo and to Stendhal (*Thomas Hardy*, p. 164).

in the English 1685 rebellion, for, as Marx observed to Engels in his letter (8 October, 1858): ° "We cannot deny that
bourgeois society has experienced its sixteenth century a
second time—a sixteenth century which will, I hope, sound
the death-knell of bourgeois society, just as the first one
thrust it into existence." Conrad, too, was disillusioned by
the false dawn "on the horizon of the Vienna Congress
through the subsiding dust of Napoleonic alarms and excur-
sions [which] has been extinguished by the larger glamour
of less restraining ideals," as he observed in his "Autocracy
and War" essay. But Conrad had seen "commerce pretty
close and knew what it was worth," and declares in his 1905
essay: "A swift disenchantment overtook the incredible infatuation which could put its trust in the peaceful nature of
industrial and commercial competition."

All of them living in the post-Napoleonic war years were
naturally absorbed in the Napoleonic wars, and in the un-
settled problems that resulted from the failure of the Revolution—the poverty and unrest created by it. Hardy's pater-
nal great-grandfather served in the Home Guard and lived

° "With the favourable turn of world trade at this moment (Oct. 8,
1858)," Marx declared "(although the enormous accumulations of money
in the banks of London, Paris and New York show that things must still
be very far from all right) it is at least consoling that in Russia *the
revolution has begun,* for I regard the convocation of the 'notables' to
St. Petersburg as such a beginning. In Prussia likewise things are worse
than in 1847, and the absurd delusions as to the middle-class propensities
of the Prince of Prussia will be dissolved in fury. It will do the French
no harm if they see that the world can move without them. At the same
time there are exceptionally big movements among the Slavs, especially
in Bohemia, movements which are indeed counter-revolutionary but still
add to the ferment. . . .
. . . The particular task of bourgeois society is the establishment of
the world market, at least in outline, and of production based upon the
world market. As the world is round, this seems to have
been completed by the colonization of California and Australia and the
opening up of China and Japan. The difficult question for us is this:
on the Continent the revolution is imminent and will also immediately
assume a socialist character. Is it not bound to be crushed in this little
corner, considering that in a far greater territory the movement of bourgeois
society is still on the ascendent?" (*Correspondence,* pp. 117–18).

through the Peasants Rebellion of the thirties. Tolstoy's father was a general on Kutuzof's staff, and Tolstoy himself was a soldier and war correspondent in the Crimean War. Victor Hugo's grandfather was a peasant farmer in the Vosges and his father a carpenter at Nancy, and later a general under Napoleon's brother, King Joseph in Portugal. His mother was an anti-Bonapartist; Hugo himself, as a boy of nine, was with his father in Madrid in 1811. The Hugos, being of different political beliefs and on the losing side, suffered more from the privations of war than Count Tolstoy's* family, or his wife's family, the Behrs, who had been on the winning side. Conrad's grandfather Prince Roman had served with the Polish legion under Napoleon, like Stendhal (Marie Henri Beyle, 1783–1842), who had participated in Napoleon's Italian and Prussian campaigns and in the retreat from Moscow, who is best known for his novel *The Red and the Black* (*Le Rouge et le Noir*, 1831). Stendhal had endured some hardships in following his hero. Conrad's "grand uncle Nicholas, of the Polish landed gentry, *Chevalier de la Legion d'Honneur*, etc, etc . . . in his young days had eaten of Lithuanian dog" on Napoleon's Moscow retreat (*A Personal Record*, p. 35). Hugo refers to Napoleon as "that butcher of Europe" (*Les Miserables*, "Waterloo"), and Hardy describes Gabriel Oak as one who had always regretted "that his flock ended in mutton." [5] The Hardys [6] had fared better than most of the yeomen class by going into the building trades.

All five writers, except Stendhal, discerned that the Napoleonic Wars had really settled nothing, and that the peasants and urban workers were in worse condition than before. The Complaint of Piers the Plowman "that successive generations must pay in years of poverty for military

---

* Count Osterman-Tolstoy was ordered at Ustorovno (July 25–26, 1812) to retard the advancing French army (see Tarlé, *Buonoparte*, p. 269, and Tolstoy, *War and Peace*, p. 608, for an account of the gentleman's "gallant action," (p. 611).

victories" [7] had been heard from Langland's time down to Hardy's. "The Tolpuddle Martyrs" had been sentenced to Botany Bay for trying to organize the starving "workfolk" of Dorset, as Hardy calls them. The condition of the peasants in Russia, which Tarlé says was "worse than that of negro slaves in America," [8] bred the unrest culminating in the 1825 Decembrist uprising for a quasi-republic ("Constantine and the Constitution") during the interregnum between the death of Alexander I and the accession of his brother Nicholas I. A greater unrest following the debacle of the Crimean War was building up during the oppressive reign of Alexander I (1824–1855). Gogol satirized it in his play *The Inspector-General* (1836) and later Stolypin's punitive military courts* under Nicholas following the abortive 1905 revolution, which were more cruel than Alexander's had been. Pushkin (1799–1837) was exiled to the Crimea and the Caucasus for his "revolutionary epigrams" that won him the title of "the Byron of Russia." Nicholas Nekrassov (1824–1877) ridiculed the autocracy in his poem "Who Can Be Happy and Free in Russia?" and Tolstoy protested in vain against the treatment of the peasants under Stolypin's un-Christian barbarity. Alexander II (1855–1881) reluctantly initiated a land-reform, by which his advisers persuaded him he would escape the fate of Louis XVI (guillotined July 21. 1793), but he was assassinated by Grenevetsky, March 1, 1881, returning from a Sunday parade. Terrorism mounted: in 1911 Stolypin, Minister of the Interior, was shot at a performance in the Kiev Opera House on September 1 honoring

---

* Apropos of this is Engel's letter to Laura Lafargue (Oct. 2, 1886): "A cowardly bourgeoisie like the German and Russian, sacrifices its general class tendencies to the monetary advantages of brutal repression. But a bourgeosie with a revolutionary history of its own, such as the English and particularly the French, cannot do that so easily. Hence that struggle within the bourgeoisie itself, which in spite of its occasional bits of violence and oppression, on the whole class drives it forward—see the various electoral reforms of Gladstone in England, of Radicalism in France. This verdict is a new stage, and so the bourgeosie in doing its own work, is doing ours" (Engels-Lafargue *Correspondence,* 1.378).

the Tsar, by Bogrov, who, like Razumov of Conrad's Russian novel, was a police agent.

Alexander II's land policy was a fraud. It allowed the peasants to buy a few desiatins of land (a desiatin is 2.69 acres) from their former masters—"too large to be buried in, too small to live on"[9]—on which they contracted to make redemption payments for forty-nine years to the Tsarist Government, which immediately paid their former masters. The average allotment was as paltry as the divisions made among the French peasants after the Revolution (which embittered the dying old French peasant in Hardy's poem "The Peasant's Confession") and those among the peasants in North Vietnam today, compared with the large estates in South Viet-Nam.—Unable to meet their payments, the peasants drifted to the large towns, where, on account of their illiteracy, they could either not obtain work or were mercilessly exploited. In 1877 Marx wrote a letter, in French, to the Editor of the *Otechestvennie Zapisky,* saying that

> if Russia is tending to become a capitalistic nation after the example of the western European countries,—and during the last few years she has been taking a lot of trouble in that direction—she will not succeed without having first transformed a good part of her peasants into proletarians. (*Correspondence,* p. 354)

He came to the conclusion that "if Russia continues to pursue the path she has followed since 1861 (serf emancipation of that year), she will lose the finest chance ever offered by history to a nation in order to undergo all the fatal vicissitudes of the capitalist regime." In a letter to Danielson[*]

---

[*] Engels had written Danielson (Sept. 22, 1892): "Another thing is certain: If Russia really required after the Crimean War a *grande industrie* of her own, she could have it in one form only: the *capitalistic form.* And along with that form, she was obliged to take over all the consequences which accompany capitalistic *grande industrie* in all other countries. . . .
. . . For it is one of the necessary corollaries of *grande industrie,* that it *destroys* its own home market by the very process by which it *creates* it. It creates it by destroying the basis of the domestic industry of the

(Feb. 24, 1893) Engels elucidated further Russia's position at the crossroads of history:

> Well, in or about 1854 Russia started with the commune on the one hand and the necessity of the *grande industrie,* on the other. Now, if you take the whole state of your country into account, as it was at that date, do you see any possibility of the *grand industrie* being grafted on the peasants' commune in a form which would, on the one hand, make the development of that *grande industrie* possible, and on the other hand raise the primitive commune to the work of a social institution superior to anything the world has yet seen? And that while the whole Occident was still living under the capitalist regime? It strikes me that such an evolution, which would have surpassed anything known in history, required other economical, political and intellectual conditions than were present at the time in Russia.
>
> No doubt the commune and to a certain extent the cartel, contained germs which under certain conditions might have developed and saved Russia the necessity of passing through the torments of the capitalistic regime.

During the Napoleonic wars and afterwards, a few land-owners had liberated their serfs like Tolstoy and the land-owning characters of *War and Peace* (1865–1869)—Pierre Bezukov, a Free-Mason convert, and Prince Alexi, an admirer of Montesquieu, who ask each other "Who is to till the land?"—a question that Araktcheev also asked Prince Alexi. They argue over the merits of the respective philanthropies, and Tolstoy observes of the outcome

> that the serfs continued to give in labour and money just what other people's serfs gave—that is to say, all that could be got out of them.

The Russian land reform of 1861 widened the cleavage

peasantry. But without domestic industry the peasants cannot live. They are ruined as *peasants;* their purchasing power is reduced to a minimum; and until they, as *proletarians,* have settled down into new conditions of existence, they will furnish a very poor market for the newly-arisen factories" (*Marx-Engels Correspondence,* pp. 499, 500).

between the gentry and the peasants as the Industrial Revolution had done in England. The shifting of the burden off the back of the gentry gave them increased ease but increased the burden on the peasants to an intolerable weight, like that of the peasants before the French Revolution depicted in Millet's painting "The Man with the Hoe," which inspired Markham's poem by the same name.

"The French peasant of the epoch of Napoleon I," historian Eugene Tarlé notes "is the same peasant of whom Karl Marx speaks in his Eighteenth Brumaire," and further: "The Bonaparte dynasty is representative not of the enlightenment of the peasants, but of their superstition; not of their understanding, but of their prejudices; not of their future, but of their past." [10]

This led in France to the twice-attempted restoration of the Empire by Napoleon's nephew Louis (president, 1848, then emperor, 1851, by a *coup d'etat*) with the backing of its senate, which was as servile as Napoleon I's. Hugo, who exiled himself during the Second Empire, was liberated on the reestablishment of the republic and returned to the Assembly to find life no better for France under the Third Republic than it had been under the Second. Marx wrote that a bourgeois monarchy is always followed by a bourgeois republic,* or words to that effect, and that the year "1848 was only child's play compared to 1870." [11]

In Russia similar conditions led to the 1825 Decembrist uprisings, as in France they had led to the rebellions of 1830 against Charles X (1824–1830), when Louis Phillipe was recalled to the throne under a constitutional monarchy such as the Decembrists asked for under Constantine. The Decembrists were only a handful of Russian officers compared to

---

* See Engels's letter to Marx from Manchester, Sept. 12, 1870:" . . . However the peace may turn out, it must be concluded before the workers can do anything at all. If they were victorious now—in the service of national defense—they would have to inherit the legacy of Bonaparte and of the present lousy Republic, and would be needlessly crushed by the German armies and thrown back another twenty years" (*Marx-Engels Correspondence,* pp. 304–5).

the Chartists in England, but in both countries the government maintained increased vigilance over the population.
Neither Russian nor English uprisings were comparable to
the uprisings in France, which successive Bonopartists put
down with bloodshed, nor with Stolypin's military courts,
which bring to mind the dictator Guzman Bento and his
"Army of Pacification" of Conrad's *Nostromo* (pp. 47, 384),
with its irrationality of the firing squad. At the bottom of the
situation was the frightful condition of the poor which Hugo
pictures in his novel *Les Miserables* (1862), the Paris poor
and their restive fear of the police enforcing the Code Napoleon.° The prefect of Police Javert, in his allegiance to

° Napoleon retained the Code Napoleon (1804) "in full force the Law
of Lichapelier (1791) identifying even the most peaceful strikes with crimes
punishable by criminal persecution," and "gave capital complete freedom to
exploit labor. And, in addition, to all this, he created the so-called 'labour
books,' which were retained in the employer's hands and without which
no worker could secure a new position. . . His criminal legislation indis-
putably marked a long step backward," Tarlé says, "when compared with
the laws of the Revolutionary period" (*Bonaparte*, p. 130).

Marx notes in criticizing Hugo's Napoleon *le petit* and Proudhon's
coup d'état, that "Hugo fails to realize that he makes the individual seem
great instead of small by ascribing to him a capacity for personal initiative
without parallel in history. Proudhon, on the other hand, tries to show that
the *coup d'état* was the outcome of an antecedent historical development.
But in his case an exposition of the *coup d'état* becomes transformed with
a historical apology for the hero who effected it (Otto Richele, *Karl Marx:
His Life and Work*, p. 193). Hardy, unlike Hugo, makes Napoleon seem
small, and recognizes the historical antecedent at the Milan Coronation
ceremony, when the Spirit of the Year replies: "Thou reasonest ever thus-
wise—even as if / A self-formed force had urged his loud career," to the
Pities, who opine: "Thus are the self-styled servants of the Highest / Con-
strained by earthly duress to embrace / Mighty imperiousness as it were
choice" (I,1,vi), and again in Marshall Ney's advice to Napoleon after
Fontainebleau: "Sire, things like revolutions turn not back / But go straight
on" III,4,iv). Hardy glimpsed Napoleon's nephew "Plon-Plon" at the funeral
of Louis Napoleon (July 12, 1878), at Chislehurst, "as he walked by, bare-
headed, a son on each arm . . . a round projecting chin, countenance
altogether remindful of Boney. . . . The recollection," Hardy says, "had
been of enormous use to him when writing *The Dynasts* in imagining the
Emperor's appearance" (*Early Life*, p. 168).

Tolstoy says in *War and Peace:* "Davout was to the Emperor Napoleon
what Araktcheev was to Alexander. . . . Not like Arakteheev, a coward
but he was as exacting and cruel and as unable to express his devotion
except by cruelty. In the mechanism of the state or organism these men
are as necessary as wolves in the organism of nature. And they are always

authority, while pursuing Jean Valjean, is as sinister a figure in literature as the Russian Stolypin. In England these "gone down, gone down under people" are the Durbyfields of Hardy's *Tess*,[12] *les joyeux va-nu-pieds*, the Jondrettes, of Hugo's *Les Miserables*, and the fever-stricken straggler Platon Karatev, with his devoted dog, who brings light to Pierre in Tolstoy's *War and Peace* (p. 989). The whole vista of history is opened up in Hardy's description of Jude's afterthoughts following a policeman's stopping him in the shade of Christminster with "You've had a wet?" Hardy says:

Whatever his wetness, his brains were dry enough. He only heard in part the policeman's further remarks, having fallen into thought on what struggling people like himself had stood at that Crossway, whom nobody ever thought of now. It had more history than the oldest college in the city. It was literally teeming, stratified, with the shades of human groups, who had met there for tragedy, comedy, farce; real enactments of the intensest kind. At Fourways men had stood and talked of Napoleon, the loss of America, the execution of King Charles, the burning of the Martyrs, the Crusades, the Norman Conquest, possibly of the arrival of Caesar. Here the two sexes had met for loving, hating, coupling, parting; had waited, had suffered for each other; had triumphed over each other, cursed each other in jealousy, blessed each other in forgiveness.

He began to see that the town life was a book of humanity infinitely more palpitating, varied, and compendious than the gown life. These struggling men and women before him were the reality of Christminster, though they knew little of Christ or Minister.[13]

---

to be found in every government; they always make their appearance and hold their own, incongruous as their presence and their close relations with the head of the state may appear" (p. 575). Denisov and Nikolay "criticize the government," and Denisov asks Pierre, "Well, what are you going to do?" Pierre explains: "This is the position of things in Petersburg: the Tsar lets everything go. He is entirely wrapped up in this mysticism [while] everything is going to ruin: 'Bribery in the law-courts,' nothing but coercion and drill in the army; exile—people are being tortured, and enlightenment is suppressed. . . . Everybody sees that it can't go on like this. The strain is too great, and the string must snap" (pp. 1090–91).

Hugo, unlike Tolstoy, did not believe in passive resistance; as embittered and disillusioned as Balzac, he had quit the Assembly and cast his lot with the Communists. Nor did he suffer from Tolstoy's exceeding religiosity,[14] which characterized Tolstoy's work after 1881 and even *War and Peace*. It took Gorki to waken Tolstoy from his theological dream and bring him back to reality. The historical fact is well summed up in Gorki's conversation with Tolstoy, whom he ran across at Gaspra, a short time before his death (1910), of which Gorki reports:

> We were walking in Yusupov Park. He had discoursed brilliantly on the morals of the Moscow aristocracy. A big Russian wench was working almost doubled over on a flower bed, showing her elephantine legs, her enormous heavy breasts shaking. He looked at her attentively:
> All this splendour and extravagance was supported by caryatids like that. Not merely by the work of muziks and peasant wenches, not by quit rent, but literally by the blood of the people.[15]

The description recalls the nouveau riche—Paula Power and her set of Hardy's *A Laodicean*—the portraits of the de Stancy ancestors and those "denied the opportunity to articulate their higher emotions" and the pauper graves of the children of a family whose "husband used to smite for Jimmy More the blacksmith till 'a hurt his arm'," who were "buried at night for a shilling a head," and their nineteenth-century compatriots in Tolstoy's *War and Peace*—old Prince Andrei's estate, stables, hounds, the embellished Italian statue in which "the face of the angel reminded them of the face of the little princess," who had died in childbirth (p. 338). There is something epochal about Hardy's Kutuzof, who is "so old," according to the Spirit of the Years, *"that even Death debates on taking him"* (III, 1, ix) in *The Dynasts*, while in *War and Peace* he is treated with purely nationalistic homage as "the savior of Russia," who "refused to sacrifice one Russian for ten Frenchmen," and who, with "the whole Russian Army was convinced that the Battle of Borodino was a victory" (p. 769).

In both works, there is, of course, much cursing of Napoleon as "the enemy of the people and the human race," and both authors put in the mouths of their leaders the battle cries of Mother Church—Hardy with mordant satire, Tolstoy reportorially. Tolstoy has Kutuzof say to his soldiers, "Christ be with you!" (p. 150), and Bagration, "With God's help" (p.165), echoed by Denisov (p. 168) and his "Serene Highness" the Tsar, in "With God's aid" (p. 253). Tolstoy depicts war as "terrible but glorious"; Hardy, as barbaric and inglorious. To be sure, there are examples of noncombatants suffering in *War and Peace*, like the Polish family with a baby that Rostov found "without clothes or food, or the strength to go away on foot" (p. 364), and the trial by a French military court of Pierre, who maintained that he was "defending a woman . . . that was the duty of every man, and so on" (p. 893), and the ravages of nature on the outskirts of Smolensk where lay "golden fields and corpses glittering in the sun"; but these lack the incisiveness of Hardy's lines on the Prussian defeat at Jena and the King and Queen's flight, commented on by the Spirit Ironic (II, 1, v), which would have weighted down Conrad's heart:

> *This monarchy, one-half whose pedestal*
> *Is built of Polish bones, has bones home-made!*
> *Let the fair woman bear it. Poland did.*

The individual tragedy is overshadowed by the collective tragedy in this speech and also in the citizens of Madrid asking "a thousand pardons" of the Spanish Princess in their speech "you, an injured wife—an injured people we!" (II, 2, ii), following the overthrow of the Bourbon dynasty in Spain. There is also the chorus of the Pities' apprehension for the fauna and flora on the eve of Waterloo (III, 6, viii), which Tolstoy seems to have forgotten.

In both *War and Peace* and *The Dynasts* blame is placed

on English gold (p. 147; I, 6, i), and there are celebrations of victories and mournings over defeats, but in *The Dynasts* they take on a collective quality as at the Brighton Pavilion celebrating the victory of Albuera and the public funeral for Lord Nelson, whereas in *War and Peace* they occur on the periphery of the characters' consciousness—the ringing of vespers in the Kremlin, which the French "supposed . . . was a call to arms" (p. 835) and the Te Deum in the cathedral (St. Petersburg) in thanksgiving for repelling the French (p. 872), and are more of a private family nature like Prince Alexi's burial, and subconscious like the children's prayer-wish "for the snow to turn into sugar" (p. 888). The scene of an old Countess of Catherine the Great's time giving a ball for Natasha (p. 418) is grandiosely unreal compared to the famished Russian soldiers feeding on "asparagus, or Mollie's sweet root, which was very bitter" (p. 363), and to money's being "plentiful if provisions were not." But these scenes do not have the reality of Hardy's ragged deserters, drunk and bedded down in straw in a cellar after the battle of Astorga. Tolstoy for the most part describes the situation; Hardy lets his soldiers speak and act. In all of Tolstoy's analogies between war and physics, there is nothing to compare to Hardy's description of "the whirlwind of the will" and the devastation following the battle of Leipzig, a matter treated fully by Amiya Chakravarty in his *The Dynasts and the Post-War Age in Poetry*. Tolstoy epitomizes nationalism; Hardy transcends it.

I find a great deal more Carlylean hero worship in Tolstoy and the opposite in Hardy. Tolstoy is for people bowing to the wills of the great men, who are instruments of God's will; while Hardy's common soldier, like the First Deserter near Astorga, exclaims: "Good Lord deliver us from all great men, and take me back again to humble life" (II, 3, ii).

The Dynasts is a much larger undertaking than either *Vanity Fair* or *War and Peace*. It has "the totality of objects," which, according to Hegel, is the *sine qua non* of the epic, and to spare. Both Tolstoy and Hardy cover the entire period of 1804 to 1815, while Thackeray covers only the hundred days and Victor Hugo only revisits Waterloo in *Les Miserables* and exhibits it as a relic, as East Germany is preserved today. Tolstoy, however, limits his canvas to the Russian-French action and pays scant attention to the continental allies, and practically ignores the English action except at Waterloo, while Hardy portrays the whole gamut of the terrestrial tragedy. There is nothing about the battle of Trafalgar in *War and Peace*, nor about the political machinery, and no meetings of the Duma to correspond to those of the House of Commons. Moreover, in *War and Peace*, war appears in the background, often as an interlude in the people's lives,* whereas in *The Dynasts* it occupies the foreground, is a continuous bombardment and cataclysmic upheaval. *The Dynasts* depicts a total all-out war effort, *War and Peace* a series of more or less rear-guard actions. The difference is due, I think, to Tolstoy's being Russian-oriented and Hardy's being anti-war oriented. One does not get the impression of war in physicist's terms from *War and Peace* that one gets from *The Dynasts:* the huge massing of Napoleon's invasion forces at Boulogne (I, l, iv): the ship-transport within whose "hulls, like sheep a-pen, are packed in thousands fighting men" (II, 2, v); the "these prim ponderosities" of Wellington's entrenchment at Calendrix, Portugal, "rearing up their foreheads to the moon" (II, 6, ii); the massive naval battle of Trafalgar; the vast armies, continental landbattles, the terrific expenditure of men's lives and money, which bankrupted France and well-nigh bankrupted their adversaries. These appear in more concentrated form in *The Dynasts* than in *War and Peace,* appear in epic pro-

---

* Tolstoy notes: "A consultation took place between the great noblemen at the table only . . . the secretary was told to write down the resolution of the Moscow nobility; that the nobles of Moscow, like those of Smolensk would furnish a levy of ten men in every thousand, with their complete equipment. . . . In the Fall of 1806 ten out of every thousand of the population were recruited for the regular army besides a further nine for the militia" (*War and Peace,* pp. 635–36).

portion, and are expressed with greater economy and cinematographic effect through Hardy's "Dumb Show," which has been likened to Dos Passos's "Camera Eye" later. Somehow Hardy, by his selection of historical ordinates and arrangement or actions has more fully fashioned the Napoleonic Wars, which might be called the first world war, into an "*Iliad* of Europe" of that time. *The Dynasts,* consequently, creates the impression of a modern work. Moreover, the various spirits' observance of and comments on the various political and sanguinary aspects of the war put Hardy's work on a higher political plane than that of the bewildered observer Pierre Bezukov, who is supposed to represent Tolstoy in part, but who, alas, is a rather pathetic Quixote, as at the battle of Borodino, the best of Tolstoy's descriptions of warfare.

Tolstoy takes his time and tends to caricature war in a Dickensenian manner; Hardy moves swiftly and satirizes war in a Swiftian vein, which is strengthened by his flashbacks to antecedent historical events and brings out more incisively Napoleon's retrogressive tendencies in the process of being corrupted by the oligarchic traditions he originally opposed. I prefer Hardy's Kutuzov, who has more of the inscrutable Asiatic about him, to Tolstoy's, in which he appears as "a pudgy," sensuous, well-fed European ((pp. 695, 1027) and as an older reflection of the young Tsar Alexander Pavlovitch, for whom young Rostov "would have been happy to die on the spot" (p. 223), and who speaks of him as " 'your Serene Highness,' as everyone called him" (p. 690). Tolstoy makes no reference to the Tsar's mother, Alexandra, Empress-of-all-the Russias, while Hardy makes her as important a personage as Queen Victoria, to whom the Tsarevitch is Prince Albert and consort. Tolstoy's Alexandra is likened to a queen bee and Moscow to her deserted hive. Hardy's common soldiers are closer to Remarque's, Barbusse's, and Arnold Zweig's later, and unlike Hacek's machinelike Good Soldier Schweik with his computerized dic tion: "Beg to report, sir," or the farcical Sergeant Bilco of TV, who is a far cry from Falstaff. In Tolstoy the officers are glorified at the expense of the *poilu* and are presented like the captain of Company III who, "never taking his eyes off his superior" (p. 99), emulates him on the battlefield.

It is easier for me to follow Hardy's account in play shape than it is Tolstoy's in novel form. I am aware that my opinion differs from that of most critics who regard Tolstoy's novel superior to Hardy's epic. Possibly their having been compelled to read Homer's *Iliad* in high-school—and sometimes not very good translations of it—has prejudiced them against poetry, in general, and epic poetry, in particular, in favor of almost any kind of novel. Webster has a preference for Tolstoy's *War and Peace* to Hardy's *Dynasts* because Tolstoy shows history as "a process whereby leaders draw sustenance from the mass," and Hardy shows it as "the old Carlylean march of great men: Napoleon, Fox, Pitt, Wellington." [16] I disagree with Webster's opinion, though he is an authority on Hardy. I find the officers' hero worship of the Tsar and Tolstoy's adulation of the little Prince, disgusting at times.* *War and Peace* is more like *Vanity Fair* in treatment, albeit of greater scope; neither of them has the stature of *The Dynasts*. The reason may partly be due to the fact that Tolstoy wrote *War and Peace* before the Franco-Prussian War and Hardy *The Dynasts* afterward, and partly to a basic difference in attitudes toward life and literary temperament: [17] Tolstoy states that he "felt enveloped in a cloud of joy" during the composition of his great novel; Hardy felt, from Nov. 17, 1885 on, "in a fit

* For example, Prince Andrie's sentimental fealty to the young Tsar which at times almost unmans him and reminds one of Tennyson's Galahad; "the handsome youthful Alexander" (p. 223), which reads like a society reporter's account; Natasha and Boris's falling in love, when they behave like children in comparison ot Turgenev's young people in love; and finally such Homeric epithets as "the beautiful Helene" and "the Little Princess Lisa of the downy upper lip," which occur over and over again, and which might be worthy of Pope's mock-heroic epic *The Rape of the Lock*, but scarcely of the *Iliad* or *The Dynasts*.

of depression, as if enveloped in a leaden cloud" most of the time. *The Dynasts* has a sense of contemporaneity that *War and Peace* lacks, obfucscated as it is with religiosity and the feudalistic past, and a depth of historicity like a paleontological palimpsest, thereby giving it a significance not to be found in *War and Peace,* which only traverses the ground between Genesis and Revelation in genealogical fashion on Russian soil. Tolstoy's omniscient method lacks the depth perception of Hardy's double vision; Hardy brings out the irony between mankind's creative arts and destructive science, between man's collective knowledge and inhuman fratricide, that raises the question of a modern English poet —was it Auden or C. Day Lewis?—who asked, "After such knowledge, what forgiveness?" Moreover, Hardy emphasizes the politico-economic aspects of the Napoleonic Wars, with scenes in the House of Commons and the Chamber of Deputies, while Tolstoy makes no reference to the Duma and only one to Tsar Alexander's conference with the landowners and merchants.

The most fundamental difference is that Hardy's pessimism is more hopeful than Tolstoy's optimism, in that Hardy sees a gradual amelioration in mankind operating through the extension of consciousness and sensibility ("Consciousness the Will informing, till It fashion all things fair"), while Tolstoy thinks that mankind is no more able to regulate history than it is to regulate the heavenly bodies:

> To history the recognition of the free wills of men as forces able to influence historical events, that is, not subject to laws, is the same as would be to astronomy the recognition of free will in the movements of the heavenly bodies.
> This recognition destroys the possibility of the existence of laws, that is, of any science whatever. If there is so much as one body moving at its free will, the laws of Kepler and of Newton are annulled, and every conception of the movement of the heavenly bodies is destroyed. If there is a single human action due to free will, no historical law exists, and no conception of historical events can be formed. (*War and Peace,* p. 1133)

And:

> If the will of every man were free, that is, if every man could act as he chose, the whole of history would be a tissue of disconnected accidents. (p. 1122)

> Man is the creation of an Almighty, All-good, and All-wise God. What is sin, the conception of which follows from man's consciousness of freedom? That is the question of ethics. (p. 1124)

> Only in our conceited age of the popularization of knowledge, thanks to the most powerful weapon of ignorance—the diffusion of printed matter—the question of the freedom of the will has been put on a level, on which it can no longer be the same question. In our day the majority of so-called advanced people—that is, a mob of ignoramuses—have accepted the result of the researches of natural science, which is occupied with one side only of the question, for the solution of the whole question (p. 1124).

One can see how far apart the mind of Tolstoy is from the mind of Hardy. To Tolstoy, faith has displaced everything; Gutenberg and the French Encyclopedists are of no consequence. All that matters is the personal relationship of one's conscience to God and humble obedience to God's immutable laws. Tolstoy's view is an eighteenth-century view, Hardy's a nineteenth-century view. His mind represents no such closed circuit as Tolstoy's. Hardy was receptive to the new science and his mind had grown from the revelations of Darwin, Huxley, Lyell, Einstein, and others, as it is plain to see that Tolstoy's had not. Tolstoy seems to have clung to the old faith of his forefathers, unlike Hardy, who tested his faith by reading both Newman and Darwin and with more courage than Tennyson did. It is as if Tolstoy had put all his trust in the Russian translation of the King James version of the Bible, which became for him, in his later days, the *Compleat Fortune-Teller*. Tolstoy makes

Serge Youriévitch's bust of Thomas Hardy, reproduced by permission of Evelyn Hardy and her agent David Higham Associates Ltd. (London) from her book Thomas Hardy's Notebooks *(Hogarth Press, London, 1955). Photographed by Bob Felling, San Jose, California.*

* "From the 25th to 30th of August 1924 Hardy was sitting to the Russian sculptor Serge Youriévitch for his bust. This was made in Hardy's study at Max Gate, and though he enjoyed conversing with the sculptor," he was tired by the sittings, probably on account of his age, and definitely announced that he would not sit again for anything of the kind" (*Later Years*, p. 239). See *Thomas Hardy's Notebooks*, ed. Evelyn Hardy (London: Hogarth Press, 1955), photograph opposite p. 106.

A pupil of Rodin, Youriévitch gave up a career in the Russian embassy in Paris for sculpture and travels, and became a master of character portraiture. His bust of Hardy has an earthy quality and one feels that he had a great liking for and appreciation of Hardy's work. Youriévitch also made a bust of Franklin Delano Roosevelt and of the American Indian. See *Art Digest*, April 15, 1931, and *Literary Digest*, April 27, 1929.

Youriévitch was born in Paris on March 31, 1873, and died there Dec. 18, 1969. He became an officer of the Legion of Honor by decree of March 3, 1913, while serving in the capacity of the Chamberlain of His Majesty attached to the Russian Embassy in Paris. (Courtesy of K. Christie Vogel and Carol Coon, Reference Librarians of the San Jose and San Francisco Public Libraries, respectively, who obtained the vital statistics from the Grande Chancellerie de la Légion d'Honneur, Paris, January 29, 1975.)

Napoleon a king in God's game of chess. Hardy makes Napoleon resemble one of Hegel's "reflex categories," that is, as Marx explains: "One man is king only because other men stand in the relation of subjects to him . . . they imagine that they are subjects because he is King" (*Capital,* p. 66), a good example of which is Shakespeare's *King Lear* (IV, 6), who boasts: "Ay, every inch a king. When I do stare see how the subjects quake." Hardy's Napoleon is a Fascist-minded opportunist who blames his vicissitudes on his star ("My star's to blame"; *Dynasts* II, 1, viii) and who after Fontainebleau laments: "By morrow dawn, I shall not have a man to shake my bed or say good-morning to!" (III, 4, iv). One wonders whether Hardy may not have read E. G. Wakefield's report of Peel's colonization at Swan River, West Australia: "Mr. Peel was left without a servant to make his bed or fetch him water from the river."*

It is to be regretted that Georg Lukacs does not mention *The Dynasts* in his discussion of Tolstoy. He makes the important distinction, however, between the writings of "the great English eighteenth century novelists" (Goldsmith, Fielding) who "lived in a post-revolutionary period" and "Tolstoy [who] was a pre-revolutionary writer . . . and still remained a pre-revolutionary writer even after the disaster of the European revolution of 1848, which left its pessimistic marks on the western writers." [18] There is, I think, despite its exaggeration, some truth in it.

Hardy attended (July 1893) a lecture by Stepniak on Tolstoy, who supervised the Russian translation of Hardy's *Tess* for a Moscow newspaper, and he admired Tolstoy's "philosophic sermon on war—his masterly indictment of war as a modern principle, with all its senseless and illogical crimes" [19] (*The Times,* June 28, 1904). Hardy had a much wider knowledge of science than did Tolstoy, who was as confused by his masters, as Marx says Mill was by his, and,

---

* Quoted by Marx in *Capital,* pp. 839–40, from E. G. Wakefield's *England and America* (1833), 2:33.

moreover, he had liberated himself from Christian mysticism as Tolstoy had not. He knew the history of the English peasantry as well as Tolstoy did that of the Russian peasantry and, what is more important, knew it from the standpoint of his forebears who had gone "down, down, down" or had turned to taking up the building trades as his father and grandfather had done. Indeed, the Wessex peasants in his novels and innumerable characters in his Napoleonic epic *The Dynasts* are in the Rainbarrow scenes perhaps the most fully alive. Hardy had, of course, read Balzac's *The Peasants* and Langland's *Piers the Plowman,* and he knew from his own family history the anti-Jacobin war of the Stuart dynasty, which had abolished feudal tenure of land, "that is," as Marx observes "they got rid of all its obligations to the State, 'indemnified' the state by taxes on the peasantry and the rest of the mass of the people, vindicated for themselves the right of modern private property in estates to which they had only a feudal title, and finally, passed the laws of settlement, which, *mutatis mutandi,* had the same effect on the English agricultural labourer, as the edict of the Tartar Boris Godonof on the Russian peasantry" (*Capital,* pp. 795–96). It is significant, I think, that Hardy viewed the torturous progress of the Wessex peasants from the time they were "thralls of Cedric, collared in brass" (A.D. 519) to their improved condition as wage-earners, through their membership in Arch's National Agricultural Workers Union (1872). Hardy did not lose sight of the imagery of their state and their travail when he copied some old notes on May 29, 1922, made before he contemplated writing *The Dynasts"*:

> We—the People—Humanity, a collective personality—(Thus "we" could be engaged in the battle of Hohenlinden, say, and in the battle of Waterloo).
> Title "self-slaughter"; "divided against ourselves."
> A battle. Army as somnambulists—not knowing what it is for.
> We were called "Artillery," etc. "We were so under the spell of habit that" (drill).

It is now necessary to call the reader's attention to those of us who were harnessed and collared in blue and brass.

These are the real reasons for Hardy's writing *The Dynasts*, and they were the reasons also behind Balzac's complaint on the peasants' eon-long servitude in his novel *The Peasants* (1844), and Lenin's plea (*in absentia*) at the Versailles Conference (1919) for "Peace, Land and Bread," and for Hardy's "pale pathetic people" of *The Dynasts*. Hardy saw as Marx saw "in the stormy youth of modern industry, especially from 1797 to 1815 . . . that the structure of the economical elements of society remains untouched by the storm-clouds of the political sky" (*Capital*, pp. 601, 394), and moreover, living in the intensified period of imperialistic history after Marx's death in 1883, saw that the situation was darkening again.

9

The Criticism of
The Dynasts

Hardy had thought that he "might express more fully in verse ideas and emotions which run counter to inert crystal-lized opinion—hard as rock—which the vast majority of men have vested interests in supporting," adding that "if Galileo had said in verse that the world moved, the Inquisition might have left him alone."[1] Hardy complained to Swinburne that critics criticized literature "with a secret eye on its political and theological propriety." Swinburne thought it would be the same 2,000 years hence; Hardy doubted it.[2] He felt, however, that he "must make an independent plunge, embodying the real, if only temporary thought of the age," but he expected to catch it "hot and strong for attempting it!"[3]

From Hardy's remark one would think he anticipated both a political and a theological assault. It appears, however, that the critics did not see any threat in a poetic account of the Napoleonic Wars, which had ended in 1815, despite Disraeli's anxiety for the occupants of the Palace and Marx's for the eviction of the cottagers during the Franco-Prussian War. And so *The Dynasts* was condemned on theological grounds. Nothing is so apparent in the criticism of *The Dynasts* as the bourgeois critics' failure to recognize Hardy's reason for writing it or to comprehend its import, and if I give more space to it than it deserves, it is to emphasize not only Hardy's preference for dramatic critics who have "less time [for] rehearsing their prejudices," [4] than literary critics, as he told Charles Morgan in 1922, but also their utter incompetence to deal with the literature of history in an unprecedented form. Most surprising is their failure to compare *The Dynasts* with Tolstoy's *War and Peace* and even Thackeray's *Vanity Fair,* and their total lack of any literary historical method. Only the *Edinburgh Review* critic (April 1908), whom I shall refer to later in this chapter, showed any knowledge of world literature, and the *Fortnightly* critic W. J. Courtney "goes so far as to find in Mr. Hardy's scheme something that corresponds with the attitude of the scientific historian," but the New York *Times* critic, quoting him (March 3, 1906), cautioned that "what the best of the critics say of this work, before it is completed, should be taken with reserve by all persons who wish to be forehanded in appraising works of art."

Yet it was an age of historiography (Macaulay, Carlyle, Green, Taine, Guizot, Sismondi, Halévy); the novelists wrote historical novels (Bulwer-Lytton, Thackeray, Dickens, Trollope, Reade, and Disraeli himself). Hardy had read *Pelham* and *Vanity Fair.* Indeed Hardy had noted in a contribution to a symposium in the *New Review* (January 1890) that

> there is a revival of the artistic instincts toward great dramatic motives—setting forth "that collision between the individual and the general"—formerly worked out with such force by the Periclean and Elizabethan dramatists, to name no other. (H. Orel, pp. 126–27)

Even the poets' muse, Clio, inspired heavy-artillery pieces befitting a Napoleon who had been a "heavy-artillery man" (Macaulay's "Battle of Naseby," Browning's "How They

Brought the Good News from Ghent to Aix," Tennyson's "Charge of the Light Brigade" and "Ode on the Death of the Duke of Wellington," and his historical plays written during his declining years: *Queen Mary* (1875), *Harold, Becket* (1884), *The Cup,* based on Plutarch's *De Mulierbus Virtutibus,* and *The Foresters* (1892), based on the Robin Hood legends. Macaulay had written a biography of William Pitt (1834) and both Hazlitt and Scott a *Life of Napoleon,* but, curiously, Jane Austen never mentioned the Napoleonic Wars in either her novels or her letters. Was it Laura or Paul Lafargue who exclaimed after Hugo's death, "Long live bourgeois poetry!"

There were the old standbys—Herodotus, Holinshed, Shakespeare, and the Bible, of course. Carlyle had supplied a galaxy of heroes in *Heroes and Hero Worship* (1841), from Goethe to Frederick the Great and from Mahomet to the greatest of all—"one whom we do not name here"—on Divine Right as Divine Might. And George Eliot had translated Strauss's *Life of Jesus* (1846) from the German. Criticism in the English-speaking world was still a belle-lettristic jeremiad of theology and aesthetics* of idealists. "Now what is of more value"—Calverton raises the question in *The Newer Spirit* (pp. 168–69)—"the charming or the true," and he points out that the aim of criticism "is not to create a work of art, but a work of analysis—of logic." Darwin was so upset by the critics that he left his defense to his disciples, Huxley and other colleagues. They explained away some of the controversy, which reached its height in Hardy's age and still breaks forth endemically today, especially after the loss of loved ones in World Wars. Prince Nikolai, at the end of

---

* Apropos is Marx's comment to Engels (July 18, 1877) on the "dilettante literary men who make the *Neue Welt, Vorworts,* etc., unsafe, necessarily form the majority of his collaborators. Ruthlessness—the first condition of all criticism—is impossible in such company; besides which constant attention has to be paid to making things easily comprehensible,, *i.e.* exposition for the ignorant. Imagine a journal of chemistry where the readers' ignorance of chemistry is constantly assumed as the fundamental presupposition" (*Correspondence,* p. 346).

War and Peace, goes home to Bald Hills and builds a new church; Hardy, more realistically, at the end of *The Dynasts* views the underworld of history from the Overworld of the Spirit of the Pities and the Years, who observe:

> And Europe's wormy dynasties rerobe
> Themselves in their old gilt, to daze
> Anew the globe!
>   (III, 7, viii)

So "the critics' appraisement" of *The Dynasts,"** Mrs. Hardy says, "was in truth, while nominally literary, at the core narrowly Philistine and even theosophic," their attitude being in general on what ground do you arrogate to yourself a right to express in poetry a philosophy which has never been expressed in poetry before?" [5]

"The cardinal error" that *The Spectator* of February 20, 1904 (which Marx called "the Philistine *Spectator*"**) found in the philosophy, was that it was "too cold, bloodless and formal." The critic declared that, although "free-will is not necessary to human interest, belief in it is necessary to human life." This was Tolstoyian, of course, and the critic might have supported it with Prince Andrei's and Pierre's agreeing "that one must believe in the possibility of happiness in order to be happy, and let the dead bury their dead, but while one has life one must live, and be happy in the thought" (p. 548). The *Spectator* critic also passed up an opportunity to contrast Hardy's fatalism with Tolstoy's predestination, or to compare the so-called free will of their respective characters, which Hardy shows as emerging into a better historical condition and Tolstoy as "pre-ordained

---

* Hardy wrote to Edmund Gosse (Jan. 17, 1904): "It is most unlikely that I shall carry the drama any further; for (as anticipated) in spite of some notable exceptions, the British Philistine is already moved by *the odium theologicum* in his regard of it, though the prejudice is carefully disguised (*vide Times* of Friday)" (see Richard Purdy, *Thomas Hardy: a Bibliographical Study,* p. 126).
   ** *Capital,* p. 363n.

from all eternity." Hardy's will was "a thousand times more distant from humanity than the Fate of other poets," the *Spectator* continued, and the effect thereby tended "to belittle mortal efforts, that the unreality of it all would become too spectral for art." Hardy pictures Napoleon as "the brazen rod that stirs the fire because it must"; Tolstoy declares that "great men—so-called great men—are but labels serving to give a name to the event, and like labels, they have the least possible connection with the event itself." [6] When has any complaint been made of the Realpolitik being "too spectral for art."? *The Dynasts*, it seems, had dissented from the political theology of Carlyle's *Heroes and Hero Worship** and Tolstoy's faith that kings were the instruments of God.

"Human drama," the critic maintained, "even on Mr. Hardy's theory, demands some illusion in its philosophy as well as in its staging." He might have found an example of Carlyle's Hero as King in the straggler's informing Prince Hohenlohe, who is with his Prussians on the Weimar road after the battle of Jena,

> The King himself
> Fought like the commonest. But nothing served . . .
> Prince William, too, is wounded. Brave Schmettau
> Is broke; himself disabled. All give way,
> And regiments crash like trees at felling-time! [7]

or have contrasted this episode with Emperor Alexander's tears in Tolstoy's *War and Peace* at seeing a dying soldier lifted into a stretcher: "say in French . . . 'what an awful thing war is!' " or with that of Young Prince Andrey's telling his father, "if I'm killed, and if I have a son . . . let him grow up with you, please." [8] Neither of these vignettes, to my mind, is as moving as our own Whitman's lines on our Civil War:

---

* Hardy has Napoleon say grandiosely: "Great men are meteors that consume themselves / To light the earth. This is my burnt-out hour!" (*The Dynasts*, III, 7, ix).

> Come up from the fields, father, here's a letter from our Pete;
> And come to the front door, mother—here's a letter from
>   thy dear son.

The critic acknowledged that "we can imagine a great drama of dignified spirits [proclaiming] in noble verse a lofty if heartless creed," but [Hardy's] spirits, "piteous, ironic and merely didactic, do not talk in noble numbers but in the worst jargon of the schools," concluding, "their espionage is in the spirit of a very young man who has just begun to dabble in metaphysics, and is imperfectly acquainted with the terminology." But he seems to have overlooked the espionage of the real spies (Sir Robert Wilson and Lord Hutchinson°) eavesdropping at the parley of Napoleon and Alexander, who were "cutting up Europe like a plum-pudding, *Par Nobile fratrum!*" the First Spy says, asking the Second "Did you get much for me to send on?":

> Much; and startling, too. "Why are we at war?" says Napoleon when they met.—"Ah—why!" said t'other.—"Well," said Boney, "I am fighting you only as an ally of the English, and you are simply serving them, and not yourself, in fighting me."—"In that case," says Alexander, "we shall soon be friends, for I owe her as great a grudge as you." [9]

The First Spy replies, "Somebody must ride like hell to let our Cabinet know!" Tolstoy, incidentally, in his rendition of the scene dwells on the disgust and hostility of Prince Rostov and others at seeing the Tsar fraternizing with Napoleon and their exchanging the Russian Order of St. George and the *Légion d'honneur* at a banquet lasting almost two hours [10] —ceremonials that Hardy passes over to get down to brass

---

° Speaking to the English Commissioner Wilson, in October of 1812, Kutuzof declared: "I will say again, as I have already said to you before, that I am not at all convinced that the complete destruction of the Emperor Napoleon and his army would be such a boon for the world. His legacy would not be destined for Russia, nor for any other continental country, but for that country which even now dominates the seas and whose sway should then become unendurable" (see Tarlé, *Bonaparte,* p. 295).

tacks of dividing the spoils and bringing in Napoleon's proposal of marriage to Alexander's sister, Anne, which Tolstoy leaves out.

"This constant harping on the Immanent Will in pseudo-scientific terms becomes in the end merely comic," the critic complained, "and these sinister spirits have indeed led Mr. Hardy into strange deeps," resulting in "the very worst lyrics and the most turgid meditations." "Yet," the critic confessed, "the outlines of a great conception rise out of the misty philosophy and awkward rhythms," in spite of "its technical faults and tortured monotony of the prosody." "It is the work of a poet, but it is rarely poetry," the critic added; "his Muse is too unskillful . . . for he has no turn for transcendental poetry." "Hardy had followed Coleridge's precept," Mrs. Hardy says, "that a long poem should not attempt to be poetical all through." [11]

The London Times° (Jan. 29, 1904), in an unsigned article by A. B. Walkley, called *The Dynasts* "a fearful sort of wild fowl . . . which clearly . . . will not go on the same shelf with either *Macbeth* or *Charley's Aunt*," and rebuked Hardy for writing a play not intended for the stage, with a particularly galling reference to Hardy's apprenticeship in architecture :

> Let us take an example from Mr. Hardy's old profession. It is an elementary principle in architecture that structure is conditioned by material. Stone demands one kind of building, iron another, wood a third. Suppose an architect were to construct an iron bridge under the limitations proper to a stone bridge, would Mr. Hardy applaud the feat? No, he would say it was bad architecture. So we say when it is attempted to build a book according to the methods of a play, or a play according to the methods of a book.

Citing Lessing's *Hamburg Dramaturgy* (1767–1769), the

° Editor, George Earle Buckle, Disraeli's biographer, who was editor of the *Literary Supplement* (1884–1912), was succeeded by Geoffrey Dawson. See *History of the London Times* 1884–1912, vol. 3 (New York: Macmillan, 1949), p. 65.

critic asked: "What is the use of building a theatre, dressing up men and women, putting their memories to the torture, crowding the whole town into a hall, if any work, when represented is only to produce some of the effects which might have been produced by a story read in a chimney corner? . . . It has, indeed, a fearful interest for those of us who, like the Shah," he chided, "prefer to have our dancing done for us," and added belittingly after a reference to the Encyclopedia, that as "a compromise between the play's fitness for the ordinary theatre and relegating it to a No-Man's-Land of 'mental performance' . . . it should be a puppet show." He jubilantly suggested that Hardy "let Brown's Theatre of Arts, which had performed Napoleonic gestes at country fairs all over Wessex, from Budmouth to Christminster, between 1830 and 1840, show him the right way."

Hardy replied in "A Rejoinder" (London *Literary Times*, Feb. 5, 1904), one of the few and rare instances, besides his preface to *Late Lyrics and Earlier* (1923), of his literary self-defense:

> Sir,—The objections raised by your dramatic critic to the stage-form adopted in *The Dynasts* for presenting a rapid mental vision of the Napoleonic Wars—objections which I had in some degree anticipated in the preface to the book— seem to demand a reply, inasmuch as they involve a question of literary art that is of far wider importance than as it affects a single volume. I regret that in the space of a letter I shall only be able to touch upon it briefly.
>
> According to it one must conclude that such productions as Shelley's "Prometheus Unbound," Byron's "Cain" and many other unactable play-like poems are a waste of means, and in his own words, may be read just as, *faute de mieux*, shoe leather may be used as an article of diet.

Hardy reminded his critic "that play shape is essentially, if not quite literally, at one with instinctive, primitive, narrative shape." Then he continued with:

This likeness between the order of natural recital and the order of theatrical utility may be accidental; but there it is; and to write scene so-and-so, instead of once upon a time, at such a place, is a trifling variation that makes no difference to the mental images raised. Of half-a-dozen people I have spoken to about reading plays, four say that they can imagine the enactment in a read play better than in a read novel or epic poem. It is a matter of idiosyncracy.

In mercy to his own argument he should have left architecture alone. Like those of a play for reading, its features are continually determined by no mechanical material, or methodic necessities (which are confused together by your critic). As for mechanical necessities, that purest relic of Greek architecture, the Parthenon, is a conventionalized representation of the necessities of a timber house, many of which are not necessities in stone, such as imitations of wood rafter -ends, beam-ends, and ceiling joists. As for necessities of purpose, medieval architects constructed church parapets with the embrasures of those of a fortress, and on the Continent planned the eastern ends of their cathedrals in resemblance of a Roman Hall of Justice. In respect of necessities of method, that art throughout its history has capriciously subdued to its service, in sheer waywardness, the necessities of other arts, so that one can find in it a *very* magazine of my own procedure in *The Dynasts.*

After referring to sculpture's borrowing from painting and to poetry's from music, and pointing out that "analogies between the arts are apt to be misleading," Hardy declared that

having said this much in defense of the form chosen, even supposing another to have been available, I have no room left for more than a bare assertion that there was available no such other form that would readily allow of the necessary compression of space and time. I believe that anyone who should sit down and consider at leisure how to present so wide a subject within a reasonable compass would decide this was, broadly speaking, the only way.

"His hankerings after actual performance of *The Dynasts*" Hardy called a misapprehension on the critic's part and suggested that "if he will look again at the last paragraph of the preface he will perceive that my remarks on perform-ance refer to old English drama only."

The critic, replying in *"The Dynasts* and the Puppets" (*London Literary Times,* Feb. 12, 1904) continued his lament on the decline of Partridge and his puppet art, and "caught with delight at the chance offered by *The Dynasts* of bring-ing them to a national entertainment once again."

The *Saturday Review*[*] (Jan. 30, 1904), to which Hardy had subscribed since his apprenticeship days, took a joking attitude toward the work. The reviewer, Max Beerbohm,[**] observed with something of Meredith's Comic Spirit that "in England during recent years, great writers in their autumn . . . have tended to write either about Napoleon or about Mrs. Meynell" (poet, essayist, and author of *A Letter from a Girl to Her Own Old Age* [1893]), citing Mr. Patmore on Mrs. Meynell and Mr. Meredith on Napoleon. "But I mislead you when I speak of Hardy as 'confining himself to Napoleon,'" Mr. Beerbohm went on; "excluding Mrs. Mey-nell would be more accurate. He is so very comprehensive." The scene of Nelson's death irresistibly reminded him of

the same scene as erst beheld by me, at Brighton, through the eyelet of a peepshow, whose proprietor strove to make it more realistic by saying in a confidential tone "'Ardy, 'Ardy,

[*] Editor (1898–1913, Harold Hodge, who succeeded Frank Harris (1894–98) (Graham, p. 330).

[**] Hardy met Mr. Beerbohm at "a memorial service to Meredith in Westminister Abbey (May 22, 1909), and Mr. and Mrs. Beerbohm, in company with Mr. and Mrs. Granville-Barker, visited the Hardys toward the end of May 1923 (see *Later Years,* pp. 137, 231). Beerbohm thought Hardy should have kept the Wessex peasants out of *The Dynasts* because they destroyed the unity of effect, but both the *Spectator* and the New York *Times* bestowed superlative praise on "his peasants, especially his Wessex men [who] have the true Shakespearean ring" (*Spectator,* Feb. 20, 1904). Hardy sat opposite Beerbohm at a dinner, and thought he had "not at all a humorous face . . . but rather melancholy expression," and Beer-bohm sent Hardy a copy of his recollection of his cartoon of him, "Mr. Thomas Hardy composing a lyric," which Mrs. Hardy showed Vere Collins, Dec. 27, 1920 (see Collins, *Talks with Thomas Hardy at Max Gate,* pp. 32–33).

I am wounded, 'Ardy.—"Not mortally, I 'ope my Lord?"—
"Mortally, I fear 'Ardy." °

One would have thought that Beerbohm, above all critics,
would have seized the chance to play off Hardy's nostalgic
deserter after Astorga saying in a cellar, "Would that I were
at home in England again, where there's old fashioned
tipple, and a proper God A'mighty instead of this eternal
'Ooman and baby" against the baby talk of Tolstoy's Prince
Denisov to Prince Rostov, who have been obliged to spend
the day in inactivity: "Wostov, lets dwink to dwoun our
gwief," or Hardy's having Napoleon grab the crown from the
Archbishop and put it on his own head, against Tolstoy's
having the writer of an ode to General Bragation grab it off
"a great silver dish" at a banquet and read it himself.[12] But
no. Instead, Beerbohm criticized Hardy for

> using a form which must always (be our dramatic imagination
> never so vivid) hamper and harass us in the study, which
> creates the effect of "*a duodecimo.*"

Although Beerbohm considered the Immanent Will "an
artistic nuisance" and the spirit puppets "mere electrons,
shifted hither and thither, for no reason, by some impalpable
agency," he admitted "yet they are exciting." "We wonder
why Mr. Hardy wrote it," he mused, "or rather, one regrets
that the Immanent Will put him to the trouble of writing it,"
and, "Wot's the good of anythink? Wy nothink' was the refrain of a popular coaster song some years ago, and Mr.
Hardy has set it ringing in our ears again."

° Perhaps that's what Hardy meant when he wrote his friend Edward
Clodd (28 Aug. 1914): "Yes: everybody seems to be reading *The Dynasts*
just now—at least, so a writer in *The Daily News* who called here this
morning tells me—T. H." (*Later Years*, p. 277). Blomfield told about a
Punch and Judy show performing outside the office in St. Martin's Square
(before Hardy came to work for him), and how the housekeeper, a woman
London-bred, came running upstairs exclaiming, "Why, Mr. Arthur—I
declare there's a man inside! And I never knew it before!" (*Early Life*,
p. 60).

The belletristic *Athenaeum** (Jan. 23, 1904) character-ized *The Dynasts* as "an attempt to combine historic chron-icle with poetic drama," in the manner of Aeschylus's and Shakespeare's plays, but the critic was of the opinion that Hardy "in adopting his new method, forfeits much . . . that has hitherto contributed to his success." The critic denied that he would "restrict a man's effort to one line, however brilliant the success achieved in it," since "were this done the author of the 'Lay of the Last Minstrel' might never have written 'Redgauntlet' or 'Rob Roy,' but the change in Mr. Hardy is in the wrong direction." He found his charac-terizations seldom more than "a thumb-nail sketch," and his blank verse, compared with Shakespeare's, which was "worthy, dignified, heroic . . . merely verse of marvelous blankness." "To convey in verse of marvelous blankness a debate in the House of Commons is work for inferior hands, and not for the author of 'Far from the Madding Crowd' and 'The Woodlanders.'" The critic might have found the conversation of the two old rustic beacon-keepers,[13] Jems Purchess and his companion John, on Egdon Heath some-thing as worthy of note as the repartee between Prince Hal and Falstaff on Flanders Fields in Henry IV and Henry V:

First Old Man:	The words of my Lord Lieutenant was whenever you see Kingsbere-Hill Beacon fired to the eastward, or Black' on to the westward, light up. . . .
Second Old Man:	I don't gainsay it. And so I keep my eyes on Kingsbere, because that's most likely o' the two, says I.
First Old Man:	That shows the curious depths of your ignorance. However, I'll have patience, and say on. Didst ever larn geography?
Second Old Man:	No. Nor no other corrupt practices.
First Old Man:	. . . Tcht-tcht!—Well, I'll have patience and put it to him in another form. Dost

* Editor (1901–1916), Vernon Rendall; poetry editor, Watts Dunton (see Graham, p. 319).

know the world is round—eh? I warrant
dostn't!

Second Old Man: I warrant I do!

Or the conversation between the two pedestrians on the
road, who see the beacon burning at daybreak on Rainbarrow tumulus:

1st Pedestrian: He's landed, westward, out by Abbott's
Beach. And if you have property you'll save
it and yourselves, as we are doing!

2nd Pedestrian:
All yesterday the firing at Boulogne
Was like the seven thunders heard in Heaven
When the fierce angel spoke.[14]

The Phantoms, whom they encounter on the road, "and before breakfast too," inform them that they have been sent
to "ease their souls," and "Even now a courier canters to
the port to check this baseless scare"; whereat the First
Pedestrian says skeptically to his companion:

These be inland men who, I warrant 'ee, don't know a ler-
ret from a lighter! Let's take no heed of such, comrade; and
hurry on!

Or the conversation on Durnover Green, Wessex, at the
burning of Napoleon* in effigy:

Yeoman: Why, you don't suppose that Boney
himself is to be burned here?

Rustic: What—not really Boney that's to be
burned?

A Woman: Why, bless the poor man, no! This is

* One recalls Rostopchin's broadsheets of the old tapster and Moscow
burgher called Karpusha Tchigirin in which he is made to jeer at
Napoleon's march on Moscow, saying that "they would be blown out with
Russian cabbage, that Russian porridge would rip their guts open, and
cabbage soup would finish them off; that they were all dwarfs, and a
village lass could toss three of them on her pitchford single-handed!"
"They were as much read and discussed," Tolstoy says, "as the latest
'bouts-rimes' of Vasily Lvovitch Pushkin" (*War and Peace,* pp. 697–98).

only a mommet they've made of him, that's got neither chine nor chitlings. . . .

Rustic: (vehemently) Then there's no honesty left in Wessex folk nowadays at all! . . .

Longways: 'Tisn't a mo'sel o' good for thee to cry out against Wessex folk, when 'twas all they own stumpoll ignorance.

Vicar of Durnover: (removes his pipe and spits perpendicularly) My dear misguided man, you don't suppose that we should be so inhuman in this Christian country as to burn a fellow-creature alive?

Rustic: Faith, I won't say I didn't! Durnover folk have never had the highest of Christian characters, come to that. And I didn't know but that even a pa'son might backslide to such things in these gory times—I won't say on a Zunday, but on a week-night like this—[15]

There are many other Hardyan "thumbnail sketches."

In America the reception of Part I of *The Dynasts* was unfavorable. The New York *Times** (Feb. 6, 1904) said: "Before such a tremendous effort criticism must pause in bewilderment," declaring "that the critics of Mr. Hardy's own land do not know quite what to make of it."

It is such a bewildering conglomeration of the real and ideal, of the pageantry of war and the commonplace of peasant life; of verse possessing appreciable poetic charm and verse that is no better or worse than so much prose; of the chattering and moaning of joyless, impotent, and undignified spirits . . . of humour and irony almost worthy of Swift, of measured moralizing quite worthy of Tupper, that the most receptive mind can make very little of it.

* Book-review editor, Edward A. Dithmar (1902–1907), John Grant Dater (1908), J. B. Gilder. See Meyer Berger's *Story of the New York Times, 1851–1951* (New York: Simon & Schuster, 1951), p. 195. A tentative plan-drawn up (Oct. 6, 1900) by W. Moberley Bell, editor of the *London Times*, for use of each orther's offices and sale of each other's stories as well as for an international edition, was turned down by Adolph Ochs "for fear it would be labelled 'Anglophile'" (pp. 133–34).

The critic complained of the burden, "as the London *Times* had done, "of this mental panorama on the reader," who must not only have from a theatrical sense but "also be prodigously interested in the English history of the opening of the nineteenth century and view all the momentous happenings on the Continent . . . from the British point of view." * It was a straw in the wind of the epidemic of patriotism that is spread by the American press from time to time in waves that sweep across the country and are carried to every flag-stop on Hearst's Fourth Estate. The critic's statement on this point was not true. Hardy's claim for his work, that it had "a tolerable fidelity to the facts of its date as they are given in ordinary records," the critic dismissed with:

> After all, historical accuracy as to the fact in such a work matters very little in comparison with accuracy of atmosphere and the pervading and authentic breath of life. To put the matter briefly, we prefer both as literature and art the fringe of the subject as touched on in "The Trumpet Major" to the texture of it as treated in *The Dynasts.* In one case we have a moving story wrought with infinite care and full of human modulations; in the other we have a drama greatly planned, but lacking in concentration and the intimacy of simple things.

If the critic had looked more carefully he might have found some of "the intimacy of simple things" in the conversation between the two postillions,[16] representative of the *lumpen-proletariat,* who side with the monarchy in the class struggle in France (p. 298), waiting on a street-corner in Avignon to glimpse Napoleon who, in custody of officers on his way to Elba, refused to go through the town, such an example as is not found in *The Trumpet-Major:* "My God these people of Avignon . . . are headstrong fools like all Provençal folk":

* Anyone who read the newspapers in 1923 will recall the hysteria of patriotism originating in the Midwest with Chicago Mayor Thompson's rabid Anglophobia, which raged on the front page and stirred up American history teachers and local school boards in a battle over American history text book (Muzzey vs. West) which the writer of this book, then entering college, well remembers (see Henry L. Mencken, *American Language* (New York: Knopf, 1838), pp. 81–84).

2nd Postillion :   Blast-me-blue, I don't care what happens to him! Look at Joachim Murat, him that's made King of Naples; a man who was only in the same line of life as ourselves, born and bred in Cahors, out in Perigord, a poor little whindling place not half as good as our own. Why should he have been lifted up to king's anointment, and we not even had a rise in wages? That's what I say.

1st Postillion :   But now, I don't find fault with that dispensation in particular. It was one of our own calling that the Emperor so honoured, after all, when he might have anointed a tinker, or a ragman, or a street woman's pensioner even. Who knows but that we should have been kings too, but for my crooked legs and your running wound?

2nd Postillion :   We kings? Kings of the underground country, then, by this time, if we hadn't been too rotten-fleshed to follow the drum. However, I'll think over your defence, and I don't mind riding a stage with him, for that matter, to save him from them that mean mischief here. I've lost no sons by his battles, like some others we know.

Their conversation is interrupted by a traveler on horseback, whom they ask: "Any tidings along the road, sir, of the Emperor Napoleon that was?" The critic seems to have forgotten that there have been other peoples besides Americans who have lived in "times that try men's souls." The critic was positive "that no attempt will ever be made toward its theatrical performance."[*] Indeed "The New York *Tribune* and other papers had been positive," Mrs. Hardy says, that the second part of *The Dynasts* "would never be heard of,

[*] Granville-Barker's production at the Kingsway Theater, London (Nov. 1914), lasted 2½ hours and ran for 72 performances; the Hardy Players: Wessex Scenes from *The Dynasts* at the Weymouth Pavilion (June 1916); and the Oxford University Dramatic Society, Oxford (Feb. 10–14, 1920), which Hardy attended. The OUDS manager Charles Morgan had read *Jude* "in a midshipman's hammock [during World War I] when to him also Oxford was a beckoning dream" (*Later Years,* pp. 135, 164–65, 203–9).

so ridiculous was the first." [17] The *North American Review*, the oldest traditionally conservative literary magazine, which featured book reviews and which had published Hardy's poem "A Trampwoman's Tragedy" (Nov. 1903), ignored it altogether; the *Atlantic Monthly* (Sept. 1905) belatedly reviewed it, the reviewer Ferris Greenslet finding the work "chiefly important as a vivid presentation of a fatalistic philosophy of history," and finding "the poetry of the piece . . . not so much in the brackish verse as in some of the stage directions in prose."

A more friendly review appeared in the *Seattle Sunday Times* (May 1, 1904), where least expected, by Ella Higginson,[18] a poet and short-story writer, who observed appreciatively:

> Although the quality of Mr. Hardy's poetry is very uneven, his drama of the Napoleonic wars, "The Dynasts," deserves a very careful reading, and when it has been read once, it will be read a second time. Only the first part of the ambitious work has been published, but the author has a second and third part in hand, and it is to be hoped that the first part will be received with sufficient favor to warrant the publication of the second and third parts.

She found "much humor among the minor characters, and some very real pathos, notably in the death of Nelson," which she quoted from.

Whether Hardy ever read this review is not known, but his reaction to the critics' attacks is given in a letter to Henry Newbolt° acknowledging his review in *The Quarterly* (Jan. 1909): "You approach the book from the right side, which so few critics have done. Instead of saying . . . 'Here is a performance hugely defective is there anything in it not-

---

° Sir Henry Newbolt (1862–1938) was the editor of the *Monthly Review* (1900–1905), professor of poetry, Oxford (1911–1921). He wrote a naval history of World War I (1920), which would have interested Hardy as much as Hardy's depiction of Trafalgar in *The Dynasts* would have interested him. See Webster's Biographical Dictionary (1971).

withstanding the huge defects?' they have mostly contented themselves with picking out the bad lines . . . there being myriads of them, as I knew too well before they said so." [19] To a critic who had accused him of putting Schopenhauer's words into Pitt's mouth, Hardy replied that he had used Pitt's actual words that were a matter of record before Schopenhauer was ever heard of." [20] Walter de la Mere noted reflectively, "Many a stone has been thrown at the blank verse; yet does not this very verse seem by some diabolical ingenuity to reveal all the sawdust that went to stuff that monstrous zanny of the fates, Napoleon?" [21] Swinburne wrote: "I never read any dialogue of yours that gave me more delight than the fifth scene of the second act [the old beacon-keepers on Egdon Heath] nor any verse of yours that I more admired than the noble song [the Boatmen's Trafalgar Song] which closes the fifth act" (Blunden, p. 123). (The *New York Times* reviewer had discovered a flaw in versification of this song, which required "the pronunciation of Trafalgar with the accent on the last syllable, as Englishmen of today do not pronounce the word"). Meredith "spoke in favour of his continuing it, now it had a commencement," although he thought that Hardy "would have made it more effective in prose, where he is more at home than in verse."[22]

"The publication of Part II (Feb. 1906) met with a more congratulatory reception," Mrs. Hardy states, "an American critical paper going so far as to say, 'Who knows that this work may not turn out to be a masterpiece?' " [23] The *New York Times* (Mar. 3, 1906), after looking "more closely and reverently" at the second part, admitted, "as its huge proportions are slowly developed the drama of the making of history takes on grandeur in this reviewer's eyes." The *Outlook* (Apr. 7, 1906) conceded that "there is an occasional lift of wing in a phrase, an occasional touch of poetry in a sentence, but as a whole, it is like a great balloon which lies collapsed on the ground," and consigned it to those curiosities "in our time by men of great gifts who were attempting to do something for which neither their gifts nor their training fitted them." Edmund Blunden felt later that the critics had treated Hardy's "harvest of a lifelong profundity . . . casually, even flippantly, above all with a tone of moral reprobation." [24] Edmund Gosse, Hardy's literary executor, wrote (Feb. 2, 1906): "Slacken not in winding the glorious poem to a noble and thrilling conclusion! " [25]

The change of attitude, which recalls that toward Tennyson's two volumes (1832 and 1842)—"adverse criticism, recantation, praise" [26]—is exemplified by the reviews of *The Dynasts* in *The Spectator* and in the *London Times*. Of the first part the *Spectator* had declared that "Hardy's reach had exceeded his grasp," and that "he has no turn for transcendental poetry." Of Part II, in acknowledging that "in spite of a hundred faults, there is a curious sublimity. . . . We can at least acknowledge the magnitude of the conception." On the publication of Part III, the recantation was complete. "We wrote in 1904 that Mr. Hardy's reach seemed to exceed his grasp," the reviewer recalled; but, "After laying down the last volume we admit that we were wrong. Taking the complete poem we feel that the poetry has obtained unity, and that the dramatic quality of the whole is his great achievement."

The *London Times* (Feb. 27, 1908) was still uncertain whether Mr. Hardy was a poet or not, comparing him, to his disadvantage, with Wordsworth, Crabbe, and Stephen Phillips, and quoting Kant's definition of words. It finally conceded that "there is something about Mr. Hardy's semi-avoidance of all literary adornment—his inherent, ingrained, unsullied originality in the conception of his subject—which could almost tempt us to believe that he has discovered a new method and invented a new formula." Its reviewer had obviously not thought so on January 29, 1904:

Apparently, Mr. Hardy himself shares the belief of his critics that he has produced something "new and strange." We believe that to be a mistake. We think that "praetorian here, praetorian there, we ken the biggin' o't."*

The play not intended for production, which had been "bad architecture" in 1904, became the inevitable milieu in 1906:

> Considering the scope of this epic, its vast extent in time and place and in the number and importance of the characters it involved—considering the necessary brief glimpses; the intense and concentrated revelations of personality and situation which is all that can be given us regarding each man and woman in turn—it is really doubtful if any less conventional literary form would have been effective.

The "puppet" vehicle disappeared in the profounder discovery that

> Nothing is more astonishing in *The Dynasts* than the subtle, the convincing way in which Mr. Hardy contrives to make the duration of time, the slow, inevitable movement of time, palpable to our imaginations; or how he detaches us from all actual contact with the drama we are watching, giving us actually the mental sensation of rising above and brooding as from a great height over the infinitely remote issues of a living and convulsed world.

The philosophy, which the critic had condemned for its disuniting effect, became the unifying force:

> It was not so clear then as it is now that this philosophic notion was to be the great bond of unity between the myriad scenes and persons of the drama. Moreover, in this last volume, more completely than in its predecessors, Mr. Hardy has answered that objection in another way. Not only are the doings more exciting—that was to be expected as the

* A quotation from Sir Walter Scott's *The Antiquary* (1816), in which the antiquarians Old Monkbarns and younger Lovel's discussion of the final conflict between Agricola and the Caledonians, "so admirably described by Beaumont," and now extinct from "the ravage of the horrid plough," is interrupted by Edie Ogilvie, the old minstrel and mendicant with, "Praetorian here, praetorian there, I mind the biggin' o't about this bit bourock, your honor" (chap. 4).

drama drew to a close and we came to Moscow, Leipzig, Elba, and Waterloo; the pity and the horror and the humour of those doings are more concentrated and more clearly exhibited.

Of the characterization, which the *Athenaeum* (Jan. 23, 1904) had disparaged as "thumb-nail sketches," *The Times* singled out for especial praise, except for the character of Napoleon:

> When Mr. Bernard Shaw wishes his readers to understand a character he prints his history, his appearance, and his views on life in a stage direction. Mr. Hardy does not; yet, if we wished to pick a character in the drama whose personal flavour and ways are not absolutely clear, we could only hit on Napoleon.
>
> Not even Mr. Hardy has succeeded in seeing Napoleon, without as well as with, his destiny, and catching him as a mere man. But with the others the case is different. . . .Wellington is no figure-head, no portrait *d'apparat,* and Picton, Marie Louise, all the persons for whom space allowed and dramatic need demanded character, even down to the nameless mother of a nameless girl who fell in love at the Duchess of Brunswick's Ball and the Vicar of Durnover, who has only to speak twice and to spit twice are as roundly human as could be.
>
> A great work of art—the title cannot be denied to *The Dynasts;* yet it is given under compulsion. By all the rules the enterprise should have been a colossal failure. . . . By all the rules *The Dynasts* should be chaos, a drama impossible to act (that, indeed, it remains); a book impossible to be read. Perusal of the three volumes together proves it to be a great work of art, unified by its philosophic conception, its vision, and its workmanship, in which poetry constantly keeps breaking in through the business-like directions of both verse and prose.

The Academy (Mar. 14, 1908) welcomed "the completion of a work in the great manner of which only a mature and powerful genius is capable," and was "yet more thankful for the profound conception . . . wherein a great theme is developed of a finer and loftier wisdom than any discovered by the noblest of his prose writings." Robert Ross, reviewing Part II ("A Close Time for Peasants," *The Academy*, March 3, 1906), had judged it "a great imperfect work of art; imperfect in the sense that the Sistine Chapel is imperfect," for "you must return to it very often before you can absorb the spaces," and concluded, "It is the spectator who is out of proportion, not the giants nor the mind which conceived them."

The New York *Times* (May 2, 1908), which had regarded it as "a bizarre design of a once great writer's declining years" (Jan. 30, 1904), reconsidered, after it "purposely delayed its review several weeks in order that any undue enthusiasm might have time to abate," and decided that it was "one of the noblest creations in literature." The reviewer pointed out that "the idea of a cosmic drama, of justifying the ways of God to man, is, of course, not new," citing the Book of Job, *Faust,* and *Paradise Lost,* which dealt with "the relation of human actions to consequences—the question of rewards and punishment, etc." Then he wrote, "But this conception of a Fate which is Unconscious of itself, which consists of That whose restless agony it itself decrees; this vision of history as the palpitation of the anatomy of a slumbering cosmic brain—had at all events not until now got itself into literature. And here is the end of it—strangely, very strangely indeed, for those who have marked the darkening of Mr. Hardy's philosophy—in a lyric of the Chorus full of joy in the hope that the gloom of slumbering consciousness in the world being shall break at last into beneficent intelligence."

Writing in the third person, Mr. Boynton of *The Bookman** (Books of the Month, July 1908), however, remained adamant in his adverse opinion and summarized with *belletristic* aplomb:

---

* Founded in 1891.

He [Boynton] thought (as he still thinks) the Hardy blank verse pretty bad and the Hardy machinery rather ridiculous. . . . His [Hardy's] blank verse is mere crabbed and artificial prose, not at all his own characteristic prose, chopped up into lines. . . . To a reverent lover of English poetry, there may even be something resembling sacrilege in this deliberate imitation in buckram and tinplate of the heroic panoply of her greatest verse.

Nor did he find anything good to say about the characterization, which showed "no deep 'creative' realization of his great historical characters," nor about his realistic scenes, his broad-speaking yokels and camp followers, which he stigmatized as "bits of red straw, the fence-rail, the veritable canteen which lead the eye almost invariably to the great stretch of canvas beyond which we behold the nations under the half-pitying, half ironical eye of the Unseen. . . . But now that he has seen the whole show he is by no means inclined to dismiss it as a fiasco," and he granted that Hardy had managed "to get a certain pictorial effect by irregular means and in that he has not failed."

In America, William Dean Howells, then editor of the *Cosmopolitan* magazine, referred to *The Dynasts*, without mentioning it by name, in "The Editor's Study" page, which he continued to contribute to *Harper's* magazine:

When we speak of the art of Thomas Hardy, of Conrad, of Hichens, of Mrs. Humphrey Ward [one is at a loss to understand how Howells could include the last two writers in the same category] we mean something quite different—something so unlike the older art that we must say that either it is not art at all or a wholly unprecedented art!

The very content of the art, the kind of human phenomena emerging at the stage of psychical evolution which we have reached, is unprecedented. All the old signs fail us; the well-worn tokens have given place to an ever-fresh coinage. The creations of the human spirit are wholly its own, born of it, not made in conformity with any logical proportions or mental notion, and they bear no stamp of extraneous authority; whatever of divinity they may have is in their purely human genesis. The whole meaning of that designation—"the son of man"—is restored to a humanity which nearly two-thousand years after the advent of the Gospel has come to the worldly instead of the other-worldly or saintly acceptance of it. "The fruits of the spirit" are not limited, as to their nature or their scope, by the narrow definition imposed by puritanical or any other arbitrary judgment as to what is the chief end of man.

The Comtean tone is unmistakable in Howell's remarks, but his overoptimism on the physical evolution is hardly reconcilable with the western side of his nature, which had defended the Chicago anarchists in 1886 and espoused Marxism, theoretically at least. He was himself investigating the rise of the American plutocracy in such novels as *The Rise of Silas Lapham* (1885) and *Through the Eye of the Needle* (1907), for, like Hamlin Garland, Howells (born in Martin's Ferry, Ohio) was a son of the middle border.

He went on in his leisurely, reflective, Cambridge manner, with intellectual discursiveness, without coming to grips with the world itself:

> If we were going on in the old way, making much of myth and of traditional fancies and symbols and customs, seeking dramatic effects that are only outwardly impressive, courting empty but picturesque splendors, our imaginative literature would still continue to create the art which has always been associated with a distorted similitude of life. But this is not the gait of that humanity which, almost within the limit of two generations, has emerged, taking its own shape and growing into full stature on the psychical plane, with interests and desires that find satisfaction only in humanly real issues and values.

Howells missed an excellent opportunity to have noted at least the effects of the psychical evolution of the Spirit of the Years and of the Pities on the French Admiral Villeneuve "off Ferrol," inditing a letter to Decrès ("I am made the arbiter in vast designs/Whereof I see black outcomes . . .

for, if I must pen it, Demoralized past prayer is the marine")
and his resolve to make for Cadiz, instead of Brest, whereby,
"Alas! I thereby fail the Emperor; but shame the Navy
less" (I, 2, ii). One can only conclude that Howells's pre-
occupation with "the New England conscience and Boston
small-talk . . . falls about his theme with the amplitude of
crinoline," as Parrington remarks; consequently his limita-
tions on dealing with an unprecedented work like Hardy's is
evident in his first paragraph.

The Edinburgh Review° (April 1908) critic was the first
one to show any understanding of *The Dynasts* in relation
to other works in world literature, or to discover a scientific
historicity in it. The critic displayed suspended judgment
on the work and recognized its originality. "It is too early
yet to decide the exact place in literature which 'The Dynasts' is destined to take. All the critics can say at present is
that it is entirely a thing apart; there is nothing beside which
it can be placed for the sake of comparison." He courageously defended Hardy's philosophy, which the other critics
had condemned: "It is no impeachment of a man's character, not even of his religious instincts, if in these times of
distracted counsels he know not which way to look . . ." and
affirmed that "the vulgar optimist is a far less vulnerable
figure than the pessimists of the type of Leopardi and Mr.
Hardy." It is the only criticism of *The Dynasts* that shows
any historical perspective or any breadth of knowledge of
the human spirit breathing in other literatures, and it is
worth quoting in full:

But there is, we have said, also an element which is of the
Time Spirit. A certain distraction from humanity along with
the impartiality which takes place in every kind of scene
and every rank of life, this is of our age; this marks all that is

° Editor (1895–1912) Arthur R. D. Elliot, who followed the practice
of signed articles (see Graham, p. 237), inaugurated by the *London Review*—"a courageous design, in an age of irresponsible criticism . . ."
Graham says (p. 239).

most vital in modern fiction, a world-sense of a new order. It was shadowed forth by Balzac in his insatiable curiosity in human things; it is almost propounded as a doctrine in the title " Comédie Humaine" which Balzac selected to comprehend all his work. Dickens, Thackeray, Flaubert, Zola, Ibsen, Tolstoi, Dostoievsky and Gorky have each in their fashion laboured to develop the same thing. But that will not be the last word. And Mr. Hardy's poem also passes beyond this. Behind this "realism" or "naturalism" Time is labouring to bring forth another birth to which, as it has not yet taken a fully recognizable shape, no just name has yet been given. "Symbolism" expresses only part of it. What it is or will be is the picturing of this drama of common life. It will show that the common-placeness of common things lies in us—in our way of regarding them—not in the things themselves. Dickens, when he spread over all his creations ("inventions" were the better word, perhaps) a weird light which is almost supernatural; Thackeray, when "without a hero" he produced one of the most tremendous dramas that literature knows; Zola, when he turned a market-hall into a grim poem; Flaubert, when he expended gems of his prose style on familiar scenes and objects; the Russians, who have shown a deeper, more poetic reading of human nature than had as yet been shown, at any rate to prose fiction. In this tendency, in this action of the Time Spirit Mr. Hardy's "Dynasts" will, we believe, in future times be acknowledged to take a great place.

Hardy had hoped to avoid "a polemic handling" of *The Dynasts* by stating in the preface that "the scheme of the drama was based on a tentative theory of things which seemed to accord with the mind of the age." [27] "I suppose I have handicapped myself," he wrote the *Times* literary critic (Feb. 5 and Feb. 22, 1904) "by expressing, both in this drama and previous verse, philosophies and feelings as yet not well established or formally adopted into the general teaching; and by thus over-stepping the standard boundary set up for the thought of the age by the proctors of opinion,[*]

[*] Marx similarly complained that "the Paris *Revue Positviste* reproaches me in that, on the one hand, I treat economics metaphysically, and on the other hand—imagine!—confine myself to the mere critical analysis

I have thrown back my chance of acceptance in poetry by many years."[28]

The London *Times*, of course, had set the pattern of criticism in the other reviews of Part I of the work, and "a large number of critics were too puzzled by it to be unprejudiced." This is evident in the qualified statements in their review of Part III (*The Times* and *Spectator*, particularly), when, rereading their reviews of Part I, they found it difficult to take back what they had said. The reception of *The Dynasts* might have been different if it had had the good fortune to have as intelligent a review as Darwin's *Origin of Species*[*] had received in that paper. The *Times*' science critic had applied to Huxley "for help in a matter beyond his competence," prefixing an introductory paragraph of his own to Huxley's article. In Hardy's case, however, the *Times* dramatic critic felt no limitation on the subject matter, and proceeded on his own. One conjectures that the science critic and Huxley would have found in Hardy's comparison of Napoleon and his army after Waterloo with "meanest insects on obscurest leaves," and the X-ray description of the Immanent Will, with souls like "pale cysts," something not seen before and worthy of note. Hardy had a liking for Huxley, "which grew with the knowledge of him," Mrs. Hardy notes in June 1878. But unlike Darwin, he had no Huxley to still the waves he had caused on Galilee.

Hardy, Mrs. Hardy says, "had probably been so far influenced by the reception of the first two parts, as not to expect the change of view which was about to give to the third part, and the whole production, a warm verdict of success, or he would not have followed the entry on 'Eve of Good Friday (Mar. 29, 1907), 11:30 P.M. Finished draft of Part III of *The Dynasts*,' by the addendum":

of actual facts instead of writing recipes (Comtist ones?) for the cook-shops of the future" (*Capital*, p. 21).

[*] A review of the American edition of the book (D. Appleton & Co. March 1860), three and a half columns long, by John Swinton, appeared in the New York *Times* of March 28, 1860 (see Meyer Berger, *History of the New York Times*, pp. 250–51).

Critics can never be made to understand that the failure may be greater than the success. It is their particular duty to point this out; but the public points it out to them. To have strength to roll a stone weighing a hundredweight to the top of the mount is a success, and to have the strength to roll a stone of ten hundredweight only half-way up that mount is a failure. But the latter is two or three times as strong a deed.

The laws of work are as operative in literature, Hardy knew, as they are in physics.

Principally in recognition of his achievement in *The Dynasts* Hardy was awarded in 1910 at the age of seventy, by the King, the Order of Merit, the greatest literary honor bestowed in England. This was the year that the Nobel prize of literature was awarded to Paul Heyse, which had gone to Selma Lagerlof the previous year, and was to go to Maurice Maeterlinck the following year, whom Hardy had criticized for his "sophistry" May 17, 1902.

The Dynasts, since then, has been praised and dispraised by a great many critics, but I shall limit myself to two whose criticism is more pertinent in the light of events of our own times. Amiya Chakravarty calls *The Dynasts* "the most lucid and cogent exposition of the mind of our Age";[29] Harvey Curtis Webster[30] observes that *The Dynasts* depicts the nations "carrying the laws of the jungle into international affairs," and says, "Behind them and led by them are what Marx called the *Lumpenproletariat,** men and women in the mass who have neither power, nor ill-will, intelligence, nor overweening selfishness."

Hardy's drama should be reread thoughtfully today in the history of our perilously extended time of the human race, when contemporary leaders seem farther from solutions for

---

* Hardy, observing the crowds at the British Museum (May Day 1891), makes the following somewhat ambiguous note: "Democratic government may be justice to man, but it will probably merge in proletarian, and when these people are our masters it will lead to more of this contempt, and possibly be the utter ruin of art and literature!" (*Early Life,* p. 309); however, in his "Memories of Church Restoration" (*Life and Art,* p. 109), he declared: "Life, after all is more than art."

their problems than the Victorians did for theirs, and when critics who, Hardy had observed in 1923, "are moved by a yearning for the reverse of that of the Athenian enquirers on Mars Hill," [31] and who show less and less understanding of the effects of the new social relations wrought by the Industrial Revolution (to use Plekhanov's insight[32]), their influences on, and their meanings to society and literature.

"As for the title" (from *The Magnificat*), Hardy wrote his friend Gosse (Jan. 31, 1904) that "it was the best and shortest inclusive one I could think of to express the rulers of Europe in their desperate struggle to maintain their dynasties rather. than to benefit their peoples" [33]—an opinion also expressed by Engels in his letter to his friend J. P. Becker (May 22, 1883), that *"the masses are far better than almost all their leaders."* [34] Neither the critics then or now, nor the historians and political leaders of Hardy's time or ours, if they have read it, seem to have comprehended that.

The storm that arose from Hardy's philosophy in *The Dynasts*, like that following publication of Darwin's *Origin of Species*, did not abate and on June 2, 1921, Hardy received a tribute originating with St. John Ervine and signed by one hundred and six young writers: "You have crowned a great prose with a noble poetry," and thanking him for all he had written "but most of all, perhaps, for *The Dynasts.*" A year before he received a letter from John Slater, secretary of the Federation of the Royal Institute of British Architects, informing him of his nomination as "an Hon. Fellow of the R.I.B.A.," to which he replied on March 7:

I really don't know what to say. Age has naturally made me like Gallio,° care for none of these things at any rate very

° Gallio, Marcus Annaeus Novatus (born at Cordoba, Spain, before 4 B.C., died A.D. 65). Elder brother of the philosopher and tragedian Lucius Annaeus Seneca, he was adopted by the Senator Lucius Junius Gallio, whose name he assumed. Made proconsul of Achaea by Emperor Claudius I, which office he held when St. Paul was at Corinth about A.D. 52 and refused to be a judge of the Jews' accusations against Paul (see *Acts of the Apostles* (18 : 12–17); whereupon a mob of angry Greeks beat Sosthenes, much, especially as I am hardly ever in London. But at the same time I am very conscious of the honour of such a proposition, and like to be reminded in such a way that I once knew what a T square was. So, shall I leave the decision to your judgement?

He was "duly nominated and elected," Mrs. Hardy says "and it was a matter of regret to him that he could not attend the meetings of the Institute, held still in the same old room in Conduit Street in which he had received the prize medal for his essay in 1863 from the hands of Sir Gilbert Scott." Slater was "almost the only surviving friend of Hardy's architectural years in London since the death of Arthur Blomfield."

It is not Hardy who is timid about facing the problems of his age, which have multiplied in ours, but his critics, who have treated his novels in general, and his poetry and *The Dynasts* in particular, with a spurious eclecticism— "the worst of all methods," in Marx's opinion, which is meant to show the extent of their knowledge and the lack of Hardy's, but actually shows that more historical insight is required if we are to extend our perception of the human condition beyond the mirror of our English-speaking consciousness and tradition that eclectic critics brought, or can bring, to the task.

In June 1913, when Hardy was at Cambridge being installed as an honorary fellow of Magdalene College, the audience in the Chapel stared at him "all ablaze in a crimson L.D.D. gown which he had put on by mistake, while the Archdeacon of Zanzibar preached a sermon on God being a God of desire, not a mild or impersonal force." [35]

The Dynasts would seem to deny that a socialistic republic could have been born into the world in A.D. 1917, when

president of the Corinth synagogue, in Gallio's presence, but he "cared for none of those things," which is indicative of "the impartial attitude of Roman officials, at the time toward provincial religions" (see *Encyclopepia Americana*).

Matthew Arnold had depicted society, earlier, as "living between two worlds—one dead and the other powerless to be born." It remains to be seen whether, with the efforts being made to encircle and destroy it, it can survive. The Pities perhaps would say Yes; the Years, No.

"A Philosophy of Experience"

What do we mean when we speak of the philosophy of Thomas Hardy? The philosophy of his novels, of his poetry, of his short stories,* or of *The Dynasts?* Or, do we mean a representative sampling of each kind of his writings, by which his view of life appears as a darker or lighter gray depending on the selections made and the critic making them? Or, do we mean an unrepresentative sample of his work from his heavier and more somber novels and poems, or an unrepresentative sample from his lighter and less somber pieces, in which the sun bursts through the mottled

* Hardy's philosophy is not that of his fictional characters, and must be separated from theirs. The two have been confused long enough. Owen and Cytherea's superstition about things happening in *threes*, or coincidence (*Desperate Remedies*); Creedle's belief that, if Giles's Christmas party were a failure, "'Twere doomed to be so"; Grace's remark on her narrow escape from the frightened horse at the tree-barking operations, "There's destiny in it, you see. . . . I was doomed to attend the picnic"; Tess's mother's dependence on the *Complete Fortune Teller;* Henchard's fear that someone has cursed a waxen image of him; etc.— these superstitions are largely refuted by Marty's disbelief in the Midsummer Night's ceremony, and by Giles's remark that Marty's neuralgic headache is due to her having shorn her hair, and that "two simultaneous troubles do not always make a double trouble." One does not find such legerdemain in the London novels.

threatening sky long enough to add a voice or two to the joyous lyrics "In the Seventies" and "The Darkling Thrush" and to the chorus of optimism expressed by the Pities ending *The Dynasts?* A recent critic* seems to have done the latter, stating that Hardy, if his writings had been written by any other man, would be considered an "optimist!" A fair-minded appraisal should be based on all his work as a token of poetic justice to those whose souls, like his, cannot rest because of their thoughts having been misrepresented by critics—of which he complains in his poem "Spectres that Grieve."

In 1922 Hardy protested to Charles Morgan, who had tea with him at Max Gate, that "critics approached his work with an ignorant prejudice against his 'pessimism' which they allowed to stand in the way of a fair reading and fair judgement," and in the preface to his posthumously published volume of poetry, *Winter Words* (1928), he mentioned that previous volume, *Late Lyrics and Earlier* (1923), "was pronounced wholly gloomy and pessimistic by reviewers—even by some of the more able class." ** and, "as labels stick, I foresee readily enough that the same perennial inscription will be set on the proceeding, not withsanding the surprises to which I could treat my critics by uncovering a place here and there to them in the volume."

A better guide to Hardy's philosophy is to be found in his appraisal of his philosophical reading (Dec. 31, 1901), for it reveals that his philosophy was more nearly what a philosophy should be, a search for a philosophy from one's experience, from which the title of this chapter is taken.

After reading various philosophic systems, and being struck

* Frank R. Southerington, *Hardy's Vision of Man*, (New York: Barnes & Noble, 1971), p. xi.
** In 1923 Hardy had taken the trouble to answer his critics, and set them right about his poems being "fugitive impressions," and concluded, "to repeat what I printed . . . twenty years ago and wrote much earlier in a poem entitled In Tenebris: 'If way to the Better there bye, it exacts a full look at the Worst.' "

with their contradictions and futilities, I have come to this: *Let every man make a philosophy for himself out of his own experience* [Hardy's italics]. He will not be able to escape using terms and phraseology from earlier philosophers, but let him avoid adopting their theories if he values his own mental life. Let him remember the fate of Coleridge, and save years of labour by working out his own views as given him by his surroundings.

This appears to be what Hardy did; it should clarify, beyond the shadow of a doubt, the obfuscations that have arisen from critics' considering the secondary sources of his thought instead of the primary source—his empirical habit of mind —out of which it grew.

There is no point at all in considering the philosophy that Hardy read after finishing *Jude the Obscure* (1896)—that is, Maeterlinck's* *Apology for Nature* (1900) and Bergson's* *Creative Evolution* (1907), with which he disagreed, and very little, if any, point in considering Schopenhauer and von Hartmann, since his own philosophy was shaped by his reading before this date and his reflections on his experiences in Wessex and London long before their works were available in English translation. Hardy subjected his philosophical reading to the same test of rationality as he had his reading of Darwin's *Origin of Species* and Newman's *Apologia* as a young man in London in 1865 (the year Lockyer discovered helium in the sun's rays) in his search for truth. His reading of John Stuart Mill's *Essay on Liberty*,[1] which he and many of the young men "knew by heart," had tempered his inquiring mind and strengthened his conviction that "no man can be a great thinker who does not

---

* See Hardy's criticism of a review of Maeterlinck's *Apology for Nature* (*Academy and Literature*, May 17, 1902), for quoting "with seeming approval his vindication of Nature's ways . . . that . . . though she does not appear to be just from our point of view, she may practice a scheme of morality unknown to us in which she is just"; and his criticism of Bergson's *élan vital* for being "our old friend Dualism in a new suit of clothes . . . "an ingenious fancy without real foundation" (*Later Years*, pp.96–98, 271).

recognize, that as a thinker it is his first duty to follow his intellect to whatever conclusions it may lead." This is reiterated in his journal note of July 19, 1883:

> In future I am not going to praise things because the accumulated remarks of ages say they are great and good, if these accumulated remarks are not based on observation. And I am not going to condemn things because a pile of accepted views raked together from tradition, and acquired by installation, say antecedently that they are bad.

Moreover, Hardy was as critical of the teleological philosophers as was Marx,[2] who declared that "with Hegel it (philosophy) is standing on its head" and it "must be turned right side up again, if you would discover the rational kernel within its mystified shell." In May 1886, Hardy noted skeptically of the teleological philosophers whom he had been "reading in the British Museum":

> Have been thinking over the dictum of Hegel—that the real is the rational and the rational the real—that real pain is compatible with a formal pleasure—that the idea is all, etc., but it doesn't help much. These venerable philosophers seem to start wrong; they cannot get away from the pre-possession that the world must somehow have been made to be a comfortable place for man. If I remember, it was Comte who said that metaphysics was a mere sorry attempt to reconcile theology and physics.

It will be remembered that Auguste Comte (1798–1857), originated a philosophy in which the whole essence of existence is concentrated into one great being whom he termed Humanity (a philosophy that interested Conrad and many Poles after the failure of the 1863 Polish insurrection), and that Hardy himself declared that his views showed closer agreement with Spencer* and Comte than with the German

* I have prized H. C. Webster's statement which, while recognizing the resemblance between Hardy's Immanent Will and Spencer's "The Unknowable" (noted by Rutland also), observes that "The creator of *The Dynasts* was quite capable of constructing a naturalistic system without Spencer's help" (*On a Darkling Plain*, p. 45).

philosophers.[3] Hardy's interest in Darwin led him to read Spencer's *First Principles* and *Principles of Biology* (1862), which strengthened his agnosticism. He began reading Comte's *Positive Philosophy* in 1863, and went on with it in May 1970, before the publication of *Far from the Madding Crowd* (1874), which caused his name to be linked with George Eliot, whose death in the winter of 1880, when Hardy lay ill, "set him to thinking about Comte's *Positivism*,* and some poems." His poem "In the Seventies"[4] (undated) is animated with a Comtean optimism:

> In the seventies nought could darken or destroy it,
> Locked in me.
> Though as delicate as lamp-worm's lucency;
> Neither mist nor murk could weaken or alloy it
> In the seventies!—could not darken or destroy it,
> Locked in me.

This autobiographical poem not only records the happiness of his early married life and literary success, but also, I think, his happiness over the brighter prospect in the workfolk's lives since their affiliation with Joseph Arch's National Agricultural Workers Union (1872). Arch was a representative of the enlightened proletariat, who in Comte's philosophy were to bring about a better life for people. The poem

* This was when Hardy was confined to his bed as the result of a cerebral hemorrhage. Comte attributes the same proportion as Marx to man's "effective action upon the external world," Henri Gouhier points out, quoting Mrs. Prenant, and both emphasize materialism, but Marx stresses the economic factors, while Comte emphasizes the intellectual aspects (see "August Comte's Philosophy of History," in *The Nineteenth Century World*, ed. Guy S. Metraux and François Grouzet [New York: New American Library, 1963], p. 482).

Pertinent is Paul Laforgue's letter to Engels (24 April 1884): "I have just been readiing H. Spencer's article on 'The Coming Slavery' (*Contemporary Review*, Apr. 1884, the old fogey is too grotesque for words: Laura and I are going to reply to him; and in *To-day* we shall use his own phrases and examples to demonstrate the opposite of his findings (*Engels-Laforgue Correspondence*). The compiler explains (p. 200) that in the article (pp. 461–62) Spencer was somewhat insulting to the working class in tone, when he denounced the slavery by state intervention in the individual's affairs under socialism, saying "all Socialism involved slavery."

curiously shows the effect of Comte on Hardy and the social relation of the poet to his art. A similar elation is found in the poem "The Voice of Things" [5] (1913), which looks back to the earlier time when Hardy had escaped from a profession he did not like and a place he did not like to find the woman of his choice and his life work:

> Forty Augusts—aye, and several more—ago,
>   When I paced the headlands loosed from dull employ,
> The waves huzza'd like a multitude below
>   In the sway of an all-including joy
>   Without cloy.

The social implications are found most clearly in the last stanza of his poem "In a Wood," in which he turns away from the apparitions of the competitive struggle in London reflected in Little Hintock forest with the resolve:

> Since, then, no grace I find
>   Taught me of trees,
> Turn I back to my kind,
>   Worthy as these.
> There at least smiles abound,
> There discourse trills around,
> There, now and then, are found
>   Life-loyalties.[6]

Hardy's experiences of Nature in Wessex had given him an understanding of Malthus's "Essay on the Increase in Population" (1798), which Marx called "a libel on the human race," and which Darwin acknowledged was the basis of his own study of the struggle for existence. Moreover, Hardy's observations in London had sharpened his knowledge of Hobbes's *bellum omnium contra omnes*, referred to by Engels in his book *The Condition of the Working Classes in England in 1844.* Hardy, "as a young man," Mrs. Hardy says, "had been among the earliest acclaimers of *The Origin of Species,*" [7] and one should add that Marx and Engels were also much impressed by Darwin's book.* Hardy's projection of the competitive struggle in London in terms of the natural struggle in Wessex ("In a Wood") is apropos of Marx's comment to Engels that it was "wonderful how Darwin had rediscovered English society in the plant and animal kingdom," and Engels's comment that "competition is the completest expression of the battle of all against all." [8] Hardy could not believe that the state in society was a necessary corollary of the state in Nature, and he questioned the motives of Disraeli's and Gladstone's rationalizations of Darwin to justify their political ends on the basis of Darwin's "struggle for existence" and Spencer's "survival of the fittest." To Hardy, "the Darwinian theory was a truth which would liberate men's minds," and he resented statesmen's misusing it as an expediency for their misgovernment in the interest of the few and the suppression of the many, who had no voice in government and no control of their history. In this respect, for Hardy at least, Darwin had as much to do with the Reform Bill of 1867 as the Reform League who campaigned for it, and both had more to do with the passage of it than the Honorable Mr. Thring who drafted it. Indeed, Darwinism and the Reform Bill were the basis of Hardy's optimism as a young man in the sixties, which were radical politically as well as scientifically. The political struggle for manhood suffrage had increased the electorate threefold, and young Hardy, in his poem "1967" (1867), looked forward hopefully to

> A century which, if not sublime,
> Will show, I doubt not, at its prime,
> A scope above this blinkered time.[9]

Darwinism had an "ethical meaning" to Hardy. Indeed, he addressed a letter to the Secretary of the Humanitarian

---

* Marx was as interested in Darwin's "history of Nature's technology" as Hardy, and wrote to Engels (Jan. 16, 1861) that the *Origin of Species* "contains the basis in natural history for our view" (*Marx-Engels Correspondence*, pp. 125–26).

League,* The Athenaeum, Pall Mall, S.W., London, on April 10, 1910, as follows:

> Sir:
> I am glad to think that the Humanitarian League has attained the handsome age of twenty years—the Animals Defence Department particularly.
> Few people seem to perceive fully as yet that the most far-reaching consequence of the establishment of the common origin of all species, is ethical; that it logically involved a readjustment of altruistic morals by enlarging as a *necessity of rightness* the application of what has been called "The Golden Rule" beyond the area of mere mankind to that of the whole animal kingdom. Possibly Darwin himself did not wholly perceive it, though he alluded to it. While man was deemed to be a creation apart from all other creations, a secondary or tertiary morality was considered good enough towards the "inferior" races; but no person who reasons nowadays can escape the trying conclusion that this is not maintainable. And though I myself do not at present see how the principle of equal justice all round is to be carried out in its entirety, I recognize that the League is grappling with the question.[10]

The letter recalls President Andrew Jackson's last words on his deathbed, while his friends in the room fought back their tears and the Negro slaves stood outside the window in lamentation: "Do not cry, I shall meet you all in heaven, yes I hope to meet you all in heaven white and black."**

---

* See Hardy's letter to "a lady of New York in answer to an inquiry she made" on vivisection (*Later Years,* p. 138); also his account of a very interesting lunch at the Bachelors Club, given by his friend George Curzon," where he met "Mr. F. C. Selous, the mighty hunter . . . wondering how such a seemingly humane man could live for killing" (*ibid.,* p. 29).

** This is reported in A. M. Schlesinger's *Age of Jackson* (Boston: Little, Brown & Co., 1945), p. 447.

But the resistance of the ruling classes to further social and economic reforms at home, and their resorting to imperialistic misadventures abroad as an outlet for unemployment and depression, disheartened Hardy. "The blinkered time" [11] of 1867 receded before the onrush of laissez-faire capitalism, which ignored the people's welfare at home and risked their lives in imperialistic wars abroad, into the darker view of his later novels of one who "waits in unhope" of his poem "In Tenebris" [12] (1895–96), and finally, following the Boer War,* into the deceptive state pictured by the Pities following Napoleon's liquidation of the Revolution:

> *The pale pathetic peoples still plod on*
> *Through hoodwinkings to light!* [13]

---

* Replying to a writer in the Parisian *Revue Bleue* (Jan. 1902), Hardy stated that "the effect of the South African War on English literature had been a vast multiplication of books on war itself and the issue of large quantities of war-like and patriotic poetry. These words naturally throw into the shade works that breathe a more quiet and philosophic spirit; a curious minor feature in the case among a certain class of writers being the disguise under Christian terminology of principles, not necessarily wrong from the point of view of international politics, but obviously anti-Christian, because inexorable and masterful" (*Later Years*, pp. 91–92). To a reader who took exception to the character of the soldier-phantom in Hardy's poem "A Christmas Ghost-Story" as "unheroic," Hardy wrote a fine letter, reprinted in W. T. Stead's *War against War in South Africa*, p. 81. Jack London quotes George Bernard Shaw's definition of a soldier "ostensibly a heroic and patriotic defender of his country, is really an unfortunate man driven by destitution to offer himself as food for powder for the sake of regular rations, shelter, and clothing" (*People of the Abyss*, p. 221). Cobden, on a trip to Sicily in 1848, observed: 'The rags and misery remind me of Ireland. The only persons I see in the small towns and villages with clean, sleek skins and good clothes on their backs are priests and soldiers" (J. Morley's (*Life of Cobden*, 2.466). And William Morris observed, "the Italian peasant is . . . worse off than his brother of Ireland" (J. W. McKail, *William Morris*, 2:78).

"One can judge of the execrable political cantmonger, Edmund Burke," Marx says angrily, who maintained that "the laws of commerce are the laws of Nature and therefore the laws of God." He continues: "This sycophant who, in the pay of the English oligarchy, played the romantic laudator temporis acti against the French Revolution just as, in the pay of the North American Colonies, at the beginning of the American troubles, he had played the Liberal against the English oligarchy, was an out and out vulgar bourgeois. No wonder that, true to the laws of God and of Nature, he always sold himself in the best market" (*Capital*, pp. 833–34n).

Hardy became a victim of "the decennial cycle of stagnation, prosperity, over-production and crisis, ever recurrent from 1825 to 1867," which, Marx observes, "seems indeed to have run its course but only to land us in the slough of despond of a permanent and chronic depression." [14] The failure of Parliament* to do anything about the deplorable condition which, in 1856, had made Dickens "quite an Infidel" in regard to politicians, made Hardy, a less angry man, only an agnostic—"a harmless agnostic" in his own words. He says as much in his preface to *Late Lyrics and Earlier* (1923) in answering the persistent charge of pessimism, which he maintained "is, in truth, only such 'questionings' in the exploration of reality, and is the first step towards the soul's betterment, and the body's also," quoting the line from his poem "In Tenebris": "If way to the Better there be, it exacts a full look at the Worst": that is to say by the exporation of reality, and its frank recognition stage by stage along the survey, with an eye to the best consummation possible: briefly evolutionary meliorism," [15]

---

* "The reforms of 1867 and 1884," observes K. B. Smellie (*A Hundred Years of English Government*, pp. 192–93), "did not suddenly transform the H. of C. The number of members of the House who could claim close relations with peers and baronets only gradually diminished; while the number of those concerned with industry and commerce gradually increased. The number of members of the House who were either sons of peers or heirs to the peerages shrank from 108 in 1860 to 51 in 1897, while the number engaged in manufacturization and mercantile operations rose from 90 in 1865 to 112 in 1880; between 1874 and 1900 the number of brewers, ironmasters, armament makers and manufacturers increased from 61 to 120. Both in 1865 and 1880 there were 80 members who had served in the Army or Navy, 250 who had attended one of the great public schools, or Oxford and Cambridge, but there was no drastic change in the House until the rise of the Labour Party and the victory of 1906."

The Third Parliamentary Reform Act (1884) granted the ballot to male agricultural workers, but the enfranchisement of women, proposed by Mill in 1866, continued to be ignored until 1919 and 1928. Public educcation, established in 1870, was not made compulsory until 1891, and then only for England and Wales. There was "fierce and prolonged debate" to the Education Act of 1902, when the Conservatives ventured to put the secatrian school on the rates as well as the taxes" (Maccoby, *English Radical Tradition*, 5:174, 200, 219). This was the reason behind the Radical Party's conference at Leeds (Oct. 17, 1883) extending the franchise to the counties, which the chairman J. Morley said was "vast proof of

The political record was anything but "evolutionary."
Gladstone told Graham (Nov. 27, 1860):

> We live in anti-reforming times. . . . I sometimes reflect how much less liberal as to democratic policy in any true sense of the word, is this government than was Sir Robert Peel's; and how much the tone of ultra-toryism prevails among a large portion of the liberal party.

and later in connection with his Home Rule Bill for Ireland, to Morley:

> Look at the whole conduct of the opposition from '86 to '85—every principle was thrown overboard, they could manufacture a combination against the government, blaming Disraeli as "the grand corrupter . . . who sowed the seed" of manhood suffrage.[16]

Parliament is indicted by Marx for its class prerogatives:

the conviction which was growing up in the Radical party that it was not enough for them to be the helpless exponents of excellent ideas, but that they must organize, they must unite" (*ibid.*, p. 186).

In 1885 George Howell, M.P. from East Bethnal Green, proposed an amendment to the Ballot Act and "triennial parliaments" towards a more equitable and representative government, which had been one of the rejected Chartist demands. In 1891 Gladstone suggested a plan of paying members of parliament to the extent of their need for money, while Morley, possibly thinking of his having rejected Hardy's *Poor Man and the Lady* in 1868, thought it was "desirable in the public interest that poor men should have access to the H. of C. and that the poor man should stand on the same footing as anyone else" (Morley, *Life of Gladstone*, 3:479).

F. A. Channing, in a speech at Kettering (July 1886), declared on the subject of Home Rule for Ireland: "I ask whether the best man in the world, Mr. Gladstone himself or Mr. Bright is entitled to choose representatives for people who should choose for themselves" (see Maccoby's *English Radical Tradition*, 5:204). In 1891 Cecil Rhodes gave Schnodhorst £5000; later, alarmed at certain speeches of Gladstone and Labouchere, he asked him to divert the money for charity. Schnodhorst exceeded his function and reassured him. By 1901 speculation was suggesting that Rhodes had given £5000 to the Liberal party in return for the promise that Uganda should not be evacuated (see Smellie's *A Hundred Years of English Government*). Gladstone's "combination of a belief in political liberty and High Church principles was a mystery to the Tories and his belief that to our landed property we owed the kindly and intimate relations between our higher and lower classes," Smellie says," [is] an exasperation to the Radicals" (*Ibid.*, pp. 208–9).

Parliament did not vote a single farthing in aid of emigration, but simply passed some Acts empowering the municipal corporations to keep the operatives in a half-starved state, *i.e.,* to exploit them at less than the normal wages. On the other hand, when 3 years later, the cattle disease broke out, Parliament broke wildly through its usages and voted, straight off, millions for indemnifying the millionaire landlords, whose farmers in any event came off without loss, owing to the rise in the price of meat. The bull-like bellow of the landed proprietors at the opening of Parliament, in 1866, showed that a man can worship the cow Sabala without being a Hindoo, and can change himself into an ox without being a Jupiter. (*Capital,* p. 632n)

Morris,[*] in 1877, made much the same observation of the period on "all the world turned bourgeois . . . and the devil take the hindmost," ending with a rustic image that should have delighted Hardy:

> How much nearer are we to the ideal of the bourgeois commonwealth than they were at the time of the Reform Bill, or the time of the Repeal of the Corn Laws? Well, thus much nearer to a great change, perhaps, that there is a chink in the armour of self-satisfaction . . . but as to approaching the ideal of that system reformed into humanity and decency, they are about as much nearer to it as a man is nearer to the moon when he stands on a hayrick! [17]

Victorian society was a society in which the incentive of surplus profit, and surplus profit alone, had set in motion

[*] Engels wrote Marx's daughter Laura Lafargue (London, Nov. 23, 1884): "Morris was here the other night and quite delighted to find the Old Norse *Edda* on my table. Morris read a piece of his poetry (a refonte of the eddaic Helreid Brynhilder, the description of Brynhilda burning herself with Sigurd's corpse etc. etc.), it went off very well" p. 245. She had written Engels (Feb. 16, 1884): "Morris is all very well as far as he goes, but it is not far . . . p. 139. Engels died Aug. 6, 1895, of cancer of the throat, and his ashes were scattered in the sea at Eastbourne.

Hardy sent gift copies of *Tess* to William Morris and also to Alfred Austin (both dated Dec. 1891), inscribing in the latter a quotation from "A Dialogue at Fiesole": ". . . Wrestlers born, Who challenge iron Circumstance—and fail" (see Purdy, *Thomas Hardy, a Bibliographical Study,* p. 74).

and viciously accelerated capitalist enterprise without any regulation, or thought of the past or future. Hardy portrays it in the scene of Ethelberta's taking her working class brothers Sol and Dan on their half-day off to Milton's tomb in Cripplegate cemetery, where Hardy gives us a picture through the "fly-wheel which afterwards," Marx says in *Capital* (p. 411) plays "so important a part in Modern Industry";

> All people were busy here: our visitors seemed to be the only idle persons the city contained; and there was no dissonance—there never is—between antiquity and such beehive industry; for pure industry, in failing to observe its own existence and aspect, partakes of the unobtrusive nature of material things. This intra-mural stir was a flywheel transparent by excessive motion, through which Milton and his day could be seen as if nothing intervened. Had there been ostensibly harmonious accessories, a crowd of observing people in search of the poetical, conscious of the place and the secene, what a discord would have arisen there." [18]

Captain de Stancy and Paula's repartee (*A Laodicean*) over his Cavalier ancestors having knocked down her Roundhead ancestors in the Civil War and the Parliamentary cannon having battered down de Stancy castle [19] reveal a farcical consciousness and recalls by contrast Marx's anger at the bourgeoisie of both countries fraternizing after the Franco-Prussian War for the common massacre of the proletariat,[20] putting down the Paris Commune and restoring the Third Empire in France as in putting down the Commonwealth and restoring the Stuart dynasty. The Thames Embankment[21] proposed by Christopher Wren to the London aldermen after the Great Fire (1666), Hardy was just then seeing built in 1862. Whether they got around to Napoleon's proposal of gilding "the dome of the *Invalides*, in best gold leaf and on a novel pattern during the Third Empire," doesn't really matter; it was like the low-cost workingmen's lodgings established in the eighties by Lord

Rowton* in London and the Mills Hotels in New York, by which philantropists of that day pumped some of their surplus wealth into welfare projects as great corporations today found foundation trusts to escape federal income taxes, and had little more effect in correcting the underlying causes than the model villages erected in the Crimea for display to Catherine the Great, or the Elizabethan Poor laws in the reign of Elizabeth who, in her travels, is said to have said, "*Pauper ubique jacet*" (*Capital*, pp. 750, 793). The Thames project, like Napoleon's, was a political device, as was also manhood suffrage, grudgingly given, of which Lord Derby wrote to Disraeli (Dec. 22, 1866):

> Of all possible hares to start, I do not know a better than the extension of household suffrage, coupled with plurality of voting.[22]

The feudal aristocracy and the rising bourgeoisie "were playing into each other's hands," as John Bright observed, "to suppress the rising proletariat, and one would think a workman never read a newspaper";[23] he might have added, a poet either.

Hardy had not read for nothing these words in Mill's *Essay on Liberty:*

> It is hardly too much to say that the right to dwell freely in a grimy street; to drink freely in the neighbouring public house, and to walk freely between the high-walled parks and the jealously preserved estates of their landowners is all that the just and equal laws of England secure to the mass of the people.[24]

"The British Constitution," Smellie says Lord Derby "sapiently said," "was still a monarchy limited, an aristocracy tempered, and a House of Commons not altogether demo-

---

* Lord Rowton (1838–1903), Secretary to Disraeli and special envoy to Berlin Conference of 1878. Hardy met Lord Rowton, "who is great on lodging houses" (*Early Life*, p. 301).

cratic." [25] Smellie observes that there were "two Englands: a democratic England of the towns and an aristocratic England of the counties." [26]

Hardy's faith in the democratic England is best shown on the positive side by his choice of working-class heroes and heroines* in his novels, for he believed, as Conrad did, that "man is a worker, or he is nothing—only a worthless adventurer," and he depicts people struggling against conditions that they did not create (a point discussed above in the chapter on his novels). It is shown on the negative side in several little poems that express the powerlessness of the individual against the powerfulness of bourgeois society. These reveal his disillusionment with political reform and the more or less resigned attitude of a person who feels himself alone. In a little-known poem "A Commonplace Day," [27] which is "turning ghost," Hardy emphasizes, in one stanza at least, through a combination of "impulse" and "intent" in some one, somewhere (suggestive of stirrings of the Will), "that enkindling ardency from whose maturer glows/The World's amendment flows"; but the impulse,

---

* Marian, Tess's friend, calls Flintcomb-Ash "a starve-acre place," and Hardy says that "the single fat thing on the soil was Marian herself; and she was an importation," and further: "Of the three classes of villages, the village cared for by its lord, the village cared for by itself, and the village uncared for either by itself or by its lord—(in other words, the village of a resident squire's tenantry, the village of free copyholders, and the absentee-owner's village, farmed with the land)—this place, Flintcomb-Ash, was the third" (*Tess*, p. 363). There are the negotiations between a farmer from a county seven miles away, who would not take the old man without the younger—the son had a sweetheart on his present farm, who "stood by waiting the issue," which was solved by Lucetta's entreaty to Farfrae, who needed a young carter and "would take the old man without the younger" (*Mayor of Casterbridge*, p. 184).

"While great owners are thus escaping from poor-rates through the depopulations of lands over which they have no control, the nearest town or open village receives the evicted labourer," Marx notes, and "these open villages form, in fact, the 'penal settlement' of the English agricultural proletariat. . . . The labourers were it not for the small owners would for the most part have to sleep under the trees of the farms which they work" (*Capital*, pp. 750, 752).

> benumbed at birth
> By momentary chance or wile, has missed its hope to be
> Embodied on the earth;
> And undervoicings of this loss to man's futurity
> May wake regret in me.

His hope, poised on the delicate Comtean balance, shifts between the short-range view of the poem "He Wonders about Himself" (1893), written before the Boer War, and the long-range view of the poem "To an Unborn Pauper Child"[28] (1901). In the former, he expresses a reasonable belief in the individual's role in histroy:

> Part is mine of the general Will,
> Cannot my share in the sum of sources
> Bend a digit the poise of forces
> And a fair desire fulfill?

In the latter poem—a hopeless one: "No man can change the common lot to rare"—Hardy grieves over the unborn pauper child: "Thou wilt thy ignorant entry make,/Though skies spout fire and blood and nations quake." He pictures such a nativity in the woman's camp near Mont Saint-Jean (*The Dynasts*) "on the sheltered side of a clump of trees," amid wounded soldiers and wives, mistresses, and small children sitting on "armfuls of straw from the adjoining farm," where "a woman has just given birth to a child," and "a camp-follower is playing a fiddle near." [29]

In the phenomenon of war, Hardy found a cogent medium for the expression of his philosophy that the individual's will is subjected to the nation's will. It is only a long time after a war has been over that he can look forward hopefully, as he did in 1915, recalling the day of the bloody battle of Gravelotte (August 18, 1870) in the Franco-Prussian War, when he and Miss Gifford observed an old horse harrowing clods in the arable field below the parsonage—to reflect with any equanimity. He does this in the last stanza of his poem "In the Time of 'the Breaking of Nations' ": [30]

> Yonder a maid and her wight
> Come whispering by:
> War's annals will cloud into night
> Ere their story die.

Hardy is closer to Engels and Marx than to Thiers* and Chateaubriand. Like Chateaubriand (1768–1848) earlier, Hardy charges Nature with indifference to man's welfare, but unlike Chateaubriand, Hardy, after the death of his parents, did not embrace Christianity as did Chateaubriand after the death of his mother in prison. Moreover, in his poem "The Peasant's Confession" (1898), suggested by a passage that Hardy "stumbled upon" that spring at the British Museum in Thiers's *Histoire du Consulat et de L'empire* [31] he shows the peasant misleading Napoleon's emissary looking for Grouchy's army, and killing him to save his farm from becoming a battlefield, a crime he afterwards regretted on his deathbed. More important is Hardy's reflection on history given in journal notes and in a letter replying to Edward Wright's question about the philosophy of *The Dynasts*, which "seems to me," he wrote, "to settle the question of Free will v. Necessity":

> The will of a man is, according to it, neither wholly free nor wholly unfree. When swayed by the Universal Will (which he mostly must be as a subservient part of it) he is not individually

*Louis Adolphe Thiers (1797–1877), a Rouen mill owner and minister of France, who took part in the *National* (1830), which aided in the downfall of the Bourbons, held several offices under Louis Philippe until 1840; after the revolution of 1848 voted for the presidency of Louis Napoleon; arrested and banished for his opposition to Napoleon's *coup d'état* (Dec. 2, 1851); returned during the crisis of 1870–71: after the fall of Paris became the chief executive; first duty imposed upon him was to assist in drawing up the treaty of peace whereby France ceded Alsace-Lorraine to Germany and suffered an enormous indemnity; chief works are a *History of the French Revolution* (6 vols., 1823–1827) and *History of the Consulate and Empire* (20 vols.).

It would be interesting to know whether Hardy read Plekhanov's essay "The Role of the Individual in History" (1898), according to which human history develops not as a process of expressing definite laws but only in accidental ways in accordance with the prescription and fantasies of critically thinking individuals.

free; but whenever it happens that all the rest of the Great Will is in equilibrium the minute portion called one person's Will is free, just as a performer's fingers are free to go on playing the pianoforte of themselves, when he talks or thinks of something else and the hand does not rule them.[32]

Marx expresses the homeostasis in economic terms:

The price of labour, at the moment when demand and supply are in equilibrium, is its natural price. . . . As soon as his labour actually begins, it has already ceased to belong to him; it can therefore no longer be sold by him. (*Capital,* pp. 589, 588)

And again:

As in religion man is governed by the products of his own brains, so in capitalistic production, he is governed by the products of his own hand. (*ibid,* pp. 589, 681)

And:

That in their appearance things often represent themselves in inverted form is pretty well known in every science except political economy. (*ibid,* p. 588)

"Since I discovered, several years ago," Hardy wrote (October 1882) "that I was living in a world where nothing bears out in practice what it promises incipiently, I have troubled myself very little about theories. Where development according to perfect reason is limited to the narrow region of pure mathematics, I am content with tentativeness from day to day." In London, on March 28, 1888, he observed: "London* appears not to *see itself.* Each individual

---

* See Hardy's observations of Londoners as automatons or somnambulists at Society gatherings and at art-salons (*Early Life,* pp. 341, 294–95), and his other observations on city life at music-halls, operas, horse-races, Lord Mayor's Show, Piccadilly, Upper Tooting, at the Marble Arch, etc., with their images of London as a Wheel and a Beast (*Early Life,* pp. 297, 180, 171, 295, 179, and 224).

is conscious of *himself,* but nobody conscious of themselves collectively, except perhaps some poor gaper who stares round with half-idiotic aspect. There is no consciousness here," he continued, "of where anything comes from or goes to—only that it is present." * "Groping tentativeness" is the distinguishing trait of the Immanent Will of *The Dynasts* as the Spirit Ironic comments on a temporary truce between the combatants at the battle of Talavera, whom the Pities observe lying down "by the bivouac embers: /There to pursue at dawn the dynasts' death-game/unto the ending!" (II, 4, iv) and the Spirit Ironic explains:

> *It is only that Life's queer mechanics chance*
> *to work out in this grotesque shape just now.*
> *The groping tentativeness of an Immanent Will*
> *(as grey old Years describes it) cannot be asked to*
> *learn logic at this time of day!* [33]

Hardy noted in his journal: "October 20 (1884) *Query:* Is not the present quasi-scientific system of writing history mere charlatanism? Events and tendencies are traced as if they were rivers of voluntary activity, and courses reasoned out from the circumstances in which natures, religions, or what-not, have found themselves." Marx, in a letter to Schweitzer (Jan. 25, 1865), comparing Proudhon with historian Raumer (1781–1875) for their charlatanism in science and accommodation to politics, declared they were "living contradictions and inseparable from such a point of view" (*Correspondence,* p. 176). Hardy went on to say, "But are they not in the main the outcomes of *passivity*—acted upon by unconscious propensity?" In the spring of 1885 he had

---

* Compare Adam Smith's description of "hand and head labour [becoming] more pronounced . . . as society becomes richer" (cited by Marx in *Capital,* p. 398), with Hardy's description of "Copse-work, as it was called, being an occupation which the secondary intelligence of the hands and arms could carry on without requiring the sovereign attention of the head, the minds of its professors wandered considerably from the object's" recounting "later chronicles and ramifications of family history . . . of a very exhaustive kind (*The Woodlanders,* p. 27).

reflected on the discussion of the misadventures of British imperialism in the Sudan at the Carnarvons' "nominally social but really political parties," that gave rise, Mrs. Hardy says, "to the following notes of that date":

> History is rather a stream than a tree. There is nothing organic in its shape, nothing systematic in its development. It flows on like a thunderstorm-rill by a road side; now a straw turns it this way, now a tiny barrier of sand that. The off-hand decision of some commonplace mind high in office at a critical moment influences the course of events for a hundred years.

This puts Hardy more in line with the school of thought from Heraclitus to Parrington, and separates him from the idealists and teleologists from Plato to Tolstoy, who saw history as the preordained working out of God's beneficent plan, even to what makes the apple fall, and even to the vicissitudes of war, in which it appears "all happens fortuitously," as Tolstoy* believed.

* "Napoleon's historian, Thiers, like others of Napoleon's historians," writes Tolstoy, "tries to justify his hero by maintaining that he was drawn on to the walls of Moscow against his will. He is as right as any historians who seek the explanation of historic events in the will of a man; he is as right as the Russian historians, who assert that Napoleon was lured to Moscow by the skillful strategy of the Russian generals. . . . In this, apart from the law of 'retrospectiveness,' which makes all the past appear a preparation for the subsequent facts, the element of mutual interaction, too, comes in confusing the whole subject. A good chessplayer, who has lost a game is genuinely convinced that his failure is due to his blunders, and he seeks the blunder at the commencement of the game, forgetting that at every move during the whole game there were similar errors, that not one piece has been played as perfectly as possible. The blunder on which he concentrates his attention attracts his notice simply because his opponent took advantage of it. How much more complex is the game of war, which must be played within certain limits of time, in which there is not one will controlling lifeless toys, in which the whole it the resultant of the innumerable collisions of diverse individual wills!"

"We are forced to fall back on fatalism in history to explain irrational events (that is, those of which we cannot comprehend the reason). The more we try to explain these events in history rationally, the more irrational and incomprehensible they seem to us. Every man lives for himself, making use of his free-will for attainment of his own objects, and feels in his whole being that he can do or not do any action. But as soon as he does anything, that act, committed at a certain moment in time, becomes irrevocable and is the property of history, in which it has a significance, predestined and not subject to free choice" (*War and Peace*, p. 565).

Tolstoy's conception is a static, eighteenth-century conception. He likens war to "the centre wheel of a great tower clock," with "the complex action of countless different wheels and blocks" (p. 234); or was what Isaiah Berlin calls in *The Hedgehog and the Fox*, on the other hand, "the differentials" of history, the unforeseen factors. Hardy's conception is more scientific and evolutionary, being an extension of Darwin's view on the life of man in the universe—the tendency of an ape to become a man. Hardy is closer to Engels and Marx, who laid "the main emphasis at first on the derivation of political, juridical and other ideological notions, and of the action arising through the medium of these notions from basic economic facts" (*Correspondence*, p. 510), and like them rejected "the bourgeois illusion of the eternity and finality of capitalistic production" (Engels's letter to Mehring, July 14, 1893). Hardy has the Spirit of the Years describe Christianity as "a local thing, which the wild dramas of this wheeling sphere include with divers other such, in dim, pathetical, and brief parentheses" (*Dynasts:* I, 1, vi), to Spirit of the Pities, who did not recognize the rites at the Coronation of Napoleon, "*though in its early lovingkindly days of gracious purpose it was much to me.*" Both Marx and Engels recognized that the Christians had renounced the problems of this world for the rewards of the next, or words to that effect, and that to them "Hegel [1770–1831] has never existed."

This passivity that Hardy observed in the phenomenon of war he also observed in the phenomena of church. Hardy's observation (July 8, 1888) at St. Mary Abbott's Church, Kensington—"the ugliest church in London," his employer's father, Bishop Blomfield called it—is interesting in this connection:

Moreover, Mrs. Howe remarks that after the Indian mutiny of 1857, "new ideas about history [began] to germinate . . . for novelists to rationalize England's position in India. The "New History had a nicer name for the situation [which] was complexity (and) lent an almost mystic sanctity to whatever was complex" (p. 66).

They pray in the litany as if under enchantment. Their real life is spinning on beneath their apparent one of calm like the District Railway-trains underground just by, throbbing, rushing, hot, concerned with next week, last week. . . . Could these true scenes in which this congregation is living be brought into church bodily with the personages, there would be a churchful of jostling phantasmagorias crowded like a heap of soap bubbles, infinitely intersecting, but each seeing only his own. That bald-headed man is surrounded by the interior of the Stock Exchange; that girl by the jeweler's shop in which she purchased yesterday. Through this bizarre world of thought circulates the recitative of the parson—a thin solitary note without cadence or change of intensity—and getting lost like a bee in the clerestory.

Hardy's observation offers a startling comparison in ideas and imagery to Engels's in a letter to J. Bloch (Sept. 21, 1890), and in some respects reads almost like a precis of it:

We make our own history, but in the first place, under very definite presuppositions and conditions. Among these the economic ones are finally decisive. But the political, etc., ones and indeed even traditions which haunt human minds, also play a part, although not the decisive one. . . .

In the second place, however, history makes itself in such a way that the final result always arises from conflicts between many individual wills, of which each again has been made what it is by a host of particular conditions of life. Thus there are innumerable intersecting forces, an infinite series of parallelograms of forces which give rise to one resultant—the historical event. This again may itself be viewed as the product of a power which, taken as a whole, works *unconsciously* and without volition. For what each individual wills is obstructed by everyone else, and what emerges is something that no one willed. Thus past history proceeds in the manner of a natural process and is also essentially subject to the same laws of movement.[34] [italics original]

Marx cites Vico on the difference between human history and natural history (*Capital*, p. 406n) and Darwin's interest in Nature's technology. He says that "the further question arises: What driving forces in turn stand behind these motives? What are the historical causes which translate themselves into the motives in the brains of these actors?" For example, he calls attention to the fact that "the East 'so called' end of London is not only the seat of iron ship-building" industry but also of a so-called "home industry always underpaid" (*Capital*, p. 736), referring to a Tory paper's editorializing on "the frightful spectacle" (1866) exposed in one part of the metropolis (the East end of London). Hardy noted in his journal (Jan. 2, 1888): "Different purposes, different men. Those in the city for money-making are not the same men as they were when at home the previous evening. Nor are these the same men as they were when lying awake in the small hours," and he observes of the farmers at the hiring Fair in *The Mayor of Casterbridge:* "Their faces radiated tropical warmth, for though when at home their countenances varied with the seasons, their market faces all the year round were glowing little fires" (p. 175) and the townsfolk understood "every fluctuation in the rustic's condition, for it affected their receipts as much as the labourer's," and they entered "into the troubles and joys which moved the aristocratic families ten miles round—for the same reason."

There are two more passages from *The Mayor* particularly meaningful. One presents abstractly, in Lucetta and Elizabeth-Jane's walking past Henchard's granary on a drizzly day, a scene in which the voices of Henchard's workmen "were borne over to them at that instant on the wind and raindrops from the other side of the wall":

There came such words as "sacks," "quarters," "threshing," "tailing," "next Saturday's market," each sentence being disorganized by the gusts like a face in a cracked mirror.

The other passage is concrete and offers a commentary on the government's Botany Bay policy toward the agricultural proletariat, from the reign of Castlereagh to Queen Victoria:

On other sides of the yard were wooden granaries on stone staddles, to which access was given by Flemish ladders, and a store-house several floors high. Wherever the doors of these places were open, a closely packed throng of bursting wheat-sacks could be seen standing inside, with the air of awaiting a famine that would not come. (p. 71)

One is reminded of Marx's critique of the "vulgar economy" of Nassau W. Senior of Manchester, who maintained "that the profit (including interest) of capital is the product of the last hour of the twelve," and who declared, "I substitute for the word capital, considered as an instrument of production, the word abstinence"* (*Capital*, p. 654). Marx comments in many places on the anomaly of want in the midst of plenty

* "An unparalleled sample this, of the discoveries of vulgar economy!" Marx exclaims. "It substitutes for an economic category, a sycophant phrase—*volia [sic] tout*" (*Capital*, p. 654). Marx comments further on Senior's hypothesis: "The more society progresses, the more abstinence is demanded—namely, from those who ply the industry of appropiating the fruits of others' industry. All the conditions for carrying on the labour-process are suddenly converted into so many acts of abstinence on the part of the capitalist. If the corn is not all eaten, but part of it also sown—abstinence of the capitalist. If the wine gets time to mature—abstinence of the capitalist" (*ibid.*, p. 654). For this he cites Scrope's *Political Economy* in a footnote; "No one . . . will sow his wheat, for instance, and allow it to remain a twelve-month in the ground, or leave his wine in a cellar for years, instead of consuming these things or their equivalent at once . . . unless he expects to acquire additional value," of which he remarks: "It has never occurred to the vulgar economist to make the simple reflection, that every human action may be viewed as 'abstinence' from its opposite. Eating is abstinence from fasting, walking, abstinence from standing still, working abstinence from idling, idling abstinence from working. These gentlemen would do well, to ponder once, in a way, over Spinoza's 'Determinatio est Negatio'" (p. 654). Marx notes, "In the face of the habitual mode of life of the old feudal nobility which, as Hegel rightly says, 'consists in consuming what is in hand,' and more especially displays itself in the luxury of personal retainers, it was extremely important for bourgeois economy to promulgate the doctrine that accumulation of capital is the first duty of every citizen, and to preach without ceasing, that a man cannot accumulate, if he eats up all his revenue, instead of speading a good part of it in the acquisition of additional productive labourers, who bring in more than they cost" (*ibid.*, p. 645). In another footnote: "Thus for instance, Balzac, who so thoroughly studied every shade of avarice, represents the old usurer Gobsec as in his second childhood when he begins to heap up a hoard of commodities" (*ibid.*).

and the law of supply and demand being enforced by the police.

Hardy's "Will" in *The Dynasts* also bears a striking resemblance to the innumerable conflicting wills of society that create a situation that invites comparison with Engels's description of unconscious Nature and Caudwell's of the Market, which appears to be "an extension of Nature" but which is nothing but "the public, blind, strange, and passive." [35] In his poem "In a Wood," Hardy depicts the one situation, the other in his poem "Hap," [36] in which the "purblind Doomsters—Crass Casualty and dicing Time"—deal out, with the colossal indifference of capitalist society, misery instead of happiness to human beings. Hardy, it will be recalled, described London in the spring of 1889 (April 5), as "Four million forlorn hopes!" and in the poem "Nature's Questioning" [37] ("The headpiece represents a broken key") the agricultural proletariat, cowed into the passivity* of natural objects, raises the question:

"Or is it that some high Plan betides
    As yet not understood,
    Of evil stormed by Good,
We the Forlorn Hope over which Achievement strides?"

There was during the nineteenth century "a continual movement of growth in productive forces, of destruction in social relations," Marx observes, "of the formulation of ideas, the only immutable thing in the abstraction of movement—*mors immortalis.*" [38] This *The Dynasts* most fully depicts.

---

* "In a village school . . . containing 75 scholars, 33 vanished thus on the Lady Day (April 6) of the present year," Hardy writes. "Some weeks elapse before the newcomers drop in and a longer time passes before they take root . . . their dazed and unaccumstomed mood rendering immediate progress impossible, while the original bright ones have by this time degenerated into the dazed strangers of other districts ("Dorsetshire Labourer," *Hardy's Personal Writings*, ed. H. Orel, pp. 182–83, 170. The situation is poetically reflected in Hardy's poem "Nature's Questioning" (see for interpretation, G. W. Sherman, on "the dull, unvarying joyless one," *Colby Library Quarterly* (May 1952), pp. 99–100.

Hardy speaks against the apologists in his observation about life's "contrarious inconsistencies": "Nature's jaunty readiness to support unorthodox social principles," [39] and the Shade of the Earth's reference to Dame Nature as *"that lay shape they used to hang phenomena upon"* (*The Dynasts,* I, 1, vi).

But Nature is nonexistent in the London novels, to confuse Hardy or his urban characters as in the Wessex novels. Indeed, they do not lay the blame on some brooding unconscious Will at the back of things (Hardy's poem "The Last Chrysanthemum"); nor does Hardy intervene like the messenger from the Earth in his poem "God-Forgotten": "Lord, it existeth still." [40] But he does transfer some of his depression acquired in London to the Wessex countryside, as Mumford [41] has observed; and what is more important, he does use Nature as a mirror in the manner Caudwell has observed Tennyson did in *In Memoriam* (1850), which immeasurably enriches his Wessex novels with psychological and philosophical overtones, particularly *The Return of the Native, The Woodlanders,* and *Tess of the D'Urbervilles.* I have commented somewhat on this in the chapter on the novels.

Caudwell [42] declares that Tennyson, "like Darwin, and even more Darwin's followers . . . projects the condition of capitalistic production into Nature (individual struggle for existence) and then reflects the struggle intensified by its instinctive and therefore unalterable blindness back into society, so that God—symbol of the internal forces of society—seems captive to Nature—symbol of the external environment of society," and he cites Tennyson's stanzas from *In Memoriam:*

> Are God and Nature then at strife,
> That Nature lends such evil dreams?
> So careful of the type she seems,
> So careless of the single life;

> That I, considering everywhere
>   Her secret meaning in her deeds,
>   And finding that of fifty seeds
> She often brings but one to bear.

> I falter where I firmly trod. . . .

Marx observed that "as the heavenly bodies once thrown into a certain definite motion, always repeat this, so it is with social production as soon as it is once thrown into the movement of alternate expansion and contraction." Effects, in their turn, become causes and the varying accidents of the whole process which always reproduces its own conditions, take on the form of periodicity." [43] Hardy frequently projects the irrationality of society into unconscious nature in this manner in a piece of Turner-like impressionism: "Crowds"—mostly women [milling in the alley of butcher stalls (*A Pair of Blue Eyes*), under the glare of gas lights—the most lucrative of all England's industries between 1846 and 1866, according to Marx] "illuminating the lumps of flesh to splotches of orange and vermilion, like the wild colouring of Turner's later paintings, whilst the purl and babble of tongues of every pitch and mood was to this human wild-wood what the ripple of a brook is to the natural forest." [44] Other instances are Winterborne's "bidding against Melbury for timber and faggots that he did not want . . . in an abstract mood, in which the auctioneer's voice seemed to become one of the natural sounds of the woodland" (*The Woodlanders*), and the somberness of Egdon Heath suggesting "the façade of a prison" rather than "the façade of a palace double its size," with his observations that "what was the tragedy of Nature to the ancient Greeks has become the tragedy of Society to modern man" (*The Return of the Native*), and that

> the time seems near, if it has not actually arrived, when the chastened sublimity of a moor, a sea, or a mountain will be all of nature that is absolutely in keeping with the moods of the more thinking among mankind." [45]

It is of such regions that Darwin observed that the struggle for existence was entirely between the elements.

A particular instance of this transfer is found in Hardy's description of Clym's face seen against the dark tanned wood of the settle, which was to the hearth of old cavernous fireplaces "what the east belt of trees is to the exposed country estate, or the north wall to the garden" and Clym's face impressed the gazer as "a natural cheerfulness striving against depression from without, and not quite succeeding." In Clym's face "could be dimly seen the typical countenance of the future . . . whose Phidias should there be a classic period to art hereafter . . . may produce such faces." He continues further:

> The view of life as a thing to be put up with, replacing that zest for existence which was so intense in early civilizations, must ultimately enter so thoroughly into the constitution of the advanced races that its facial expression will be accepted as a new artistic departure.[46]

One could discount Hardy's interest in the development of genetic individuality* to social differentiation** if he had not expressed it before and afterwards. Stephen Smith, the architect, has a constitution that, rare in the springtime of civilization, seems to grow abundant as a nation "gets older, individuality fades and education spreads"; he also has "a brain with extraordinary receptive powers, and no great creativeness." George Somerset (*A Laodicean*) has a "mature forehead . . . now growing common, and with the advance of juvenile introspection it probably must grow commoner still." [47] The development is most fully portrayed in Clym Yeobright who, like the heath, has "a lonely face, slighted

---

* Lysenko, Trofim Denisovich (1898–), Soviet agronomist, who disregards the distinction between genotype (genetic endowment) and phenotype (physical appearance), insisting that all parts of the organism are involved in heredity (*Encyclopaedia Britannica*).

** For this terminology I am indebted to the late Dr. Joseph Kramer of the Biology Department of the University of Montana, to whom I described Hardy's comment on Clym's face.

and enduring, suggesting tragical possibilities." Susan Henchard has "the hard, half apathetic expression of one who
deems anything possible at the hands of Time and Chance,
except fair play." Hardy emphasizes the difference between
the remediable and the irremediable ills in his comment on
Susan that "the first phase was the work of Nature, the
second probably of civilization," and in his comment on the
caroling girls in his poem "Music in a Snowy Street."

Hardy's philosophy was a curious amalgam of Darwin
and Comte, and his pessimism was in a large measure the
result of his disillusionment with the promise of his age
after 1867. On February 7, 1881, he noted: "To conserve the
existing good, to supplant the existing bad by good, is to
act on a true political principle which is neither Conservative nor Radical."* "As to my pessimism," he wrote later

* It is interesting to compare Hardy's view with the views of George
Howell, secretary of the Reform League, during Hardy's employment at
Bloomfield's. Howell declared in his election speech at Bethnal Green
(1885): "As a fervent believer in representative government, I am opposed
to the existence of a hereditary House of Peers. The House of Lords is
non-representative and irresponsible. It represents class interest and pro-
motes class legislation. It is the embodiment of a caste and of privileges.
It has resisted all measures of reform as long as it dared. . . . The members
of the peerage, their families and relatives have for generations monopolized
place, power, privileges, pay and pensions. Within a period of 35 years
some 350 peers, with their families and relatives, numbering 8,523 persons,
have held 13,880 offices and have drawn salaries and pensions of
£108,614,632 from the revenue of the country, and this too, while thousands have been in a starving condition from want of employment and
food. And be it remembered, these recipients of state pay never their full
share of taxation according to their means." He expressed himself as opposed to the present union of the Church and State, and as favouring "a
thorough reform of the land laws, the abolition of primogeniture and
entail and of all the settlement tying up land and preventing its free
sale, and of the entire sweeping away of the game laws"; and also "the
enfranchisement of leasehold and the cultivation of waste land, so as to
give employment to surplus labour, and at the same time to increase the
quantity of home grown food for the people." And: "I am in favour of
retrenchment as well as reform. Our national expenditure is enormous and
expensive, and yet we are told by 'experts' that the country is in a defense-
less state. A large increase of military and naval expenditure is now taking
place—the result of panic and jingo bluster and defiance." But he had
faith in the democracy, and believed that "when we have obtained a
truly representative system of government . . . we shall hear of no more
such crimes as the bombardment of Alexandria, or consequent blunders

(January 16, 1918): "My motto is, first correctly diagnose the complaint—in this case human ills,—and ascertain the cause; then set about finding a remedy if one exists. The motto or practice of the optimists is," he declared: "Blind the eyes to the real malady, and use empirical panaceas to suppress the symptoms." "When we have got rid of a thousand remediable ills," Hardy told William Archer, "it will be time enough to determine whether the ill that is irremediable outweighs the good;[46] that is life itself." He has projected quite a lot of himself into Jude's reflections on the sculptured notables in the Christminster Quad; and on the procession:

> the most real to Jude Fawley were the founders of the religious school called Tractarian: the well-known three, the enthusiast, the poet, and the formalist, the echoes of whose teachings had influenced him even in his obscure home. The scientists and philologists followed in his mind-sight in an odd impossible combination, men with meditative faces, strained foreheads and

like the war in the Soudan." He also declared: "I am strongly opposed to hereditary pensions and to expenditures on royal palaces, yachts, and retainers, the latter being mere courtiers, basking in the presence of royalty and reclining in indolence under the shadow of the court, draw their annual salaries as if for useful work" (Maccoby, *English Radical Tradition*, 5:392–94). The foregoing description offers an interesting comparison with Hardy's description of the tourist resort of Knollsea (*The Hand of Ethelberta*) in summer and in winter: "This was the time of year to know the truth about the inner nature and character of Knollsea, for to see Knollsea smiling to the summer sun at was to see a courtier before a king; Knollsea was not to be known by such simple means. The half dozen detached villas used as lodging-houses in the summer, standing aloof from the cots of the permanent race, rose in the dusk of this gusty evening, empty, silent, damp, and dark as tombs" (p. 384).

Hardy says of Ethelberta's dilemma on which suitor to marry: "It might be pleasant to many a modern gentleman to find himself allied with a lady, none of whose ancestors had ever pandered to a court, lost an army, taken a bribe, oppressed a community, or broken a bank; but the added disclosure that, in avoiding these stains, her kindred had worked and continued to work with their hands for bread, might lead such an one to consider that the novelty was dearly purchased" (p. 224).

Hardy has Pitt on his deathbed remark on the trifling pensions to his kin" in *The Dynasts* (I, 6 viii) to this friend Bishop Tomline, whose spiritual "mediocrity" he comments on in *The Return of the Native*, pp. 204–5).

weak-eyed as bats with the constant research; then official characters—such men as Governor-Generals and Lord-Lieutenants, in whom he took little interest; chief-Justices and Lord Chancellors, silent, thin-lipped figures of whom he barely knew their names.

Hardy may have shown Jude's admiration for "the enthusiast," Sir Robert Peel, but he never would have subscribed to Peel's admission of futility to Croker, as reported in Morley's *Life of Gladstone* in the 1840s:

> If you had to constitute new societies, then you might on moral and social ground prefer cornfields to cotton factories, and you might like an agricultural population better than a manufacturing one; as it was, the national lot[,] was cast, and statesmen were powerless to turn back the tide.[49]

Hardy's thoughts seem more inclined to those expressed by Marx in the preface to *Capital,* at least in respect to the following observation:

> In the domain of Political Economy, free scientific enquiry meets not merely the same enemies as in all other domains. The peculiar nature of the material it deals with, summons as foes into the field of battle the most violent, mean and malignant passions of the human breast, the Furies of private interest. The English Established Church, *e.g.,* will more readily pardon an attack on 38 of its 39 articles than on 1/39 of its income. Now-a-days atheism itself is *culpa levis,* as compared with criticism of existing property relations. Never-the-less there is an unmistakable advance. I refer, *e.g.,* to the bluebook published within the last few weeks: "Correspondence with Her Majesty's Missions Abroad, regarding Industrial Questions and Trades' Unions. (p. 15)

The issues regarding capital and labor, urged on Parliament in 1866 by J. S. Mill, Hardy saw likewise as largely negated in practice. The Trades Union Act (1881) proclaimed that "a strike was legal," [50] but anything done in pursuance of a strike, as the Webbs observed, was "criminal"; in Germany Herr Wagner "was for factory laws in principle but not in practice." The Factory and Workshops Consolidated Act (1878) raised the employable age of children to eleven and limited the employment of women to twelve hours a day with an hour and a half for meals. The Companies Act (1871) fully protected them against liability, but the Employers Liability Act (1880) fell short in protecting the employees. The former stimulated commercial enterprises, or "so-called home industry," which Marx pointed out was "always underpaid";[51] the latter was thwarted in practice by the employers' resort to the negligence of fellow employees, or "common employment," and perhaps get out of awarding damages to complaining employees. In July 1886 Hardy wrote: "As to the architecture of the courts, there are everywhere religious art-forces masquerading as law-symbols; The leaf, flower, fret, suggested by spiritual emotion," he declared, "are pressed into the service of social strife." And on a trip with his brother Henry (April 1911) to visit the English cathedrals at Lichfield, Worcester, and Hereford, he noted: "View the matrices rather than the moulds." In *Jude* he wrote: "Intellect in Christminster is pushing one way, and religion the other, and so they stand stockstill, like two rams, butting each other." [52] He had described the debate in the House of Commons on the Irish question in these images and also Wellington's ramparts at Torres Vedras, Portugal, as "their outer horns and tusks to keep his foothold firm in Portugal." (*The Dynasts*, II, 6, ii). In 1890 Hardy lamented that "in the past century material growth has been out of all proportion to moral growth," and hoped "that during the next hundred years the relations between our inward and outward progress may become less of a reproach to civilization." [53] A further comment on his notes of February 16, 1882, on human automation "viz., an account of human action in spite of human knowledge showing how very far conduct lags behind the knowledge that should really guide it."

Hardy read the daily papers—"Cheap Jack," [54] as he

called the British press in *The Dynasts,* which bore out Morris's contempt for the bourgeois press, which Carlyle had extolled earlier as "the True Kings and Clergy" of Society. He continued to read the *Saturday Review** and *Punch*** to get contrasting views of what was going on. Since the death of George Eliot (1880), he had become acquainted with the *Positivist,* edited (1893–1900) by Edward Beesly, in which he found views closer to those in the weekly trade-union paper *The Beehive**** (1861–1877) (which he had first come across during his years at Blomfield's), which advocated political reform. In it Beesly wrote in 1873: "The result of the Greenwich election is highly satisfactory. . . . The workman has at last come to the conclusion that the difference between Liberal and Tory is pretty much that between the upper and nether millstone. The quality of the two is essentially the same." Morris had said that the two parties "are sections of the wealth-possessing class and on all parliamentary questions affecting the interests of labour they play into one another's hands so systematically and imperturbably that one would suppose they thought workmen never read a newspaper or hear a speech," [55] or, Morris might have added, that a poet does either. In a letter to Hardy (Nov. 1884) Beesly relates his particular encounter with the upper millstone following his defeat at the Westminster poll: "I suppose there is not a more hopeless seat in England. We might have made head against its Toryism alone, or the clergy, or the Baroness's legitimate influence from her alms-giving of old

---

* Macmillan condemned the *Saturday Review* in his letter to Hardy (Aug. 10, 1868) rejecting *The Poor Man and the Lady* "for its mocking tone, paralyzing noble effort and generous emotion" (see Morgan, *House of Macmillan,* p. 90).

** Hardy (on Jan. 5, 1890) noted, "Looking over old *Punches.* Am struck with the frequent wrong direction of satire, and of commendation, when seen by the light of later days."

*** Largely written by Robert Hartwell, an old Chartist, and edited by George Potter, which numbered among its contrbutors Frederick Harrison, Henry Crompton, E. S. Beesly, Lloyd Jones, Robert Applegarth, George Howell, and George Shipton. Succeeded by *Labour Standard,* a penny weekly in 1881 (see Maccoby, 3:86 and the Webbs, p. 298n).

date there (it being her special preserve), or the tap of philanthropy turned on for the occasion. But all united were much too strong for us. I return to my work in much contentment." [56] Beesly's letter to Hardy offers an interesting comparison with Engels's letter to Bernstein (Nov. 11, 1884) on the situation:

> The 1884 elections are for us what the 1866 was for the German philistine. At that date, without doing a thing to bring it about, indeed against her own will, she suddenly became "a great nation"; Now, however, by our own hard work and heavy sacrifices, we have become a "great party!" *Noblesse oblige!*

The working classes in London, as a consequence of their political enfranchisement, were organizing for a shorter working day, better working conditions, and a livable wage. Between 1810 and 1830 money wages were falling, from 1849 to 1874 rising, while money wages were practically "stationary," and prices had risen. The 9-hour day (1859) —it had been 12 hours in 1832—had reduced the working week from 58½ hours to 54 hours by 1870—it had been 15 hours since 1833 (5:30 A.M. to 8:30 P.M.—but not without the combined opposition to the trades-union demands by employers, learned societies, Parliament, and *The Times*.[57] At an international May Day celebration (May 4, 1890), over 100,000 persons turned out to support the 8-hour day.

William Morris declared in his address to workingmen (1877): "I doubt if you know the bitterness of hatred against freedom and progress that lies at the hearts of a certain part* of the richer classes in this country: their newspapers

---

* Hardy may have recalled Robert Lowe's slandering them in the House of Commons as "repulsive, unreflecting violent people . . . guilty of venality, ignorance, drunkenness, and intimidation" (Lionel Trilling, *Matthew Arnold*, p. 248). Morris's "Address" is a good answer to Granville Hicks's being a little dubious about the Socialism [of Hardy's *Poor Man and the Lady*] if Sir Alexander Macmillan could find wisdom in Will's speech to workingmen," and his conclusion, "we may suspect that Hardy went no further than, say, George Eliot in *Felix Holt*" (*Figures of Transition*, p. 120).

veil it in a kind of decent language, but do but hear them talking among themselves, as I have often, and I know not whether scorn or anger would prevail in you at their folly and insolence. These men cannot speak of your order of its aims, of its leaders, without a sneer or an insult: these men if they had the power (may England perish rather!) would thwart your just aspirations, would silence you, would deliver you bound hand and foot for ever to irresponsible capital." [58] In 1888 trade-unionists (Burns, Mann,* and Eleanor Aveling, Marx's daughter) organized East London, which had been regarded as unorganizable, in the fight for the 8-hour day, and the Socialists led the girls at Bryant and Mays Match factory in a successful strike and got the gas companies to reduce the working day from 12 to 8 hours, and a wage increase to boot of sixpence a day. The theosophist Annie Besant and Bradlaugh raged against Socialism because, as Engels wrote Laura Lafargue (Feb. 5, 1884) "It threatens to cut short their wittles" (p. 169). The Great Dock Strike led by Burns shook society to its underpinnings and resulted in improved conditions for maritime workers, swelling union membership to a hundred thousand in a year. The Great Lockout in the English coal industry in the winter of 1893 created fearful unrest and untold misery.

Morris was much affected by the Pall Mall demonstration (Feb. 8, 1886), for which Hyndman had mobilized the Socialist Democratic Federation members at a supportive meeting of the Labourers League and Fair Trade League in "the street of big political aristocratic and big capitalistic clubs, the centre of English political intrigue," in Engels's words (*Engels-Lafargue Correspondence*, p. 447), and a huge crowd from the East end had engulfed the Fair-traders. Police violence was met with mob resistance, and there were ex-

---

° Tom Mann (1856–1941), also leader of the great transport strike, Liverpool, 1911; was imprisoned in 1912 for his leaflet to soldiers "not to shoot down" members of the working classes and again in 1932–33 for agitation in behalf of the unemployed, tried for sedition in 1934, but acquitted owing to mass agitation (*Marx-Engels Correspondence*, p. 462).

cesses on both sides. An eyewitness recorded the incident in his diary; his sympathies went first to those in the mob and then to those in the carriage, and he related how, returning home, he was greeted by his landlady—"Poor shabby thing"—who said to him:

> The Poor's rose at last, Sir, I ses, ses I, to my husband, Lord knows we're poor, but you keep out of it. What with 'Indman breaking up the gov'ment and Bradlaugh breaking up the Church, it's awful.[59]

Not since 1848 had there been such violence. The Trafalgar Square riot (Nov. 13, 1887)—"Bloody Sunday"—was even more violent and tragic. Many persons were severely injured when the Police attacked the marchers. John Burns and Cunninghame-Graham, M.P. (later Joseph Conrad's friend) were sentenced to six weeks' imprisonment for breaking through the police line.[60] Three persons died of their injuries, among them the socialist Alfred Linnell, who was marching next to George Bernard Shaw, then unknown. Morris wrote a poem honoring Linnell, "A Death Song," which was sold as a penny pamphlet for the benefit of Linnell's family, and spoke at his graveside rites in Bow Cemetery, Cheapside.

There is no mention in the official biography of Hardy's attitude towards Burns's and Mantle's organizing the London dockyard workers, but it would be strange indeed if he did not approve of their union activities since he approved of Joseph Arch's in getting a decent and livable wage for the agricultural proletariat. Hardy describes Arch, whom he had heard speak, "to be rather the social evolutionist—what M. Émile de Laveleye (1822–1892) would call a Possibilist than the anarchic irreconcilable." [61]

The suppression of labor's reasonable demands by capital during these years amounted to tyranny. For inducing a man not to accept employment at a struck shop, trade unionists were imprisoned at hard labor, while employers were

allowed to make all possible use of "blacklists" and "character assassination notes"; [62] in short, boycotting by employers
was freely permitted; boycotting by the men was put down
by police. Dan Cullen was blacklisted for his participation
in the Great Dock Strike (Aug. 13-Sept. 15, 1889), and died
in misery in the Temperance Hotel, London, as he had
lived in misery in a London slum—one of the "Municipal
Dwellings not far from Leaman Street." Jack London refers
to him as "A Jude the Obscure," who "reached out after
knowledge," who knew his Shakespeare, and "who toiled . . .
in the day and studied . . . at night." [63] The Labor Act of
1871, which had recognized the Union's legal right to strike,
was almost wholly negated in practice, and a flagrant attempt was made by the capitalist press to crush the unions
in the Taff Vale case of 1900. A number of employees of the
Taff Vale Railway Company in South Wales went on a
strike in August 1900 for wages and union recognition. The
company imported nonunion workers to break the strike.
The Amalgamated Society of Railway Servants (ASRS) held
that it was not responsible for damages caused during the
strike since it was neither a corporation nor an individual,
but Justice Sir George Farwell decided that it was a cor-
porate body and therefore liable and imposed a fine of
£23,000 on the Union in favor of the Company—an opinion
sustained by the House of Lords in July 1901. After a hearing in December 1902, the Company was awarded £23,000
damages and the total cost to the Union amounted to more
than £40,000.*

Hardy had received "a touch or two on my speckled
hide" in the cause of literary truth, he wrote on July 16,
1896, for his explorations of reality in *Jude* and *Tess,* by such
reviewers of the bourgeois press as Jeannette Gilder, who
called *Jude* "immoral" in the *New York World,* and Bishop
How, who called it "garbage" in the *Yorkshire Post.* Few

---

* For a comprehensive account, see Sidney and Beatrice Webb, *History
of Trade Unionism,* p. 600–8.

critics, then or now, took cognizance of the socioeconomic fabric* of Hardy's novels, and his sadness over the hard lot of the agricultural and urban proletariat in bourgeois society. His having written "the Battle of the Nations" in *The Dynasts* gives stature to even such anoymous characters as the old shepherd, for whom "the battle of life had been a hard [one]" in *The Mayor of Casterbridge,* and to the obscure Jude in his struggle and failure to realize his inborn potentiality in the greatest city in the world. After the bloody Trafalgar Square Riot (1887) and after "a bloody battle" of the Boer War (Dec. 1899), when Hardy saw "the Lists of Killed and Wounded" posted "At the War Office, London," he was moved to reflect in his poem "Christmas Ghost-Story" (Christmas-eve 1899):

> And what of logic or of truth appears
> In tacking "Anno Domini" to the years?
> Near twenty-hundred liveried thus have hied,
> But tarries yet the Cause for which He died.

How fast Hardy held on to his Darwinism to the very end is clear from his "Epitaph" for G. K. Chesterton, the converted Catholic who had maliciously reviled him for his scientism, published for the first time in J. O. Bailey's recent book, *The Poetry of Thomas Hardy* (1970):

> Here lies nipped in his narrow cyst
> The literary contortionist
> Who prove & never turn a hair
> That Darwin's theories were a snare.
> He'd hold as true with tongue in jowl

* See Hardy's note, Feb. 22, 1893: "There cannot be equity in one kind. Assuming, *e.g.*, the possession of £1,000,000 sterling or 10,000 acres of land to be the coveted ideal, all cannot possess £1,000,000 or 10 000 acres. But there is a practical equity possible: that the happiness which one man derives from one thing shall be equalled by what another man derives from another thing. Freedom from worry, for instance, is a counterpoise to the lack of great possessions, though he who enjoys that freedom may not think so" (*Later Years,* p. 15).

> That Nature's, geocentric rule
> . . . true & right
> And if one with him could not see
> He's shout his choice word "Blasphemy." [64]

Hardy was not interested in Christ's miraculous birth nor in his promise of rewards in the next world, but in Christ as "a young reformer" in this world, as he wrote Israel Zangwill on November 10, 1905. He had regretted in 1880 that Comte had not introduced Christ among the worthies of his calendar for practical purposes, and in 1923 he had thought that there must come about "an alliance between religion, which must be retained unless the world is to perish, by means of the interfusing effect of poetry—"the breath and finer spirit of all knowledge; the impassioned expression of science [quoting Wordsworth] as it was defined by an English poet who was quite orthodox in his ideas" (Preface to *Late Lyrics and Earlier*, p. 531).

In the meantime the country had been kept in a state of constant alarm over the threats of rival imperialisms in Europe and Africa—the Suez Canal (1875), the annexation of the Boer Republic (1877), the intervention in Egypt (1882), the Boer War (1899–1901), the Russo-Japanese War (1904–5)—years that were too much like those he was writing about in *The Dynasts*, leading up to World War I. In 1899 he reflected in his poem "At the War Office" on the "hourly posted sheets of scheduled slaughter." The great war all but destroyed his hope for mankind. "It was seldom," Mrs. Hardy says, "that he had felt so heavy of heart," and he said that he would not have ended *The Dynasts* as he did if he had written it after the war. He had been deceived into wishful thinking that war had become an anachronism and that "The Sick Battle-God" [65] of his poem who, though sometimes he looms "bespatched with paint and lath . . .was no more." In his poem "The Blow," [66] he even blames the Immament Will, "the inscrutable, the hid," for hurling "the stone into the sunshine of our days" rather than "anyone of my kind," or Comte's God of Humanity. Hardy could not retreat into the love of the beloved, as Matthew Arnold did in his poem "Dover Beach"* (1867), "where ignorant armies clash by night as on a darkling plain," and he was too realistic to envision a glorious Armageddon "in the central blue" initiating, in one stanza, "the Parliament of the World," as Tennyson did in "Locksley Hall" (1842), nor could he accept Browning's view that "God's in his Heaven, all's right with the world," a "smug Christian optimism," in Hardy's opinion, "worthy of a dissenting grocer." [67] Instead, he viewed a gradual ameliorative process through the extension of consciousness and sympathy through mankind. This is conveyed in Jude's reverie following his visit to Christminster's Hall of Fame before he falls asleep, in which the phantom voices of historical personages speaking to him suggest the historical and spiritual levels of *The Dynasts*, and by his recognition in the retinue of phantoms of "the man whose mind grew with his growth in years, and the man whose mind contracted with the same." [68] Jude "had joined" for this purpose "an Artisans' Mutual Improvement Society, established in the town about the time of his arrival there, its members being young men of all creeds and denominations, including Churchmen, Congregationalists, Baptists, Unitarians, Positivists and others," agnostics having "scarcely been heard of at this time—their one common wish to enlarge their minds." [69] Jude's tribute to Sir Robert Peel, who

---

* In the last three lines of "Dover Beach," the "whole country traversed in Arnold's *Culture and Anarchy* is revealed in a lighting flash," says Dover Wilson in his preface to that work.

Both Marx and Engels believed that "nationalism" and its concomitants, religion and militarism, were so many anachronisms—by-products and bulwarks of capitalism, which with the passing of their foundation, would automatically disappear. Marx's own criterion was to consider in a given case whether they operated for or against the proletarian cause. Thus he favoured it in India and Ireland, because it was a weapon in the fight against imperialism, and attacked the democratic nationalism of Mazzini and Kossuth, because it seemed to work merely for the replacement of a foreign by a native system of capitalistic exploitation, and to obstruct the social revolution (Berlin, *Karl Marx: His Life and Environment*, p. 202).

reversed his stand on the Corn Laws and voted for repeal ("Sir: I may be wrong, but my impression is that my duty toward a country threatened with famine, etc.") at the risk of his political future, recalls the Chorus of the Pities' paean of hope ending *The Dynasts* that it is Man's consciousness that will bring about mankind's improvement. Marx notes that the Irish famine of 1846 "killed more than 1,000,000 people, but it killed poor devils only." [70]

In 1909, in response to an invitation of Dr. Max Dessoir, "a professor at the University of Berlin, who wished to have an epitome of the culture and thought of the time—the 'Weltanschauung' of a few representative men in England and Germany—" Hardy wrote:

> We call our Age an age of Freedom. Yet Freedom, under her incubus of armaments, territorial ambitions smugly disguised as patriotism, superstitions, conventions of every sort, is of such stunted proportions in this her so-called time, that the human-race is likely to be extinct before Freedom arrives at maturity.

His and Mrs. Hardy's happy courtship is recalled in the poem "Lines to a Movement of Mozart's E-Flat Symphony" (1898), and though he observed that "love lures life on . . . We eyed each other and feared futurity." Mrs. Hardy was active in the suffragette cause, and Hardy must have been heartened by the resolution introduced by Keir Hardie, British Socialist and labor leader, and Edward Vaillant, French Socialist, at the International Labour Congress* at

---

* It represented 27 federations of trades or industries with over seven million in nineteen countries (see Barbara Tuchman, *The Proud Tower* [New York: Macmillan, 1966], p. 452). Engels had foreseen it in 1883 (letter to Borkheim): "And finally no war is any longer possible for Prussian Germany except a world war indeed of an extension of violence hitherto undreamt of" (Preface to Borkheim, *In Memory of the Suppressed German Patriots 1806–1807*. "Eight to ten millions of soldiers will mutually massacre one another and in doing so devour the whole of Europe until they have stripped it barer than any swarm of locusts has ever done . . . only one resultant is absolutely certain: general exhaustion and the establishment of the condition of the ultimate victory of the working classes" (*Correspondence*, pp. 456–57), concluding: "This is the prospect when the system of

Copenhagen in August 1910 calling for a general strike[71] of labor in all countries on the threat of a world war. Samuel Gompers, who had gone to affiliate the American Federation of Labor with the International Federation in 1909, had been so encouraged by the tenfold increase in trade-union membership in Germany and Austria that he was sure the working classes and their sons would never slaughter each other again as they had done in the Napoleonic wars. The German and Austrian delegates, however, whose working-men were busy producing munitions for Krupp and the Prussian state, put nationalism above internationalism, and the Hardie-Vaillant resolution was tabled with catastrophic effect.

In 1910 Hardy, with Mrs. Hardy, saw from the balcony of the Athenaeum Club the funeral procession (May 6) of Edward VII ("the typical monarch," Morton says, "of the new era of monopoly capitalism" [p. 458]), which Hardy commemorated in his poem "A King's Soliloquy on the Night of His Funeral":

> From the slow march and muffled drum,
>   And crowds distrest,
> And book and bell, at length, I have come
>   To my full rest.

and on this occasion recalled having seen from the same spot in July 1891 "the German Emperor William II pass to the city." [72]

In 1914 Hardy declined an invitation from men of letters and art in Germany, who were "honouring the memory of Friederich Nietzsche on the seventieth anniversary of his

mutual outrages in armaments, driven to extremity, at last bears its inevitable fruits. This, my lords, princes and statesmen, is where in your wisdom you have brought old Europe."

"It would be difficult to compute what Edward owed to the friendship of Sir Ernest Cassell but such a computation if made would be most suitably recorded on cash-ruled paper" (see Morton, p. 458, quoting from E. Wingfield-Stratford, *The Victorian Aftermath* [New York: Morrow, 1934]).

birth," because "it is a question whether (at this date) Nietzsche's philosophy is sufficiently coherent to be of great value, and whether those views of his which seem so novel and striking appear thus only because they have been rejected for so many centuries as inadmissable under humane rule." Hardy had not reckoned until the German invasion of Belgium "on the power still retained there by the governing castes whose interests were not the people's." [73]

Unlike Robert Frost, Hardy was hopeful toward the League of Nations and receptive toward President Wilson's "Fourteen Points." The League, it seemed to him, was "all that stood between Civilization and a new Dark Ages," and "it behoves young poets and other writers to endeavour to stave off such a catastrophe," he wrote in 1920. Replying to the New York *World* (Dec. 23, 1920), he declared: "Yes I approve of the international disarmament, on the lines indicated by the *New York World.*" In the reflection of the Franco-Prussian War, he had cogitated on history in *The Return of the Native:*

> Had Philip's warlike son been intellectually so far ahead [as] to have attempted civilization without bloodshed, he would have been twice the godlike hero that he seemed, but nobody would have heard of Alexander.

Engels makes a similar observation in his letter to Mehring (14 July, 1893) on Richard the Lion-Hearted's career, from which one might infer that no one would have heard of Bismarck or of Good King Edward VII either. In 1923, on the failure of the League, "when comment on where the world stands," he wrote, "is very much the reverse of need-

---

° Of a German prisoners' camp in Dorchester (1916), "Men lie helpless here from wounds: in the hospital a hundred yards off, other men, English lie helpless from wounds—each scene of suffering caused by the other"; and he wrote of his going to adjudicate at the Police Court (May 23, 1918) "on several food profiteering cases, undertaken by me as being 'the only war-work I was capable of'" (*Later Years,* pp. 173, 187).

less in these disordered years of our prematurely afflicted century," he expressed his apprehension for the future:

> that whether the human and kindred animal races survive till the exhaustion or destruction of the globe, or whether these races perish and are succeeded by others before that conclusion comes, pain to all upon it—tongued or dumb, shall be kept down to a minimum by loving-kindness, operating through scientific knowledge and actuated by the modicum of free will, conjecturally possessed by organic life when the mighty necessitating forces—unconscious or other—that have "the balancings of the clouds," happen to be in equilibrium, which may or may not be often.[74]

In the same year he wrote in reply to a letter from John Galsworthy that "the exchange of international thought is the only possible salvation for the world," and reaffirmed that he "hoped to see patriotism not confined to realms but circling the earth," [75] as he had said at the beginning of the South African War. World War I, "horrible as it seems to us," he reflected, "was nothing compared to what with scientific munitions-making only in its infancy, the next war would be. I do not think a world in which such fiendishness is possible to be worth the saving," he had written in 1918. "Better let western 'civilization' perish, and the black and yellow races* have a chance," adding, "However, as a meliorist (not a pessimist as they say) I think better of the world." [76]

During the years 1920 to 1925 he was interested in "conjectures on rationalizing the English Church" that would be "comprehensive enough to include the majority of thinkers of the previous hundred years who had lost all belief in the supernatural," but when "the new Prayer Book appeared . . . he found that the revision had not been in a rationalistic direction, and from that time on lost all expectation of seeing the Church representatives of modern thinking minds." [77]

---

* "All sovereigns, except the Chinese, wear a military uniform," exclaims Prince Andrey to Pierre, "and give the greatest rewards to the man who succeeds in killing most people" (*War and Peace*, p. 725).

Hardy's hope was always reborn of despair. He did not lose his faith in the potentialities of people—his novels and poems are testimony to that—and he clung forlornly to Comte's theory "that advance is never in a straight line, but in a looped orbit." He tried to maintain his belief in evolutionary meliorism in the anti-reforming era between World War I and World War II as Dickens had tried to do between the Crimean War and the Franco-Prussian war, expressed in a public speech a year before his death, in which "he affirmed that his faith in the people who do the governing of the country was 'infinitesmal' while his faith in the people they govern was 'illimitable.'" [78] Hardy's writings show that he was further to the left of the Liberals than to the right of the Radicals, and that he was sensitive to the distinction between Art and Science, as put by Christopher Caudwell: "Art is the science of feeling, science the art of knowing. We must know to be able to do, but we must feel to know what to do." [79] He had little use, like Marx, for "the so-called 'practical men' and their wisdom," and like him he could not turn his back on "the agonies of mankind and look after his own skin" (Marx to S. Meyer, Hanover, 30 April 1867, *Correspondence*, p. 219), pending publication of *Capital*, "without completely finishing my book, at least in manuscript."

Hardy was as weary as Marx of the philosophers' attempts to interpret the world, but not so impatient as Dickens to change it. He recognized the need to change it, as Marx did, but the problem was, as he had observed in *Jude*, a difficult one.

"An illness, which at the commencement did not seem to be serious," Mrs. Hardy says, "began on December 11, 1927." Sitting at the writing table as usual in his study that morning, he "felt totally unable to work"—a feeling that he had never experienced before. "From then on his strength

waned daily." His wife copied his poem "Christmas Eve in
the Elgin Room" and posted it to the *Times,* in which it
appeared on December 24. He continued to come down-
stairs and sit for a few hours till Christmas day; after that he
came down no more. The window in the adjoining bedroom
was opened so that he might hear the bells welcoming in
the New Year, as "that had always pleased him," Mrs. Hardy
says, "But now he said that he could not hear them, and
did not seem interested." On January 10, 1928, he rallied
and insisted on writing a cheque for his subscription to the
Pension Fund of the Society of Authors. "For the first time
in his life he made a slightly feeble signature . . . and then
laid down his pen." That evening his wife read aloud to him,
at his request, Browning's poem "Rabbi Ben Ezra"—all
thirty-two stanzas, which he listened to "with wistful in-
tentness." He spent a restful night and the next morning
seemed much stronger. He received "an immense bunch of
grapes" from a friend in London, and remarked "quite
gaily" to his wife, "I am going on with these." That evening
he asked her to read the stanza from FitzGerald's *Rubaiyat**
beginning:

> O Thou, who Man of Baser Earth didst make,
> And ev'n with Paradise devised the Snake;
> For all the Sin wherewith the Face of Man
> Is blacken'd—Man's forgiveness give—and take!

"He indicated that he wished no more to be read." A little

---

* Terhune notes that Cowell, in a letter to Aldis Wright, complained
of there being "no original for the line about the snake," and says of
this "much discussed" 81st quatrain that "FitzGerald's answer to Cowell's
criticism has survived." FitzGerald wrote: "As to my making Omar worse
than he is in that stanza about Forgiveness, you know I have translated
none literally . . . and when you look at such Stanzas as 356, 436, and
many besides, where 'La Divinité' is accused of the Sins we commit, I do
not think it is going far beyond by way of Corollary to say—'Let us forgive
one another.' I have certainly an idea that this *is* said somewhere in the
Calcutta MS. But it is very likely I may have construed, or remembered
erroneously. But I do not *add* dirt to Omar's face." Terhune notes that
"Herron-Allen traced the lines to an apologue in Attar's *Mantik-ut-tair,*"
(p. 229).

later that evening, he had "a sharp heart attack of a kind he had never had before," and he "remained conscious until a few minutes before the end," which came shortly after nine o'clock with the doctor and Mrs. Hardy at his bedside.

His heart, which was removed from his body, was buried on January 16 in the grave of his first wife among the Hardys' moss-covered tomb under the great yew tree in the corner of Stinsford Parish cemetery, in the presence of his brother, Henry, and sister, Katherine, and Dorset friend. On the same day the ashes of his cremated body were buried in a niche in the Poet's Corner of Westminster Abbey, next to Dickens and a vacant crypt in which Kipling, one of the pall-bearers, was interred in 1936. A spadeful of earth sent by a Dorset farm laborer, Christopher Corbin, had been sprinkled on the casket in the presence of his wife, Florence, and his sister, Katherine. A throng filled the streets outside in the wet and cold.

It was discovered, in his will, that Hardy had left a sum of money to two humanitarian societies for lessening the sufferings of animals in transit to the slaughterhouse, and provided, also, that the cottage in which he was born should remain "the house of an ordinary labourer living in an ordinary labourer's world."

that bright kingdom where the souls who strove
Live now forever, helping living men
                              —John Masefield
                              (1878–1966)

Appendix
Chart of Thomas Hardy's Serialized Novels

Thomas Hardy's first serialized novel was *A Pair of Blue Eyes* and his last one *The Well-Beloved*. They were all serialized in monthly magazines except *The Mayor of Casterbridge*, *Tess of the D'Urbervilles*, and *The Well-Beloved*, which appeared in weekly periodicals. Book publication followed soon after the serialization was completed.

Novel	Date of Book Pub. and price	Magazine	Editor	Dates	No. of Installments
A Pair of Blue Eyes	1873 May 31s 6d	*Tinsleys'*	Tinsley brothers	Sept. 1872–July 1873	11
Illus. by J. A. Pasquier, Hardy providing sketches.		Sept. 1872: Chaps. 1–5; Oct., 6–8; Nov., 9–11; Dec., 12–14. Jan., 1873: Chaps. 15–18; Feb., 19–21; Mar., 22–25; Apr., 26–28; May, 29–31; June, 32–36; and July, 37–40.			
Far from the Madding Crowd	1874 Nov. 21s	*Cornhill*	Leslie Stephen	Jan.–Dec. 1874	12
Illus. by Mrs. Helen Patterson Allingham (Hardy sketches)		Jan. 1874: Chaps. 1–5; Feb., 6–8; Mar., 9–14; Apr., 15–20; May, 21–24; June, 25–29; July, 30–33; Aug., 34–38; Sept., 39–42; Oct., 43–47; Nov., 48–51; Dec., 52–57.			

The Hand 1876 Apr. 3	*Cornhill*	Leslie	July 1875–May	
of Ethelberta 21s		Stephen	1876	11

Illus. by George
Du Maurier

July 1875: Chaps. 1–4; Aug., 5–9; Sept., 10–15; Oct., 16–21; Nov., 22–26; Dec., 27–30; Jan. 1876: 31–34; Feb., 35–38; Mar., 39–42; Apr., 43–46; May, 47–50.

The Return 1878 Nov. 4		M. E.	Jan.–Dec. 1878	13
of the Native 31s	*Belgravia*	Braddon		

Illus. by Arthur
Hopkins

Jan. 1878: Bk. I, Chaps. 1–4; Feb., I:5–7; Mar., I:8–11; Apr., II:1–5; May, II:6–8; June, III: 1–4; July, III: 5–8; Aug., IV:1–4; Sept., IV:5–8; Oct., V:1–4; Nov., V:5–8; Dec., V:9 & VI:1–4.

The Trumpet- 1880	*Good Words*	Donald	Jan.–Dec. 1880	12
Major Oct. 26		Macleod		

31s 6d Jan. 1880: Chaps. 1–4; Feb., 5–7; Mar.,
Illus. by John   8–10; Apr., 11–14; May, 15–17; June,
Collier   18–21; July, 22–24; Aug., 25–27; Sept., 28–30; Oct., 31–34; Nov., 34 cont'd–37; Dec., 38–41.

A Laodicean	*Harper's*	Henry M.	Dec. 1880–Dec.	
1881 Dec.	*New Monthly*	Alden	1881	13

31s 6d Dec. 1880: Bk. I, Chaps. 1–4; Jan., 1:4
Illus. by George cont'd 8; Feb., 1:9–13; Mar., I:13 cont'd
Du Maurier   and II:2; Apr., II:3–7; May, II: cont'd 7 and III:1–3; June, III:4–7; July, III:8–12; Aug., IV:1–5; Sept., V:1–5; Oct., V:6–10; Nov., V:11–14; Dec., VI:1–5.

Two on a Tower	*Atlantic*	Thomas	May–Dec. 1882	8
1882 Oct.	*Monthly*	Bailey		
31s 6d		Aldrich		

May 1882: Chaps. 1–4; June, 5–9; July, 10–15; Aug., 16–21; Sept., 22–27, Oct., 28–32; Nov., 33–37; Dec., 38–41.

The Mayor of   Arthur   Jan. 2, 1886-May
Casterbridge   *The Graphic* Locker   15, weekly   20

        1886 May 10 Jan.   2,   1886:   Chaps.   1–2;   Jan.   9,
                21s 3–5; Jan. 16, cont'd 5–7; Jan. 23, 8–9,
Illus. by Robert   Jan. 30, 10–12; Feb. 6, 13–15; Feb. 13,
Barnes   15–17; Feb. 20, 18–19; Feb. 27, 20–21;
                    Mar. 6, 22–23; Mar. 13, 24–25; Mar. 20,
                    26–27;   Mar.   27,   cont'd   27–29;   Apr.   3,
                    30–32; Apr. 10, 33–34; Apr. 17, 35–36;
                    Apr. 24, 37–38; May 1, 39–41; May 8
                    cont'd 41–43; May 15, 44–45.

The Woodlanders   *Macmillan's* Mowbray May 1886–Apr.
      1887 Mar. 15   Morris   1887   12

                21s May 1886: Chaps. 1–4; June, 5–8; July,
Without illus.   9–13; Aug., 14–18; Sept., 19–22; Oct.,
                    23–25; Nov., 26–29; Dec., 30–33; Jan.,
                    1887: 34–37; Feb., 38–40; Mar., 41–43;
                    Apr., 44–48.

Tess of   1891 Nov. 29 *The Graphic* Arthur   July 4, 1891–Dec.
the D'Urbervilles   6s   Locker   26, 1891, weekly   24

Illus. by Hubert von   July 4, 1891: Chaps. 1–3; July 18, 3
Herkomer & some of   cont'd 6; July 24, 6–8; Aug. 1, 9–11; Aug.
his pupils: Daniel   8, 12–14; Aug. 15, 15–16; Aug. 22,
A. Wehrschmidt,   17–18; Aug. 29, 19–21; Sept. 5, 22–23;
E. Borough Johnson,   Sept. 12, 24–26; Sept. 19, 27–28; Sept.
or J. Syddall   26,   29   cont'd   30;   Oct.   3,   31–55;
                        Oct.   10,   33   cont'd   35;   Oct.   17,
                        35 cont'd 37; Oct. 24, 37 cont'd 39; Oct.
                        31, 40–41; Nov. 14, 42–44; Nov. 21,
                        45–46; Nov. 28, 47–48; Dec. 5, 49–50;
                        Dec. 12, 51–52; Dec. 19, 53–56; & Dec.
                        26, 57–59.

Jude the   1895 Nov. *Harper's*   Henry   Dec. 1894–Nov.
Obscure   (postdated *New Monthly* Mill   1895   12
              1896)   Alden

                31s 6d Dec., 1894: Bk. I, Chaps: i–vi; Jan.,
Illus. by W.   1895: I: vii–xi; Feb., II, i–v; Mar.,
Hatherell   II:vi–III, iii; Apr., III:iv–vii; May., III:

viii–IV, ii; June, IV:iii–v; July, IV:vi–V, iii;
Aug., V:iv–vii; Sept., V:viii–VI:iii; Oct.,
VI:iv–vii; Nov., VI:vii cont'd xi.

The	1897 Mar. 16	*Illustrated*	Clement	Oct. 1–Dec. 17,	
Well-Beloved	6s	*London News*	Shorter	1892, weekly	12

Illus. by Walter
Paget

Oct. 1, 1892: Part I, Chaps. i–iii; Oct.
8, I:iv–vii; Oct. 15, I:vii–II:i; Oct. 22,
II:i–II, iii; Oct. 29, II:iv–vii; Nov. 5,
II:vii–II:ix; Nov. 12, II:x–II:xii; Nov.
19, II:xii–III:i; Nov. 26, III i (cont'd):iii;
Dec. 3, III:iv–III:vi–viii (largely re-written;
and the closing chaps, but chap. III, vi–viii
were new) Dec. 10, XXVIII (cont'd)–XXX;
Dec. 17, XXXI–XXXIII.

Source: Richard L. Purdy, *Thomas Hardy: A Bibliographical Study* (London: Oxford University Press, 1954).

Notes

CHAPTER 1

1. Vere H. Collins, *Talks with Thomas Hardy at Max Gate* (London: Duckworth, 1928), p. 63.
2. Florence E. Hardy, *The Later Years of Thomas Hardy* (New York: Macmillan, 1930), p. 183; *Collected Poems* (New York: Macmillan, 1940), "In Tenebris, II," p. 154. The official biography, *The Early Life of Thomas Hardy* (1928) and *The Later Years of Thomas Hardy* (1930) —hereinafter referred to as *Early Life* and *Later Years* in the Notes— "was not carried beyond the year 1918," Richard Purdy states, "and the four concluding chapters are Mrs. Hardy's work, although Hardy provided frequent paragraphs and continued to select details." See R. Purdy, *Thomas Hardy, a Bibliographical Study*, pp. 272–73.
3. Granville Hicks, *Figures of Transition* (New York: Macmillan, 1939), p. 113.
4. Evelyn Hardy, *Thomas Hardy, a Critical Biography* (New York: St. Martin's Press, 1955).
5. F. E. Hardy, *The Later Years*, p. 122.
6. *Collected Poems*, p. 204.
7. *Ibid.*, Preface to *Late Lyrics and Earlier*, p. 531.
8. Dona Torr, ed., *Marx-Engels Correspondence: 1846–1895* (New York: International Publishers, 1936), p. 182.
9. *Early Life*, p. 49; Karl Marx, *Letters to Kugelmann* (New York: International Publishers, 1934), p. 33.
10. I have searched in Charles Morgan's *House of Macmillan* (London: Macmillan, 1934) and in John Morley's *Recollections* (N.Y.: Macmillan, 1917) where one would expect to find this reference, but cannot locate it.
11. W. F. Monypenny and G. E. Buckle, *Life of Benjamin Disraeli* (New York: Macmillan, 1929), 2: 709.

12. *Ibid.*, p. 236.
13. *Tess of the D'Urbervilles*, Wessex ed. (London: Macmillan, 1912), p. 415; Karl Marx, *Capital* (New York: Modern Library, n.d.), p. 518.
14. Sidney and Beatrice Webb, *History of Trade Unionism* (London: Allan & Unwin, 1924), p. 334.
15. A. L. Morton, *A People's History of England* (New York: International Publishers, 1938), p. 340.
16. Isaiah Berlin, *Karl Marx: His Life and Environment* (London: Clarendon Press, 1963), p. 184.
17. Webb, *History of Trade Unionism*, pp. 144–45.
18. *Ibid.*, p. 146.
19. *Ibid.*, p. 144.
20. *Later Years*, pp. 93–96; Royden Harrison, "Beesly's St. James Speech," *Science & Society* (Fall 1963).
21. See Hardy's "Dorsetshire Labourer," in *Hardy's Personal Writings*, ed. Harold Orel (Lawrence, University of Kansas Press, 1966).
22. *Poems of William Blake*, ed. William Butler Yeats (New York: Book League of America, 1938), p. 202.
23. Morton, p. 331.
24. David Erdman, *Blake: Prophet against Empire* (Princeton, N.J.: Princeton University Press, 1954), pp. 305–6, 312.
25. Arnold Kettle, *Introduction to the English Novel* (London: Hutchinson Universal Library, 1953), 2: 58; Ray Morrell, *Thomas Hardy: The Will and the Way* (Kuala Lumpur: University of Malaya Press, 1965), p. 2.
26. G. M. Trevelyan, *Life of John Bright* (New York: Houghton Mifflin, 1925), pp. 367–68.
27. *Early Life*, p. 27.
28. Trevelyan, pp. 92–93.
29. Torr, ed., *Selected Correspondence of Marx and Engels*, pp. 126, 125.
30. *Ibid.*, 125.
31. *Collected Poems*, p. 569.
32. *Ibid.*, pp. 56–57.
33. Richard Purdy, *Thomas Hardy, a Bibliographical Study* (London: Oxford University Press, 1954), p. 297.
34. Karl Marx, "Eighteenth Brumaire," *Basic Writings on Politics & Philosophy of Marx and Engels*, ed. Lewis S. Feurer (New York: Doubleday, 1959), p. 330.
35. *Ibid.*, p. 331.
36. Karl Marx, *Capital*, trans. Ernest Untermann (New York: Modern Library, n.d.), pp. 823–24.
37. Morton, p. 452.

458   THE PESSIMISM OF THOMAS HARDY

38. K. B. Smellie, *Great Britain since 1688* (Ann Arbor: University of Michigan Press, 1962), p. 208.

39. Susanne Howe, *Novels of Empire* (New York: Columbia University Press, 1949), p. 94.

40. William James, *Letters,* ed. Henry James (Boston: Atlantic Monthly Press, 1920), 2: 94.

41. Joseph Conrad, *Heart of Darkness* (New York: Doubleday, 1924), p. 61.

42. Irving Howe, *Politics and the Novel* (New York: Horizon Press, 1967), p. 102.

43. Feodor Dostoevsky, *Winter Notes on Summer Impressions,* trans. R. L. Renfield (New York: Criterion Books, 1955), p. 89.

44. Hicks, pp. 118, 115.

45. Barbara Tuchman, *The Proud Tower* (New York: Bantam Publishers, 1972), p. xiii.

46. *Life & Letters of Joseph Conrad,* ed. G. Jean-Aubry (New York: Doubleday-Page, 1927), 1: 246.

47. *Collected Poems,* "In Tenebris III," p. 155. There is the following preface to this poem: *"Heu mihi, quia incolatus meus prolongatus est! Habitavi cum habitantibus Cedar; Multum incola fuit anima mea,"* which Hardy lists as *Ps.* cxiv." It corresponds to Ps. 120; v. 5: "Woe is me, that I sojourn in Mesech, that I dwell in the tents of Kedar." "My soul hath long dwelt with him that hateth peace" (v. 6) and "I *am* for peace; but when I speak, they *are* for war" (vi 7) are significant of the times. "In Tenebris I" is prefaced by a Latin quotation also: *"Percussus sum sicut foenum, et aruit cor meum"* (Ps. 101, Hardy says) and likewise "In Tenebris II": *"Considerabam ad dextram, et videbam; et non erat qui cognoscere me. . . . Non est qui requirat animam meam—Ps.* xcli." Are not the former, Ps. 102, v. 3: "For my days are consumed like smoke and my bones as an hearth" and the latter, Ps. 110, v. 1: "The Lord said unto my Lord, sit then at my right hand, until I make thine enemies thy footstool."

48. J. W. McKail, *Life of William Morris* (London and New York: Longmans Green, 1901), 2: 25.

49. Jacob Korg, *George Gissing: a Critical Biography* (Seattle: University of Washington Press, 1964), p. 35. Korg refers to Gissing's never-published article "Hope of Pessimism," in which Gissing called "the philosophy of nineteenth-century Radicalism, based on the standards drawn from Schopenhauer, 'Agnostic Optimism.'" Gissing maintained that it is a mistake to believe, as the Comtists did, that science can eliminate "the metaphysical instinct, for even after people have been educated

out of their religious ideas, they will still think in religious terms unconsciously. . . . When the scientist and the Philistine are on their deathbeds, both will be forced to acknowledge the futility of their beliefs," says Gissing, coining one of his best phrases "the convincing metaphysics of death" (pp. 51–52). Hardy wrote to C. W. Saleeby (Feb. 2, 1915): "I am utterly bewildered to understand how the doctrine that, beyond the knowable, there must always be an unknown, can be displaced" (*Later Years*, p. 168). This was in reference to a passage from an article in the *Cambridge Magazine* concerning Herbert Spencer's doctrine of the "Unknowable," in which the writer had written: "We doubt if there is a single philosopher alive today who would subscribe to it. Even men of science are gradually discarding it in favour of Realism and Pragmatism."

50. Georg Lukacs, *Studies in European Realism* (New York: Grosset & Dunlasp, 1964), pp. 191–92.
51. *Ibid.*, pp. 246–98.
52. C. Wright Mills, *The Power Elite* (New York: Oxford University Press, 1956), chap. 8.

CHAPTER 2

1. Evelyn Hardy, *Thomas Hardy*, illus. opposite p. 224.
2. *Early Life*, p. 15.
3. *Ibid.*, p. 281.
4. *Ibid.*, pp. 303, 7.
5. *Ibid.*, p. 9.
6. *Collected Poems*, p. 236.
7. *Ibid.*, pp. 623–24.
8. *Early Life*, pp. 5–6.
9. *Ibid.*, p. 19; *Later Years*, p. 176.
10. *Early Life*, p. 19.
11. *Tess*, p. 68.
12. *Far from the Madding Crowd*, Wessex ed. (London: Macmillan, 1912), p. 22; *The Later Years*, p. 263.
13. Evelyn Hardy, pp. 20–21.
14. *Under the Greenwood Tree*, Wessex ed. (London: Macmillan, 1912), p. 69.
15. *Later Years*, p. 199. "In one of them lived an old man who was found one day rolling on the floor, with a lot of pence and halfpence scattered around him. They asked him what was the matter, and he said he had heard of people rolling in money, and he thought that for once in his life he would do it, to see what it was like."

16. *Collected Poems,* p. 444.

17. *Early Life,* p. 31.

18. *Ibid.,* p. 32.

19. *Evelyn Hardy,* p. 42.

20. See Hardy's poem "The Abbey Mason," inscribed "With Memories of John Hicks, Architect," *Collected Poems,* pp. 379–86.

21. *Early Life,* p. 211.

22. Giles Dugdale, *William Barnes of Dorset* (London: Cassell & Co., 1953), p. 89. E. P. Thompson, *The Making of the English Working Class* (New York, Pantheon, 1964), p. 778.

23. *Ibid.,* pp. 249, 165.

24. *Early Life,* p. 39.

25. *Tess,* p. 121.

26. *Early Life,* p. 230.

27. *Ibid.,* p. 165.

28. *Ibid.,* p. 153.

29. *Poetical Works of Ebenezer Elliott* (London: Henry S. King, 1876), 1: 372.

30. *Early Life,* pp. 279–80.

31. John W. Bowyer and John L. Brooks, *The Victorian Age* (New York: F. S. Crofts & Co., 1941), p. 3.

32. Joseph Conrad, *Nostromo* (New York: Doubleday, 1924), p. 198.

33. Arthur Adrian, *Mark Lemon: First Editor of Punch* (London: Oxford University Press, 1966), pp. 41, 57.

34. *Early Life,* p. 43.

25. Harvey Curtis Webster, *On a Darkling Plain* (Hamden, Conn.: The Shoestring Press, 1973), p. 30.

36. Evelyn Hardy, p. 53.

CHAPTER 3

1. Edmund Blunden, *Thomas Hardy* (London: Macmillan, 1942), pp. 18–19, 21–22.

2. *Early Life,* p. 22; see H. P. Clunn, *Face of London* (London: Simpkin Marshall, 1932), p. 396.

3. *Early Life,* pp. 46–47.

4. *Ibid.,* p. 47.

5. *A Pair of Blue Eyes,* Wessex ed., p. 126.

6. *London in Dickens' Day,* ed. Jacob Korg (Englewood Cliffs, N.J.: Prentice-Hall, 1960), p. 159

7. Marx, *Capital,* p. 257.

8. Henry Collins, "Karl Marx, The International & the British Trade Union Movement," *Science & Society* (Fall 1962), p. 400.

9. John W. Dodds, *Age of Paradox* (New York: Rinehart, 1952), p. 267.
10. *Early Life,* p. 55; Clunn, pp. 116–17.
11. Clunn, p. 94.
12. *Collected Poems,* p. 544.
13. A club of Whig wits, painters, politicians, and men-of-letters, which took its name from Christopher Cat, keeper of a pie-house in which the Club met in Shire Lane, near Temple Bar, and in the summer at Upper Flask, Hampstead Heath. Founded in 1703, it dissolved in 1720. See *Encyclopedia Britannica.*
14. Berlin, *Karl Marx: His Life and Environment,* p. 198; also see Franz Mehring's *Karl Marx: The Story of His Life,* trans. Edward Fitzgerald, which describes the Marx family Sunday picnics at Hampstead Heath.
15. *Early Life,* p. 54.
16. A. McK. Terhune, *Life of Edward FitzGerald* (New Haven, Conn.: Yale University Press, 1947), p. 234; F. Dostoevsky, *Winter Notes on Summer Impressions,* pp. 87ff.
17. Berlin, p. 222.
18. Dodds, p. 468.
19. Thomas Hardy, *The Dynasts* (New York: Macmillan, 1944), I, 5, iv.
20. *Early Life,* p. 49.
21. *The Hand of Ethelberta,* Wessex ed., pp. 89–90, 139.
22. *Desperate Remedies,* Wessex ed., p. 354.
23. *Early Life,* p. 59.
24. Evelyn Hardy, pp. 57, 63.
25. See Hardy's poem on Swinburne's death, "A Singer Asleep," *Collected Poems,* pp. 304–5.
26. Swinburne's poem "Hymn to Proserpine."
27. *Later Years,* p. 111.
28. *Early Life,* p. 82.
29. *Ibid.,* p. 295.
30. *Desperate Remedies,* pp. 353, 350. Marx and his family lived in lodgings on Dean Street, Soho, the first seven years of his exile in London, described by a Prussian spy as follows: "He lives in one of the worst and cheapest neighbourhoods in London. He occupies two rooms. There is not one clean or decent piece of furniture in either room, everything is broken, tattered and torn, with thick dust over everything . . . mss., books and newspapers lie beside the children's toys, bits and pieces from his wife's sewing basket, cups with broken rims, dirty spoons, knives, forks, lamps, and inkpot, tumblers, pipes, tobacco ash, all piled on the same table." See Isaiah Berlin, *Karl Marx: His Life and Environment,* p. 194.

31. Robert Blatchford, *Merrie England* (New York: Monthly Review Press, p. 57.

32. *The Hand of Ethelberta*, Wessex ed., p. 364.

33. *A Pair of Blue Eyes*, p. 141.

34. Quoted in Jack London's *People of the Abyss* (New York: Macmillan Company, 1904), p. 263; Herman Melville, *Journal of a Visit to London and the Continent: 1849–1850*, ed. Eleanor Melville Metcalf (Cambridge, Mass.: Harvard University Press, 1948), p. 25; *Life of William Morris*, 2: 14.

35. *The Hand of Ethelberta*, p. 184; *Desperate Remedies*, p. 201.

36. Hicks, p. 19.

37. *The Hand of Ethelberta*, p. 364.

38. *Early Life*, pp. 58–59.

39. Marx, *Capital*, p. 716.

40. *Ibid.*, p. 722.

41. Dodds, p. 266.

42. *The Hand of Ethelberta*, pp. 329, 418, 215.

43. *Ibid.*, pp. 365, 364.

44. Vachel Lindsay's poem "William Booth Enters into Heaven."

45. *Early Life*, p. 68.

46. Marx; *Letters to Dr. Kugelmann*, p. 33. An advertisement of the organizational meeting of the Reform League appeared in the *London Times* of Feb. 21, 1865. See J. H. Park's *English Reform Bill of 1867* (New York: Columbia University Press, 1920), pp. 89, 266. "The Reform League's papers show that by May 1866 it claimed 51 provincial and 20 metropolitan branches, and that its income from April 1865 to May 1866 had been £621 13s. 7½d., a good deal of this . . . coming in relatively large donations from 'advanced Liberals' whose help had been sought" (Simon Maccoby, *English Radicalism*, 3: 85. League papers are in the Howells Collection of the Bishopgate Institute (*ibid.*, p. 88). Edmund Beales (1803–1881) espoused Polish Exiles Society and Garibaldi's visit to England; George Odger (1820–1877) was a shoemaker and trade unionist, president of the International Association of Working Men in 1870, who had been dubiously praised by Matthew Arnold as a representative of "the beautiful and virtuous mean of our present working class." See Arnold's *Culture & Anarchy*, ed. J. Dover Wilson, p. xxi. Feargus O'Connor (1794–1855) was a Chartist leader and editor of the *Northern Star*, official organ of Chartism. See Maccoby, *English Radicalism*, 2: 193.

47. Joseph Park, *English Reform Bill of 1867* (New York, Columbia University Press, 1920), pp. 110–11. The League disbanded in 1867 but was revived in 1876. *Ibid.*, p. 266.

48. Maccoby, *English Radicalism,* 3: 91.
49. E. K. Brown, *Matthew Arnold* (University of Chicago Press, 1948), pp. 119, 207, n 6; K. B. Smellie, p. 363.
50. Monypenny and Buckle, 2: 236.
51. John Morley, *Life of Gladstone* (London: Macmillan, 1903), 2: 29.
52. Marx, *Capital,* p. 733.
53. Lionel Trilling, *Matthew Arnold* (New York: Columbia University Press, 1958), p. 244.
54. Marx *Capital,* p. 433. "The demand for children's labour," Marx notes, "often resembles in form the inquiries for negro slaves, such as were formerly to be read among advertisements in American journals," and he quotes an English factory inspector's saying, "My attention was drawn to an advertisement in the local paper of one of the most important manufacturing towns of my district, of which the following is a copy: Wanted, 12 to 20 young persons, not younger than what can pass for 13 years. Wages, 4 shillings a week. Apply &c. The phrase 'what can pass for 13 years' has reference to the fact that, by the Factory Act, children under 13 years may work only 6 hours. A surgeon official appointed must certify their age. The manufacturer, therefore, asks for children who look as if they were already 13 years old. The decrease often by leaps and bounds in the number of children under 13 years employed in factories, a decrease that is shown in an astonishing manner by the English statistics of the last 20 years, was for the most part, according to the evidence of the factory inspectors themselves, the work of the certifying surgeons, who overstated the age of children to the capitalist's greed for exploitation, and the sordid trafficking needs of parents."
55. K. B. Smellie, *A Hundred Years of English Government* (London: Duckworth, 1937), p. 150.
56. Jack London, *People of the Abyss,* p. 252.
57. *Early Life,* p. 285.
58. *Ibid.,* p. 65.
59. *Ibid.,* p. 64.
60. *Ibid.,* p. 54.
61. *Collected Poems,* p. 203.
62. *Early Life,* pp. 71–72.
63. *Ibid.,* pp. 74–75.
64. *Collected Poems,* p. 204.
65. Park, p. 111.
66. Smellie, *A Hundred Years of English Government,* p. 192; E. L. Woodward, *Age of Reform: 1815–1870* (London: Clarendon Press, 1962), p. 642. Hardy met Lord Goschen later in the eighties. See *Early Life,* p. 262.

67. Norman St. John Stevas, *Walter Bagehot* (Bloomington, Ind.: Indiana University Press, 1959), p. 20.

68. *Ibid.*, p. 56.

69. Edgar Johnson, *Charles Dickens,* 2: 825.

70. John Morley, *Life of Gladstone,* 2: 56.

71. Monypenny and Buckle, 2: 308, 790–91.

72. Webb, *History of Trade Unionism,* p. 269.

73. *An Indiscretion in the Life of an Heiress,* ed., Carl J. Weber (Baltimore: Johns Hopkins University Press, 1935), p. 67.

74. Marx, *Capital,* preface, p. 21 n. *Saturday Review* (Jan. 1868) declared: "The author's views may be as pernicious as we conceive them to be, but there can be no question as to the plausibility of his logic, the vigour of his rhetoric and the charm with which he invests the driest problems of political economy. . . ." Courtesy of Dr. William Allen, General Reference Department, Stanford University Library. A review written by Engels and signed by Samuel Moore was rejected by John Morley, the then editor of the *Fortnightly Review.* See *Engels on Capital: Synopsis, Reviews, Letters and Supplemental Material* (New York: International Publishers, 1937), p. vii.

75. Simon Maccoby, *English Radical Tradition* (London: Nicholas Kaye, 1952), 5: 169; Morton, p. 383.

76. F. E. Halliday, *Thomas Hardy: His Life and Work* (Bath, England: Adams & Dart, 1972), p. 22.

77. T. A. Jackson, *Charles Dickens: The Progress of a Radical* (New York: International Publishers, 1931), p. 295.

78. Morton, p. 437.

79. Monypenny and Buckle, 2: 801.

80. Halliday, p. 199.

CHAPTER 4

1. Thomas Hardy, "Candour in English Fiction," *Thomas Hardy's Personal Writings,* ed. Harold Orel, p. 128.

2. Christopher Caudwell, *Illusion and Reality* (New York: International Publishers, 1947), p. 245.

3. *Early Life,* p. 135.

4. *Ibid.,* 143.

5. *Later Years,* p. 77.

6. *Early Life,* p. 81. Hardy called it long afterwards, Purdy says, "the most original thing (for its date) that I ever wrote" (p. 276). More detailed accounts of this never-published novel will be found in the following books: Evelyn Hardy, *Thomas Hardy;* W. R. Rutland, *Thomas Hardy: A Study of His Writings and Their Backgrounds,* and Carl Weber, *Hardy of Wessex.*

7. *Ibid.*, p. 83.

8. Morgan, *House of Macmillan*, pp. 87–88.

9. Dodds, *Age of Paradox*, pp. 425–26.

10. Morgan, p. 91.

11. *Early Life*, p. 80.

12. *Desperate Remedies*, p. 183.

13. Richard Purdy, *Thomas Hardy, a Bibliographical Study*, p. 4. The reader, John Morley, advised Macmillan: "Don't touch this, but beg the writer to keep away from such incidents as violation, and let us see his next story." The incident referred to was "violation of a young lady at an evening party and the subsequent birth of a child," which Morley pronounced "too abominable to be tolerated as a central incident from which the action of the story is to move," and "also some other scenes (*e.g.*, between Miss Aldclyffe and her maid in bed), which are highly extravagant." Charles Morgan, *House of Macmillan*, p. 94.

14. *Early Life*, p. 116.

15. *Desperate Remedies*, p. 431.

16. R. Purdy, p. 7.

17. Weber, *Hardy of Wessex*, p. 73.

18. *Under the Greenwood Tree*, p. 85.

19. *Early Life*, p. 110

20. *Ibid.*, p. 111

21. *Ibid.*, p. 112; R. Purdy, facsimile opposite p. 5.

22. R. L. Purdy, *Thomas Hardy, a Bibliographical Study* (London: Oxford University Press, 1954), p. 8.

23. *Early Life* p. 115; Evelyn Hardy, Thomas Hardy and Horace Moule, *London Times Literary Supplement* (Jan. 23, 1969), p.89.

24. *Early Life*, p. 18. That afternoon Hardy "went to a law-bookseller, bought *Copinger on Copyright* . . . and sat up half the night studying it. The next day, he called on Tinsley," and after some discussion of their contract, agreed to Tinsley's request to "throw in the three-volume edition of the novel with the magazine rights," Mrs. Hardy says, "having . . . some liking for Tinsley's keen sense of humour even when it went against himself. . . . (*ibid.* pp. 118–19).

25. *Ibid.*, pp. 120–21.

26. *Ibid.*, pp. 101–2. Raphael and David Brandon had published *Analysis of Gothic Architecture* in two quarto volumes, and *Open Timber Roofs of the Middle Ages* (1849), both books "familiar to Hardy, having been textbooks for architects' pupils till latterly, when their absorbing interest given to French Gothic had caused them to be superseded by the works of Norman Shaw, Nesfield, and Viollett-le-Duc." Brandon "was convinced that the development of modern

English architecture should be based on English Gothic and not on French," Mrs. Hardy says, "as was shown in his well-known design for the Catholic Apostolic Church in Gordon Square; and that his opinion was the true one was proved in the sequel, notwithstanding that the more fashionable architects, including Blomfield, were heart and soul of the other opinion at this date. . . . Brandon's practice had latterly declined, and he had drifted into a scheme for unifying railway-fares on the principle of letter-postage. Hardy was in something of a similar backwater himself—so far as there could be a similarity in the circumstances of a man of twenty-nine and a man of sixty." Hardy helped Brandon with his architecture, "which had fallen behind," and sometimes with the details of his railway schemes, though, having proved to himself its utter futility, he felt in an awkward dilemma: whether to show Brandon its futility and offend him, or to go against his own conscience by indulging him in the hobby." *Early Life,* pp. 101–2. Knight's chambers in *A Pair of Blue Eyes* were drawn from Brandon's in Clement's Inn.

27. *A Pair of Blues Eyes,* p. 142.
28. R. Purdy, p. 336.
29. *Early Life,* pp. 134–35.
30. *Ibid.,* pp. 95–96, 131.
31. "Candour in English Fiction," *Hardy's Personal Writings,* ed. Harold Orel, (Lawrence, Kan.: University of Kansas Press, 1966), pp. 128, 130.
32. Smellie, *A Hundred Years of English Government,* p. 129; Engels, *Condition of the Working Class in England in 1844,* p. 298.
33. *Far from the Madding Crowd,* pp. 328, 61; *Tess,* p. 442.
34. *Far from the Madding Crowd,* p. 72; *Collected Poems,* pp. 194–95; *Later Years,* p. 8.
35. *Collected Poems,* p. 195.
36. "Dorsetshire Labourer," *Hardy's Personal Writings,* ed. H. Orel, pp. 183, 181.
37. *The Mayor of Casterbridge,* pp. 211–12.
38. *Far from the Madding Crowd,* p. 32.
39. *The Mayor of Casterbridge,* p. 331.
40. *Ibid.,* p. 103.
41. *Ibid.,* p 82.
42. *Ibid.,* pp. 253, 261, 258.
43. *Ibid.,* p. 315.
44. *Ibid.,* p. 231.
45. *Ibid.,* pp. 114, 265. ("He was kind-like to mother when she was here below, sending her the best-ship coal and taties and such-like that were very needful to her," Abe recalls. P. 383).

46. *Ibid.,* p. 295.

47. *Ibid.,* p. 294.

48. *Far from the Madding Crowd,* p. 331; *The Mayor of Casterbridge,* p. 60.

49. Marx, *Capital,* p. 432.

50. *The Mayor of Casterbridge,* p. 192.

51. *Early Life,* p. 125.

52. Marx, *Capital,* p. 342.

53. *Far from the Madding Crowd,* p. 446.

54. *Ibid.,* p. 328.

55. *The Woodlanders,* p. 206.

56. *The Mayor of Casterbridge,* pp. 96–97.

57. *Ibid.,* p. 245.

58. *Ibid.,* p. 40.

59. *Ibid.,* p. 45.

60. *The Return of the Native,* p. 241.

61. *Ibid.,* p. 199.

62. *Ibid.,* p. 207.

63. Brown, *Matthew Arnold,* p. 68.

64. *The Return of the Native,* p. 75.

65. *Two on a Tower,* p. 265.

66. *The Woodlanders,* p. 59.

67. *Ibid.,* p. 61.

68. *Ibid.,* p. 10.

69. *Ibid.,* p. 114.

70. *Ibid.,* p. 117. Such an old contract is salvaged from a bureau drawer after the fire and read by Edward Springrove Sr. and his son Ted:

> Aṅò the said John Springrove for himself his heirs executors and administrators doth convenant and agree with the said Gerald Fellcourt Aldclyffe his heirs and assigns that he the said John Springrove his heirs and assigns during the said term shall pay unto the said Gerald Fellcourt Aldclyffe his heirs and assigns the clear yearly rent of ten shillings and sixpence . . . at the several times hereinafter appointed for the payment thereof respectively. Aṅò also shall and at all times during the said term well and sufficiently repair and keep the said Cottage or Dwelling-house and all other the premises and all houses or buildings erected or to be erected thereupon in good and proper repair in every respect without exception and the said premises in such good repair upon the determination of this demise shall yield up unto the said Gerald Fellcourt Aldclyffe his heirs and assigns. (*Desperate Remedies,* pp. 209)

71. *The Woodlanders,* pp. 117, 124.

72. *Ibid.*, p. 214.
73. *Ibid.*, p. 55.
74. *Ibid.*, pp. 81, 124.
75. *Ibid.*, p. 13.
76. *Ibid.*, p. 108.
77. *Ibid.*, p. 121.
78. *Ibid.* p. 123.
79. *Ibid.*, p. 185.
80. *Ibid.*, p. 192.
81. *Ibid.*, p. 276.
82. *Ibid.*, p. 52.
83. *Ibid.*, p. 305.
84. *Ibid.*, p. 145.
85. *Ibid.*, p. 167.
86. *The Return of the Native*, pp. 204–5.
87. *The Woodlanders*, p. 264.
88. *Later Years*, p. 10.
89. *The Woodlanders*, p. 213.
90. *Tess*, p. 41
91. *Ibid.*, Preface.
92. *Ibid.*, p. 297.
93. *Ibid.*, p. 298.
94. *Ibid.*, p. 416.
95. *Ibid.*, pp. 48–49.
96. *Ibid.*, p. 242.
97. *Ibid.*, p. 240.
98. *Ibid.*, p. 34.
99. *Early Life*, pp. 289–90.
100. *A Pair of Blue Eyes*, p. 145; *Tess*, p. 14.
101. *The Woodlanders*, p. 196.
102. *Ibid.*, p. 46.
103. *Ibid.*, p. 196.
104. *Ibid.*, p. 77
105. *Ibid.*, p. 204.
106. Blatchford, *Merrie England*, pp. 224–25. 47.
107. Morley, *Life of Gladstone*, 1: 282–83.

CHAPTER 5

1. *The Mayor of Casterbridge*, pp. 258–59.
2. George Gissing, *The Nether World* (New York: E. P. Dutton, 1929), p. 11.

3. *Ibid.*, p. 21
4. *Jude the Obscure*, (Wessex ed.) p. 342.
5. *Desperate Remedies*, p. 347; *Tess*, p. 485.
6. *A Pair of Blue Eyes*, p. 141; London, *People of the Abyss*, pp. 204–9, 237.
7. *Hardy's Personal Writing*, p. 181.
8. *A Pair of Blue Eyes*, p. 96.
9. *The Hand of Ethelberta*, pp. 110–11.
10. *Jude the Obscure*, p. 113.
11. *Ibid.*, p. 111.
12. *A Pair of Blue Eyes*, p. 96.
13. *Jude*, p. 372.
14. *Far from the Madding Crowd*, pp. 45, 71.
15. *The Hand of Ethelberta*, p. 225.
16. *Ibid.*, p. 203.
17. *The Woodlanders*, p. 8.
18. *The Hand of Ethelberta*, p. 424.
19. *Jude the Obscure*, pp. 180–81.
20. *Tess*, pp. 204, 285.
21. *The Mayor of Casterbridge*, p. 205.
22. "Dorsetshire Labourer," pp. 174–78.
23. *Collected Poems*, pp. 358–59, 627.
24. Webster, *On a Darkling Plain*, p. 119.
25. Samuel C. Chew, *Thomas Hardy* (New York: Alfred Knopf, 1929), p. 20.
26. *Early Life*, p. 131.
27. *Desperate Remedies*, p. 358.
28. *Ibid.*, p. 431.
29. *A Pair of Blue Eyes*, p. 160.
30. *The Hand of Ethelberta*, pp. 141–42; *Later Years*, p. 93.
31. *Desperate Remedies*, p. 350.
32. *A Pair of Blue Eyes*, p. 156; *Jude*, p. 376.
33. *The Hand of Ethelberta*, p. 354.
34. *A Pair of Blue Eyes*, p. 292.
35. *Ibid.*, p. 100.
36. *Ibid.*, pp. 156, 89.
37. *Ibid.*, p. 145.
38. *The Woodlanders*, pp. 68, 63.
39. *A Pair of Blues Eyes*, pp. 261, 264.
40. *Ibid.*, pp. 239–41.
41. Torr, ed., *Selected Marx-Engels Correspondence*, p. 235.
42. *Early Life*, p. 149.

43. R. Purdy, p. 12.
44. *A Pair of Blue Eyes*, p. 281.
45. *Ibid.*, p. 278.
46. *The Hand of Ethelberta*, pp. 182, 119–20, 146.
47. *Ibid.*, pp. 311, 129, 111.
48. *Ibid.*, pp. 277, 418.
49. *Ibid.*, pp. 185, 77.
50. *Ibid.*, p. 425.
51. *Ibid.*, pp. 183, 320–21.
52. *Ibid.*, p. 191.
53. *Ibid.*, p. 201.
54. Morley, *Life of Gladstone*, 2: 247.
55. *The Hand of Ethelberta*, pp. 155, 200.
56. Louis Adamic, *My America* (New York: Harper's, 1938), p. 473; *The Hand of Ethelberta*, p. 473.
57. *A Laodicean*, pp. 38, 212, 164.
58. *Ibid.*, pp. 124, 101, 105.
59. *Ibid.*, pp. 154–55.
60. *Ibid.*, p. 403.
61. *Ibid.*, pp. 20, 54, 195.
62. *Ibid.*, pp. 309.
63. *Ibid.*, pp. 348–49.
64. *Ibid.*, pp. 22, 114, 392.
65. See Newman's *Apologia pro vita sua*, Bowyer and Brooks, *The Victorian Age*, p. 236.
66. *Later Years*, p. 147.
67. *A Laodicean*, pp. 314, 188.
68. *The Hand of Ethelberta*, p. 366. Replying to a friend (Sept. 1926) about a proposed dramatization of *Jude the Obscure*, Hardy wrote: "Would not Arabella be the villain of the piece? . . . more than Blind Chance. Christminster is of course the tragic influence of Jude's drama in one sense, but innocently so, and merely as crass obstruction. By the way it is not meant to be exclusively Oxford, but any old-fashioned University about the date of the story, 1860–70, before there were such chances for poor men as there are now. I have somewhere printed that I had no feeling against Oxford in particular" (*Later Years*, pp. 248–49). On October 30, 1919, in reply to an inquiry "if *Jude the Obscure* is autobiographical," he wrote, "I have to answer that there is not a scrap of personal detail in it, it having the least to do with [my] own life of all [my] books" (*ibid.*, p. 196). At the Masefield's (June 1923) "Hardy was asked a question or two about Jude's village, which it was thought he might have passed on the road from Dor-

chester, and he spoke briefly and depreciatingly of 'that fictitious person if there ever was such a person. . . .' " (*ibid.*, p. 233).

69. *Jude the Obscure,* pp. 91, 100.

70. *Ibid.,* p. 314.

71. *Ibid.,* p. 482.

72. *Ibid.,* p. 180.

73. *Ibid.,* pp. 251ff.

74. *Ibid.,* p. 294.

75. *Ibid.,* pp. 74–75.

76. Arthur Quiller-Couch, *Poet as Citizen and Other Papers* (New York: Macmillan, 1935), p. 207.

77. Lloyd Eshelman, *A Victorian Rebel* (New York: Scribner's & Sons, 1940), pp. 345–46.

78. *Later Years,* p. 50.

79. J. O. Bailey, *The Poetry of Thomas Hardy* (Chapel Hill; University of North Carolina, 1970), p. 99.

80. *Later Years,* p. 48.

81. *Ibid.,* pp. 39–40. Hardy notes on his visit to Swinburne (June 1905); "We laughed and consoled with each other on having been the two most abused of living writers: he for *Poems and Ballads,* I for *Jude the Obscure*" (*ibid.,* p. 112).

82. *Ibid.,* pp. 40–41. 50.

83. *Ibid.,* p. 44.

84. *A Collection of Letters of Thackeray 1847–1855,* ed. Jane Octavia Brookfield (New York: Scribner's Sons, 1887), p. 174.

85. Edgar Johnson, *Charles Dickens: His Tragedy and Triumph* (New York: Simon & Schuster, 1952), 1:89. Dickens reported for *Mirror of Parliament,* a sort of predecessor of *Hansard* and the U.S. *Congressional Record.*

86. *Early Life,* p. 129.

87. *Later Years,* p. 74.

88. *Early Life,* p. 292.

89. *Ibid.,* p. 277.

90. "The Profitable Reading of Fiction," *Hardy's Personal Writings,* ed. H. Orel, pp. 112, 121.

91. V. L. Parrington, *Main Currents in American Thought* (New York: Harcourt Brace, 1939), p. 326.

92. *Early Life,* p. 224; *Later Years,* p. 92.

93. Lukacs, *Studies in European Realism,* p. 36.

94. *Tess,* pp. 160–69.

95. See Kettle's quotation from D. H. Lawrence on Hardy, *Introduction to the English Novel,* 2:60 (from *Phoenix,* 1936).

96. *Later Years,* p. 65.
97. Marx, *Capital,* p. 387.
98. *Tess,* p. 242.

CHAPTER 6

1. Collins, *Talks with Thomas Hardy at Max Gate,* pp. 22–23.
2. "On the Western Circuit," *The Short Stories of Thomas Hardy* (London: Macmillan, 1928), p. 352.
3. *An Indiscretion in the Life of an Heiress,* ed. Carl Weber, p. 76. An emasculated version of *The Pood Man and the Lady,* with the characters' names changed, and the narrator's point of view shifted from the first person to the third person. (See Weber's *Hardy of Wessex* or Evelyn Hardy, *Thomas Hardy,* for further details.)
4. *Ibid.,* pp. 73–74.
5. *Ibid.,* p. 60.
6. *Ibid.,* pp. 272, 40.
7. *Desperate Remedies,* p. 272; *A Pair of Blue Eyes,* pp. 78, 80.
8. *A Pair of Blue Eyes,* p. 99.
9. *Ibid.,* p. 91.
10. *Ibid.,* p. 156.
11. *The Hand of Ethelberta,* p. 312.
12. *Far from the Madding Crowd,* pp. 41, 53.
13. *The Woodlanders,* pp. 94, 100.
14. *The Hand of Ethelberta,* pp. 182, 66, 361.
15. *The Return of the Native,* pp. 240, 239.
16. *The Woodlanders,* pp. 166–67.
17. *A Laodicean,* p. 43.
18. *Two on a Tower,* pp. 11–12.
19. *The Mayor of Casterbridge,* p. 182.
20. *A Laodicean,* p. 464.
21. *The Hand of Ethelberta,* p. 89.
22. *An Indiscretion. . . ,* p. 23.
23. *Tess,* p. 209.
24. *An Indiscretion. . . ,* pp. 46–47.
25. *Tess,* p. 4.
26. *Ibid.,* p. 44.
27. *Ibid.,* p. 60.
28. *Ibid.,* pp. 242–43.
29. *Ibid.,* pp. 43, 29.
30. *The Hand of Ethelberta,* pp. 183, 331–32.
31. *The Woodlanders,* p. 59. In the preface Hardy states: "In respect

of the occupations of the characters, the adoption of iron utensils and implements in agriculture, and the discontinuance of thatched roofs for cottages, have almost extinguished the handicrafts classed formerly as 'copsework', and the type of men who engaged in them."

32. *The Mayor of Casterbridge*, p. 195.
33. Webster, *On a Darkling Plain*, p. 148.
34. *The Hand of Ethelberta*, pp. 141, 210.
35. *A Laodicean*, p. 37.
36. *A Pair of Blues Eyes*, p. 134; *The Woodlanders*, p. 67.
37. *The Mayor of Casterbridge*, p. 223; *Jude the Obscure*, p. 130, 288.
38. *The Mayor of Casterbridge*, p. 368.
39. *The Woodlanders*, p. 163; *Tess*, pp. 415–17.
40. *Jude the Obscure*, pp. 392–93.
41. *Ibid.*, p. 395.
42. *Ibid.*, p. 100.
43. *Early Life*, pp. 223, 231–32.
44. *Ibid.*, p. 76.
45. Morton, p. 390.
46. R. Purdy, *Thomas Hardy, a Bibliographical Study*, p. 34.
47. *Early Life*, p. 235.
48. Joseph Warren Beach, *The Technique of Thomas Hardy* (Chicago: University of Chicago Press, 1922), p. 12.
49. *Early Life*, pp. 285, 223.
50. Michael Millgate, *Thomas Hardy: His Career as a Novelist* (New York: Random House, 1971). p. 162.
51. Georg Lukacs, *Studies in European Realism*, p. 70.
52. *Early Life*, p. 232, 197.
53. William Archer, *Real Conversations* (London: Heinemann, 1904), p. 30.
54. Webster, p. 137.
55. *The Trumpet-Major*, p. 102.
56. *Under the Greenwood Tree*, pp. 70–71.
57. *The Dynasts*, II, 2, iii.
58. *The Trumpet-Major*, p. 204.
59. *The Dynasts*, I, 4, i.
60. *The Trumpet-Major*, p. 310.
61. *Ibid.*, pp. 121–22.
62. *A Pair of Blue Eyes*, p. 241.
63. *Two on a Tower*, pp. 31–32.
64. *Ibid.*, p. 33.
65. *The Dynasts*, III, After Scene, I, 1, vi.
66. *Two on a Tower*, pp. 34–35.

67. R. Purdy, p. 44.
68. *Two on a Tower*, p. 136.
69. *Ibid.*, p. 79.
70. *The Well-Beloved*, title page.
71. *Later Years*, p. 59.
72. R. Purdy, p. 95.
73. *A Pair of Blue Eyes*, Preface, p. viii.
74. *The Well-Beloved*, p. 62.
75. *Early Life*, p. 232.
76. *The Well-Beloved*, p. 148.
77. *Later Years*, pp. 261–62.
78. Chew, *Thomas Hardy*, pp. 110–11.
79. *The Well-Beloved*, p. 24.
80. *Far from the Madding Crowd*, pp. 43, 165.
81. *The Hand of Ethelberta*, p. 254.
82. *The Well-Beloved*, Preface.
83. *The Dynasts*, I, 6, vii.
84. *The Well-Beloved*, p. 3.
85. *Ibid.*, p. 92.
86. *Early Life*, p. 232.
87. Arthur Macdowall, *Thomas Hardy* (London: Faber & Faber, 1931), p. 167.
88. *Later Years*, pp. 59–60.
89. *Ibid.*

CHAPTER 7

1. *Early Life*, p. 4; José Yglesias, "Pablo Neruda," *The Nation* (July 11, 1966).
2. *Early Life*, p. 65. He regretted that Scott, "the author of 'the most Homeric poem in the English language—*Marmion*—should later have declined on prose fiction, ibid., p. 64.
3. R. Purdy, *Thomas Hardy, a Bibliographical Study*, p. 98.
4. *Later Years*, p. 65.
5. *Ibid.*, p. 207.
6. *Ibid.*, p. 66.
7. *Ibid.*, p. 80.
8. *Ibid.*, p. 77.
9. I. A. Richards, *Science and Poetry* (New York: W. W. Norton, 1926), p. 80.
10. *Collected Poems*, p. 222.
11. *Ibid.*, p. 505.
12. *Ibid.*, pp. 293–94; *Early Life*, p. 156.

13. *Collected Poems*, pp. 43–44.
14. *Ibid.*, pp. 111–12.
15. *Ibid.*, pp. 61–62.
16. *Ibid.*, pp. 182–85.
17. *Later Years*, p. 93; R. Purdy, pp. 138–39.
18. *Early Life*, p. 216; *Later Years*, p. 201.
19. R. Purdy, p. 166. Some friction seems to have developed in their middle years: Whether it was due to dissimilarities in temperament and beliefs, or the childless marriage, it is difficult to say. There is a note of disappointment in Hardy's diary entry for August 13, 1876: "We hear that Jane, our late servant, is soon to have a baby. Yet never a sign of one is there for us" (*Early Life*, p. 153). Hardy's poem "The Division," written in the 1890s (*Collected Poems*, p. 205), has been cited as evidence of the growing estrangement between them, but whether the woman referred to is Emma Hardy, as Evelyn Hardy suggests (p. 265), or Mrs. Arthur Henniker, as Purdy intimates (p. 141), is conjectural.
20. *Collected Poems*, p. 325.
21. *Ibid.*, p. 320.
22. *Ibid.*, p. 538. There is a reproduction of a drawing of the second Mrs. Hardy, by W. Strang, R.A., in *Later Years*, opposite p. 160.
23. *Ibid.*, pp. 7, 8.
24. *Ibid.*, p. 798.
25. "On the Western Circuit," *The Short Stories of Thomas Hardy*, p. 352.
26. *Collected Poems*, p. 759.
27. *Ibid.*, p. 8.
28. *Ibid.*, p. 11.
29. Collins, *Talks with Thomas Hardy at Max Gate*, p. 23.
30. *Collected Poems*, pp. 56–57.
31. *Ibid.*, p. 154. "Original title was 'De Profundis'; it was altered to to 'In Tenebris' in subsequent editions" (R. Purdy, p. 116).
32. Friedrich Engels, *Condition of the Working Class in England in 1844*, ed. W. O. Henderson and W. H. Chalomer (New York: Macmillan, 1958), p. 31; *Early Life*, p. 51.
33. *Early Life*, pp. 283–84.
34. *The Return of the Native*, pp. 266ff, 272.
35. *A Pair of Blue Eyes*, p. 141.
36. *Desperate Remedies*, p. 268; *Hardy's Personal Writings*, p. 184.
37. *The Mayor of Casterbridge*, p. 212.
38. *The Woodlanders*, p. 88.
39. *The Dynasts*, I, 6, v; III, 4, iii.
40. *Ibid.*, I, 4, vi.

41. *Collected Poems*, pp. 78–79, 80–81.

42. *Ibid.*, pp. 620–21.

43. *Ibid.*, pp. 8, 10, 177–81.

44. *Ibid.*, p. 468.

45. *The Dynasts*, III, 6, viii; *Later Years*, p. 276.

46. *Collected Poems*, pp. 330, 138, 300–301.

47. *Ibid.*, pp. 228–29.

48. *Ibid.*, p. 533.

49. *Ibid.*, p. 436.

50. *Ibid.*, pp. 101, 106, 110.

51. *Early Life*, pp. 4–5.

52. *Return of the Native*, p. 131. See Hardy's diary note, Sept. 10, 1888: "Destitution sometimes reaches the point of grandeur in its pathetic grimness: *e.g.*, as shown in the statement of the lodging house keeper in the Whitechapel murder: 'He had seen her in the lodging-house as late as half past one o'clock or two that morning. He knew her as an unfortunate, and that she generally frequented Stratford for a living. He asked her for her lodging-money, when she said, "I have not got it. I am weak and all, and have been in the infirmary." He told her that she knew the rules, whereupon she went out to get some money' (*Times* report), O richest City in the world! 'She knew the rules.'" P. 280.

53. *Collected Poems*, pp. 424–26.

54. *Ibid.*, p. 246; *Early Life*, pp. 203–4.

55. *Collected Poems*, pp. 423, 67–68, 444, 253–54, 279–80, 412. Of interest in connection with his poem to Shakespeare are Hardy's remarks at the laying of the foundation stone of the Dorchester Grammar School, founded by his ancestor and namesake Thomas Hardy, who died in 1599: "though he must have had a modern love of learning not common in a remote country in these days, Shakespeare's name could hardly have been known to him, or at least vaguely as that of a certain ingenious Mr. Shakespeare who amused the London playgoers," adding, "that he died before Milton was born" (*Later Years*, pp. 254–55). The date was July 21, 1927; Hardy was in his eighty-seventh year.

56. *Collected Poems*, pp. 96–97, 288–89, 659; *Later Years*, pp. 30–31.

57. *Collected Poems*, p. 512; *Later Years*, pp. 169, 261.

58. *Collected Poems*, p. 513; Siegfried Sassoon, *Siegfried's Journey, 1916–1920* (New York: Viking, 1946), p. 96.

59. *Collected Poems*, p. 83.

60. *The Dynasts*, II, 3, iv.

61. *Ibid.*, I, 6, vi.

62. *Collected Poems*, p. 269. At the head of the poem in its magazine

publication (*Harper's Weekly,* Nov. 8, 1902) and *The Sphere* (Nov. 22, 1904) "appeared the following subtitle 'Scene: The settle of the Fox Inn, Stagfoot Lane. Characters: The speaker (a returning soldier) and his friends, natives of the hamlet.'" See R. Purdy, p. 147.

63. See Siegfried Sassoon's "Counter-Attack" and Edgar Lee Masters's "Knowlt Hoeheimer," *Spoon River Anthology.*

64. *The Dynasts,* I, 1, i. Conrad makes some interesting observations on the factors of weather and wind in connection with the battle of Trafalgar:

> Had the last great fight of the English navy been that of the First of June, for instance, had there been no Nelson's victories, it would have been well-nigh impassable. . . . The fleet tactics of the sailing days have been governed by two points: the deadly nature of a raking fire, and the dread, natural to a commander dependent upon the winds, to find at some crucial moment part of his fleet thrown hopelessly to leeward . . . these two points have been eliminated from the modern tactical problem by the changes of propulsion and armament. . . . . Except at the Nile, where the conditions were ideal for engaging a fleet moored in shallow water, Lord Nelson was not lucky in his weather. Practically it was nothing but a quite unusual failure of the wind which cost him his arm during the Teneriffe expedition. On Trafalgar Day the weather was not so much unfavourable as extremely dangerous . . . My well-remembered experience has convinced me that, in that corner of the ocean, once the wind has got to the northward of west (as it did on the 20th, taking the British fleet aback), appearances of westerly weather go for nothing, and that it is infinitely more likely to veer round to the east than to shift back again. It was in those conditions that, at seven in the morning of the 21st, the signal for the fleet to bear up and steer east was made . . . for some forty minutes, the fate of the great battle hung upon a breath of wind such as I have felt stealing from behind, as it were, upon my cheek while engaged in looking to the westward for the signs of the true weather *Mirror of the Sea,* pp. 189–91.

65. *Collected Poems,* p. 15.

66. *The Dynasts,* III, 2, i.

67. *Collected Poems,* p. 428.

68. *The Dynasts,* III, 5, vi. Hardy told Edmund Gosse "that the poem 'would have been enough in itself to damn me for the Laureateship, even if I had tried for or thought of it, which of course I did not'" (Purdy, p. 163).

69. *The Dynasts,* III, 7, iv.

70. G. K. Chesterton, *Victorian Age in Literature* (New York: Henry Holt, 1913), p. 43; *Later Years*, pp. 214–16.
71. *Later Years*, pp. 217–18.
72. *Collected Poems*, p. 439.
73. *Ibid.*, p. 112.
74. *Ibid.*, p. 266.
75. H. C. Duffin, *Thomas Hardy* (Manchester, England: University of Manchester Press, 1937), p. 336.
76. *Collected Poems*, pp. 621–22.
77. *Ibid.*, p. 616.
78. *Ibid.*, pp. 310–11, 63–66, 537.
79. *Early Life*, p. 167.
80. *Later Years*, p. 79.
81. John Walker (1732–1807), English actor, philologist, and lexicographer; born at Colney Hatch, Middlesex; left stage in 1868, taught elocution published *Rhyming Dictionary* in 1775. Hardy had a copy of it, according to Evelyn Hardy, p. 76.
82. *Later Years*, p. 85.
83. *Collected Poems*, p. 199.
84. *Ibid.*, p. 765.
85. *Ibid.*, p. 96.

CHAPTER 8

i. "EUROPE IN THROES"

1. R. Purdy, *Thomas Hardy, a Bibliographical Study*, p. 122.
2. Collins, *Talks with Thomas Hardy at Max Gate*, p. 43. The books were Archibald Alison, *History of Europe 1789–1815;* Beatty, *Death of Wellington;* E. P. Brenton, *Naval History of Great Britain;* Elliott *Life of Wellington;* Fitzgerald, *Life of George IV;* C. H. Gifford, A *History of the Wars Occasioned by the French Revolution;* J. S. Memes, *Memoirs of the Empress Josephine;* W. F. P. Napier, *History of the War in the Peninsula;* William Siborne, *The Waterloo Campaign;* and Stanhope, *Life of William Pitt;* and of course, the periodical *A History of the Wars*, belonging to his grandfather "with their melodramatic prints of serried ranks, crossed bayonets, huge knapsacks and dead bodies," which "were the first to set him on the train of ideas," Mrs. Hardy says, "that led to *The Trumpet-Major* and *The Dynasts*" (*Early Life*, p. 21). These books are examined in scholarly fashion but without critical insight in Walter F. Wright's *The Shaping of the Dynasts* (1967), listed on pp. 321–22.
3. *Early Life*, pp. 140, 150.

4. *Ibid.*, pp. 188, 290, W. F. Wright, *The Shaping of the Dynasts* (Lincoln: University of Nebraska Press, 1967), pp. 222–23.

5. Michael Howard, *The Franco-Prussian War* (London: Rupert Hart-Davis, 1961), p. 77.

6. See the account of Hardy and Mrs. Hardy's meeting "a delightful old campaigner John Bentley" at Chelsea Hospital on Waterloo Day, 1875, and his shaking hands, October 27, 1878, with "a palsied pensioner—deaf, [who] served under Sir John Moore in the Peninsula, through the retreat and was at Waterloo" (*Early Life*, pp. 140, 161–62). Hardy inscribed two ballads on his Napoleonic geste to veterans, "Valenciennes" (in memory of S. C.) and "San Sebastian" (with thoughts of Sergeant M—), *Collected Poems*, pp. 15–19. See the footnote on John Bentley, who "used to declare that he lay down on the ground in such weariness that when food was brought to him he could not eat it and slept till next morning on an empty stomach. He died at Chelsea Hospital ,187–, aged eighty-six" (*The Dynasts*, III, p. 343).

7. *The Dynasts*, III, 6, viii.

8. *Early Life*, pp. 188–89.

9. *Ibid.*, p. 188.

10. *Collected Poems*, pp. 105–6.

11. *Ibid.*, pp. 96–97.

12. *The Dynasts*, I, 3, ii; III, 7, i. See descriptions of Nature in *Early Life*, pp. 3–4, 72, 141, 144, 147, 149–50, 199, 205–6, 241, and in *Later Years*, pp. 70–71, 76, 201, 212–13, 241; and heath scenes in *The Return of the Native*.

13. *The Dynasts*, II, 6, i; III, 7, ix.

14. *Early Life*, p. 191; Walter Wright, p. 83.

15. *Later Years*, p. 125.

16. *Ibid.*, p. 105.

17. *The Dynasts*, I, 4, vi.

18. III, After Scene.

19. *The Dynasts*, p. vii.

20. I, 1, iii.

21. I, Fore Scene.

22. I, 1, vi.

23. W. R. Rutland, *Thomas Hardy, a Study of His Writings and Backgrounds* (London: Blackwell, 1938), p. 341.

24. Edmund Blunden, *Thomas Hardy*, p. 20.

25. Byron, *Don Juan* (1819–1823), Canto IX, stanzas viiii, iv, and ix.

26. *Later Years*, p. 104.

27. *The Dynasts*, I, Fore Scene; III, 2, ii; III, 7, vii.

28. III, 7, v.
29. I, 6, vi.
30. Walter F. Wright, Preface, p. ix.
31. *Later Years,* pp. 110–11.
32. *The Dynasts,* p. ix.
33. I, Fore Scene.
34. III, After Scene.
35. I, Fore Scene.
36. I, 1, vi.
37. I, 6, i; II, 3, iii.
38. II, 3, iii; II, 4, viii.
39. I, 6, i.
40. II, 5, ii.
41. II, 5, iii.
42. III, 3, ii; III, 1, vii; III, 5, iii; III, 6, viii.
43. III, 5, v.
44. Karl Marx, *The Civil War in France,* ed. Lewis S. Feurer, *Marx and Engels: Basic Writings on Politics & Philosophy* (New York: Doubleday, 1959), p. 389.
45. *The Dynasts,* I, 6, viii.
46. I, 1, iii.
47. II, 5, iii.
48. II, 5, iii.
49. Eugene Tarlé *Bonaparte,* trans., John Cournos (New York: Knight Publications, 1937), p. 406. (Reprinted by Octagon Books, 1970, as *Napoleons Invasion of Russia, 1812.*)
50. Marx, *Capital,* pp. 820, 823ff, 837.
51. *The Dynasts,* I, 1, vi.
52. III, 7, iv.
53. II, 6, iii.
54. II, 5, ii.
55. II, 5, viii; III, 4, iv.
56. III, 5, iii.
57. III, 7, ii.
58. III, 7, ix.
59. I, Fore Scene.
60. III, 7, ix. Francis says to Marie Louise, "Have you seen/What the Allies have papered Europe with?", and at her request Metternich takes out a paper and reads:

> The Powers assembled at the Congress here
> Owe it to their own troths and dignities,
> And to the furtherance of social order,
> To make a solemn Declaration, thus:

By breaking the convention as to Elba,
Napoleon Bonaparte forthwith destroys
His only legal title to exist,
And as a consequence has hurled himself
Beyond the pale of civil intercourse.
Disturber of the tranquillity of the world
There can be neither peace nor truce with him,
And public vengeance is his self-sought doom.—

to which Marie Louise (pale) says, "O God, how terrible! What shall—
(she begins weeping)" (III, 5, iv).

61. I, 4, iii.
62. I, 4, iii.
63. II, 2, vi.
64. II, 5, vii.
65. II, 6, vii.
66. II, 5, iv; II, 5, v.
67. III, 5, v.
68. I, 1, ii.
69. I, 6, i.
70. II, 1, viii.
71. II, 1, viii.
72. I, 6, v; II, 3, ii.
73. III, 2, iv.
74. II, 1, vi; II, 1, viii.
75. II, 6, iii; II, 6, iv.
76. III, 1, iv.
77. III, 1, i.
78. III, 1, i.
79. II, 5, vii.
80. III, 1, vii.
81 III, 1, xii.
82. III, 1, xii.
83. *The Return of the Native*, p. 204. Hardy wrote his sister Mary (Aug. 17, 1862) that he was reading extracts from Ruskin's *Modern Painters* (*Early Life*, p. 50) and elsewhere took her to task for saying that she was not concerned with art, for art was everyone's concern. William Morris said in his Ipswich address in 1884: "The cause of art is the cause of the people. We well-to-do-people, have for our best work the raising of the standard of life among the people" (McKail, *Life of William Morris*, 2:84–85).
84. *The Dynasts*, III, 3, ii.
85. III, 3, i.
86. II, 3, ii.

87. II, 6, v.
88. III, 1, iv.
89. I, 6, iii; III, 5, i.
90. III, 7, viii.
91. II, 6, iii; II, 5, viii; III, 2, iii.
92. III, 2, iii.
93. II, 3, ii; I, 5, v; III, 4, iii.
94. III, 1, v; II, 2, v.
95. II, 6, iv.
96. I, 5, iv; II, 3, iv; II, 3, v.
97. III, i, xi; III, 1, xi.
98. III, 1, xi.
99. II, 3, i.
100. Siegfried Sassoon, *Siegfried's Journey: 1916–1920*, pp. 5, 27.
101. *The Dynasts*, I, Fore Scene; III, After Scene, 2, iii.
102. II, 2, iii.
103. III, 4, iv; I, 1, vi; III, After Scene.
104. I, 6, iii.
105. *Ibid.*
106. III, After Scene.
107. III, 7, ix.

ii. "THE PALACE AND THE COTTAGE"

1. T. A. Jackson, *Charles Dickens: The Progress of a Radical* (New York: International Publishers, 1938), p. 248.
2. *The Dynasts*, I, 6, v.
3. Monypenny and Buckle, *Life of Disraeli*, 2:1276.
4. *Ibid.*, pp. 1367–68.
5. *Ibid.*, pp. 1371–72.
6. Maccoby, *English Radical Tradition*, 5:158.
7. Lukacs, *Studies in European Realism*, p. 42.
8. Monypenny and Buckle, 2:470.
9. Tarlé, pp. 136–37.
10. Monypenny and Buckle, 2:289–90.
11. *Later Years*, p. 95; "Dorsetshire Labourer," p. 174. Richard Jeffries had an article, "The Wiltshire Labourer," in *Longman's Magazine* (Nov. 1883), in which he observed: "Ten years have passed away, and the Wiltshire Labourers have only moved in two things—education and discontent." He blamed neither the landowner nor farmer, but found the root of the trouble in the fact that the labourer has no fixity of tenure (see Keith, *Richard Jeffries, A Critical Study*, p. 37.

12. Monypenny and Buckle, 2:1265.
13. *Ibid.*, p. 1112. Julian Symons says that Dickens offered "no explanation" for his action (*Charles Dickens*, p. 21), but suggests that it was to found the magazine *Household Words* (1850). Dickens wrote Forster (Feb. 9), after 17 issues, that he was "tired to death and quite worn out" (see Fox Bourne, *English Newspapers*, 2:143). Dickens's father handled the Parliamentary beat for his *Daily News*.
14. Mackail, *Life of William Morris*, 1:358.
15. Monypenny and Buckle, 2:901.
16. *Ibid.*, p. 778.
17. Maccoby, 3:20.
18. Morton, p. 374.
19. Owen Lattimore, *Inner Asian Frontiers of China* (Irvington-on-Hudson, N.Y.: Capitol Pub. Co. & American National Geographic Society, 1951), p. 144.
20. *The Dynasts*, III, 4, vi; III, 7, ix.
21. Erdman, *Blake: Prophet against Empire*, pp. 306, 312. Disraeli wrote Queen Victoria (New Year's Day 1879): "The authority of yr. Majesty's throne stands high again in Europe . . . and yr. Majesty's arms have achieved, in Asia, a brilliant and enduring success" (Monypenny and Buckle, 2:1271).
22. Monypenny and Buckle, 2:709.
23. *Ibid.*, pp. 473–74.
24. Marx, *Civil War in France*, pp. 389–98; Conrad, *Notes on Life & Letters*, pp. 106–7.
25. Monypenny and Buckle, 2:765–66.
26. *Under the Greenwood Tree*, p. 158.
27. Monypenny and Buckle, 2:765–66.
28. Eshelman, *Victorian Rebel*, p. 192.
29. *Ibid.*, p. 159.
30. Maccoby, *Radical Tradition*, 5:181–82.
31. *The Dynasts*, I, 1, iii; I, 6, v.
32. *Early Life*, p. 225.
33. Maccoby, *English Radical Tradition*, 5:166–67.
34. *Eshelman*, pp. 135–36.
35. *The Dynasts*, I, 4, vi.
36. *Eshelman*, p. 215.
37. Marx, *Civil War in France*, p. 390.
38. "Dorsetshire Labourer," p. 189.
39. Marx, *Civil War in France*, p. 389.
40. *The Dynasts*, I, 2, v.

iii. THE PEASANTS

1. *The Dynast*, Preface, p. v.
2. *Ibid.*, p. vi.
3. "Dorsetshire Labourer," p. 189.
4. Wright, *The Shaping of The Dynasts*, pp. 222–23.
5. *Far from the Madding Crowd*, p. 41.
6. *Early Life*, pp. 10, 35.
7. Otis and Needleman, *An Outline History of English Literature*, (New York: Barnes & Noble, 1952), 1:58.
8. Tarlé, *Bonaparte*, p. 289. Tarlé goes on to say: "That the Russian serfs more nearly resembled negro slaves than the serfs of any of the other defeated feudal absolutist countries of Europe Napoleon knew well enough." He enumerates unspeakable cruelties meted out to them during the reign of Catherine II (1762–1796) and especially following the peasant rebellion led by Pugahev (1773–1774).
9. Anatole G. Mazour, *Czarist and Communist Russia* (Princeton, N.J.: Van Nostrand, 1962), p. 257.
10. Tarlé, pp. 406–7.
11. Marx, *Eighteenth Brumaire*, p. 327.
12. *Tess*, p. 5. Victor Hugo, Les *Miserables*, "Marius," and Tolstoy's War *and Peace*. Douglas Labaree Buffum notes that "in *Les Miserables* he (Hugo) has given Romanticism, Realism and even Naturalism" (*Les Miserables par Victor Hugo*, ed. Buffum, Introduction, p. xiv). One recalls the notable paragraph describing the homeless Jondrettes (Troisieme Partie, "Marius"):

    > Cette famille était la famille du joyeux va-nu-pieds. Il y arrivait et il y trouvait la pauvreté, la détresse, et, ce qui est plus triste, aucun sourire; le froid dans l'âtre et la froid dans, les coeurs. Quand it entrait, on lui demandait:—D'où viens-tu? Il répondait;—De la rue. Quand il s'en allait, on lui demandait:— Où vas tu? Il répondait:—Dans la rue. Sa mère lui disait: Qu'est-ce que tu viens faire ici? (p. 150)

13. *Jude the Obscure*, p. 139.
14. *Journal of Tolstoy: 1895–1899*, almost any page.
15. Maxim Gorki, *On Literature*, trans, from Russian by Ivy Litvinov (Moscow, U.S.S.R.: Foreign Language Pub. House, n. d.), p. 301. Gorki continues:

    > Clearly the idea that destroys his peace of mind more frequently than any other is the idea of God. Sometimes this seems to be not an idea, but a tense resistance to something by which he feels he is dominated. He does not speak about it as much as he would like to, but thinks about it continually. I don't think this is a sign

of age, or due to a presentiment of death, more likely it comes from a fine human pride. A little from a sense of injury, too, perhaps—that he, Lev Tolstoy, must shamefully submit to the will of some streptoccous. . . . His favourite subjects of conversation are God, the peasant, and woman. Of literature he speaks seldom and little as if it were an alien subject to him. And his attitude toward women, as far as I can see, is one of obstinate hostility. There is nothing he liked so much as to punish them—unless they are just ordinary women like Kitty and Natasha Rostova. (pp. 292, 305)

16. Webster, *On a Darkling Plain,* p. 214.
17. Preface to *War and Peace* (Penguin Classics, 1); *Early Life,* p. 230.
18. Lukacs, *Studies in European Realism,* p. 246.
19. *Later Years,* p. 107.

CHAPTER 9

1. *Later Years,* pp. 57–58.
2. *Ibid.,* p. 183.
3. *Ibid.,* p. 104.
4. *Ibid.,* p. 208. Charles Morgan, who conducted Hardy around Oxford at the time the Oxford Dramatic Society presented scenes from *The Dynasts* (1920), and who later visited Hardy at Max Gate in 1922, recalls that Hardy spoke of literary criticism "with a bitterness that surprised me. . . . sadly rather than querulously; but he was persuaded . . . that critics approached his work with an ignorant prejudice against his 'pessimism' which they allowed to stand in the way of fair reading and fair judgement."
5. *Later Years,* p. 103.
6. *The Dynasts,* III, 7, iv; Tolstoy, *War and Peace,* (Modern Library ed.), p. 566.
7. *The Dynasts,* II, 1, iv.
8. Tolstoy, *War and Peace* (Modern Library ed.), pp. 232, 95.
9. *The Dynasts,* II, 1, vii.
10. Tolstoy, *War and Peace,* (Modern Library ed.) pp. 381–82.
11. *Early Life,* p. 266.
12. *The Dynasts,* I, 1, vi; *War and Peace,* (Modern Library ed.) p. 281.
13. *The Dynasts,* I, 2, v.
14. I, 2, 5.
15. III, 5, vi.
16. III, 4, vi.
17. *Later Years,* p. 114.

18. Ella Higginson, born in Council Grove, Kansas, *circa* 1862; died in Bellingham, Washington, Dec. 27, 1940. She conducted a literary column "Clover Leaves," in the Seattle *Times* and wrote, besides poetry and short-stories, a book entitled *Alaska the Great Country* (Macmillan, 1908). She was a cousin, by marriage, of Col. T. W. Higginson (1863–1911), a captain in the Civil War and commander of the 33rd U.S. Colored Infantry, the friend and literary adviser of Emily Dickinson (see Anna Wells's *Dear Preceptor*). Hardy and his wife accidentally met "Colonel T. W. Higginson of the United States (August 10, 1897), who is staying at the same hotel as ourselves introduced himself to us. An amiable, well-read man, whom I was glad to meet. He fought in the Civil War. Went with him to hunt up the spot of the execution of the Duke of Buckingham, whose spirit is said to haunt King's House still" (*Later Years,* pp. 71–72).

19. Weber, *Hardy of Wessex,* p. 249.

20. *Ibid.,* p. 239.

21. Blunden, *Thomas Hardy,* p. 124.

22. Weber, p. 248.

23. *Later Years,* p. 117.

24. *Blunden,* p. 113.

25. *Ibid.,* p. 118.

26. Harold Nicolson, *Tennyson* (London: Constable & Co., 1923), pp. 111–12, 122, 154–55.

27. *Later Years,* p. 103.

28. *Ibid.,* p. 104.

29. Amiya Chakravarty, *The Dynasts and Post-War Age in Poetry* (New York: Octagon Books, 1970, p. 9.

30. Webster, *On a Darkling Plain,* p. 211.

31. *Late Lyrics and Earlier,* Preface, p. 528.

32. V. F. Calverton, "The Impermanence of Esthetic Value," *Newer Spirit,* (New York: Boni & Liveright, 1925), pp. 146–47.

33. R. Purdy, *Thomas Hardy, a Bibliographical Study,* p. 122.

34. Torr, ed. *Marx-Engels Correspondence,* p. 419.

35. *Weber,* p. 226.

CHAPTER 10

1. See Hardy's letter to the London *Times* (May 21, 1906) "on how one of the profoundest thinkers of the last century appeared forty years ago to the man in the street [which] may be worth recording as a footnote to Mr. Morley's admirable estimate of Mill's life and philosophy in your impression of Friday."

It was a day in 1865, about three in the afternoon, during Mill's candidature for Westminster. The hustings had been erected in Covent Garden, near the front of St. Paul's Church, and when I—a young man living in London—drew near to the spot, Mill was speaking. The appearance of the author of the treatise, *On Liberty* (which we students of that date knew almost by heart) was so different from the look of persons who usually address crowds in the open air that it held the attention of people for whom such a gathering in itself had little interest. Yet it was, primarily, that of a man out of place. The religious sincerity of his speech was jarred on by his environment— a group on the hustings who, with a few exceptions, did not care to understand him fully, and a crowd below who could not. He stood bare-headed, and his vast pale brow, so thin-skinned as to show the blue veins, sloped back like a stretching upland, and conveyed to the observer a curious sense of perilous exposure. The picture of him as personified earnestness surrounded for the most part by careless curiosity derived an added piquancy—if it can be called such—from the fact that the cameo clearness of his face chanced to be in relief against the blue shadow of a church which, on its transcendental side, his doctrines antagonized. But it would not be right to say that the throng was absolutely unimpressed by his words; it felt that they were weighty, though it did not quite know why. (*Later Years*, pp. 118–19)

Hardy's portrait of Mill offers an interesting contrast to that of Marx, who criticized his economic theories as a "strange optical illusion to see everywhere a state of things which as yet exist only exceptionally on our earth," and taking stock of his position to conclude: "On the level plain, simple mounds look like hills; and the imbecile flatness of the present bourgeoisie is to be measured by the altitude of its great intellects" (*Capital*, pp. 567–68).

2. Marx, *Capital*, Preface, p. 25. Marx mentions Mill's claiming superiority over the mercantilists (p. 566), but criticizes his misinterpretation of profits (p. 567) and excessive generalizations and viewed him as "an apologist of the wage-fund theory" (p. 669).

3. Wright, *The Shaping of the Dynasts*, p. 28; *Early Life*, p. 101. Comte's *Positive Philosophy* (1839) provided "the version of a secular religion," having "a morality, a cult, a dogma, and a hierarchically organized clergy." Comte believed that the nineteenth century would be "characterized by the preponderance of history in philosophy, in politics and even in poetry. Science had foresight as its end and for the positivist, social science was the science of history." Comte came to dismiss his old employer Saint-Simon (1760–1825) as "a depraved juggler,"

"a vague and superficial writer," and "a charlatan," whose influence was "one of the characteristic symptoms of the mental and moral anarchy of our times" (see John F. Laffey, "August Comte: Prophet of Reconciliation and Reaction," *Science & Society* [Winter 1965]); but "Comte never quite abandoned Saint Simon's final view," Laffey says, "of the potentialities of the proletariat" (*ibid.*, p. 47). Nor did Hardy. Hardy noted in his journal (1880–81):

> If Comte had introduced Christ among the worthies in his calendar it would have made Positivism tolerable to thousands who, from position, family connection, or early education, now decry what in their heart of hearts they hold to contain the germs of a true system. It would have enabled them to modulate gently into the new religion by deceiving themselves with the sophistry that they still continued one-quarter Christians, or one-eighth, or one-twentieth, as the case might be: This as a matter of *policy,* without which no religion succeeds in making way. (*Early Life,* p. 189)

4. *Collected Poems,* pp. 430–31.
5. *Ibid.,* pp. 401–2.
6. *Ibid.,* p. 57.
7. *Early Life,* p. 198.
8. Marx, *Capital,* p. 391.
9. *Collected Poems,* p. 204.
10. *Later Years,* pp. 141–42.
11. *Collected Poems,* p. 204.
12. *Ibid.,* p. 153.
13. *The Dynasts,* III, 4, iv.
14. Marx, *Capital,* p. 31.
15. *Collected Poems,* Preface to *Late Lyrics and Earlier,* p. 526.
16. Morley, *Life of Gladstone,* 2: 37.
17. Eshelman, *Victorian Rebel,* p. 214.
18. *The Hand of Ethelberta,* pp. 213–14.
19. *A Laodicean,* p. 86.
20. Marx, *Civil War in France,* pp. 388–89.
21. Clunn, *Face of London,* p. 107; *Early Life,* p. 49.
22. Monypenny and Buckle, *Life of Disraeli,* 2: 218.
23. Maccoby, *English Radical Tradition,* 5: 181–82.
24. Mill, *On Liberty.*
25. Smellie, *Great Britain since 1688,* p. 224.
26. *Ibid.,* p. 244.
27. *Collected Poems,* pp. 104–5.
28. *Ibid.,* pp. 479–80, 116–17.
29. *The Dynasts,* III, 7, v.

30. *Collected Poems*, p. 511. Hardy noted (Oct. 1917) on this poem:
    I believe it would be said by people who knew me well that I have
    a faculty (possibly not uncommon) for burying an emotion in my
    heart or brain for forty years, and exhuming it at the end of that
    time as fresh as when interred. For instance, the poem entitled
    'The Breaking of Nations' contains a feeling that moved me in 1870,
    during the Franco-Prussian war, when I chanced to be looking
    at such an agricultural incident in Cornwall. But I did not write
    the verses till during the war with Germany of 1914, and onwards.
    Query: where was that sentiment hiding itself during more than
    forty years? (*Later Years*, p. 178)

31. *Later Years*, p. 74. Collected Poems, pp. 26-30. The poem is prefaced
    by the following excerpt from Thiers, *Histoire de l'Empire*, "Waterloo":
    Si le maréchal Grouchy avait été rejoint par l'offiicer que Napoléon
    lui avait expédié la veille à dix heures du soir, toute question eût
    disparu. Mais cet officier n'etait point parvenu à sa destination,
    ainsi que le maréchal n'a cessé de l'affirmer toute sa vie, et il faut
    l'en croire, car autrement il n'aurait eu aucune raison pour hésiter.
    Cet officier avait-il été pris? avait-il passé à l'ennemi? C'est ce
    qu'on toujours ignore.

32. *Later Years*, p. 125.

33. *The Dynasts*, II, 4, iv. II, 4, v.

34. Torr, *Marx-Engels Correspondence*, pp. 475–76.

35. Caudwell, *Illusion and Reality*, p. 102. The literary pseudonym of
    Christopher St. John Sprigg, born Oct, 20, 1907, in Putney, Surrey,
    England, who before he was twenty-five published several books on
    aeronautics and detective novels as well as some poems and short
    stories. He enlisted in the International Brigade and was killed in
    action on the Jarama, February 12, 1937. Caudwell's death was a loss
    to literary criticism. He was the author also of *Studies in a Dying
    Culture* (1938) and *The Crisis in Physics* (1939), published pos-
    thumously.

36. *Collected Poems* pp. 56–57, 7.

37. *Collected Poems*, pp. 58–59. The poem "Nature's Questioning" offers
    an interesting instance of projection. See the writer's interpretive note in
    Colby College Library Quarterly (May 1952).

38. Sweezy, *Theory of Capitalist Development*, p. 20.

39. *The Mayor of Casterbridge*, p. 368.

40. *Collected Poems*, pp. 136–37, 112.

41. Lewis Mumford, *Sticks and Stones* (New York: Boni & Liveright,
    1924), p. 113.

42. Caudwell, p. 99.

43. Marx, *Capital,* p. 695.

44. *A Pair of Blue Eyes,* pp. 148–49.

45. *The Return of the Native,* p. 5.

46. *Ibid.,* pp. 197, 161.

47. *A Pair of Blue Eyes,* pp. 101–2; *A Laodicean,* p. 5.

48. Archer, *Real Conversations,* pp. 46–47.

49. Morley, *Life of Gladstone,* pp. 192–93.

50. Webb, *History of Trade Unionism,* p. 284.

51. Marx, *Capital,* p. 736.

52. *Jude the Obscure,* p. 181.

53. *Later Years,* p. 86. This statement was made in reply to the representative of the American Red Cross Society, whom Hardy declined to be interviewed by in Oct. 1900.

54. *The Dynasts,* I, 4, vi.

55. Webb, *History of Trade Unionism,* p. 288.

56. *Early Life,* p. 220. Edward Spencer Beesly (1831–1915), professor of history at London University (1859–1889), who presided at the organizational meeting of the First International at St. James Hall, London, on Sept 28, 1864, and also helped to organize the Social Democratic Foundation (1884). He was the author of some historical works: *Cataline, Clodius and Tiberius* (1878), *Queen Elizabeth* (1892), and *A Strong Second Chamber* (1907).

57. Smellie, *Great Britain since 1688,* pp. 15, 181.

58. MacKail, *Life of William Morris,* 1 : 359–60.

59. Lloyd Eshelman, pp. 259–60.

60. Webb, *History of Trade Unionism,* pp. 385–86. Cunninghame Graham, Conrad's friend, was chairman of the Scottish Labour Party; elected to Parliament as a Liberal but became a socialist. Burns, born in Battersea in 1859, became leader of London unemployed agitation. "Morris disliked the Fabians," says George Bernard Shaw, "not because they were intellectual superiors, but because they represented one more 'species of Socialism.' Like Dickens, Morris saw Parliamentarism as the way of failure and was constitutionally opposed to Parliamentary bickerings and obstructionist tactics" (Shaw, "William Morris as I Knew Him," pp. 1–7).

61. "Dorsetshire Labourer," p. 184.

62. Webb, *History of Trade Unionism,* p. 284.

63. London, *People of the Abyss,* pp. 158–165.

64. Bailey, *The Poetry of Thomas Hardy,* p. 647.

65. *Collected Poems,* pp. 88–90; *Later Years,* pp. 162–65.

66. *Ibid.,* p. 449.

67. Weber, *Hardy of Wessex* (1940 ed.) p. 190. See Hardy's letter to Edmund Gosse dated Mar. 6, 1899:

The longer I live the more does Browning's character seem the literary puzzle of the nineteenth century. How could smug Christian optimism worthy of a dissenting grocer find a place inside a man who was so vast a seer and feeler when on neutral ground? You, from your intimacy with Browning, could probably answer all that, if any living man can, and don't think me officious if I say that you ought to give an explanation to the world. One day I had a theory which you will call horrible—that perceiving he would obtain a stupid no hearing as a poet if he gave himself in his entirety, he professed a certain mass of commonplace opinion as a bait to get the rest of him taken. Well, 'the Riddle of Browning' is what I want to read from your pen (p. 49).

Caudwell finds the optimism of Browning "even sadder" than "the pessimism of Arnold and the young Tennyson" because they fell "a victim to commodity fetishism" (*Illusion and Reality*, p. 101).

68. *Jude the Obscure*, pp. 95, 93.
69. *Ibid.*, p. 366.
70. Marx, *Capital*, p. 774.
71. Tuchman, *The Proud Tower*, pp. 529ff. World War I came as a shock to Hardy, he having doubted

the coming so soon of such a convulsion as the war. . . . When the noisy crew of music-hall Jingoes said exultingly, years earlier, that Germany was as anxious for war as they were themselves, he had felt convinced that they were wrong. He had thought that the play, *An Englishman's Home*, which he witnessed by chance when it was produced, ought to have been suppressed as provocative, since it gave Germany, even if pacific in intention beforehand, a reason, or excuse for directing her mind on a war with England. . . . War, he had supposed, had grown too coldly scientific to kindle again for long all the ardent romance which had characterized it down to Napoleonic times, when the most intense battles were over in a day, and the most exciting tactics and strategy led to the death of comparatively few combatants. Hence nobody was more amazed than he at the German incursion into Belgium, and the contemplation of it led him to despair of the world's history thenceforward. (*Later Years*, pp. 161–62.).

72. *Later Years*, p. 142; *Collected Poems*, pp. 350–51.
73. *Later Years*, p. 162.
74. *Collected Poems*, Preface to *Late Lyrics and Earlier*, p. 527.
75. *Later Years*, p. 230.
76. *Ibid.*, p. 190.
77. *Ibid.*, p. 225.
78. Jackson, *Charles Dickens*, p. 247.
79. *Caudwell*, p. 265.

Bibliography

Adrian, Arthur A. *Mark Lemon, First Editor of Punch*. London: Oxford University Press, 1966.

Archer, William. *Real Conversations*. London: Heinemann, 1904.

Arnold, Matthew. *Culture and Anarchy*. Edited by J. Dover Wilson. Cambridge: Cambridge University Press, 1932.

Auden, W. H. "A Literary Transference." *Southern Review*, Summer 1940.

Bailey, J. O. *Thomas Hardy and the Cosmic Mind*. Chapel Hill, N.C.: University of North Carolina Press, 1956.

———. *The Poetry of Thomas Hardy: A Handbook and Commentary*. Chapel Hill, N.C.: University of North Carolina Press, 1970.

Baker, Howard. "Hardy's Poetic Certitude." *Southern Review*, Summer 1940.

Barzun, Jacques. "Truth and Poetry in Thomas Hardy." *Southern Review*, Summer 1940.

Beach, Joseph W. *The Technique of Thomas Hardy*. Chicago: University of Chicago Press, 1922.

Berlin, Isaiah. *Karl Marx and His Environment*. London: Oxford University Press, 1963.

———. *The Hedgehog and the Fox* (an essay on Tolstoy's view of History). New York: New American Library of World Literature, 1957.

Blackmur, R. P. "The Shorter Poems of Thomas Hardy." *Southern Review*, Summer 1940.

Blatchford, Robert. *Merrie England*. New York: Monthly Review Press, 1966.

Blunden, Edmund. *Thomas Hardy*. London: Macmillan, 1942.

Bourne, Randolph. *History of a Literary Radical.* New York: B. W. Huebsch, 1920.

Bowra, C. M. *Inspiration and Poetry.* London: Macmillan, 1951.

Bowyer and Brooks. *The Victorian Age.* New York: F. S. Crofts, 1941.

Brennecke, Ernest, Jr. *Thomas Hardy's Universe.* Boston: Small Maynard, 1924.

Calverton, W. F. *The Newer Spirit.* New York: Boni & Liveright, 1925.

Camroe, Viscount. *British Newspapers and Their Controllers.* London: Cassel, 1948.

Carpenter, Richard. *Thomas Hardy.* New York: Twayne Publishers, 1964.

Caudwell, Christopher. *Illusion and Reality.* New York: International Publishers, 1947.

Chakravarty, Amiya. *The Dynasts and the Post-war Age in Poetry.* New York: Octagon Books, 1970.

Chase, Mary Ellen. *Thomas Hardy From Serial to Novel.* Minneapolis, Minn: University of Minnesota Press, 1927.

Chesterton, G. K. *The Victorian Age in Literature.* New York: Henry Holt, 1913.

Chew, Samuel C. *Thomas Hardy: Poet and Novelist.* New York: Knopf, 1919.

Clunn, Harold P. *The Face of London.* London: Simpkin Marshall, 1932.

Cole, G. D. H. *A Short History of the British Working Class Movement.* London: Allen & Unwin, 1948.

———. *British Working Class Politics: 1832–1914.* London: Routledge & K. Paul, 1965.

Collins, Henry. "Karl Marx, the International and the British Trade Union Movement." *Science & Society,* Fall 1962.

Collins, Vere H. *Talks with Thomas Hardy at Max Gate.* London: Duckworth, 1928.

Davidson, Donald. "The Traditional Basis of Thomas Hardy's Fiction." *Southern Review,* Summer 1940.

Davies, Donald. *Thomas Hardy and British Poetry.* New York: Oxford University Press, 1972.

Dobrée, Bonamy. "The Dynasts." *Southern Review,* Summer 1940.

Dodds, John W. *Age of Paradox.* New York: Rinehart, 1952.

Dostoevsky, Feodor. *Winter Notes on Summer Impressions.* Translated by R. L. Renfield. New York: Criterion, 1955.

Douglas, Sir George. "Thomas Hardy: Some Recollections." *Hibbert Journal* 26, April 1928.

Duffin, H. C. *Thomas Hardy.* Manchester, England: University of Manchester Press, 1937.

Dugdale, Giles. *William Barnes of Dorset.* London: Cassell, 1953.

Elliott, Ebenezer. *Poetical Works of Ebenezer Elliott.* London: Henry S. King, 1876.

Engels, Friedrich. *The Condition of the Working Class in England in 1844.* Translated by W. O. Henderson and W. H. Chaloner. New York: Macmillan, 1958.

———. *Ludwig Feuerbach.* New York: International Publishers, 1947.

———. *Engels-Lafargue Correspondence.* vols. 1 & 2. Translated by Yvonne Kapp. Progress Publishers, Moscow, USSR. 1959 and 1960.

Erdman, David. *Blake Prophet against Empire.* Princeton, N.J., Princeton University Press, 1954.

Eshelman, Lloyd W. *A Victorian Rebel.* New York: Scribner's Sons, 1940

Firor, Ruth A. *Folkways in Thomas Hardy.* Philadelphia: University of Pennsylvania Press, 1962.

Garwood, Helen. *Thomas Hardy: An Illustration of the Philosophy of Schopenhauer.* Philadelphia: J. C. Winston, 1911.

Gissing, George. *The Nether World.* New York: E. P. Dutton, 1929.

Gorki, Maxim. *On Literature.* Translated by Ivy Litvinov. Moscow, USSR.: Foreign Language Publishing House, n.d.

Graham, Walter James. *English Literary Periodicals.* New York: T. Nelson & Sons, 1930.

Guerard, Albert J. *Thomas Hardy: The Novels and Stories.* Cambridge, Mass.: Harvard University Press, 1949.

Halliday, F. E. *Thomas Hardy: His Life and Work.* Bath, England: Adams & Dart, 1972.

Hardy, Evelyn. *Thomas Hardy, a Critical Biography.* New York: St. Martin's Press, 1954.

———, ed. *Thomas Hardy's Notebooks.* London: Hogarth Press, 1955.

Hardy, Florence E. *The Early Life of Thomas Hardy.* New York: Macmillan, 1928.

———. *The Later Years of Thomas Hardy.* New York: Macmillan, 1930.

Harrison, Royden. "Beesly's St. James Speech." *Science & Society,* Fall 1963.

Hedgecock, F. A. *Thomas Hardy, Penseur et Artiste.* Paris: Hatchett & Cie, 1911.

Hicks, Granville. *Figures of Transition.* New York: Macmillan, 1939.

Hornbock, Bert C. *The Metaphor of Chance, Vision and Technique in the Works of Thomas Hardy.* Athens, Ohio: Ohio University Press, 1971.

Howard, Michael. *The Franco-Prussian War.* London: Rupert Hart-Davis, 1961.

Howe, Irving. *Thomas Hardy.* New York: Macmillan, 1967.

Howe, Susanne. *Novels of Empire.* New York: Columbia University Press, 1949.

Howell, George. *Conflicts of Capital and Labour.* vol. 1. London: Macmillan, 1890.

Jackson, T. A. *Charles Dickens: The Progress of a Radical.* New York: International Publishers, 1938.

James, William. *Letters of W. James.* Edited by his son Henry James. vol. 2. Boston: Atlantic Monthly Press, 1920.

Johnson, Edgar. *Charles Dickens: His Tragedy and Triumph.* New York: Simon & Schuster, 1952.

Johnson, Lionel. *The Art of Thomas Hardy* (with a chapter on his poetry by J. E. Barton). New York: Dodd Mead & Co., 1928.

Karl Marx Dictionary. Edited by Morris Stockhammer. New York: Philosophical Library, 1965.

Kettle, Arnold C. *Introduction to the English Novel.* vols. 1 and 2. London: Hutchinson Universal Library, 1951, 1953.

Korg, Jacob. "Hardy's *The Dynasts:* A Prophecy." *South Atlantic Quarterly* 63, January 1954.

———. *George Gissing, a Critical Biography.* Seattle, University of Washington Press, 1963.

———, ed. *London in Dickens' Day.* Englewood Cliffs, N.J.: Prentice-Hall, 1960.

Lattimore, Owen. *Inner Asian Frontiers of China.* Irvington on Hudson, N.J.: Capital Publishing Co. & American National Geographic Society (New York), 1951.

Leavis, F. R. "Hardy the Poet." *Southern Review,* Summer 1940.

Lewis, C. Day. "The Lyrical Poetry of Thomas Hardy." Proceedings of the British Academy, 37 (1951).

London, Jack. *People of the Abyss.* New York: Macmillan, 1904.

Lukács, Georg. *Studies in European Realism*. New York: Grosset & Dunlap, 1964.

Maccoby, Simon. *English Radicalism*. vol. 3. London: Allen & Unwin, 1938.

————. *The English Radical Tradition*. vol. 5. London: Nicholas Kaye, 1952.

Macdowall, Arthur. *Thomas Hardy*. London: Faber & Faber, 1931.

Mackail, J. W. *The Life of William Morris*. London & New York: Longmans Green, 1922.

Maitland, Frederic. *Life and Letters of Leslie Stephen*. London: Duckworth, 1906.

Marx, Karl. *Capital*. Translated by Ernest Untermann. New York: Modern Library, n.d.

————. *Selected Correspondence: Marx and Engels*. Translated by Dona Torr. New York: International Publishers, 1936.

————. *Marx and Engels Selected Correspondence*. Translated by the late I. Lasker. Moscow, USSR: Progress Publishers, 1965.

————. *Letters to Kugelmann*. New York: International Publishers, 1934.

————. *Basic Writings on Politics and Philosophy of Marx and Engels*. Edited by Lewis S. Feurer. New York: Doubleday & Co., 1959.

————. *Marxist Social Thought*. Edited by Robert Freedman. New York: Harcourt Brace & World, 1968.

Marzials, Frank T. *Charles Dickens*. London: W. Scott, 1887.

Mazour, Anatole. *Tsarist and Communist Russia*. Princeton, N.J.: Van Nostrand, 1962.

Mehring, Franz. *Karl Marx: the Story of His Life*. Translated by Edward Fitzgerald. London: Allen & Unwin, 1951.

Melville, Herman. *Journal of a Visit to London and the Continent*. Edited by Eleanor Melville Metcalf. Cambridge, Mass.: Harvard University Press, 1948.

Métraux, Guy and Crouzet, François. *The Nineteenth Century World*. New York: Mentor Books, 1963.

Mill, John Stuart. *Autobiography* (Harvard Classics edition). New York: Collier & Sons, 1909.

Miller, Joseph Hillis. *Thomas Hardy: Distance and Desire*. Cambridge, Mass.: Belknap Press, 1970.

Mizener, Arthur. "Jude the Obscure as a Tragedy." *Southern Review*, Summer 1940.

Monypenny and Buckle. *Life of Benjamin Disraeli.* vols. 1 and 2. New York: Macmillan, 1929.

Morgan, Charles. *The House of Macmillan: 1843–1943.* London: Macmillan, 1944.

Morley, John. *Life of Cobden.* vols. 1 and 2. London: Macmillan, 1908.

——. *Life of William Ewart Gladstone.* London: Macmillan, 1903.

Morrell, Roy. *Thomas Hardy: The Will and the Way.* Kuala Lampur: University of Malaya Press, 1965.

Morton, A. L. *A People's History of England.* New York: Random House, 1938.

Muller, Herbert J. "Novels of Thomas Hardy To-day." *Southern Review,* Summer 1940.

Mumford, Lewis. *Sticks and Stones.* New York: Boni & Liveright, 1924.

Nevison, Henry W. *Changes and Chance.* New York: Harcourt Brace, 1941.

Nichols, C. *History of the English Poor Law: 1714–1853.* Revised by H. G. Willink. London: S. King & Sons, 1904.

Nicolson, Harold. *Tennyson.* London: Constable & Co., 1923.

Orel, Harold. *Thomas Hardy's Epic Drama: a Study of The Dynasts.* Lawrence, Kan.: University of Kansas, 1963.

——, ed. *Hardy's Personal Writings.* Lawrence, Kan.: University of Kansas Press.

Page, William. *The Victoria History of the County of Dorset.* London: Archibald Constable & Co., 1908.

Parks, Joseph H. *The English Reform Bill of 1867.* New York: Columbia University Press, 1920.

Parrington, Vernon L. *Main Currents in American Thought.* New York: Harcourt Brace, 1939.

Perkins, David. "Hardy and the Poetry of Isolation." *E.L.H. (Journal of English Literature)* 26 (1958).

Plekhanov, George. *Essays in Historical Materialism.* New York: International Publishers, 1940.

Porter, Katherine Ann. "Notes on a Criticism of Thomas Hardy." *Southern Review,* Summer 1940.

Purdy, Richard L. *Thomas Hardy, a Bibliographical Study.* London: Oxford University Press, 1954.

Quiller-Couch, Arthur. *The Poet as Citizen and Others Papers.* New York: Macmillan, 1935.

Ransom, John Crowe. "Honey and Gall." *Southern Review,* Summer 1940.

Richards, I. A. *Science and Poetry*. New York: W. W. Norton, 1926.

Rutland, W. R. *Thomas Hardy: a Study of His Writings and Their Backgrounds*. London: Blackwell, 1938.

Sassoon, Siegfried. *Siegfried's Journey: 1916–1920*. New York: Viking, 1946.

Schwarts, Delmore. "Poetry and Belief in Thomas Hardy." *Southern Review,* Summer 1940.

Sherman, G. W. "The Influence of London on *The Dynasts.*" *PMLA (Publication of the Modern Language Association)* 63, September 1948.

———. "A Note on One of Thomas Hardy's Poems ("Nature's Questioning"). *Colby Library Quarterly* 3. May 1952.

Smellie, K. B. *A Hundred Years of English Government*. London: Duckworth, 1937.

———. *Great Britain since 1688*. Ann Arbor, Mich.: University of Michigan Press, 1959.

Southerington, Frank R. *Hardy's Vision of Man*. New York: Barnes & Noble, 1971.

Southworth, James Granville. *The Poetry of Thomas Hardy*. New York: Columbia University Press, 1947.

Stevas, Norman St.-John. *Walter Bagehot*. Bloomington, Ind.: Indiana University Press, 1959.

Stewart, John Innes Mackintosh. *Thomas Hardy, a Critical Biography*. New York: Dodd Mead, 1971.

Stratford-Wingfield, Esme. *The Victorian Aftermath*. New York: Morrow, 1934.

Sweezy, Paul. *Theory of Capitalist Development*. New York: Monthly Review Press, 1942.

Symons, Julien. *Charles Dickens*. New York: Roy Publishers, 1951.

Tarlé, Eugene. *Bonaparte*. Translated by John Cournos. New York: Knight Publications, 1937.

Tate, Allen. "Hardy's Philosophic Metaphors." *Southern Review,* Summer 1940.

Tennyson, Charles. *Alfred Tennyson*. New York: Macmillan, 1949.

Terhune, Alfred McK. *The Life of Edward FitzGerald*. New Haven, Conn.: Yale University Press, 1947.

Thackeray, William Makepeace. *Vanity Fair*. New York: Dodd Mead & Co., 1943.

Thompson, E. P. The Making of the English Working Class, New York: Pantheon, 1964.

Tolstoy, Leo. *War and Peace*. Translated by Constance Garnett. New York: Modern Library, n.d.

————. *Journal of Leo Tolstoy: 1895–1899*. Translated by Rose Strunsky. New York: Knopf, 1927.

Trevelyan, G. M. *Life of John Bright*. New York: Houghton Mifflin, 1925.

Trilling, Lionel. *Matthew Arnold*. New York: Columbia University Press, 1958.

Tuchman, Barbara. *The Proud Tower*. New York: Macmillan, 1966.

Van Ghent, Dorothy. *The English Novel*. New York: Rinehart, 1953.

Von Thunen Johann. *Von Thunen's Isolated State*. Translated by Carla Wartenberg. New York: Pergamon, 1966.

Webb, Sidney and Beatrice. *History of Trade Unionism*. London: Allen & Unwin, 1924.

Weber, Carl J. *Hardy of Wessex*. New York: Columbia University Press, 1940 (revised 1960).

Webster, Harvey Curtis. *On a Darkling Plain*. Chicago: University of Chicago Press, 1947 (reprinted by Shoestring Press, Hamden Conn., 1972).

Williams, Merwyn. *Thomas Hardy and Rural England*. New York: Columbia University Press, 1972.

Woodward, E. L. *The Age of Reform 1815–1870*. Oxford: Clarendon Press, 1962.

Wright, Walter F. *The Shaping of The Dynasts*. Lincoln, Neb.: University of Nebraska Press, 1967.

Zabel, Morton Dauwen. "Hardy in Defense of His Art." *Southern Review*, Summer 1940.

Zachrison, Robert E. *Thomas Hardy as Man, Writer and Philosopher*. Stockholm: Almquist & Wiksell, 1928

Index

501